johnny depp starts here

JOHNNY DEPP

RUTGERS UNIVERSITY PRESS
NEW BRUNSWICK, NEW JERSEY, AND LONDON

STARTS HERE

Murray Pomerance

Third paperback printing, 2005

Library of Congress Cataloging-in-Publication Data
Pomerance, Murray, 1946–
   Johnny Depp starts here / Murray Pomerance.
     p. cm.
   Filmography: p.
   Includes bibliographical references and index.
   ISBN 0-8135-3565-4 (hardcover : alk. paper) — ISBN 0-8135-3566-2 (pbk. : alk. paper)
   1. Depp, Johnny—Criticism and interpretation.   I. Title.
   PN2287.D39P66   2005
   791.4302′8′092—dc22

                                    2004016422

A British Cataloging-in-Publication record for this book is available from the British Library.

Manufactured in the United States of America

for LESLIE FIEDLER (1917–2003)
scholar, teacher, friend, spirit, guide, dreamer

CONTENTS

Acknowledgments

I was writing this book before I knew it. In the late summer and early autumn of 2001, sometime before the World Trade Center collapsed, I was invited by David Sterritt and Mikita Brottman to join a panel on screen performance that they were going to propose to the Society of Cinema Studies, as it was still known. For some reason I will never fathom, I suggested Johnny Depp. I certainly liked his work, and perhaps fancied, along with Kemmons Wilson, the founder of Holiday Inn, "that I'm so damn normal that anything I like, everybody else is going to like too" (Halberstam 1993, 174). I hadn't really thought about Depp, except that he was someone worth watching. David and Mikita warmed immediately to the suggestion, and I sat down to write. In the late winter of 2002, in Denver, the panel happened, in front of what turned out to be an enthused and jovial audience, many of whom shared my sense that Depp was a figure to be contended with. I am particularly grateful to David and Mikita, as well, for sharing both published and unpublished material of theirs on Johnny Depp; and to David and also to William Luhr for inviting me to present some of this material to the Columbia University Seminar on Cinema and Interdisciplinary Interpretation. That my musings should have become a book is due to a suggestion, made with his usual infectious good humor, by Barry Keith Grant; this is probably not the book he had in mind, but I hope it is close enough to bring pleasure.

To think of Depp at all I was led, first by the perspicacity of the editors of *Cahiers du cinéma* and later by the generous hospitality of Leslie Barker and Adelaide Barker Karaskas. In various ways, they made it possible for me to want to see, and then actually to see, *Edward Scissorhands,* which really did open the door. My dear friend and colleague Michael DeAngelis reflected my suspicion that Depp was to be taken seriously, but also moved me to a much deeper stratum of thought through his patient and meticulous analyses of star personae in *Gay Fandom and Crossover Stardom* and in his brilliant essay on Depp, so generously offered to me for publication in an anthology on screen gender at the end of the twentieth century (DeAngelis 2001).

I have been encouraged, assisted, provoked, and enthralled like a kid at a magnificent carnival through many conversations with Tom Gunning. And I have received travel directions of inestimable value from Ann Kaplan. Jane Hoehner has been a gracious and loyal friend. Jay Glickman helped me shop. Further, many friends and students have opened their thoughts to me and I am extremely grateful: Jennifer Brayton, Michelle Czukar, Slobodan Drakulic for knightly courtesy, Craig Fischer, Lester D. Friedman, Giovanna di Girolamo, Eve Goldin of the Cinemathèque Ontario Film Reference Library in Toronto, Peter Higdon, Andrew Hobbs, Maureen Holloway, and Chuck Hsuen, Halifax, for *Dead Man*. I owe debts of gratitude as well to Michael Anderson and Mike Orlando of the Hollywood Canteen, Toronto, Chanda Curtice, Andrew Horton, Susan Hunt, Howard Kaufman, Martin Landau, Kenny Moi of the *New York Post,* Wayne Pittendreigh, Susanne Meyers Sawa of the University of Toronto Music Library, John Simon, J. David Slocum, Milos Stehlik at Facets, Chicago, Alan Walker, and Leslie Witol. Invaluable assistance has been provided me by Carla Cassidy, Dean of Arts at Ryerson University.

My book-loving partners at Rutgers University Press are in these pages as much as I am. My gratitude to Leslie Mitchner, Marilyn Campbell, Anne Hegeman, Arlene Bacher, Gary Fitzgerald, and Molly Baab; to Adam Bohannon, the designer; and to Eric Schramm for his customary keen eye. And Ron and Howard Mandelbaum at Photo-Fest, New York, have been generous with their wisdom and knowledge. My friend Jamie Thompson has been most encouraging and helpful in secret ways. Curtis Maloley and Nathan Holmes have gone overboard in their spirited and exhausting work on this project. I thank Curtis for his nonstop discoveries and suggestions, his taste in books, and his speedy fingers; and I thank Nathan for considerable research, for unflagging wit, and for preparing the filmography that ends this book.

Ariel Pomerance is involved with unstinting love in every aspect of my writing. I hope and trust that in some way these pages reflect his fascinations as much as my own. Nellie Perret's wisdom, courage, and brilliant observation are my beacon, my ground, and my delight. But she is also the best detective a writer could hope to know. Aware that, as Truffaut's Montag says, "in order to find, one must first know how to hide," she has again and again helped me to find what I have hidden from myself, thereby gifting me with not only love but also understanding.

johnny depp starts here

Players and painted stage took all my love,
And not those things that they were emblems of.

William Butler Yeats

I just want to know who you are.

Scottie Ferguson, in *Vertigo*

INTRODUCTION: A TRICK OF LIGHT

The rumor about Johnny Depp—that is, the story one is urged over and over to accept when by the popular media one is told about him—is this . . .

Born in Kentucky he was particularly attached to his mother. His brother introduced him to heavy rock music:

I was daydreaming of taking her out behind the 7-Eleven to drink Boone's Farm strawberry-apple wine and kiss until our mouths were raw. ZZZZRRRIIIPP!! was the sound I heard that ripped me from that tender moment. My brother Danny, ten years my senior and on the verge of committing fratricide, having had more than enough of "Do you feel like we do?," promptly seized the vinyl off the record player and with a violent heave chucked the sacred album into the cluttered abyss of my room.

"No more," he hissed. "I can't let you listen to that shit anymore!"

I sat there snarling at him in that deeply expressive way that only teens possess, decompressing too fast back into reality. He grabbed a record out of his own collection and threw it on.

"Try this . . . you're better than that stuff. You don't have to listen to that shit just 'cause other kids do."

"OK, fucker," I thought, "bring it on . . . let's have it!"

The music started . . . guitar, fretless stand-up bass, flutes and some Creep pining away about venturing "in the slipstream . . . between the viaducts of your dreams. . . ." "Fuck this," I thought, "this is pussy music—they're not even plugged in!" The song went a bit further . . . they didn't play that kind of stuff on the radio, and as the melody of the song settled in, I was starting to get kind of used to it. Shit! I even liked it.

. . .

My life had been metamorphosed when Danny put Van Morrison's *Astral Weeks* onto the turntable that day. (Depp 1999, 69; 70)

A boyish voice—even a little dirty—unpolished—authentic—from the streets.

He later became enchanted with Jack Kerouac's *On the Road* ("life-changing for me" [Depp 1999, 70]) and got a television acting job on "21 Jump Street," where as an "undercover cop with a pouty demeanor" (Kaylin 2003, 95) he became a teen idol (who could "see his mug grinning back at him from the covers of magazines" [Nashawaty 2003, 30]), at once despondent and constrained by mediocre scripts and a gnawing sense of having been typecast that irked and depressed him. "It was a very difficult situation," Depp writes,

> bound by a contract doing assembly-line stuff that, to me, was borderline Fascist (cops in school . . . Christ!) . . . Dumbfounded, lost, shoved down the gullets of America as a young Republican. TV boy, heart-throb, teen idol, teen hunk. Plastered, postered, postured, patented, painted, plastic!!! Stapled to a box of cereal with wheels, doing 200 mph on a one-way collision course bound for Thermos and lunch-box antiquity. Novelty boy, franchise boy. Fucked and plucked with no escape from this nightmare. (Depp 1995, ix)

He became rambunctious ("at one point, unemployed and recently evicted, he crashed in the Hollywood Boulevard apartment of his young actor friend Nic Cage, where he stole Mexican money Cage had tossed in a drawer" [Kaylin 2003, 95]). He more or less fell into movies (one of his biographers calls him an "accidental actor" [Heard 2001, x]), thanks to John Waters, who cast him in *Cry-Baby* (finding him "the least homophobic hetero boy I ever met" [Heard 2001, 53]); then he went from film to film, bizarre character part to bizarre character part, acting out the role of a delinquent offscreen by trashing hotel rooms, drinking too much, and being rude to reporters. He had a chain of girlfriends, at least two of them, Winona Ryder and Kate Moss, internationally celebrated. He fiercely maintained an independent and self-directed personality, choosing his own roles, often to the detriment of achieving financial success. Shooting *The Ninth Gate* in Europe for Roman Polanski he met Vanessa Paradis, fell immediately in love, and fathered two children, so that, having transformed "from heavily moussed and packaged newcomer to reflective expatriate" (Kaylin 2003, 95), he now lives in domestic bliss in a small town in France, doting upon his kids and lovely partner and looking back with a rueful and understanding smile on the outrageous rake he used to be. With *Pirates of the Caribbean: Curse of the Black Pearl, Once Upon a Time in Mexico, Secret Window, Finding Neverland,* and *The Libertine,* his most recent films, he seems to have broken into the mainstream and become at last a hugely successful star (who can still get away with some pirate gold on his teeth), a turn of affairs that occasions numerous stories about him in the press, all of which repeat this litany with quiet understanding as though it is the single pathway by which boys, or at least movie star boys, become men in the West. Johnny, once a hellion, has grown up. Johnny, once a rebel, has become bourgeois. "Now the former hotel-trasher, who turned 40 in June, doesn't even go out to the cinema any more" (Caron 2003, 86), or know where the nearest movie theater is ("I have absolutely no idea . . . no idea at all" [Nashawaty 2003, 34]), or, for that matter, read newspapers: "I don't want to know who is up, who is down, who is a success or who is a failure. These things don't interest me. I prefer to spend time with my children" (Caron 2003, 89).

So it is that if he remains beautiful, mysterious, enchanting, and epigrammatic—indeed, as *People* magazine recently had it, "The Sexiest Man Alive" (Russell 2003)—his career can also remain something of a moral lesson, neatly configuring him as "first in a generation of blessed young actors who understand the capriciousness of success, know how lucky they were to find it so fast and ease their guilt by paying regular homage to old guys" (Kaylin 2003, 97).

His "old guys" include Hunter S. Thompson—"There's really not an ugly bone in the guy's body"—as well as Roky Erickson and the 13th Floor Elevators: "If you listen to old 13th Floor Elevators stuff—Roky Erickson especially, his voice—and then go back and listen to early Led Zeppelin, you know that Robert Plant absolutely copped everything from Roky Erickson. And it's amazing. And Roky Erickson is sitting in Austin, Texas; he's just there. And Robert Plant had a huge hit. It always goes back to those guys, you know? I love those fucking guys" (Richardson 2004, 99)—and, it need hardly (at least for fans of *Benny & Joon*) be said, Charlie Chaplin, about whom he expresses great adoration in Richard Schickel's *Charlie: The Life and Times of Charles Chaplin* (2003), noting sadly, "We've definitely lost comic patience. . . . What Chaplin did was milk a gag and really stretch it out, really draw it out. Even if you knew what the result was going to be, it was still hilarious." The pumpernickel roll dance from *The Gold Rush* that Chaplin made up more or less spontaneously, Depp vowed, took him a month to work out, working over and over and over.

So be it. For a number of reasons, this myth of the civilized savage is (too) convenient. It reflects once again an oft-told story of Hollywood, thus reifying that story, solidifying it, entrenching it in what seems historical "fact" and social "reality." For example, the "actor's career"—passing from obscure and strange performances during a period of "wild" youth to more conventionally structured and comprehensible, hermetically bourgeois performances in middle age—also typified Marlon Brando (Johnny's friend and sometime mentor) and Humphrey Bogart (dead six years before Johnny was born). Indeed, if we look at Michael Curtiz's *Yankee Doodle Dandy*, we see a (sparkling) cinematic retelling of this myth as the "life story" of George M. Cohan. Johnny did only what many great actors do, then, in sowing his youthful wild oats with a list of lovers and in proffering a charm box of strange and inexplicable performances, then in settling down to something the mass media could deftly package and handle. It is important to note, indeed, that the very image of Johnny the rake become Johnny the reasonable is itself a mediated package, a way of putting a frame around him so that we can be comforted by his apparent stillness and presence (when he is always in motion, and not present to us at all). His performance as a singing gypsy who likes cocoa in *Chocolat*, one that occupies relatively little space in this book, can be seen as a transitional role for Depp, the gateway through which he left the flaky *monde* of Edward Scissorhands and Co. and became the gentle husband and father he is today. If Hollywood actors are weird, they are only weird as youths, our myth seems to say; and finally they, even they, grow up. Seeming for a while to be Peter Pan, Johnny finally became—as all wayward boys do—Mr. Darling. His recent title performance as J. M. Barrie in Marc Forster's *Finding Neverland* was therefore to be anticipated with some real excitement (and also with tranquilized reassurance, since instead of performing onscreen with the untamed Vincent Gallo, Charlie Sheen, Anthony Michael Hall, Al Pacino, or Brando he had graduated to the genteel well-bonded company of Dustin Hoffman and Julie Christie).

Johnny as middle-class parent also nicely addresses the aura of shapeless eroticism that followed him "in his youth," his adoring yet somewhat inwardly turned audiences of both genders and virtually all persuasions,* his penchant for feelingful unpredictability and political devotion. All this can be swept aside as jejune, as rudimentary, now rarefied and modified—shaped and burnished—into a conventional adulthood that should apparently, like religion, be the pathway for all. He proves that one can look back and say, "I didn't know shit," thus not only excusing whatever one did or didn't do in one's youth but also erasing it, defining it as beneath mature interest.

But the myth of the tamed Johnny Depp has for me an outcome still more pernicious. By amalgamating his many fascinating screen performances into a single package of "previous," and therefore relatively immature, work, the wrap-up of Johnny as a family man who has found truth has the potential to obscure from critical appreciation and serious reflection all of what Depp committed to the screen before "finding" love and family, that work now constituting in retrospect just a preparation for the "real" challenges of bourgeois life. The myth not only amalgamates performances, it diminishes each of them into a link in a progressive chain; it renders the screen appearances superficial and casual by positing in the bourgeois present a special depth, a gravity, and a purpose. What Depp onscreen showed us about the screen itself, then; about performance; about masculinity; about recognition and understanding—all this is apparently to be disregarded, unexamined, flushed away as preliminary to a present condition the well-socialized adult viewer is very unlikely to find galvanizing and important even if strange.

Our sense of need to grasp, hold, own, define, bound, isolate, and realize Johnny Depp—we live in a world where everything is flying past us, where we might sense a need to grasp virtually anything, yet he is especially desirable, it seems—is comforted, not challenged, by the public relations material that recounts that boyhood-to-manhood legend over and over, that America-to-Europe legend, that legend of being lost and being found. As I will try to argue in many

---

* I am grateful to Joe McElhaney for recollecting that lesbians, while Johnny was young, had a particular fondness for the boyishness of his girlishness.

ways in these pages, what makes Depp so peculiar and so vitally interesting is exactly that he is ungraspable, that he throws in our face any attempt to use theory to net him. This is partly because he is continually morphing, but I mean something else—something to do with the self he presents onscreen and the exercise we must endure to come to terms with it. This is not, at any rate, a conventional study of a movie star. The conventional star study has a clear biographical line as its center—I more or less neglect that here. Or else it suggests a salient link between an actor's characterizations onscreen and important social, political, historical, or cultural happenings. I write often as though there are no happenings of any kind except on the screen where the Depp image resides. As a celebrity, Depp is certainly an ultimate figure of the publicity machinery of high capitalism, which traffics in surfaces and phantom images, packages, expendables, transferables. In such a culture, even for a flash we wish to own our experience, and to own things. So, we want to possess Depp. Depp can be understood *this* way . . . or Depp is definitely an example of *that* . . . or: there is no doubt that Depp really and truly is. . . . Of Jimmy Stewart one could say he was the common man epitomized. Of Marlon Brando one could have thought, "Rebel." Of Depp, no such objectification is possible and that impossibility is the message.

A psychological approach I reject, since we do not meet Depp and can have very little, if anything, to say about him as a familiar. Another, more current, approach has been taken by star theory from Richard Dyer and James Naremore to Paul McDonald, Richard Corliss, Thomas Austin, and others. The audience's methods of interpretation, in this kind of work, become the center of the analysis, Depp's acting playing to, and also deriving from, audience expectations about performance and dutiful acceptance of its social conventions. If psychological criticism mythologizes every aspect of performance as legend and spirit, as personality; audience reception criticism rationalizes performance as reflection, or image, or the social world, neglecting that there is another world, a world of theatricality—in this case, the world of the screen—in which still another complex arrangement of forces, intentions, mobilizations, alignments, pointers, memories, and moves is taking shape entirely outside considerations of who the actor really is, hiding behind the mask, or what current events and social structures get reflected in his staged actions.

What this book is *not,* then, is: (a) the story of Johnny Depp's life,

(b) the plots and production histories of Johnny Depp's films, all his films, one by one, starting at the beginning and moving forward, (c) what Johnny Depp's characterizations say about the society in which they are sold, or (d) who Johnny Depp truly, really, actually, sincerely, authentically, fundamentally, profoundly, originally, and personally really is. I do not methodically cull through every performance he ever gave, recounting his conversations with his director, his personal anxieties, or his opinions about his character, or giving an in-depth analysis of his DVD commentaries. All these approaches are too easy. By this I don't mean writing any of those books would be an easy task. Writing any of them would be difficult. But the accomplishment would settle too easily upon us; we would be too much at ease in, and with, it. And—not to give too much away before the right moment—Johnny just isn't comprehensible in the conventional terms used for writing about actors or screen acting, because there are aspects of his performances that render his screen presence, taken in all, and to summarize it in a single word, circulatory. His screen presence is not objective, not rotund, not actually there, in a way that cannot be said of other actors—for example, Sean Penn or Russell Crowe. A more precise way of putting this is that in watching Johnny Depp we reflect upon him and wonder, and my single guiding principle here has been to try to spell out the wonder that has been mine when I have watched him. It is hardly a private wonder, and to make it plain is to give others the opportunity to recognize it as their own and possess it more fully. What is it precisely that can intrigue us— I want to ask—about Depp's presence onscreen? What can we learn about looking, thinking, understanding, and watching cinema by watching him?

Not "Who is he?" or "What does he mean?" but "What is going on when we are watching him?" Now one thing is true that may not be immediately apparent to every reader: what is going on is unavoidably musical. I know that the first time I had that realization was in listening to the opening credit sequence of Emir Kusturiça's *Arizona Dream* where we hear a long Deppish raga to music by Goran Bregovic. He immediately struck me as first and foremost a musician, who sings his roles. In structuring these pages it seemed necessary, implicitly, and from the outset, to be musical as well. I therefore begin with a suite in nine movements, called "Depp Positions." I think Johnny's acting both makes and implies certain formal statements— philosophical claims, if you will—about being, about social life, about performance itself, about our contemporary world. It makes "depositions." In each movement I try to tease out and discuss one such deposition and move in my discussion back and forth among the films. And all the movements circle around the theme of Depp's manner of playing to his audience's desire for approximation, knowledge, and touch.

In "Hungarian," to begin, I treat Depp's curious forays into ethnicity with some specific reference to Tim Burton's *Ed Wood*. What is the curious ethnicity Ed seems to be able to manifest in company with Béla Lugosi? What is it to understand that Depp is producing this quality, this aura, given that we know that neither Johnny nor Ed is discernably an ethnic type? Discussed here, as well, is John Badham's *Nick of Time,* where Johnny is a kind of double of himself. In "Apprehending," the discussion addresses itself specifically to our desire for proximity, for possession, and for fixation; and muses, in fact, about getting into Johnny Depp's mouth as a way of permeating his shell. Contrasting some curious moments in *Ed Wood* and *Donnie Brasco* with Dustin Hoffman's torture in the dentist's chair in *Marathon Man,* the argument moves to establish what can be meant by "interiority" in the case of Johnny Depp. "Not Finished" discusses the performance in *Edward Scissorhands* in terms of Goffman's dramaturgical ecology, the need for actors to open to the audience aspects of interaction that might not ordinarily be seen, suggesting that Depp forecloses interaction here and produces exactly a sense of distance. Meditation and the relationship between the image and the mind is worked through in terms of Ortega's proximal and distal vision in "One Drag," a movement that also finds room for a reflection upon Depp and smoking. "No Thing" and "Disappearance" discuss Depp's screen performances in terms of Marx's "derealization" and Robert Jay Lifton's "protean man." Depp has established a star career with the performance history of a character actor. "Blanc" is a meditation on various nuances of Johnny Depp's whiteness, playing with such groundings as Jim Jarmusch's impressions of the actor, Gwendolyn Audrey Foster's analysis of colonialism, and Tom Gunning's discussions of the detective, and with such films as *What's Eating Gilbert Grape, L.A. Without a Map, The Brave,* and others. Baudelaire's *flâneur* inevitably comes up in the case of Depp's touring the world of characters and social forms; "The Outsider" presents a discussion of *Pirates of the Caribbean, From Hell, Fear and Loathing,* and other material in terms of Walter Benjamin's approach to Baudelaire and modern life. "Light and Darkness" is about Depp's eyes, notably in *Once Upon a Time in Mexico,* focusing on his tendency to gaze outward—to make the audience his object—and on his performance as a step toward a "cinema of the absolutely presentable."

In all these pieces, and all through the book, my modality is jazz and my method is an extended riff. I would not go so far as to call this "bop" but it is true that I do play with themes and variations and that I try to "blow"—yet, to be precise, not really to *blow*. In my own musical training, which preceded my training as a writer and thinker, I was a pianist, which means that instead of blowing I struck. I am trying to strike a sequence of notes and note groupings, to make passages, to unfold.

After "Depp Positions," I give a brief "Interlude" as a way of shaking myself out and also as a preparation for what is to come. In this I discuss Roland Barthes's theory of the *punctum* and apply it to Depp's performances. No one who is not interested in Roland Barthes's theory of the *punctum* need read this short passage and anyone who reads it may feel free to jump around at leisure. Barthes's point, in a nutshell, is that a photograph is a kind of field and that it always contains a mark or point, the *punctum,* that stands out, even leaps out, and centralizes our engagement; I try to suggest there are also cinematic *puncta* in order to prepare the reader for the next section, "Johnny Depp Starts Here."

This is a set of "études," in which I work by locating ideas not in theory as inspired by or recollected in performance but in some of Depp's performances themselves. "Études" I call them in homage to Frédéric Chopin, who wrote two opus groups of such pieces choosing a different aesthetic problem to resolve with each—as it were, a different spatio-temporal form. In this section, including discussions of Gilbert Grape, Spencer Armacost, Johnny Depp (as played by Johnny Depp in *Lost in La Mancha*), Raoul Duke, Don Juan De Marco, Donnie Brasco, Glen Lantz, Axel Blackmar, William Blake, Edward Scissorhands, George Jung, Jack Kerouac, Bon Bon, Captain Jack Sparrow, the Native American Raphael from *The Brave,* and Mort Rainey, I address the actor through his roles, attempting to elicit broader thematic discussions as inspired by particular—often quite minuscule—aspects that have hitherto gone unremarked upon. A caveat. Since at least as much as it is a study this volume is also a composition, I needed to work not in some matrix of required moves and adaptations but out of inspiration and curiosity. So it is that not every Depp performance gets treated, and that my treatments may focus on only limited aspects of a performance. My aim is to be revealing and to encourage further thought about Depp in particular and film performance in general, not to catalog all the actor's work. While it is a sad truth that the book cannot address everything, the fact that films of Depp's are being shot, edited, packaged, advertised, or planned even as this sentence is being written makes comprehensiveness impossible anyhow.

Two relatively brief essays follow and conclude the volume. In "Depp Theory," I examine Depp's screen style as an avatar of forces and energies not encountered before in screen performance, a response—decidedly enigmatic—to a certain well-worn and desiccated style of motion picture presentation and reception. To do this I begin by considering the "pleasure of the view" that encountered other historically placed forms of visual culture only to be replaced by a pervasive and bitter critical dissatisfaction. What Depp offers to viewers, I argue, is what early photography and early cinema also offered, namely, an opportunity for stunned regard. Finally, in "The Image Views Himself Disappear" I offer a kind of coda upon the theme that Johnny Depp will stop acting one day.

Let me raise an interesting and important problem. If the Johnny Depp who starts here has been, and remains, my Johnny Depp—since as a phenomenology this can be nothing if not personal—of what use, then, and of what significance can this book be to anyone else? Fundamentally, this is what has been labeled by semiotic scholarship the problem of intersubjectivity, applied to cultural, social, historical experience. It is also the problem of language. In what way, one could wonder, can this sentence that I am writing be intelligible, meaningful, useful, and perhaps pleasurable to any person other than myself? And the answer is that language invokes shared meaning, shared reference (whatever it is that we take "sharing" to mean; yet, most simply, we could say that it means many can successfully make claims upon the selfsame territory). As you read these sentences that I am composing, you recognize—and own—the words I am using just as quickly as I do when I compose with them. They do not have *only* private and unitary meaning for me, and I am not inventing or originating them; I am choosing them. I am, as it were, writing from the outside in, not from the inside out. While my body, my mind, my personality, my emotions, my memory, and my convictions are all affected when I see Johnny Depp in a film, in order to make clear to you what is happening to me I must search among the words, phrases, and references that are already available (and that I know will resonate with you because you, too, know they are already available) in order to find the ones that will bridge the chasm between us. We are all of us not only sitting at the edge of an abyss, but sitting there, as Kenneth Burke once wrote, "nervously loquacious" (1965, 272).

A brief pause. Clearly, I am addressing the problem of language for transmitting *subjective* experience, and I am taking "subjective experience" to be a reality, not a myth in itself. One could also argue that all experience is objective, indeed material, and that the very notion of a subjective, idiosyncratic, individual, personal "take" on Johnny Depp is little more than an opiate to keep me from seeing that whatever I see everybody else sees, since it is completely, *and only*, out there. This is ultimately an Althusserian critique. I would not take issue with it. From my point of view, even if Johnny is taken to be objectively real and nothing else, even if his performances are interpreted as an economically based signal system and nothing more, even if we neglect the problems of subjectivity and intersubjectivity and stand upon the conviction that there is no chasm at all separating one viewer from another when they are bound together by the strictures of class and geography; still, the task of writing these sentences, conditioned as it is by the external constraints and formulations of grammar, all publicly shared and learned, falls upon my own frail self, bearing the weight of autobiography and mortality. It is true, in other words, that we were all born and we will all die, yet saying this truth in this particular way in this particular paragraph in this particular book is my way of speaking, my way of being in the world (on this, see Goodman 1972). I must come to terms with Johnny Depp, then, in this exact way, in order to say my piece; and I think if I struggle to make sense I will also be struggling to be accessible and clear to someone else—someone who is "not me," whatever that can be taken to mean. Dear reader: it is in this exact way that I find myself writing to you.

I believe that if fully, sufficiently, penetratingly, precisely, rhythmically, colorfully, sensitively, self-consciously, mnemonically, incisively, constructively, and beautifully I can manage to say what I see on the screen, you, too, can recognize that construct and perhaps be informed. In short, my Johnny Depp can be anybody's Johnny Depp. Being a mechanically reproduced visual record, the screen performance is somewhat subject to language (given the tremendous difficulty of using words upon images), its reception by me therefore not wholly a subjective matter; or at least, what's onscreen can be related by one viewer to another in such a fashion that each indication successfully solicits a recognition, not, if you will, a wholly objective state of affairs and yet as much objectivity as ever we need or hope to achieve. To put this differently: whether I can say enough of what I have seen to make you think, "Yes, that is exactly what I have seen, too," is doubtful; but in trying to write I can evoke your attempt to read, and in that mutuality of endeavor is our conversation. In this way, not only Johnny Depp but also the screen and also film itself can start here, start in the sense of leaping into discourse—and not for the first time, either, but again and again. Film must start for us again and again, in order that we may see it more clearly, more penetratingly, more rhythmically, more self-consciously. Not Depp himself but this saying of mine about Depp starts here, and if I conjure him for the reader then he is conjured now, and in these pages, for the first time in just this way and also not exclusively here. They who read may see.

If the reader asks why I have chosen Johnny Depp, because I might have chosen any actor, any film, any era, perhaps these pages will bring the answer. In one, perhaps too flattering, sentence, his is the preeminent motion picture image of our time and motion picture images are both fascinating and culturally central. On the cultural centrality more people have written than on the fascination, and it is the fascination that holds my interest—not simply in itself, in the sense that I am curious about the way Depp fascinates—but also structurally, in the sense that I am curious about the way fascination happens and works, and Depp is the model *par excellence* in terms of our screen life. Depp's magnetism will recall that of Montgomery Clift and James Dean a little; his ability to use his body, to dance, will bring up memories of the performances of Marlon Brando; his ability to disappear into a character will remind many of Dustin Hoffman or Laurence Olivier. His physical beauty and the intensity of his gaze are nonpareil, the eyes moving in the same direction, yet not as brutally far, as Tyrone Power's, being not as hopelessly liquid as Sal Mineo's, seeming to be less fiendishly playful, indeed, than Cary

Grant's. But he can muster the sensuality of Mineo, the extraordinary grace of Grant, the dash of Power, together, all in a breath. Though one can typify performers and acting styles in this way, one is rarely helped by doing this in appreciating the subtleties of any particular performed moment, since inevitably what we see onscreen resonates for us with thoughts and experiences in the private and social realms that extend far outside the limits of the performance. While to some extent one's response to what is onscreen is personal, yet still it can be informed by sensitivity to, and knowledge about, one's culture, the history of screen performances, and the reservoir of other screen performances that may link to what one is seeing. And in the end, any attempt to say fully and clearly what one is seeing is a challenge in its own right, the richness of theories and languages of analysis entirely notwithstanding. Alexander Herzen wrote that each generation must find its own fullness; each writer about the screen must find his own way of seeing and speaking.

In order to read this book for pleasure it is not a requirement that one watch the films being written about before reading, although it's not a bad idea. The prose is intended to be interesting on its own. But the ideal circumstance, also one that is impossible, is this: that I am reading this at the same exact moment as I am writing it, yet also at the same moment that I am watching what I am writing and reading about; and that you have joined me. We can hope to approximate this, if we wish.

While I worked on this book, many of my friends and colleagues asked me the obvious question: was I intending to meet Johnny Depp? The answer to that extremely provocative question is, of course, the text in these pages. The Johnny Depp that I write about here cannot be met, that is certain, at least, not met in the sense my friends had in mind. And what about the Johnny Depp with whom one *can* sit and drink a glass of wine, chattering about his family and his home in France, his intended movie roles, perhaps even the roles from his past? That Johnny Depp, when he brings himself to such meetings, is part of a publicity construction. But there is another obstruction more interesting. Of all the movie-goers in the world, the one who is incapable of appreciating the screen performances of Johnny Depp is Johnny Depp. This book is in part written to him as a salutation and appreciation, and as such he could have no part in it. Yet, most profoundly for me, he is here already.

What is central is this one fact: it is the Johnny Depp we see onscreen who is my focus here, not the Johnny Depp who enacts that Johnny Depp even though I must attempt to write about both of them in order to say the first. It is the performing performer. I have been interested in actors and performance as long as I can remember, and in the context of this moment I will reveal a secret about my introduction to film, a secret that is possibly not only mine. Johnny Depp invokes this secret to me repeatedly and I put it forward at this moment in order that it may also be invoked for you.

I was in a very large theater, one of those places with gilding and painted cherubim on a domed ceiling and plush seats—I think, maybe, the Palace Theater on King Street in Hamilton, Ontario. It was early in the 1950s. The film, whatever it was, was in black and white. It had, to be sure, love scenes. Figures moved back and forth in the radiant, shimmering, hot silver light, eyes twinkling and so on. But I thought—I was certain beyond question—that what I was seeing was actual people who were behind the screen, somehow gathered under the roof of this august building and enacting this drama, and who, in certain moments and through some process beyond my imagination, had been turned into giants. Something I did not understand, would never understand, and in fact did not wish to contemplate, had inflated them, *but only inflated them,* so that still, even if they were huge, they were *there,* real, living out what they were living out, and the wonderful screen was permitting me to see them. It was only much, much later that I understood film was a projection coming from a booth, that it was a trick of light, and that in the theater darkness I was not in the company of those wonderful beings at all. I was alone in a crowd.

I suppose for me Johnny Depp today is still and always *there* behind the screen when I watch him, there but also untouchable, a supreme trick of light.

DЄPP POSITIONS

Hungarian

And though she may have studied with an expert dialectician and grammarian,
I . . . can . . . tell . . . zat . . . she . . . vas . . . borrrrrn . . . Hungarian!
Lerner and Loewe, *My Fair Lady*

Johnny Depp is not Hungarian. Not long into Tim Burton's *Ed Wood* (1994), however, he participates in a strange "Hungarian event." As the title character, a happy-go-lucky Hollywood studio greensman's assistant who dreams of making it big as a film director, he has accidentally encountered the celebrated horror star Béla Lugosi (Martin Landau, also not Hungarian) and they have quickly become friends. Lugosi is seventysomething, jaded, faded, masqueraded. Wood à la Depp is brash, bright, bungling, and bizarre—a man with not only a penchant for angora and high heels but also a knack for affectionate self-mockery, as though to say, "I'm an odd one, aren't I? And it's fun, isn't it, that I'm odd?" We find him one night, seated on Lugosi's divan as the two film addicts gaze at the television personality Vampira (Lisa Marie) who is hosting a late-night screening of Lugosi's *Dracula*. "I think she's a honey," coos the old star, as he begins to wave his fingers at the screen while whispering a mantra of seduction. "My gosh, Béla! How do you *do* that?" says Wood, terribly impressed at the lulling tones of the basso voice and the fingers curling outward again and again like so many waves running onto a beach. "You must be double-jointed," instructs Lugosi, as pale as a sheet. "And you must be Hungarian." As he whispers these words, we see the two friends, side by side, flicking their fingers out in perfect unison like so many tentacles, and the haunting gazes from their dark eyes are perfectly matched as their fingers "dance" in the eerie glare of the cathode light.

This is a very Deppish moment. The eerie zaniness, the simplicity and sincerity in an act of complete irrationality, the dramatic flair . . . the apparent apprenticeship, as though Johnny is drinking in the actions of Martin Landau in precisely the way that Ed is drinking in the actions of Lugosi. It is clear enough that characters and actors are onscreen together in a scene that is constructed through layering. Indeed, there is no way to appreciate the very deep complexities of Johnny Depp's screen work without seeing that it inevitably involves layering. In this case, we have Depp the performer donning the mask of Wood the character, Landau the performer donning the mask of Lugosi the character, and then, behind all this, Wood and Lugosi the historical actual beings who lived in Los Angeles in the 1950s when this movie is set. Edward D. Wood, Jr. (1924–1978) was the writer, director, producer, and frequently the star of *Glen or Glenda* (1953), *Jail Bait* (1954), *Bride of the Monster* (1955), *Plan 9 from Outer Space* (1959), *Shotgun Wedding* (1963), *Orgy of the Dead* (1965), *Class Reunion* (1970), *The Only House* (1971), *Necromania* (1971), *Cocktail Hostesses* (1973), *Five Loose Women* (1974), and many other far-from-celebrated films that intrigue more people today than they ever did while he was alive. Béla Lugosi (1882–1956) made 108 films directly (and was represented through the cutting-in of archival footage in an additional 14), including *The Veiled Woman* (1929), *Dracula* (1931), *Murders in the Rue Morgue* (1932), and *Ninotchka* (1939). Since the Lugosi onscreen in *Ed Wood* is meant to be understood as a direct representation of the Lugosi who died in 1956 and worked with Ed Wood in actuality, the Lugosi sitting on the divan and seducing Vampira through the airwaves is both a character (in Tim Burton's film) and a person (who predated Tim Burton). And the same can be said for Wood. Since Lugosi was an expatriate Hungarian, the claim made by Martin Landau on camera and in character that "you must be Hungarian" reads as a direct authentication of that historical, actual ethnicity, and therefore as a verification, too, of the relationship between the screen characterization and the real historical figure who underpins it. The character seems like a Hungarian character because the real person it is based upon was especially marked as a Hungarian person—hence the famous slow drawl in which the actor performed the annunciation of himself as "de Cowwwwwwnt!" (The Count on "Sesame Street," indeed, is an elegant parody not of Dracula the fictional, mythical being but of Dracula, the practical creation of Béla Lugosi.) But what is it that we are perceiving when, as Lugosi intones, "You must be Hungarian," we see Johnny Depp with waving fingers and saucer eyes in that flickery darkness?

What is this "Hungarian" quality emanting from Johnny Depp?

Or: what do I mean when, perceiving this film, I use the word "Hungarian"? Do I mean something historical, ethnic, geographic, something that implies heritage and inheritance, what Burke would have called (in *Permanence and Change*) the "genetic motive"? In that sense, after all, "Hungarian" is an ethnic marker, like "Italian," "Malaysian," "Portuguese." In an important sense, I do not mean to invoke ethnicity at all but, instead, to conjure what it is that Landau, as Lugosi, is conjuring when he uses the word exactly in the way that he uses it. Landau, "Hungarian," is also not Hungarian. And I take Landau to have concocted his performance in large part from viewing Lugosi films, therefore to be imitating Lugosi (the Hungarian) in his speech. Since many have drawled the word "Hungarian" softly as he does, indeed imitating him in doing this (many, to be sure, including Rex Harrison in *My Fair Lady* [1964] when he invokes the lines quoted above while performing "You Did It"), the word as thus intoned is a performing construction, part of a staging. It is meant to suggest a morbid and passionate, nostalgic and pained, appreciation and yearning (such as an appreciation for a concentration of Magyar blood and yearning for a supremacy of Magyar feeling and experience) that can be associated with a certain mythology, a certain topography, a certain characteristically melancholic personality, linking, for example, the cities of Buda and Pest and the cultural bubble blown outward from the river that divides them into the literature and imagery of the Gothic as defined in the West. The "Hungarian" strains to reach an always receding apogee of pleasurable intensity, stretches for a thread that is too impossibly high and stretched too taut while also tickling. As Lugosi's Count Dracula constitutes, in fact, the epitome of that definition, he is the paramount symbol of an aggregation of symbols. Yet he is *only* a symbol.

John Cawelti notes how in the construction of the western, a "relatively brief stage in the social evolution of the West when outlaws or Indians posed a threat to the community's stability has been erected into a timeless epic past in which heroic individual defenders of law and order without the vast social resources of police and courts stand poised against the threat of lawlessness or savagery" (1974, 58). The screen Lugosi, too, is extending and expanding a limited historical and cultural moment, indeed a moment refracted through the lens of particular interests, as he generalizes about "Hungarian" character. And it is of this generalization that he is himself the paragon, a figure who is happy to stretch vowels in lazy delight or gnawing hunger, happy to scowl and stare. In saying, "You must be Hungarian," then, he is meaning, "You must be such as I am." In one phrase, the character Béla Lugosi is beckoning the character Ed Wood to inherit him; and the older, experienced actor Martin Landau is beckoning the younger, aspiring actor Johnny Depp to imitate, duplicate, eradicate him.

Further, when Ed starts to imitate the "Hungarianness" of Lugosi's bewitching gestures, he is in truth imitating not so much the structure of the gestures as Lugosi's performance of them, his styling, his inflection. Thus it is that the scene captures the quality of apprenticeship and personal affiliation, a quality that suffuses Depp's screen work altogether. The imitation is an intimacy.

Can we believe that, at this screen moment and perfectly in tune with Lugosi's gestures, Ed Wood is actually Hungarian, too—has actually assimilated an ethnicity by contagion? Ed Wood is and can only be from Poughkeepsie, once and forever—a young man around whose dazzled perspective one Vassar girl too many has pranced. He is a creature of the lumpenbourgeoisie, a migrant to Hollywood, sucked up in the Hollywood dream, fired by a passionate belief that he can do what Orson Welles does: write, direct, produce, and star in his own fabulous motion pictures. Far from laying onto himself the mysterious dark cloaks of esoteric Hungarian history, like his buddy Lugosi, he flits around in a blonde wig and an angora sweater. But as Depp plays him at this moment in Lugosi's little house, there is "Hungarianness" in the dancing of Wood's fingers, and a distinct sense that the ethnicity of Lugosi has traveled through the air and infected his friend and neighbor to the core. Depp's Ed Wood is so impressionably ravenous for Lugosi's "Hungarianness," he has imbibed it like a potion, and, further, in doing this he is devouring the essence of his friend in something of an echo of Lugosi's screen devourings. He is a kind of Dracula of the evening. For an instant, indeed, our feeling of the dark mysticism is so intense that the "Hungarianness" seems absolutely inherent in Johnny Depp; that on "Lugosi's" instructions, moved, that is, not merely by Landau's performance but also by the knowledge of the historical Lugosi, he has willed it into being. If for Landau the characterization of this ethnicity proceeds outward and forward—from some "Lugosi" within and behind toward a surface we see onscreen—for Depp it proceeds inward and backward, the screen "Ed Wood" appropriating the "Hungarian" spirit he catches from "Lugosi" and conferring it upon the actor who plays him, Depp. For there is hardly a doubt: it is not Ed Wood who seems to have become what "Lugosi" would have him become, it is Johnny Depp. Landau finds the character in himself and in his memory, and brings it out. Depp finds himself in the character.

Another way to put this: the "Hungarian" infection can only pass from Lugosi to Depp—Lugosi, not Landau, because Landau is completely hidden inside his characterization. And Depp, not Wood, because Johnny Depp is never completely hidden inside his characterizations, not even, as we shall see, in the remarkable Edward Scissorhands, who is surely a triumph of makeup (by Irene Aparicio, Fern Buchner, Bridget Cook, Selena Miller, Matthew W. Mungle, Ve Neill, Rick Provenzano, Kim Santantonio, Susan Schuler-Page, Werner Sherer, Liz Spang, Rick Stratton, Yolanda Toussieng, Mary Ann Valdes, Lynda Kyle Walker, Brad Wilder, and Stan Winston) and costuming (by Colleen Atwood) to rival the most exquisite concoctions of Hollywood. There is for the viewer a sense of a double life onscreen with Johnny Depp, as though he is bonded through an invisible bridge of tissue to the character he is playing in such a way that what becomes of the character inevitably, and soon, becomes of him as well. Since Ed Wood has "become" Hungarian for the moment, Johnny is infected, and our sense is that while shooting this scene, at least, Johnny must also have "become" Hungarian.

To clarify: by "Hungarian" I refer, of course, not to the datum of historical, geographical, and ethnic circumstance, nor merely to attributes that seem to float off the surface of the character and evaporate around him, indications that he has been embedded in historical, geographical, or ethnic circumstance—say, the propensity to drama and romance, the sensitivity to profound sublimity, the revolutionary fire, the taste for *gulyás*. "Hungarian" is not factual. When Lugosi says, "You must be Hungarian," he means a mystique must float away from you, a chill must invade the air; he means to point to not so much a concrete experience as a fantasy of experience, that one affiliates oneself with a certain body of imagery and narration, a certain library. One adopts a certain conviction, a dominance over circumstance, a pride in silence, a mask of seriousness in the face of life covering, perhaps, a regretful smile of loss and treasured hope. All this constitutes together something of a public performance, a waving of fingers. All this is couched in an inexplicability, a tempestuousness, something very far from bright cool rationality and method. One dances one's "Hungarianness," and so for all that it is civilized it is also primitive and young. To bring off this "Hungarianness," Depp exercises his hands, fixes his gaze, and widens the apertures of his eyes, forces himself to make no expression (and no hint of expression) with the mouth but to desire only optically, with heroic restraint, so that the desire is burning and consuming. Whether any of this would make sense to an actual Hungarian as "Hungarianness," of course, is hardly the point (I find it hard to imagine that it would); a transformation has taken place in the character, one commensurate with the very arbitrary label "Hungarian" that a history of watching popularizations from Hollywood has conditioned us to use, and a transformation, indeed, that has infected the actor, who is also, it seems, an aficionado of the silver screen in the depths of his heart. To a certain mystical and entrancing fixation of attention, a certain passionate and joyous belligerence, a certain nobility we have applied the label "Hungarian," and if "Hungarian" one has to be to wave one's fingers powerfully and seductively at the "honey" who inhabits the television screen, then "Hungarian" Lugosi and Wood—Landau and Depp—have surely become.

Of how many other actors can it be said that the acts of the characters they play seem to rub off on them? Brando, surely, who forever might have been a contender. Cary Grant. Bogart. Lugosi. Like these, Depp is present himself onscreen alongside his characters, one might even say in a playful bond of love with them. If there is a sense of homoeroticism in Depp's performances, and I think it unquestionable that there is, perhaps it inheres exactly in this delicate business of affiliation and affection that is evident between him and the character he plays. When, much later in the film, Wood meets Orson Welles (Vincent D'Onofrio) in Musso and Frank's Restaurant, it is Welles, not the talented D'Onofrio, we sense in the encounter; yet it remains Depp, not just Wood, who seems exhilarated to be "meeting" him. To the argument that if this is true, Depp is simply not much of an actor, since he does not know how to embed himself fully in his performance, I would rejoin that Depp has his characteristic way of relating to the character he is playing and also that Depp is far more than an actor and also that in a blink of an eye, a breath, suddenly he *is* Ed Wood and then, just as suddenly, Ed Wood is gone.

What Grant, Brando, Lugosi, Bogart, and Depp have in common is a quality that has been depreciated in recent years by the grinding of the global publicity machine and by the pervasive mass-production of celebrity: stardom. Stars seize us *in* and *through* their characters, but also *in spite of* them, *beside* them, *over and above* them. Clint Eastwood has shown star quality, although not absolutely invariably—one sees it in *High Plains Drifter* and in *Blood Work* but not so much in *Space Cowboys* or in *The Bridges of Madison County*. The star never displaces the actor who is crafting a character, but he often sides with him. Dustin Hoffman has never gone beyond being an actor—one of astonishing range and insight. Tom Cruise has never gone beyond being a celebrity. Like Robert DeNiro before him, Leonardo DiCaprio began as an actor of chilling strength but allowed himself to be devoured by celebrity—contrast the steely *Mean Streets* or *Taxi Driver* with DeNiro's recent work, for example, *Analyze This;* and *What's Eating Gilbert Grape* or *The Basketball Diaries* with *Titanic*. Jeff Bridges has the look of a star but is, through and through, and notably, an actor; for example in *Fearless* or *Starman* or *The Big Lebowski*. And not all stars are immense—it is not the size of the stardom that is its essence. Something of the actor and something of the character must co-exist in a field of boundless fascination and pleasure, so that we find ourselves looking without needing to find, observing without calculation, reaching and yet hoping never quite to grasp. Johnny Depp isn't a broad canvas like Brando, or a dazzling array of lights like Astaire, or a paragon of classlessness like Grant, or an eternal enigma like Bogart, or a monument to loss like Lugosi, but he has the wonder of an innocent, the passion of a person who has been much denied, the wit of a juggler, and a commanding physical technique to rival James Dean's.

As to ethnicity, Johnny Depp has many times taken upon himself its mantle: a Romanisch horseman in *The Man Who Cried,* a Sicilian cop in *Donnie Brasco,* a Mexican soldier in *Before Night Falls,* a Spanish psychotic in *Don Juan DeMarco,* a French-Canadian author in *The Source,* a French balladeer in *Chocolat*—thus in a way privileging what Steven Alan Carr calls "voices that had heretofore spoken from the margins" (2001, 2). While Allen and Albert Hughes acknowledged that their *From Hell* is a "white movie" (Overpeck 2002, 41), Depp's Inspector Frederick Aberline is an opium addict living his life in a dream-state, thus, like Edward Scissorhands, everything of an alien, so very marginalized as to be almost voiceless. Nor is ethnicity alien to Depp offscreen. On his mother's side, one of his biographers writes, he is the grandson of a Cherokee, a young man who inherited "the sharp cheekbones and sculptured visage that was to grace a thousand magazine covers the world over as he grew to maturity in the public gaze" (Robb 1996, 16). As well, writes another, there is "a fair amount of Irish and German in [Johnny's] background" (Heard 2001, 2). Onscreen, to be sure, his "Hungarian" and other ethnic moments are fashioned, and also dispensed with, so casually and with so little apparent effort (Depp has a keen ear for linguistic nuance) that ethnicity seems to become fluid and fleeting, entirely of the moment.

Ethnicity for the Depp we see onscreen, indeed, is situational tincture more than historical affiliation, and so it is that his performances are continuous modulations in ethnic being, this possibly because his extreme idiosyncrasy alienates him perpetually from our complete identification, estranges him from our familiarities. In *From Hell* he lapses frequently into that opiated stupor, inhabiting a dreamland inaccessible to us as we inhabit the hyperrational territory of the narrative; as opium-eater he inhabits a radically separated *ethnos*. In *Blow,* by contrast, he affronts our pleasure-seeking sensibility by meandering through the story in an obsessive hunger for profit. As Ed Wood, when he responds to the tacit invitation to try being "Hungarian," the speed and delicacy of his response suggest immediately a desperation to try being anything else than what he is, to voyage. One hears an echo of T. S. Eliot: "Not fare well, /But fare forward, voyagers."

If ethnicity can be an anchor and lock, a basis for organizing powerlessness and hence a means of constraining and limiting freedom and opportunity, it is also a marker, a means of fixing both identity and experience in the oceanic field of variation and flux. The desire to attach a stable identity to human experience, which is constantly in motion, to call someone "this" but not "that," aims for a hierarchy of value in which statuses are aligned vertically and rewards distributed unequally, even as affiliations and loyalties based on ethnic identification systematically operate to render some institutionalized pathways accessible, give basis for shared history and experience, and mount a platform for convivially interconnected sentiment. But no one has ethnicity before humanity. And the search to pin ethnicity on us is also an attack, an attempt to apprehend. That Johnny Depp's identity onscreen is so very hard to establish within a matrix of ethnicities suggests that his film form is in combat with hierarchizing tendencies, labels, fixed approaches, historical imprisonments. He persists in being one of "Those drowsy ships that dream of sailing forth;/ It is to satisfy/ Your least desire" (Baudelaire 1983–85).

Yet it is also true, and odd to note, that only in a very few performances does Depp build for his audience a distinct sense of otherness and unfamiliarity, that he creates a being in meeting whom we can discern in ourselves an awkward feeling of strangeness and distance. Most of the time, whatever he is pretending to be, Romanisch (Cesar) or German American (Glen Lantz) or Italian (Dean Corso) or English (Frederick Aberline), we are instantly at home with him in a kind of postmodern space that Vivian Sobchack describes, following Fredric Jameson, as depthless, simulacral, and one in which "our social and ethnic affinities have been supplanted by affinities of consumption and cosmetic display" (1991, 335). In other words, we recognize the codes being used in his performance, standing outside them so that they are indeed intelligible to us and instantly identifiable and yet also finding them sufficiently familiar from repetitive use that they hardly seem strange, hardly seem like characteristics of the "other" anymore. "In an earlier time," Sobchack asserts, "being ethnic meant being part of a marginalized, yet coherent and relatively stable social group—one both perceived and represented by the dominant (and unethnic or assimilated) culture and by its own members as exclusively different and other from that dominant culture by virtue of its maintenance of specific codes of language, dress, manner, kinship, social and religious structure, and of its particular history and mythology" (1991, 332); and so she stands at once on two sides of the line that separates the one who sees ethnicity from the ethnic one he sees. Kinship, religious and social structure, and manner are "codes," after all, only for those who do not experience them directly, those who stand apart to label. Being "part" of a "coherent" group was antithetical to using codes of display. That ethnicity can be seen as "codes" would seem itself to be part of the flattening and consumerist logic of postmodernism. If Depp's "ethnic" actions are not necessarily predictable or easily accommodated to, still his character, his presentation, and his personality tend to seem comfortable for us, even neighborly, in part because they are rendered as images—first, images like all other images; and secondly, images to which we have become increasingly habituated and which are therefore every day less alien and strange. Indeed, he seems proximate, as though his performance is being whispered gently in our ear. This is, perhaps, an effect not so much of his being at ease before the lens as of his manifesting exactly the kind of dis-ease we might expect to feel, ourselves, in his place: in an extended interview about the making of *Lost in La Mancha,* he is continually picking shreds of tobacco from his lip, rubbing his chin, touching his mouth as though to ascertain whether it is moving when he speaks. Yet these self-conscious gestures we share, too. In front of an interviewer's camera, he is suddenly camera-shy.

The sense of otherness that is present in Depp onscreen so much less than we expect it to be finds a clear description in Simone de Beauvoir, for whom "otherness is a fundamental category of human thought":

> No group ever sets itself up as the One without at once setting up the Other over against itself. If three travelers chance to occupy the same compartment, that is enough to make vaguely hostile "others" out of all the rest of the passengers on the train. In small-town eyes all persons not belonging to the village are "strangers" and suspect; to the native of a country all who inhabit other countries are "foreigners"; Jews are "different" for the anti-Semite, Negroes are "inferior" for American racists, aborigines are "natives" for colonists, proletarians are the "lower class" for the privileged. (1989, xxiii)

Like De Beauvoir, when I invoke otherness, I do not mean to connote any particular visible or performable characteristic, or any salient quality presumed by those who label otherness to be present beyond the field of direct perception. The qualities or characteristics attributed to "others," of course, can neatly follow from the act of creating an alien category in order to define a self: once one has the category, one fills it with attributes. And usually with Depp, as in the characters I have listed above, although plenty of historical, cultural, or racial reasons are given through the performance to merit categorization of his onscreen personality as other, it is also true that he manages to draw himself to us as a distinct familiar, a self of our own, an innocent. It is in this sense that he is chameleon-like, and that his presence is so globally accessible (both aesthetically and in marketing). A few of his characters, further, drink strangeness from their surround: Gilbert Grape from his family and friends, George Jung from his business, Ichabod Crane from the setting in which he must act—but even these seem instantly recognizable or knowable; their strangeness is entirely a cozy and comprehensible strangeness.

But Ed Wood's Hungarian moment is of another order altogether. Perhaps it is the simplicity of him saying nothing, arching his immense black eyebrows, and waving his fingers in the eerie light, something just as direct as this *unheimlich* gesture, that pushes us back. It is certainly not that Depp seems "Hungarian" for even a moment. Yet he manages to acquire the flavor of someone who is no longer Johnny Depp, thereby dislodging us from the previous character personalities we brought to the viewing experience.

It is precisely a gesture of the *unheimlich,* what Freud called "the uncanny" (1919), that we see in Ed Wood. And I would claim that in *Nick of Time,* in the persona of Gene Watson, the father whose child is kidnapped and who has but ninety or so minutes to find her (the same ninety or so minutes that constitute the running time of the film), Depp reaches a kind of apotheosis of cinematic uncanniness. The "uncanny," writes Freud, "belongs to all that is terrible—to all that arouses dread and creeping horror; it is equally certain, too, that the word is not always used in a clearly definable sense, so that it tends to coincide with whatever excites dread" (368).

Further, as Freud shows, the uncanny is very closely related to the canny, the familiar, and "leads back to something long known to us, once very familiar" (369–370). In order to see how Gene Watson, the dutiful father who risks his life to save his child, has about him this bloodcurdling quality, we must make a brief diversion.

It is astonishing to think how, in theatrical performance, the smallest details of the organization of activity can rip through the screen of fiction for members of an audience, causing the drama to momentarily collapse. A small barrette falls accidentally from a character's coiffure and instantaneously, as the object gleams in the stage light upon the floorboards, it assumes the pungent and devastating quality of belonging *to the actress* who is performing the character, not to the character at all; and the hair out of which it fell suddenly transforms into part of the actress's body, the coiffure done up in a dressing room backstage and not in a character's boudoir. The character entirely, and instantaneously, melts away. So it is that a performer onstage will trouble herself to kick such an object under the furniture, that it may not persist within the viewing field of the audience to disrupt the show and the very being of the entity the actress is engaged in offering. An actor muffs a line or a syllable of a word, and suddenly the world of the stage is punctured by the persistent factuality of speech and its vulnerabilities, lips, throats, the actors' presence together onstage, their having rehearsed, the script they rehearsed, their knowledge of the language, of words, the structure of the lines in the script, the tongue of the actor and its sluggishness around the syllables of the threatening word, the very presence of the embarrassed audience sitting around in the darkness observing this catastrophe in a paralysis of transformation and horror. Or an actor, walking into his scene, must bend suddenly and seize from the floor a barrette, glowing in the stage light, that fell off a character's head in the scene before and that a foot did not quite manage to kick under a chair. What is significant here is a present and observable fact, a reality, that is out of the actor's momentary control; something totally unintended; something continuously present, and yet unseen, not looked for, not noticed, but always existing: as Freud quotes from Grimm's dictionary, *"The further idea is developed of something withdrawn from the eyes of others, something concealed, secret, and this idea is expanded in many ways"* (376). The reality of fiction may slip, is anxious.

In his essay on "Architectural Anxiety in Digital Culture" (2001), Anthony Vidler writes of anxious space, nervous space, as related to Freud's uncanny. One sees in *Nick of Time* inpouchings and tunnelings of a kind of modernist nervous space. In all his films, as a matter of fact, Depp exhibits an extraordinary grace in his movement and pose, so that narrative space unfolds around him in a measured, even baroque, way. But in *Nick of Time,* he is forced in an extended desperation to grope through space. His personality is like that of the camera in *L'Année dernière à Marienbad,* ceaselessly wandering in fear.

In *Nick of Time,* Depp manifests one particular aspect of Freud's *unheimlich,* which is that of the double. "The 'double' has become a vision of terror, just as after the fall of their religion the gods took on daemonic shapes," writes Freud (1919, 389). And one particularly chilling aspect of doubling is a "factor of involuntary repetition which surrounds with an uncanny atmosphere what would otherwise be innocent enough" (390). In this film, alone of all his work, Depp plays what might be called an untransformed character—untransformed in the surface, technical, discernible sense associated with make-up, costume, accent, gesture, posture, and so on. Captain Jack Sparrow in *Pirates of the Caribbean: Curse of the Black Pearl* slinks, and this slinking is what I am referring to as a transformation; transformations, too, are his teeth, his braided beard, his gleaming gaze. Edward Scissorhands is a masterpiece of make-up and costuming, and so in becoming him, Depp is transformed. But aside from a tidy haircut and a pair of expensive prescription eyeglasses—eyeglasses chosen specifically to fit with the clothing and presentation of the character and not in any way to make themselves obvious—the character of Watson is a version of Depp onscreen that seems non-racial, non-ethnic, and unothered. It is thus a kind of double of all the other Depps, which are in some sense one and the same in their manifestation as transformed Depps. Gene Watson is little other than a bourgeois, contemporary, suburban young adult—close, in fact, to what Johnny can be presumed to be by those who have no access to him, and at a distance from the other screen characterizations Johnny has made. (Conversely, we can identify "weird" Johnny with those other screen characterizations; then Gene stands out as the hollowed, too tame stranger.)

If Depp onscreen typically presents us with a mask, then the Depp in this film is the double of that mask. Gene Watson is colorless, flavorless, utile, and agile but without his own impetus, civil to a fault. In all of this film he is like the secret revealed in the disturbing moment when performance is disrupted; yet at the same time he is engaged wholly and fluidly in a performance. Thus, watching this film (in the context of other Depp films, not on its own) seems to have the chilling effect of presenting formally the denuded actor who otherwise appears only by accident. Gene is a perfectly choreographed happenstance. It is as though, in a film of a stage performance, an actor suddenly stoops to pick up a barrette, glowing in the light, that fell out of a character's hair in the scene before; and the bending, the retrieval, the deft placement of the object on a table next to a dictionary, constitute not the salvage of a performance but the performance itself.

One further twist. When an actor is performing—it may seem stunning to audiences to realize—he does not see himself. (We are so utterly wrapped up in watching him, it does not occur to us to imagine the limits imposed on his own ability to watch himself.) His appreciation of the performance, therefore, is at a great remove from what is possible for the audience. It is also true that he has in mind, and in his care, certain arcane technical matters that might be beyond the audience's ken (as they are not accustomed to, or professional at, mounting performance), and certain dramaturgical concerns the revelation of which would collapse or ruin the performance for them. But beyond this, even to the degree that he is relaxed into, and infused with, the performance, it is not a construction he is placed *to observe*. All acting is thus blind acting in a sense. One fashions a face and corrects it, modulates it and navigates with it, without seeing what one is accomplishing. So it is that in performing Gene Watson, in playing his part in the construction of *Nick of Time,* Depp can hardly have been anything but innocent of the uncanniness of his role. Screen actors may see dailies, or may attend a screening of the film, thus having a chance to see themselves as audiences will see them, but only after the fact of the performance is sealed. Yet there is no reason to suppose that Depp watches either his dailies or his films, and so there is no reason for supposing that the uncanniness I write about here would be part of his regard or self-knowledge. He has claimed, indeed, that he does not watch his films, or, generally, films at all, except to take his children. When nominated for the Academy Award for *Pirates of the Caribbean,* "he saw none of his fellow nominees' performances and guesses the last movie he saw was *Pirates*—and only because he had to" (Tyrangiel 2004, 78).

If, however, none of us is placed precisely to see what we do, most of us are not judged exclusively on the basis of that appearance. For actors to perform at all, then, is an act of extreme courage. When the performance is uncanny, it strikes at once the very strange—the surface of the role that is, above all, phantasmagorical—and the very homely and familiar, the body of the actor actually committed to public action, and in this case, a body relatively untransformed (in the way Depp's body typically is onscreen) but at the same time also not untransformed in a way the actor is in a position fully to appreciate. Gene Watson is rather like the costume that has fallen off one of the other characters Johnny plays and that must swiftly, somehow, be swept offscreen. Our sense that this is true is what gives us a chill.

Apprehending

You cannot step into the same river twice.

Heraclitus

At the very least, a scene like the "Hungarian" episode in *Ed Wood* nicely illustrates the sort of problem that confronts the viewer's paramount need to apprehend the screen Depp, to discover—grasp, penetrate, be satisfied with—him by finding and exploiting the elusive, even intangible, boundary that separates his person from his characterization. Regarding that boundary, take, for example, teeth. A few times in *Ed Wood,* Ed opens his mouth to reveal (terrifyingly) that just beneath the cuddly angora exterior, the face with skin as smooth as that of a teenage girl, wait Draculaic teeth, misshapen, sharp, obscene (teeth from the world of Jerry Lewis's Julius Kelp in *The Nutty Professor*): once he shows them to teasingly frighten a little boy at Lugosi's door on Halloween eve, later again in full femme array at the end of a party scene. When we see these fangs, we have absolutely no doubt that they are fake, that they are artificial appendages applied by Wood for an exaggerated comic and dramatic effect in some non-theatrical everyday situation (Depp, of course, using prostheses to simulate Wood using prostheses). The teeth *under* these teeth on the screen are Ed Wood's "authentic" teeth, presumably, badly out of alignment and not well cared for. But are *these* underteeth—the teeth of "Ed Wood"—in fact Johnny Depp's teeth, just as "Ed Wood's" body is Johnny Depp's body? Or has Johnny Depp implanted in himself "Ed Wood" dentures over which, in the persona of Ed Wood, he further, and ostensibly, implants Dracula fangs?

These questions are far less material as regards the narrative, to be sure, than as regards the viewer's apprehension of that narrative. What is it that I am seizing as I gaze at the screen—a view of the inside of Johnny's real mouth for and as itself, or a view of his mouth as the setting of an unreal dramaturgical place, the buccal cavity of a character? If I am optically entering Johnny's actual mouth, not Ed's; if I am seeing Johnny's teeth, not Ed's, the filmic experience is intimate in a way that exceeds the experience I have if all the dentistry I see is part of an elaborate set-up. The configuring of the actor's personal body as the character's, through makeup and prosthetics, can seem to be extended inward, the performance of Wood being given not only by the transformation of Depp's exterior surfaces but also by the transmogrification of his interior ones. Or is the impenetrable inside world of the performer *not* excitingly extended outward at all? Do the interior linings of cavities, in such a case, rather than revealing, continue the limiting presentation that begins with face and costume and continues with skin, being themselves not secrets but coverings of secrets? To apprehend Depp, must we go even beyond what is presented when he opens his mouth?

Surely the mouth we see is both Depp's and Wood's, in that Wood is the nexus of our interpretation while Depp is the origin of the manifestation. But how can we understand it, in the quick of being presented with it, except as an interior space co-extensive and co-present with all the surfaces on the screen—that is, as "Wood's" mouth? What we see, after all, is the picture of the inside of a mouth, something which, like any picture, is withdrawn even as it appears to protrude. It is a provocation, a sign of the absence of Depp. Like every image of Depp, it is a sign of his replacement.

Here is the kind of knot one gets tied up in with Johnny Depp, even though, in truth, one could very well be tied up in the same way with any other actor who does mouth work; *except that, oddly, one isn't.* Dustin Hoffman in the dentist's chair in *Marathon Man* does not provoke these musings because he presents at no time such a challenge of surfaces as does Depp. When Depp opens his mouth as Ed Wood, he is also opening his mouth as Johnny Depp, saying, in effect, "Here's my mouth. What do you make of it?" in precise expectation that indeed we will make something. Depp has Wood open his mouth in a certain way in order that he, Depp, may open his mouth. The mouth is at once Wood's and Depp's, yet as it opens and we concentrate on the teeth, thanks to a skillfully placed keylight, it is Depp the present performer, not Wood the extinct subject of performance, the teeth invoke. Quickly the mouth closes, the body moves off—Wood, not Depp.

Symbolically, the attempt to get into Johnny Depp's mouth, as it were, is the general quest to find him, to commit apprehension, which permeates all the popular journalism that has been devoted to this actor (in lieu of serious scholarship), and permeates, indeed, most backstage journalism altogether in this simulacral age. But with Depp, apprehension goes beyond entry. At issue, too, is Depp in flight from the hungry grasp of the narrative that persists in trying to net him. He is always present, as it were, beside as well as inside his character; what happens to the character happens to him. In Mike Newell's *Donnie Brasco,* for example, he is an undercover FBI agent masquerading as a hoodlum in order to assist in putting a sting on a coterie of mafia thugs. It is more than evident that betrayers and informers are sure targets for execution among the thugs, and so the viewer's easy affiliation with Depp is put in continuing jeopardy by the precarious structure of situations in which his true identity may inadvertently be revealed. One day, at the Miami airport, he is encountered by a former acquaintance who calls him by the "wrong" name in front of the wrong people: to escape from this near catastrophe, he is forced to dramatize himself as the unwilling victim of a homosexual pickup, rolling his old colleague in a particularly brutal way. Another time, asked to remove his shoes in a Japanese restaurant, he is forced by the coincidence of having planted an FBI wire on his foot to adamantly refuse, finally, indeed, to participate in a brawl in which a poor man is beaten to a pulp in the men's room. And his wife (Anne Heche) is so distraught and devastated at his prolonged absences from the family (he misses Christmas dinner and his daughter's first communion) for reasons she cannot be permitted to know, she forces him into marital therapy at the hands of a smug practitioner who attacks him with platitudes in total ignorance of the generalized flight that is his present way of life. As Donnie Brasco, then, Depp is being chased by the gang, in the sense that he must survive their relentless and systematic vigilance for traitors all the while possessing the sure knowledge that he is one; and as FBI Special Agent Joe Pistone, he is being chased by his wife, and also by his superiors in the Bureau—men who are increasingly removed from the action they are monitoring.

The effect of this complex structure is to induce on Johnny's part and on ours a deep apprehensiveness about apprehension, so that as the film progresses we find ourselves becoming panic-stricken at every human encounter he has (and fearful of what might happen to those who come too close to him). His tight relationship with Lefty Ruggerio (Al Pacino) is a locus of diffuse panic, heightened by Pacino's deftly manic performance. Donnie's contacts in the government are frighteningly inept and untrustworthy: the managers are exactly the sort of well-meaning boobs likely to compromise his secrecy without the least self-awareness. His young colleagues, amicable and adoring, are green and terrified, reliant upon a professional-

ism he must struggle continuously to mount in migraine-producing
and traumatic circumstances. We fear for his life, therefore, every
time he is to be found with Lefty, regardless of how humorous or ba-
thetic the scene; we fear for his life every time he encounters his
wife, since her frustrations and anger will surely increase his own
high-strung emotion and perhaps carry him over the edge; we fear
for his life when he is with other agents, since they are so maladroit
by comparison; and we fear for his life when he begins to rise in stat-
ure among the Mafiosi, since the new boss, Sonny Black (Michael
Madsen), and his crowd are colder than Lefty, less affectionate, less
trusting, and any tiny hint of a false move will be a death sentence. In
this taut and vitiating narrative, then, we are torn between a desire
to grasp Johnny and a frantic hope that he will elude grasping.

If he eludes grasping we may continue in our desire to grasp him,
we may keep running. And the pleasure world of the film can be
extended.

In Jeremy Leven's *Don Juan DeMarco,* the quest to apprehend
Johnny is given a bizarre twist. Here the issue is framed in ideological terms. Don Juan (Depp) is a young man who has made love to
fifteen hundred and one women, but who, on the verge of suicide,
falls under the legal and interpersonal control of an aging psychiatrist (Marlon Brando). The psychiatrist is entrusted with the bureaucratic job of committing the young man, but something about
Don Juan's seductive manner and astonishing worldliness leads him
instead to become his patient's ally against the institution, even his
patient's pupil. Where the potential grasp in *Donnie Brasco* is execution, in *Don Juan* it is a diagnosis, literally a signature on an institutional document. What makes the film fascinating as a document
about its star is that Don Juan is avowedly helpless to prevent Dr. Jack
Mickler from signing the paper that will commit him, except through
his powers of speech and persuasion. There is a kind of cat-and-
mouse game played out between Depp as embodiment and Depp as
agent of the script, since his every action of self-defense is constituted as a retreat into the dialogue provided for his character. Yet it
is also the speech—that is, the script, the metadiegesis—that keeps
Dr. Mickler's page unturned, his decision unmade, his curiosity alive,
perhaps as much in the curiously serious Spanish accent through
which Depp delivers it as in the flowery phrases with which it is
composed. If Don Juan can but be persuasive, Mickler will hold back
for a few days, then a few more days, and so on—will keep him off

the tranquilizers that will dissolve his romantic mind. Medication is the sword that can attack Don Juan. Words are his defensive parry. His romantic spirit, his engagement of love—that is to say, Depp as the incarnation of carnality—is the object of our apprehension, the thing we would stab. And we must make a judgment as to where Don Juan really is, in Johnny's body or in his talk. If we attempt to approach him rationally, we are reduced to the status of an institutional worker whose signature can be damning. Like Dr. Mickler, our choice is whether to give in to rational dictates or to deny them and respond out of poetry and emotion. If the film is about Dr. Mickler's decision to accept Don Juan as the physical and sentimental being he claims to be, it is also a venue whereby we can accept Johnny Depp as a galvanizing presence *notwithstanding* what he says onscreen. Everything he says, after all—poetic as it may be—can be rationally taken by us as script. Can we, like Mickler, transcend our script?

The word "apprehend" has at least two distinct readings, both of which I mean to engage when applying it to Depp's screen performance. It is a laying hands upon, or grasping, in the physical sense; and an intellectual seizure, a tying up or bordering, an encapsulation of a substance or field within some perimeter of understanding and discourse. In both the physical and the intellectual sense, apprehension is learning, in that we come into ownership of knowledge that potentially alters the way we go on to experience and understand the world. To apprehend is also to fear, to hold back from. That, too, is a way of learning and having the world.

What brings apprehension into consideration as we engage with Johnny Depp onscreen is precisely his unremitting elusiveness, not only that he shifts and transforms himself radically from film to film and role to role but also that even in any given scene, as we watch him move and interact in character, we sense a presence that is, above all, fluid. He is like the Heraclitean river into which one cannot step twice, always changing, always running away.

To think of John Wayne is not to have the same sense, for example; Wayne is a solid: recall him splayed on the ground contentedly, like a plump old owl, as he observes John Ireland and Montgomery Clift going at one another in the finale of *Red River*. To think of Cary Grant is to encounter a vapor: Roger O. Thornhill dancing along the station quay with Eve Kendall's overnight case under his arm in *North by Northwest* or appraising an appraiser, his ex-wife Rosalind Russell, in *His Girl Friday*. But Depp tantalizes physically exactly inasmuch as he hides or escapes—delivering ice cream to Mary Steenburgen in *What's Eating Gilbert Grape*—so that every line reading, every pose, every gesture is an ambiguity once it is set in the mise-en-scène. I am thinking in particular of a scene in *Blow* where Depp, as George Jung, and Jordi Mollà, as his buddy Diego Delgado, have amassed so much money—literally so many pieces of printed currency—they are having difficulty locating a niche in which to store it all in their modest apartment. We watch Johnny trekking from room to room with boxes of bills piled in his arms, money drifting away from him and floating like so much manna to the floor. In his bouncing gait is happiness and astonishment, pure boyish spirit and innocence even in the fact of the colossal illegality in which he has involved himself to produce this fortune. In his desperation to hurry to move the money, to hurry to find more space, is a mature urgency, the thrust of a producer hard upon a finished work. His furtive eyes and his springy body do not match, and create a kind of time field in which he migrates back and forth as we watch—is he a boy or is he a man? Is the money dangerous or is it the stuff of pure fun? To see the material floating around the room, piled in box after box after box after box, to see the room overflowing, is to have a sense of capacity, fulsomeness, plenitude, even excess, and delightful monstrosity. But to transform the objective wads of cash into bank balances is to perform a summation, a mathematics of desire, a foxtrot of collection, appropriation, entitlement, and investment—in short, to distance oneself from the momentary pleasures of the body and the eye. There is no single, fixed reading of Depp's persona or motive here.

I think the scene important for another reason, however. Since it is Johnny Depp being articulated onscreen, and also at the same time innumerable boxes of hard cash, an equation is being offered that links Depp directly to currency in two senses—Establishment (that is, wealth) and continual motion (that is, play). The project of setting ourselves productively within the antimony of fixity and currency, of drawing a line around Depp even as he never stops moving, is thus both embodied and signified by this scene in which the material currency—the cash—and the condition of currency—Depp and Jordi Mollà frenetically pacing back and forth to pick up and store more and more and more and more and more money—are entirely superimposed. To bring fixity to this scenario, one would have to stop the boys in their tracks and count the money, thus itemizing the stockpile for the record and ending the seemingly endless multiplication of profit by capping it, while at the same time leashing Johnny, petrifying his energy, positioning him once and for all. This is precisely the "positioning" that occurs with a too-sumptuous finality at the end of the film, a source of immense dissatisfaction for the audience as well as for the character.

NOT FINISHED

In his book *Frame Analysis,* among other things an excellent approach to the structure of stagings, Erving Goffman describes a feature of theatrical events that is of particular interest to me here: "Spoken interaction is opened up ecologically; the participants do not face each other directly or (when more than two) through the best available circle, but rather stand at an open angle to the front so that the audience can literally see into the encounter" (1974, 140).

In motion pictures, of course, the audience, as John Van Druten once put it, *is* the camera, seeing into the encounter because literally interposed in the space theatrical audiences dream of inhabiting. Film action is in general "opened up ecologically" exactly to the degree that the camera is ideally placed to facilitate seeing-into. But in *The Presentation of Self in Everyday Life,* Goffman prepared the "stage" upon which he struts in *Frame Analysis,* arguing that conventional situated interaction is itself typically structured dramaturgically, according to the same principles and with a view to addressing the same constraints as guide and face professional theatrical performers; yet within a different defining frame and with correspondingly different consequences. If everyday interaction is already microstructurally dramatic, dramatic staging dramatizes the dramatic, is in effect hyperdramatic. Already in dyadic interaction, each participant must open out his concerns, alignments, intentions, motives, and interpretations through stylizations of various kinds. As staging opens up interaction to the perception of the third who guards (Simmel's *tertius gaudens*), so does film, but by transporting the audience into the interaction rather than reconfiguring the interactional alignment along sightlines. So it is that in *The Glass Menagerie,* Tennessee Williams can have a character say, "We go to the movies instead of moving." In terms of characters' interaction, film's relation to everyday life can be seen as similar to theater's, in that it constitutes a reconstitution of operational space, both an invasion and an invitation that "open up" to experience and perception what had earlier been a relatively closed world.

Hypothetically at least, then, the camera brings us as close to Johnny Depp as we could come in everyday life if, in some charged dance of recognition, intimacy, and feeling he disclosed himself to us; it constructs an intimate space in which we can share habitation with him. This is accomplished filmically through lens manipulation—the medium shot and the close-up—and also through the staging convention of the intercutting of reverse shots in conversations. Yet what is striking is how little, inside this circuit of proximity, we manage to learn. This is because of the curious silences, and more curious utterances, we hear when Johnny presents himself. The spoken interaction involving Johnny Depp, in short, is *not* opened up ecologically in the way filmgoers have come to expect the interaction of screen characters will be. We are presented with typical close-ups and medium shots, but in them we are likely to find the Depp character entranced, stymied, staring outward in fascination, silenced by thought or wonder, introspective, even demonical, turned away from our curiosity to an inner world of experience.

Instructive in this regard is the moment of his introduction in Tim Burton's *Edward Scissorhands,* a scene where the neighborhood Avon lady, Peg Boggs (Dianne Wiest), has taken it upon herself to visit a castle on the hill no one has visited before. Upstairs in an attic illuminated by daylight streaming through a torn-away roof, she sees him huddled in a corner, barely distinguishable from a pile of darkened fluttering rags. Her attention is attracted in his direction, as is ours, by his first expressions, the indefinable sounds of polished metal shears lightly (that is, nervously) snipping at the air.

"I can see that I've disturbed you," says she, catching sight of him and backing away. "How stupid of me! I'll just be going now."

"*Don't go,*" he pleads, but very timidly.

It is an invitation, a prayer, a plaintive whisper, offered by Depp in an unaccented treble register like two soundings of the same high note on a flute. In his utterance there is nothing of command, alignment, intentionality, status, capability, muscularity, direction. A worn old door opening upon a squeaky hinge could produce the same two helpless tones.

Now he is fully lit and Peg sees the long scissors that are his hands. "Oh my! What happened to you?"

"I'm not finished," says the boy, inconclusively, as though even his thought of being unfinished is unfinished. Here we see that with dark purple lipstick a Betty Boop pout has been painted on his lips against a face covered with white. His hair is stiff, sticking up in all directions. His eyes are two saucers, unblinking, huge, filled with ... what? Fear? Wonder? Apprehension? Hunger? And then what, precisely, can we take to be the meaning of "I'm not finished"? Surely it suggests with exquisite compactness and directness a diegetic reality and field of possibility: that this character is the result of someone's tinkering; that the tinkering was interrupted; that therefore the character's life, not unlike that of Pinocchio, is shaped and dictated by his circumstance. The boy has scissors for hands because his maker didn't get around to putting the "real" hands on yet, and all of the film is a discursion into what is left to him as a life when he must go through the day with this ability/debility. He can become a fabulous haircutter and topiary artist. More: he can inadvertently cut people, cut himself, cut his world (he is a born editor, a walking homage to Hitchcock, who proclaimed, "Scissors are the best way" [Truffaut 1985, 346]).

But that is only the *story* in the film. What more are we given by the knowledge that he is not finished, as we struggle to grasp not only Edward Scissorhands but Johnny Depp who is playing him, Johnny Depp who was convinced, indeed, that he *"was Edward"* (Depp 1995, x)? Is it not true that as much as the "I" who is speaking is Edward, Peg's interlocutor, he is also Edward, the fictive creation of Tim Burton? "I am not finished" also means that the script for the film is hanging, that the character is only partially worked out, that the film is nothing but a hypothesis among many other possible hypotheses. In short, it is not by accident that Burton crafts for his protagonist a boy who has been partially "made" since he, too, is incapable—and admittedly so—of entirely fashioning the creatures who inhabit his films. It is Burton speaking through Scissorhands here, saying in effect, "I had the idea and I could work it out so far, but only so far." In that, he is no different than any author with any idea. But here he explicitly avers this fact, thus reilluminating authorial fiction as an achievement that is perforce incomplete: not, by the way, because it requires the interpretation of the audience to fill it in but because all stratagems, all statements, go only so far. Even the audience's interpretation is unfinished.

Of all characters in the film, however, this expression is given to Edward, which is to say, the words are organized to come out of Johnny Depp's (painted) mouth. Given that the "I" is Johnny as much as Edward, we must hear Johnny telling us that he, too, is not finished. He is not finished as a performer, but only in the process of becoming; his work on this role in the context of this film contract is not finished, but only in the process of becoming; his being Johnny Depp, the person who takes work as an actor and inhabits roles like Edward, is not finished but only in the process of becoming.

"Not finished" in this way, Edward/Johnny is in some ways an existential paragon, a creature entirely of the moment and hence of time and space. Introducing Jean-Paul Sartre's *La Nausée,* Hayden Carruth addresses the Sartrean notion of freedom: "Man, beginning in the loathsome emptiness of his existence, creates his essence—his self, his being—through the choices that he freely makes. Hence his being is never fixed. He is always becoming, and if it were not for the contingency of death he would never end. Nor would his philosophy" (in Sartre 1964, xiii).

Seen in this light,* Edward incarnate and Johnny incarnating him constitute the Existential Man, imperceptible because in continual motion. "A philosophy is not a body of propositions," indeed, wrote Abraham Kaplan, "but a way of life. . . . Existentialism sets itself quite firmly against any system or school—so much so, indeed, that existentialists don't like to be identified as 'existentialists'" (1961, 99). The cinematic nature of our affiliation with Depp existentializes him, in the sense that films by nature intend, proceed, and unfold, reflecting, in this way, life that also intends, proceeds, and unfolds. The Depp we see is a filmed Depp, caught in perpetual flux, bringing himself always forward just as Truffaut said** in general of film: "Les films avancent comme un train, tu sais, comme un train dans la nuit." While the offscreen Depp performs a denial of static recognizability in explicit terms, consistently rejecting propositions that categorize and limit him, that solidify him into an object of con-

---

* For bringing Carruth to my attention in this context, I am grateful to Curtis Maloley.

** Through the lips of his character, the metteur-en-scène Ferrand in *La Nuit Américaine* (*Day for Night,* 1973).

sideration, here Edward Scissorhands involves himself in denial through the melodious silence in which he develops his wonder at the curious Peg.

Peg, meanwhile, for her part, is completely nonplussed. "Those are your hands? (*And then, because the reality has struck:*) *Those are your hands!*" With her we stare frightened and also hypnotized at Edward's scissors, overwhelmed by the extraordinary length of their blades, their perfect symmetry, their manifold character—since considerably more than two blades are set at angles and deftly interposed at the bottom of each arm. What a blaze of desecration and fragmentation can be achieved by these creative "hands"! Edward (Johnny) is a freak of nature, to be sure, but a *monstre par excès,* a prodigy, as much as a *monstre par défaut,* an object of pity (Fiedler 1978). If Edward is flesh and metal, indeed, if he begins as flesh and ends as metal, does he not resemble Johnny Depp who begins as flesh and ends, for us at least, as celluloid? The nervous swishing of the scissors speaks for Edward, warning Peg to keep her distance. Johnny's awestruck silence keeps us at a distance, too, while at the same time constituting an apotheosis of good manners.

PEG: Where are you parents? Your mother? Your father?
EDWARD: They didn't wake up.

He was born, then, in a dream; he is a dream-child. What is pregnant about this is its connection to our own oneiric state as we are watching, watching and giving birth and credence to Edward frame by frame. For us, too, he is the child of a dream state, and to the extent that we are connected to him through the agency of this film, we do not wake up either. To wake up is to leave the theater, to lose Edward, and at the same time to lose Depp.

Peg is not only gaining courage in the face of this not-me, but finding at last a memory of who she is. She came to the castle on the hill, after all, hoping to make a sale: "Are you alone? Do you live up here all by yourself? . . . What happened to your face?— No, I won't hurt you. But at the very least, let me give you a good astringent and this will help to prevent infection . . . (*She dabs him gently*)." This handily centralizes the narrative. Regardless of the shears, the incompleteness, the blending of flesh and metal, and Edward's unfathomable orphanage, it is the face that is central to our concern, Edward's face and Johnny's. The scissors may nick at it, bring on infection. This is a face of extreme purity, the *tabula rasa* that is the ultimate fount of nostalgia. Edward is also not finished in that he has no facial expressions, no lines. He is not a reservoir of expressions and experience but only the capacity to express and to experience. The pout is painted on his mouth, not an agency of feeling. The eyes never squint in suspicion. Diegetically we are presented with an explanation: Edward has spent his life so far hiding up here at the top of the mountain, looking down from an impassable distance upon the human world. But there is a sense we must be filled with, at the same time, that Johnny Depp has done something similar. Not as an actual person, remote from our consideration, but as a screen figure, Depp has spent his life up there in front of us, illuminated, notably seen, framed, and thus, as Paul Goodman had it, especially valued. While Peg drives up the hill and enters the cloistered gate, we only dream of entering the castle, meeting the recluse, dabbing mercifully at his face.

But it is a face that cannot be touched. If the camera has opened Edward and Johnny to us ecologically, what we meet is a process and a phrase, not a being and a moment. The space in which we find ourselves seems to move as we gaze at the "not finished," move as though alive itself.

one Drag

There are very few actors who can make you believe they think—not that they're thinking about what they're saying, but that they think outside of the scene.

Orson Welles to Peter Bogdanovich

In a Blink

In Alfred Hitchcock's *The Man Who Knew Too Much* (1956), there is a startling moment in which a man (James Stewart) must cradle a dying Arab (Daniel Gélin) who is whispering a secret into his ear. Hitchcock shoots the moment from a position looking up into Stewart's face, registering his shifting expression as he hears the dying words and tries to decipher them. It is a stunning extended macro-close-up, shot in VistaVision for projection on an enormous screen that will be utterly filled with this querulous face. In *The Prince of the City* (1981), Sidney Lumet recapitulates this shot, using his camera to dolly forward and stare into the face of a crooked detective (Carmine Caridi) who, once his features are swollen enough to fill the entire screen, uses his gun (just out of frame) to blow his brains out. Both these shots tremble on the screen, perdure, breathe; and both of them court death. In each, the face is so magnified as to make accessible to us each detail as though it were a nook in a landscape. And as the face is transformed into a territory, the perilous beauty of life (the human face, expression, vulnerability, responsiveness) is revealed as a gamble and choreography against the deadly finale. There is also something relentlessly objective about the two shots, different as they are in their placement in two completely unrelated films yet similar as they are in form: they typify the treatment of a special object as the center of a field of vision, and because these shots are so distinctive in twentieth-century cinematography, so elastic and expansive, they stand as exemplars of such treatment.

The persuasive, seductive forms of the face that organize these two shots and these two sequences have bulk, seem entirely corporeal, are "filled volumes," as Ortega puts it, and are regarded, therefore, as something real (1968, 111). Like the painting of the Quattrocento, these two cinematic shots frame, elicit, and structure what Ortega called "proximal vision." So, too, does the body of Joe Gillis (William Holden) floating dead in Norma Desmond's pool in *Sunset Blvd.* (1950) seem corporeal and bulky; so does Ingrid Bergman's face when, as Ilsa Lund Laszlo, she hears Humphrey Bogart tell her they will always have Paris at the end of *Casablanca* (1942); so, in fact, does the shoe of Audrey Hepburn, when as Princess Anne she manages to lose it inside her regal gown in front of all the reporters of Europe in William Wyler's *Roman Holiday* (1953); and so does Montgomery Clift's shiny pistol in *Red River* (1948). All these are central and centralizing objects, principals of the domain of the screen that they inhabit.

By the time of the Impressionists, however, as Ortega has it, the age of "distant vision," the eye of the perceiver has withdrawn from the bulky object to concentrate on the volume of space that extends outward from itself to include that object, and then circled back to the point of the gaze's origin. In such a mode of vision, objects recede into planes, and the visual field, no longer a dispensation of things, is turned to "hollow space." Looking at the modern field of vision we have only "those side views 'from the tail of the eye' which represent the height of disdain" (123). To put this a little differently, "the field of vision tends to convert itself entirely into surface." And this modern field of vision is obtained, as the objects formerly attractive to us in their "reality" continue to recede and recede, by a process in which "we avoid focusing the eyes as much as possible" (112). In this kind of seeing, "blinking the eyes" (123), a mode not unrelated to what Wolfgang Schivelbusch later called "panoramic perception" in the context of a discussion of the train journey—

> as speed caused the foreground to disappear, it detached the traveler from the space that immediately surrounded him, that is, it intruded itself as an "almost unreal barrier" between object and subject. The landscape that was seen in this way was no longer experienced intensively, discretely (as by Ruskin, the critic of rail travel), but evanescently, impressionistically— panoramically, in fact. More exactly, in panoramic perception the objects were attractive in their state of dispersal. (1986, 189)

—we also lose a thrilling sense of distance that was made possible by the prominent, heroic object of yore. "In pure distant vision, our attention, instead of being directed farther away, has drawn back to the absolutely proximate" (112), which is the eye itself, since now we see all of the space—the screen space—and the hollow (of darkness) that includes it.

Let us consider the erotic potential of these two ways of seeing. For surely in proximal vision, repeated again and again through the history of film, it is the star and the star object—Bergman, her face; Hepburn's wayward shoe—key-lit and perfectly framed, that attract our desire. We can think of Bette Davis smoking one of Paul Henreid's cigarettes in *Now, Voyager* (1942), Grace Kelly bending forward to stare into James Stewart's face in *Rear Window* (1954) with her face partly Greek sculpture and partly magazine cover, Gene Kelly's red carnation at the end of the *American in Paris* ballet (1951). These visions we appropriate by gazing in tranquillity, extending our eye-beam, as Ortega would have it, until it embraces the Thing that stands out against its background, the "luminous hero, a protagonist standing out against a 'mass,' a visual *plebs,* and surrounded by a cosmic chorus" (110). Our sight is touch, indeed a clinch, and the object gives itself up to us by virtue of its curious placement and relation, its independence, its openness to remark, its receptivity to illumination.

Yet, if in its thingness the bulk seems a resistance to our hands, still in truth our hands are not extended. What is erotic here is precisely our keen sense of denial, our recognition of the boundary that forces a replacement of hand by eye, and this is nothing if not the product of stance. The film is seen by a standing audience, an audience drawn away from its own power of grasping by the ability to take a (dominating) point of view. We know, in desiring, that it is the eye, not the hand, by means of which we can possess; that it is light, not heat, we can experience. Perhaps the image brings up a memory of touch. So it is that the eroticism of proximal vision, and of the traditional movie star, is the eroticism of looking backward.

But the eroticism of distal vision is different. Here there is motility and rhythm, because it is only by constant motion of the eye, by the structure of interrupted apprehension, that the entire visual field is seen. Distal eroticism is more involving, more stimulating, more personal. All motion picture—even the close-up upon the favored object as highlighted above—is based on distal vision to the extent that it depends upon the flicker produced as frames race past a lit aperture (see Gunning 2004). Johnny Depp is an ultimate figure of distal perception, the limit of cinema, in that he can be traced back to the star figures of the 1930s and 1940s in his grace and penetrability (as though he is another Garbo, yet he only recalls Garbo) while he persists in shuddering before us, always transmogrifying, enjambing himself from situation to situation, redeveloping, squinting, looking askance, turning himself even as we stare at him so that he can be caught only at the corner of our gaze. We see and understand him in motion, as we do a wild animal.

The eroticism of Johnny Depp onscreen, then, is momentary and fleeting, a swath of light passing across our eyes. We exactly lack the sense of being able to touch, or remember touching, him. Instead, he makes us conscious of the entire space in which he moves. His presence is a dance, and his meanings are in rhythms.

Smoking with Thought

But what can be the meaning of this comment? There is certainly no rigorous international conspiracy to blink the eyes when Depp arrives onscreen. In what way, precisely, can his figuration be considered an example of Ortega's distal perception, and in what way can we imagine to ourselves that Johnny Depp onscreen has the character of an Impressionist painting, or else that his image generates a concavity, permits our eye to extend outward and then back again until it meets itself? For if it is true, as I have suggested, that all film is fleeting, flickering, pulsive, and evanescent, still typically something of the nature of the character's gaze or the picturing of an object yet convinces us we are looking at things that could be touched, worlds that could be experienced, people who dominate time and movement and decay in a rotund stasis.

Consider: In James Ivory's *A Room with a View* (1985), there is a piazza in Florence where a boy is stabbed to death, suddenly, out of the blue. As we watch, the place seems to us, even though the film is set in the early twentieth century, to be a location in which we could perambulate now. So, and in the same way, does the exotic alien beach on which Jodie Foster meets her dead father again in Ron Howard's *Contact* (1997). John Huston's Maltese falcon seems a bird we could take in hand; likewise Tom Cruise's guru hair in Paul Thomas Anderson's *Magnolia* (1999) or the bowl of cherries that Danielle Darrieux and her family are sweetly eating on the patio in André Téchiné's *Le Lieu du crime* (1986), or the grip of Indiana Jones's whip, or Elliott's forehead, when E.T. reaches out with his glowing finger to connect with it. Coppola's Don Corleone seems carved in stone, immobile, eternal—possibly because he is also Marlon Brando; Kurtz in *Apocalypse Now* (1979) has that effect on us, too; as does Dr. Mickler in *Don Juan DeMarco*. Depp, however, is never eternal, localized, material. Though one may wish to put one's finger on his forehead and whisper, "I'll be right here," one never feels any hope of succeeding.

In his untouchability, Depp, indeed, is like no other star of his era—or of any other. There are certain features of his presence in front of the camera that effectively produce a sustained experiential blur for the viewer, a sense that neither the face nor the persona can be grasped even in the imagination. He is, perhaps foremost, the embodiment of trepidation. Yet at the same time he is poised. How can this be? We must remember that motoricity is not propulsion. Schivelbusch writes of our culture that it is "permeated by nervousness." For him, it is exactly in this respect that the penetration of our cultural life from the seventeenth century onward by smoking, what he calls an "ersatz act" that enhances conception but not performance, "demonstrates" the culture itself (1993, 129). Schivelbusch describes in some detail the behavioral and cultural effects of tobacco use in the eighteenth, nineteenth, and twentieth centuries in a way that calls to mind central aspects of the characteristic screen performance of Johnny Depp:

> The brain is the part of the human body of greatest concern to bourgeois civilization. It alone was developed, cultivated, and cared for in the seventeenth and eighteenth centuries. The rest of the body, necessary evil that it was, merely served as a support for the head. Coffee and tobacco, each in its particular way, assisted this reorientation. Coffee functioned *positively,* arousing and nourishing the brain. Tobacco functioned *negatively,* calming the rest of the body—that is, reducing its motoricity to a minimum—as was necessary and desirable for mental, i.e., sedentary, activity. In smoking, the mentally active person works off those functionless, indeed dysfunctional bodily energies that had formerly been released in the physical work of prebourgeois man, in hunting, or in jousting. In this sense, smoking is an ersatz action. (1993, 110)

Whether or not he is utilizing a cigarette—onscreen it is not so very frequent that he is, one notable exception being *Fear and Loathing in Las Vegas*—watching Depp act is like watching a person smoke; to put this more bluntly: it feels as if he is smoking. One has the sense when watching him, and when watching smokers, of three distinct and prominent qualities: a sharply reduced motoricity, a steady working of the mind facilitated by a body under disciplined control, and a shaping of an exceptionally hard-working (and thus bourgeois) personality by an intellectual presence. Depp is the epitome of the rare actor cited by Welles who gives the impression that he thinks—thinks not only when we are looking at him but also when we are not—and it is precisely in this sense, whether he is smoking onscreen or abstaining, that he invokes the hyperrational, the dry, the reflective, the sober, the calculating—and thus the bourgeois—world that smoke brings on. Even more than he thinks while he is acting, more than he acts by thinking, Depp's screen presence is a thought.

The persona of Johnny Depp, let us remember, was born into a screen world already teeming with action-oriented bodies, not mentalities: bodies conventional (Gregory Peck, John Wayne) and ghostly (Burt Lancaster, Montgomery Clift) but also bizarre and fleshy. Among the latter one need think of only Harrison Ford as Indiana Jones or as Dr. Richard Kimble, Sean Penn as Meserve in *Casualties of War* (1989), Bruce Willis as John McClane in *Die Hard* (1988) or as Peter Fallow in *The Bonfire of the Vanities* (1990), Arnold Schwarzenegger in *Twins* (1988), *Total Recall* (1990), *Kindergarten Cop* (1990), or *Terminator 2* (1991), Christopher Reeve as Superman or as Frederick Dallas and Philip Brent in *Noises Off* (1992), Mel Gibson in *Lethal Weapon* (1987, 1989, 1992, 1998) or *The Man Without a Face* (1993), Tom Cruise as Cole Trickle in *Days of Thunder* (1990) or Mitch McDeere in *The Firm* (1993), or Keanu Reeves in *Point Break* (1991), *My Own Private Idaho* (1991), *Dracula* (1992), or *Little Buddha* (1993) to have a sense of the glowing, yet also embodied, range of personalities against which one began to discern the lines of him.

Depp's was from the very first (a supporting role in Wes Craven's *A Nightmare on Elm Street* [1984]) a sedate and self-absorbed appearance, highlit by a feline drowsiness that still figures upon his eyes and a gentleness that redefined contemporary screen masculinity. His Glen Lantz is a paragon of baby-faced and disciplined heterosexual desire. Called upon by his girlfriend Nancy to stand guard with her against creepy nocturnal noises while two of their friends "converse" in a bedroom upstairs, and then hearing the love moans of the couple, Glen retreats into a dreamy and lingering rejection of morality: in scene after scene, he seems to be slipping into a world of the imagination, so much so that he betrays Nancy's trust by falling asleep when, their two friends having brutally been murdered, she is convinced a sadistic killer is residing in her dreams and the only way to catch him is to drag him out of sleep and into the light of reality where Glen will be waiting. Here as much as in later films, but played for innocent comedy, we see Depp's amused interiority as a withdrawal from, even a rejection of, the active world outside him. Finally sleep—that is, mentality dominant over physical life—claims him. Stretched out on his own bed, earphones blocking his ears and a midnight television broadcast of Miss Nude Teenage America boggling his cupidinous teenage eyes, Glen is murdered himself, sucked brutally down into his own mattress and converted off-camera into what can only be called a wretched rotting geyser of consomméd boyishness that swirls nauseatingly around his ceiling.

Indeed, in *Nightmare,* Depp's screen persona entails, much more than a capacity for reflection, ideation, or interrogation, an ability to listen, this flagged ostentatiously by the huge earphones in which he is killed. Watching him here, and later in *What's Eating Gilbert Grape, Sleepy Hollow, Arizona Dream, The Ninth Gate, The Brave, Once Upon a Time in Mexico,* and many other films, one has the profound sense that he is listening to those who address him, and their voices are plumbing his depths. He becomes something like an auditorium, in which the voices of others echo and find form. His face, registering speech, is like James Stewart's face registering the secret that the dying man is confiding to him in *The Man Who Knew Too Much,* a face in which the motion of the eyes plays out the action of the soul; in which the mouth is sealed in preparation for a comment that need not come. The mouth of Johnny Depp is often reminiscent of Brando's mouth in *On the Waterfront*—a mouth ready to speak, but silent—and perhaps this is the feature that links him to Brando in many an imagination.

Depp has characteristics in common with many actors who went before him. In some ways he brings to mind Cary Grant's eloquent self-possession, since, like Grant, he never commits to a spurious or excessive motion, but even in his youth Grant (in, say, *Arsenic and Old Lace* or *Suspicion*) never managed to let loose a projection of such rawness. He was always a graceful bug trapped in the amber of social form and proper circumstance, the Cockney who had risen. Depp has moved, to be sure (from roots in Owensboro, Kentucky), but not climbed. As a star whose presence consistently invokes the belief that he is wondering, taking in the world through a screen of doubt, inquisitiveness, calculation, philosophical speculation, and incomprehension, Depp contrasts with Montgomery Clift, in whom one had the feeling of focused inspection, of a force closely regarding its own cycle of experience. Clift understood, or was on the verge of understanding; but Depp is considering. Clift stared directly into the camera in the trysting scene with Anne Baxter in Alfred Hitchcock's *I Confess.* His is the beauty of completely open feeling, of using his eyes to express the willingness to be seen and fathomed. Depp's eyes penetrate without allowing penetration. James Dean's body was excitingly uncomfortable with itself. In a blend far from common in late-twentieth-century culture, Depp projects the lively mind at home in the resting body, the body disciplined and relaxed, the body in place, yet eager to move—and this is one of the central conundra of his screen presence, that the body, like Brando's, rests but also, like Dean's, is hungry to move. Depp also reflects Alan Ladd in *Shane,* the young man with the steady gaze whose mind is turning. Yet if Ladd moved awkwardly, when Depp moves it is often for the pure ecstatic delight of movement, not to accomplish a trajectory. He is no Clint Eastwood, whose motion is always purposeful. Yet his movement is never apparently out of control (Jerry Lewis) or self-reflexively expressive (Jim Carrey).

It is not motion but the promise of motion that is uplifting and engaging about him. He is, accordingly, perfectly cinematic, resting and reflecting within the frame, yet always incompletely, insufficiently, so that at the same time he wears the implication that one frame is not enough and that motion is inevitable and deliciously necessary. He is not an icon of the cinema so much as an example of it. As Gary Cooper stood for the society of the plains, with his squinting, far-reaching gaze that could seize a prospect of any horizon; as John Wayne stood for the society of the stranger, with his unrelenting jaw and mapper's posture; as Humphrey Bogart stood for the society of the city, with his shadowy brow and cynical smile that denied what it understood; as Brando stood for the society of the factory, with his capacitous shoulders and dutiful lips; so Depp stands for the society of the screen, his precarious watching invoking the gap between presentation and motive.

Legato

The reduction yet intensification of motoricity is uniformly apparent in all Depp's screen work as a peculiar (in this stuttering culture) smoothness and functionality of movement and an enunciatory poise. He has the elegance of the nineteenth century without the mannered affectation. The desperate pulsation or unremitting athleticism of hard rock performance (available to Val Kilmer, Tom Cruise, Mark Wahlberg) or of modern dance (Kevin Bacon in *Footloose*) is antithetical to the carriage Depp manages. The stress of frustration is absent from his limbs. He does not produce an excess of posture or expression (a personality) yet remains utterly convincing by virtue of what seems a mentality devoted heroically to the moment. While one can see the statuesqueness and deliberation in virtually any scene Depp plays, these qualities are certainly made emphatic in particular dramatic moments. Sally Potter casts him as a Romanisch horseman apprenticed to a cirque in Paris, for example, in *The Man Who Cried;* when he appears onstage during the circus performance, in bearing, fire, and dignity he is indistinguishable from the horse at his side.

When subsequently he is moved to stand upon the horse's saddle and be carried through the noctural streets at a gallop, his posture makes it evident it is not through the agency of the strained body, through the dispensation of musculature, that he achieves the feat but through the concentration of mind. He is willing himself to maintain his balance, and willing the horse to carry him into the night.

In the "Forget about it" scene in Mike Newell's *Donnie Brasco*, Depp as Joseph Pistone is seizing a moment to rest in a Miami motel room, exhausted from his undercover work as Donnie Brasco and angry at the inefficiencies of the agent who is working him. He has flopped on a sofa, a chilled Bud can pressed to his temples and a pair of neophytes at his side. There is very little movement of his body, just a polite turn of the head to acknowledge the young men's presence, occasionally a gesture with his free hand to imitate the insiders whose language he has mastered. "What does 'Forget about it' mean?" asks one of the young agents, confused about a phrase he has heard over and over on the surveillance tapes produced by the secret recorder Pistone has been wearing. To answer this, Depp/Pistone achieves a meticulous sociolinguistic analysis, an act of cerebral precision, devotedly accompanied by a careful, musical use of the voice to convey the subtlest nuances of tone that differentiate one reading of this ambiguous phrase from another:

> "Forget about it" it's like, uh . . . if you agree with someone, you know . . . like "Raquel Welch is one great piece of ass, forget about it," but then, if you disagree, like "A Lincoln is better than a Cadillac—forget about it!" You know? But then, it's also like if somethin' is the greatest thing in the world, like "Those peppers! Forget about it!" You know? But it's also like saying "Go to hell," too. Like you know like uh, "Hey Paulie you got a one-inch pecker" and Paulie says, "Forget about it!" . . . Sometimes it just means forget about it. . . . Let me tell you somethin', I don't get this boat for Lefty—fuck'n forget about it.

While Brasco/Pistone is *invoking* actions in his speech, since each different nuanced reading of the key phrase is prototypically situated by him in a different realistic social circumstance, nevertheless the speech reveals him to be a man of thought, not a man of action. Even when, early in the film, he beats up a thief in order to impress Lefty Ruggerio (Al Pacino), it is evident—at least in retrospect—how manipulative he is being: how calculated. Here, and in the disturbing brawl in a Japanese restaurant where Pistone cannot remove his shoes lest he be caught with a planted microphone on his leg, the scene contains action that is the direct outcome of Pistone's deliberative process: he does not act out of emotion, out of instinct, out of the need to vent energy. His actions are self-choreographed tactics in a broad strategic battle to construct a reality with the unwitting collaboration of men it is his duty to lure to justice. I would call this generally distributed choreographic smoothness and fondness for stillness in Depp's appearances his preference for *legato* performance: *legato* is the musical term for a smooth, convicted, deliberate, and processual way of playing and is from the Italian meaning "bound, tied up." Johnny is bound in contemplation, tied up in the work of the mind.

In a sequence in Roman Polanski's *The Ninth Gate,* a film in which Depp's performance struck the director as "completely instinctual" (Heard 2001, 202), the protagonist, Dean Corso, is racing through the French countryside on a motorcycle. The camera is bolted to the front of the bike, so that we stare into Depp's face as the green forest rapidly disappears behind him to the sound of the revving motor. Here is a concentrated example of his continual pulsion—a pulsion that becomes a blur—coupled with a static, contemplative, focused quality that suggests a mind at work. Rather than lose himself to the road, he is fixed with concentration on his purpose, but the space in which he moves is designed to recede from us into a hollow. Even here, in rapid motion at an urgent time, Corso/Depp is frozen, bound up, in thought. So, he is both the central object of proximal vision and the blurred, shimmering field of distal vision at once.

Beyond his tendency to *think* through, rather than *move* through, a scene, disciplined control of the body is also typically evident in Depp's work—a kind of dance. His way of walking in *Nightmare on Elm Street,* for instance, recalls the lithe and balletic Jean-Claude Drouot in Agnès Varda's stunning *Le Bonheur* (1965). In *The Ninth Gate* he spends many scenes in the cinematically obscene act of reading, and through the fixation of his concentration upon the page we are also brought into the experience of reading, sharing his opticality (as though it were Johnny, indeed, watching this film instead of being watched, an ultimate address to our "pure distal" vision, in which, as Ortega emphasizes, "the object of sight is not farther off . . . but on the contrary is nearer, since it begins at our cornea" [112]).

In *From Hell,* he is typically opiated, a calm, even objective, presence in the bustling East End nocturnal streets; his method is dispassionate observation, rational argument, and conclusion. In *Cry-Baby,* action is epitomized for "Cry-Baby" Walker by a gelatinous tear frozen upon his cheek. This signals a perduring melancholia, not a momentary bout of crying. It is "Cry-Baby's" deep spirit that weeps, not his body. We have the sense, too, of a social critique implicit in "Cry-Baby's" stance toward the school, the authorities, and the hyper-uptight Mrs. Vernon-Williams (Polly Bergen), whose boarding school represents everything he (and every true Beat) abhors and fears while at the same time housing the girl he loves, the social harridan's daughter Allison (Amy Locane). This teenager is a philosopher, molded in the shape of Jim Stark from *Rebel* yet in the end even less active—his commitment is to pose, not act. In *Benny & Joon,* as Depp imitates Chaplin and then Buster Keaton, we have the sense of a character infused with mental images of the clowns who ground his imitation, as though he is watching them lovingly on an internal movie screen while duplicating their performance. In *Arizona Dream,* he actually *does* watch Jerry Lewis on a screen, drinking in the images with an effusive pleasure.

The hard-working personality, the concentration, of Depp's screen presence is configured by the charming seriousness he displays: Gilbert Grape's devotion to delivering Betty Carver's (Mary Steenburgen) groceries, bringing them into the house, unpacking them, and his ingenuous surprise when, for the thousandth time, she puts the make on him while feeding him ice cream with her finger; Spencer Armacost's intensity and single-minded aggressiveness in *The Astronaut's Wife;* the desperation and then the depravity of the two characters Depp plays in *Before Night Falls;* the well-intentioned, even pathetic, seriousness of his Inspector Ichabod Crane in *Sleepy Hollow:* a man committed to the intellect but now out of his league in a territory of passionate movement—all of these characters are people who think their way through situations and seem always onscreen to be calculating, appreciating, weighing, comparing, navigating, deciphering, intellectually *taking in* the complexities of their world.

Pondering Everything Well

Depp persistently composes himself with a kind of studiousness reflected in an eighteenth-century text about tobacco-smoking quoted by Schivelbusch: "Here straying thoughts are recollected, this being most beneficial for students, in that while smoking they can grow accustomed to pondering everything well" (1993, 107). Depp onscreen is a student of situations and people, a pensive (rather than a reaching and feeling) observer. It is the viewer's privilege to share his (alienated) view. So, for example, in *Edward Scissorhands,* through the eyes of Edward we see the pristine and chilling atmosphere of suburban life. In *Donnie Brasco,* through Pistone's desperate and sharp perceptions we see the organization of criminal life in New York. Through Agent Sands in *Once Upon a Time in Mexico* we observe political corruption and violence. Through George Jung in *Blow* we come to understand the consumer frenzy that is America of the 1970s.

Cigarettes and smoking have been central in Depp's offscreen persona, to be sure, not always happily: "Smoking. I keep trying to quit smoking cigarettes. I actually did quit when we were finishing *Donnie Brasco.* I quit for six weeks. And I did it by smoking these really cheap great, real sweet cigars—like 25 cents a pack. And it worked fine. And then I was on vacation for about a week and I took a drag off my girlfriend's cigarette, and it was all over. One drag" (Granger 2002, 46).

In his interviews he is ritualistically described as a smoker. To one writer he proclaims, "I love to smoke. I want to have another mouth grafted on so I can smoke more. Instead of three packs a day, I want to smoke six packs a day" (Diamond 1993). Another writer watches him as he "reaches into a pouch of Bali Shag tobacco and begins rolling a cigarette with chocolate brown papers" (Nashawaty 2003, 31), a routine he also performs for a smugly smiling James Lipton on "Inside the Actors Studio." An interviewer for *Gentleman's Quarterly* watches him "producing a pouch of Bali Shag and rolling the first of innumerable cigarettes" (Kaylin 2003, 95). Still another confides to his readers,

> I will tell of our adventures together: the time we found Jesus, or a guy who said he was Jesus, on Santa Monica Boulevard and Depp gave him cigarettes. . . . "You want a cigarette for the road?" Depp asked him. Jesus assented, and together the robed one and the young actor smoked for a while. "Take the pack," Depp told him. "I can buy some more." Afterward, Depp seemed thrilled. "I smoked with Christ!" he said, not a little boastfully. "Jesus is a Marlboro man!" (Zehme 1991, 32; 75)

and reports on Johnny's condition in a coffee shop when Winona Ryder went off to do some errands: "He was very much alone. He was smoking too much and drinking too much coffee, but who could blame him? He said he was enslaved by caffeine and nicotine and didn't sound proud of it. 'I like to be pumped up and hacking phlegm at the same time,' he said wryly" (32).

So devoted was he to smoking when *Edward Scissorhands* was being filmed, indeed, he "learned to hold his cigarettes between the scissors' blades" (32). Much later, at a recording session where he was reading the "211th Chorus" from Jack Kerouac's *Mexico City Blues,* he met Allen Ginsberg, who tried unsuccessfully to coach him:

> I was smiling nervously, my eyes sort of wavering between his face and the floor. I sucked down about half of my 5,000th cigarette of the day in one monster drag and filled the air around us with my poison. It was at that point that I remembered his "Don't Smoke!" poem . . . oops . . . too fucking late now, boy, you done stepped in shit! I looked at Ginsberg, he looked at me, and the director looked at us both as the crew looked at him, and it was quite a little moment, for a moment there. Allen's eyes squinted ever so slightly and then began to twinkle like bright lights. He smiled that mystic smile, and I felt as though God himself had forgiven me a dreadful sin. (Depp 1999, 70)

By 2001 he is photographed at the high point of a toke for *Details* and described as a "maladjusted, long-haired, chain-smoking horn-dog" (Compton 2001, 149). Nevertheless, smoking may be on the way out for him. Asked at the time of the release of *Pirates of the Caribbean* whether he has given up smoking for his children he replied, "Not totally, but almost—for my children and for my future grandchildren. They make me want to live a long time! Not smoking is a small sacrifice" (Caron 2003, 87).

But we must remember that "pondering everything well" is also the claim of the distal perceiver envisioned by Ortega, whose eye has retreated slowly from the rounded curves of the central object in order to take in, ray by ray, the expanse of the visual field that terminates at the eye. In this curious way, smoking is seeing; or, more precisely, smoking from the seventeenth century onward facilitated the development of this new and rational form of sight that, failing to attach itself to a favored object, democratized the field. Now, with a blinking eye, light itself, as it leaned forward to touch the surfaces of objects, was the focus and subject of vision. If one has the feeling in Johnny Depp's films that this is the way his character sees the world—as a modernist—it is also the way he leads us to see him, since far from being a figure of adoration and exclusion he announces himself to us, with his hesitations and convictions, his intensities of focus and intellectualities, his gazes and views askance, his contemplative articulations and provocative silences, his movements of body that configure movements of mind, as an ideal subject to be viewed at a distance. What we adored about Clark Gable, John Wayne, Cary Grant, Ingrid Bergman is what we adore about Tom Cruise, Tom Hanks, Leonardo DiCaprio, Kirsten Dunst—they are stimulations to the recollection of the proximal vision of the Quattrocento. Depp leads us into a different world—our world, to be sure, and yet one very far from the ancient trace that modern man continues to fixate upon in his conventional practices. This is why Depp has only begun to attract a larger audience: in a time when audiences hunger for antiquities that can be grasped, fondled, tasted, and known he embodies too much of the contemporary world, is too democratic, too elusive, too fragmentary, too shimmering to be touched. If, as Ortega warns, "an age-old habit, founded in vital necessity, causes men to consider as 'things,' in the strict sense, only such objects solid enough to offer resistance to their hands. The rest is more or less illusion. So in passing from proximate to distant vision an object becomes illusory" (111)— then Johnny Depp is the first movie star to be an authentic illusion.

NO THING

Nothing will come of nothing.

King Lear

Johnny Depp is the first movie star to be an authentic illusion: this is surely a bizarre statement to make in a postmodern climate, in the shadow of a popular culture that fills the atmosphere twenty-four hours a day with what Baudrillard has called *simulacra*. For surely it has come to be a commonplace of cultural criticism that we live in a world of the unreal, the extraordinary, the illusory, the insubstantial, in which the absence of honor, dignity, form, meaning, desire, value, and principle have left a mammoth cultural vacuum, what Fredric Jameson has called, with perhaps too little force, a "waning of affect." If our culture is regarded as a hollow, however, this is not the hollow to which I allude in citing Ortega and suggesting that Depp onscreen is an image that terminates in our eye and is thus a part of a concavity, a new distal space. From the time of the Impressionists onward, the distally perceived world has been alive with stimulation; and its form has been illumination itself; and its value has been participation. The simulacrum of Baudrillard, by contrast, is conceived most centrally as an absence, a lack. The world we live in is thought pervaded by such absence, pitifully, in the sense that a value has been tragically withdrawn, an objective reality pulled away. But Ortega shows a more thrillingly realistic approach to the withdrawal from objects by suggesting they become more intimately connected to us precisely when they *cease* to hover rotundly in our grasp. This is the leap suggested by Jean-Paul Sartre, from *having* to *being* (1956). Depp is sadly not a celebrity we can possess, and this is confounding to an audience with a post-Victorian sensibility for collecting its images. Yet at the same time Depp is gloriously not a celebrity that can be possessed, and this is a source of delirium to an audience with a postmodern sensibility for bathing in the light reflected from images, seeing them out of the corner of the eye. Baudrillard's *simulacrum,* indeed, is only uncollectable—that is its curse and its blessing.

Marx's derealization, the replacement of use value by exchange value, is described by Schivelbusch in terms of tobacco advertising:

> A new sort of smoking ritual evolved for the cigarette: no longer related to the thing—for that was now masked by advertising—but related to the advertisement. The cigarette smoker's gestures, which constitute the pleasure of smoking, are reenactments of the advertising images. Whether as adjective or noun, "the commercial" pervades our entire culture industry. To hold a cigarette like Greta Garbo, or to screw it into the side of your mouth like Humphrey Bogart—these were the ritualistic smoking gestures for smokers of the 1930s and '40s. (1993, 187)

How romantically Victorian, and how bourgeois, how possessive is the thought that tobacco itself, or the cigarette itself, might constitute the essence of the act of smoking rather than the style of the advertising image, which is the skin of the experience! Withdrawn by centuries of rapturous gazing from the heroic object, we no longer need to fantasize ownership and control of the thing we admire; but can be fulfilled through a distant vision by seeing it in its context, as a part of the shimmering field. Where the Victorians wished for possession, and feared it, the modern sensibility delights in recognition. It is precisely derealization that occurs when we enter the domain of the image, but only the romantic sensibility finds derealization a reason for chagrin—derealization that makes us note the referential scintillations of a thing in order to place it in a field of information rather than grasping at the bulk of a thing in order to put it to use. The "commercial" sensibility that adheres to the hollow image of contemporary life, the advertising sense, is merely its exploitation by capitalism. The objects of proximal vision were capitalized as products, submitted to the processes of manufacture and exploitation. The hollow of distal vision can be capitalized as simulacrum, as advertisement, as logo. But there is no necessary relation between experiential withdrawal from the object and capitalizing upon it, no necessary link between distal vision and lack. Only the ritualistic perceiver who clings to proximal vision and possession regards the withdrawal of the object as a problem and experiences lack. The optical hollow is itself a plenitude, just as much as the object ever was, although it is not a thing. A plenitude but not a thing. Thus, we lose our objectivity.

We retreat from an adoration of things, a navigation by things, an architecture of things, a bureaucracy of things, a choreography of things, a hierarchy of things, and a social hierarchy based on unequal distribution of things, the aggregation of things, the privatization of things, and the denial of things, into a social organization of space. What comes of this nothingness is precisely the thought of the world, thought which is no thing.

Movie stars have always been illusory in the sense of being social constructs. The star is not a person as such, but a socially organized personal formation based on the delimitations of a contract (for example, the seven-year studio contract of the 1930s and 1940s, which helped shape Garbo and Bogart smoking); the artful machinations of studio publicity operatives, writers, hairdressers, costumers, photographers, and lawyers; carefully tended interfaces with the press; the shaping vision of directors and producers; and the canniness of agents. The human being, the living armature, upon whom all this was laid, and whose energies and capabilities structured and maintained it, the person who was the substrate and substance of this persona, had no reason to perdure coherently through its construction, its refinement, or its broadcast. Indeed, given the extremely pervasive nature of the studio contract—Warner Bros. had this clause, also to be found in star contracts, put into the contract of even chorines going out on the *42nd Street* publicity tour: "It will be particularly required that all persons upon such tour . . . shall conduct themselves with special regard to *public convention and morals* and that no action which will tend to degrade Artist or the tour, will bring either Artist or any member of such tour into public hatred, contempt, scorn or ridicule, or which will tend to shock, insult or offend public morals or decency, or prejudice the Producer or the motion picture industry in general, will be tolerated" (Clark 1995, 98)—stars had little if any room in which, independently of stardom, to breathe.

There lingered at the fringes of stardom, however, or as an excrescence upon the glittering skin of the star image, a faint trace and reminder of the very process by benefit of which the star existed. This trace was the glimpse of the machine made accessible in the glow of the extended close-up, the artful balance of the poster, the fastidious lines of a garment, the glib bit of dialogue, the posture of the kiss. The viewer at once felt elevated, removed from the practical, enchanted; and saw the palpable material residue of the procedure which had produced the enchantment, itself a byproduct hotly to be consumed. Richard Widmark fingers the purse of a dreamy woman on an El train in *Pickup on South Street* (1953). In his shifting eyes in the medium shot there are pinpoint keylights to draw us away from his torso, even as the woman onscreen is being drawn away by her daydreams as the train rattles along, and we see this illumination exactly as clearly as we see the deftly probing fingers in a cutaway close shot of the purse. As to the fingers: they move just slowly enough for us to decipher what they are doing. A shot of the woman's faraway stare telegraphs openly that posturing is going on between the actors. All this mechanism is there to be regarded but also disattended, seen with a denying attitude. This is 1953. Thirty years later, Martin Scorsese has the television comedian Jerry Langford (Jerry Lewis) come home from shooting his nightly show to a lonely, desperately silent apartment on East 53rd Street. He stops in front of a television screen where *Pickup on South Street* is playing. He watches this scene, staring intently at Widmark's moves, and at the moves of the director, Sam Fuller, in bringing all this action to light. He has pulled back, aware that the stardom of Widmark is a construct, knowledgeable (doubly so, because the actor is Lewis, also knowledgeable) of the metatechnique that has made it possible in *Pickup* for us to both see the action and see the technique of the action, and now caught by fascination for that metatechnique even as he recognizes aspects of it. (And what is this staggering technique of Scorsese's, that he shows us Lewis's performance of Langford's recognition of Fuller's metatechnique?)

If originally the star was a construct, then, that construct radiated (and now the radiation itself can radiate). Widmark radiates, his fingers radiate in the purse. And in the Scorsese, the radiation of Widmark radiates to Langford/Lewis. Garbo with Melvyn Douglas in *Ninotchka* has cheeks that do not seem human: at once we are struck by the alabaster smoothness of her and by the makeup and lighting that achieve it, all this no matter how much we know about the achievement. The illusory quality of stardom is therefore best described as a phase, in the sense that while viewing stars, audiences shifted in and out of absorption. Crawford in *Mildred Pierce* was touching and captivating as a working woman but she was also a highly paid star taking up a role that became utterly unbelievable only to the extent that she could be seen playing it. The fiction of *Mildred Pierce* alternates between believable "truth" and pure hokum. But in the sense that audiences did not meet Joan Crawford or Richard Widmark as anything but star constructs, stardom was an illusion, a necessary illusion if the system that maintained it was to cohere. Since that system was the national ethos, it did need to cohere, and the illusion was a necessary one—that is to say, it did underpin the social hierarchy. Mildred the waitress buys a restaurant and makes herself successful: a national monument to achievement and class mobility. Widmark the petty thief gets his: punishment and retribution as sanctification.

The Crawford who plays the waitress, however, is not taken to be a working woman (although she is). If Mildred must lower her status to become a waitress, and if she then can climb again into ownership of the restaurant, the Crawford who plays her apparently has no such obligations and opportunities. She is merely investing herself in a persona out of a need to participate in make-believe. And indeed this Crawford who takes up roles is nothing but the illusion created by the publicity department (who insisted, in the case of this film, that she really did have a penchant for domestic labor and good common sense with a pocketbook [see Haralovich 1999]). In the golden age of stardom, however, if the Crawford portraying this Crawford is unavailable for comment, and the Widmark who plays the Widmark behind the thief unavailable, too, neither is actually invoked in star construction. Neither exists. And thus it is that the studio's Widmark construction becomes the public's Richard Widmark. He is never seen to do anything that contradicts his performances as a star.

In the illusion of the star, however, we have a substitution of a thing for a thing, not a replacement of the thing by nothing. What is substituted is the public persona, the elaborate and expensive mask, made by a system of manufacture (the studio system), rabidly distributed, exhibited through a complex of arrangements for optimally exploiting a product in order to profit from its exposure to every conceivable audience. What the persona is substituted *for* is the biography. I have argued above that this "derealization" both affects us directly and shows itself affecting us. But in any event, it is composed of a substitution. Arguments about the hollowness, vapidity, or vulgarity of the star construct, then, rely upon some romantic valuing of the biography, as though biographical reality had no aspect of performance. In the same way it is possible to argue against theatricality by holding up against its "falseness" the authenticity of the unconstructed day-to-day, *as though in the day-to-day there is no performance of social life.* The glitzy film star is an illusion in contrast with the "authentic" person residing under, or behind, him. Illusion being a lack of reality, the star is a lack of personality, a lack of essence, a lack of biographical and material substance.

But substance is the product of a very old system of vision, one which, as Ortega wrote, privileged as "real" only objects that apparently could be touched. In proximal vision, the eyebeam extends and embraces the "heroic" object, privileging it as both desirable and as real in the optical moment. All movie stars before Depp are privileged in this way, and also disparaged, since they are reviled as constructs and illusions in the same breath as they are worshiped as exceptionally desirable things. All movie stars before Depp are owned by their publics.

When I say that Depp is "no thing," I mean only that his presence onscreen operates for us precisely *not* to establish his rotundness, his three-dimensionality, his reality in a world outside, before, or beyond the screen, his biographical sincerity, his palpability as an object upon whom the craven institution of Hollywood can do its dirty work, his essence as a love object, his materiality. Since Johnny Depp must have *some* material presence, the presentation of this distal, dematerialized image therefore entails a new order of screen construction entirely, one that utterly blots out not only the star biography itself but the dream of a star biography. With his dominating mentality evident through his acute perceptivity, his bodily discipline, and his continual preparation for action that displaces action by overwhelming it, he manages a style of screen performance that is an "ersatz action," exactly in the way that for Schivelbusch smoking is an "ersatz action." Smoking was sedentary reflection replacing—that is, recollecting, or even evading—movement. Depp's performance is a constant evasion of presence. He is not the object to be apprehended through grasp and ownership, instead he is to be seen through the blink of an eye, and thus at a distance. He is to be juggled, not fondled. In this distance, he comes closer to us than stars have ever come, so close he ends at the eye of the beholder, unfathomable, undesirable, unsatiating.

But if earlier stars, being illusory, were no things when they should—presumably could—have been things, and thus frustrated the viewing public, Depp is no thing in a world where things are only memories. He is not an illusion in the same way as Garbo and Bogart and Widmark and Crawford are, then, a tantalizing and galling illusion, but in an entirely new way, an oneiric, not a practical, way. As Edward Scissorhands puts it, he is the child of two people who "didn't wake up."

Disappearance

Is there, or should there be, one face which should be authentic?
                    Anonymous patient, quoted by Robert Jay Lifton

Depp is a curiosity in the history of screen stardom in still another respect, one that has attracted more popular and critical attention than any other facet of his performances. This is the fact that he has made a career of playing many quite different roles, presenting to the public anything but a unified persona. The traditional movie star, who lingers in the background as we consider Depp and against the qualities of whose career we evaluate his, is quite a different presence, indeed was for years a person necessarily typecast. In Hollywood this happened in a systematic and dominant process of institutionalized filmmaking whereby, as Danae Clark points out, "by detaching the image from the person the studio could reconstruct the relation between the two into a unified subject position called the 'persona'" (22). The viewer was led to desire what Barry King terms transfilmic personality in the star (1986, 168). Clark shows the relation between this coherence and the traditional arrangements for profit-making in the studio system:

> By individualizing actors' labor power under separate contracts, producers could regulate the division of labor under the star system and enforce the use of typecasting. Since most contracts stipulated that actors must accept the roles "offered" to them, most actors found themselves playing the same type of role over and over again. The repetition of roles reinforced the illusion of a unified persona. To break from this illusion and to challenge studio regulation of the persona often resulted in suspension from the studio without pay, and, upon readmittance, the forced acceptance of even less desirable roles. (1995, 23)

Almost all the stars of the Golden Age of Hollywood filmmaking were more or less locked into the personae that were constructed by negotiation between them and the studio with recourse to the highly expert professional resources the studio controlled and used. (For example, an extremely detailed analysis of the contribution of scenic designers to the shaping of the onscreen persona is to be found in Vertrees 1997, which is an account of the making of David O. Selznick's *Gone With the Wind*. Selznick is altogether a noteworthy subject of study in this regard, a man who had an eye for every aspect of star construction.)

The intense variegation of performance we see in Depp's career is characteristic of a particularly stable and important studio asset, the character actor: Everett Sloane, Una O'Connor, Agnes Moorehead, William Demarest, Niall MacGinnis, and Thelma Ritter are but some of the luminaries whose careers literally depended on their ability to shift their presentations and appearances almost without limit. In contemporary screen work, Emmet Walsh, Philip Baker Hall, Judith Ivey, John Heard, Toni Collette, and John Turturro come to mind, and indeed, when he made *What's Eating Gilbert Grape* with Johnny Depp, Leonardo DiCaprio was an actor of exceptional promise for character work, a promise effectively erased after his star career was established with *Titanic*.

Johnny Depp has been able to sustain a star career with the performance history of a noteworthy character actor. The dominating aspect of his persona is that it is unpredictable, that he will to some
usually surprising degree disappear inside his roles and they will be
unlike the roles he has played before. Even to restrict the glance to
Depp's eponymous roles (in a substantial list which seems to have
ended around 1998) is to see immense forces of variation, renovation, instability, and volatility in the presence he brings to the screen:
the hyper-sincere "Cry-Baby" Walker; the hyper-naïf Edward Scissorhands; the genteel and dutiful Gilbert Grape; the ambitiously
kinky Ed Wood; the seductively wise Don Juan DeMarco; the "obedient" "Donnie Brasco." Add to these innocent and horny Glen Lantz
in *A Nightmare on Elm Street,* confused Axel Blackmar in *Arizona
Dream,* the charming buffoon Sam in *Benny & Joon,* William Blake,
the quintessence of whiteness, trepidation, and European civilization in *Dead Man,* neurotic, bourgeois Gene Watson in *Nick of Time,*
jaded philosophical Jack Kerouac in *The Source,* the victimized and
noble Raphael in *The Brave,* Johnny Depp, the man of the world, in
L.A. Without a Map, the madly intense Raoul Duke (Hunter S.
Thompson) in *Fear and Loathing in Las Vegas,* the malevolent alien in
The Astronaut's Wife, the obsessive sheister Dean Corso in *The Ninth
Gate,* meticulous and timid Ichabod Crane in *Sleepy Hollow,* passionate
and poetic Cesar in *The Man Who Cried,* folksy Roux in *Chocolat,*
craven and tortured George Jung in *Blow,* anal-retentive cross-
dressing Bon Bon in *Before Night Falls,* opiated, narcissistic Frederick
Abberline in *From Hell,* the foppish pirate Jack Sparrow in *Pirates of
the Caribbean: Curse of the Black Pearl,* Machiavellian Agent Sands in
Once Upon a Time in Mexico, and woozy, wacky Mort Rainey in *Secret
Window* and you have a portrait of a cinematic chameleon.

While the conventional movie star has succeeded—both in an individual career and as a useful asset of the studio—by maintaining a
coherent and *recognizable* face that can be marketed at the box office
and appreciated onscreen in terms of its own history, the star career
of Johnny Depp has to some significant degree rested on his ability to
persist as a box office attraction in spite of the fact that his screen face
is constantly changing.

He is therefore a fine example of Robert Jay Lifton's protean
man. The "protean self" is described by Lifton as a "new style of
self-process" that "is emerging everywhere" as a response to the
Holocaust and the explosion of atomic devices at Hiroshima and

Nagasaki. "Even the image of personal identity," he suggests, "insofar as it suggests inner stability and sameness, is derived from a vision of traditional culture in which man's relationship to his institutions and symbols is still relatively intact. And this, of course, is hardly the case today" (1969, 25). For those who exemplify the protean condition, the self, by contrast with the traditional unitary stable personality, is assembled from "an extraordinary set of . . . identity fragments—of combinations of belief and emotional involvement—each of which they could readily abandon in favor of another" (26).

For Lifton, the "protean personality" is a signal product of the A-bomb experience, and therefore a feature of the atomic age, with its pervasive sense of "psychohistorical dislocation" and its "flooding of imagery" (29). It is constituted of an engagement of self that is fragmented and ever-modulating in an action space that has become desperately unpredictable and subject to instantaneous wholesale destruction and renovation. One patient Lifton quotes described himself as "wearing a number of masks" and anticipates Johnny Depp when framing this pregnant question: "Is there, or should there be, one face which should be authentic?" Another young Japanese man Lifton describes reflects the ever-shifting inconsistencies and profound attitudinal shifts characteristic of post-nuclear trauma, and prefigures Johnny Depp's performing career:

Before the age of twenty-five he had been all of the following: a proper middle-class Japanese boy, brought up in a professional family within a well-established framework of dependency and obligation; then, due to extensive contact with farmers' and fishermen's sons brought about by wartime evacuation, a "country boy" who was to retain what he described as a lifelong attraction to the tastes of the common man; then, a fiery young patriot who "hated the Americans" and whose older brother, a kamikaze pilot, was saved from death only by the war's end; then a youngster confused in his beliefs after Japan's surrender, but curious about rather than hostile toward American soldiers; soon an eager young exponent of democracy, caught up in the "democracy boom" which swept Japan; at the same time a youthful devotee of traditional Japanese art—old novels, Chinese poems, kabuki and flower arrangement; during junior high and high school, an all-round leader, outstanding in studies, student self-government and general social and athletic activities; almost simultaneously, an outspoken critic of society at large and of fellow students in particular for their narrow careerism, on the basis of Marxist ideas current in Japanese intellectual circles; yet also an English-speaking student, which meant, in effect, being in still another vanguard and having strong interest in things American; then, midway through high school, experiencing what he called a "kind of neurosis" in which he lost interest in everything he was doing and, in quest of a "change in mood," took advantage of an opportunity to become an exchange student for one year at an American high school; became a convert to many aspects of American life, including actually being baptized as a Christian under the influence of a minister he admired who was also his American "father," and returned to Japan only reluctantly; as a "returnee," found himself in many ways at odds with his friends and was accused by one of "smelling like butter" (a traditional Japanese phrase for Westerners or Westernized Japanese); therefore reimmersed himself in "Japanese" experience—sitting on *tatami,* indulging in quiet, melancholy moods, drinking tea, and so on; then became a *ronin*—in feudal days, a samurai without a master, now a student without a university—because of failing his examinations for Tokyo University (a sort of Harvard, Yale, Columbia, and Berkeley rolled into one), and as is the custom spending the following year preparing for the next round rather than attend a lesser institution; once admitted, found little to interest him until becoming an enthusiastic *Zengakuren* activist, with full embrace of its ideal of "pure Communism" and a profound sense of fulfillment in taking part in the planning and carrying out of student demonstrations; but when offered a high position in the organization during his junior year, abruptly became an ex-*Zengakuren* activist by resigning, because he felt he was not suited for "the life of a revolutionary"; then an aimless dissipator, as he drifted into a pattern of heavy drinking, marathon mah-jongg games and affairs with bar-girls; but when the time came, had no difficulty gaining employment with one of Japan's mammoth industrial organizations (and one of the *bêtes noires* of his Marxist days) and embarking upon the life of a young executive or *sarariman* (salaried man)—in fact doing so with eagerness, careful preparation, and relief, but at the same time having fantasies and dreams of kicking over the traces, sometimes violently, and embarking upon a world tour (largely Hollywood-inspired) of exotic and sophisticated pleasure-seeking. (26–28)

The cynical observer, confronted today with this panoramic view across the span of a young life at the turning point of the twentieth century, will surely think, "But virtually all young people could be described this way," and it is true that by the end of the twentieth century they could. And not only young people. Writing at the end of 2002 about a real-life investigator of "X-Files"-type paranormal events, Burkhard Bilger describes his subject's past as follows:

> After his boyhood worship of J. Edgar Hoover, he grew to despise what the government stood for. He opposed the Vietnam War, even when his older brother became a captain in the Marines. (The two didn't speak for thirty years.) In 1967, he was teargassed beside the steps of the Pentagon, in the protest described in Norman Mailer's "The Armies of the Night." He marched with Martin Luther King, Jr., and kept the draft board at bay for a while by becoming a VISTA volunteer in the Deep South. When he was finally called for military service, in 1968, he fled to Canada.
>
> It was in Toronto that he fell back on the tricks he had learned as a boy. He put together shows as Janus the Magician, Mendell the Mentalist, and Mister Twister the Magic Clown. In the summer, he worked as the house magician at the Houdini Magical Hall of Fame, in Niagara Falls. In later years, he headed out to the Yukon Territory, where he dealt cards, prospected for gold, ran riverboats, and m.c.'d the cancan show at Diamond Tooth Gertie's casino. "God help us if Nickell ever has an identity crisis," one of his friends joked at the time. "There'll be twenty of him running around not speaking to each other." (93)

Thus, in general, a world culture of economic uncertainty set against a backdrop of unstable peace and rapid social and technological change has made for biographies full of career shifting, attitude changing, community dissolution, and personality fragmentation, with the result that the "protean personality" Lifton found so troubling and so fascinating is now omnipresent and commonplace. Yet it is also true that these conditions are not reflected in the most celebrated screen careers. Stars seem to be out of this world, in the particular sense that they call up stabilities and permanences akin to the cultural scene before World War II. But Johnny Depp has formed a screen career that resonates with the lives of the people in his audience, that approximates him to the everyday.

Indeed, while Lifton's description will be apparent to any of Depp's fans as a reflection of his screen career—if not precisely of the exact roles he has chosen to play then certainly of the fragmented, uncommitted, and bizarre quality of his transition through them—it is also, in its seismic shifting and variegated flavoring, an image of the career of the "Johnny Depp" beneath that screen career. For we are hardly now—and have not been since at least the 1940s—content to possess the screen image alone. National magazines touted the "boy genius" Orson Welles concomitant with the release of his *Citizen Kane* in 1941. *Life* magazine featured the "home life" of Alfred Hitchcock and the offscreen world of Ingrid Bergman as part of publicity for *Spellbound.* As Mary Beth Haralovich puts it, writing about the promotion of *Mildred Pierce,* "Production stories played a complex role in the publicity process" (1999, 197). Intended in such stories was more than the broadcasting of the "high level of expertise involved in the production of a film" (197); film publicity "concentrates on story and stars" (200) and the press material for *Mildred Pierce* about Joan Crawford in fact dubbed her "one of screenland's most important ladies" (200) and suggested that her performance as Mildred "was born of human experience as well as professional acumen" (200). Publicity stories "highlight her experiences—as a woman, mother, and actress—that provide the basis for her 'truthful' interpretation of Mildred." One story quoted by Haralovich goes so far as to claim that "Miss Crawford *is* the sacrificing, doubt-ridden, incorruptible Mildred Pierce, squaring off against the world, true to what she conceives to be a duty to her daughter, for whom she unflinchingly undergoes every privation." Mildred Pierce *in herself* was hardly a complete satisfaction to moviegoers of the mid-1940s (at a time, indeed, when movie attendance was peaking); the Joan Crawford beneath her was apparently required urgently, and swiftly filled in for avid readers by the opportunistic publicity department exactly as, today, the stars behind their performances are filled in for hungry viewers through interview clips with Mary Hart or Larry King, or through guest spots with Jay Leno, David Letterman, Conan O'Brien, or any of a large group of television "hosts" who "invite" film personalities into their television "homes" ("homes," to be sure, linked directly to the homes of those who watch).

If the surface presentation of virtually anyone in the post-Hiroshiman world might be described as protean—certainly at the beginning of the twenty-first century—yet even today we do not actually find the public idealizations known as movie stars described often in this way; and the history of the star is largely a contradiction of the idea of the shifting face. For example, the media publicity surrounding Winona Ryder's 2002 conviction for shoplifting, which reacted with a certain ritualistic glee to the fact that she was now a felon and her identity would never be quite the same, nicely reflects the traditional, conservative, even static persona that had been functioning very well for her, and other stars, up until then. Star transitions are made much of, in other words, as though they are outside the order of nature. Through marriages and break-ups, through changes of politics and hairstyle, through controversy at work and controversy in private life, most stars manage to retain a single persona for years, even through a full career, a persona that functions for them and those who produce their films the way a brand label functions for any other factory-made consumable product. Usually, stars linger for us as perduring figures, repetitions of what they have long been, images of consistent, typified, recognizable (thus merchandisable) personalities, stand-ins for those instantly identifiable, commercially oriented, offscreen "real people" we expect to meet for a charged moment each year at the Academy Awards or the Golden Globes. As Richard Dyer writes, "Certainly there is no requirement that a star image should change, and a star's apparent changelessness over a long period of time can be a source of charisma. Apart from growing older, the image of Cary Grant or Bette Davis has not really 'deepened' since the period in which they were established as stars. Equally, attempts by a star to change may meet with box-office failure—Ingrid Bergman is the *locus classicus*" (1999, 98).

Following Leo Braudy's analysis of "open" and "closed" films, Dyer suggests a dichotomy between "theatrical" and "doubling" acting styles. The "theatrical" style, typified in the films of Renoir, reveals an existential "choice" of role, as though the beings we meet onscreen, living their lives before the film began, *decided* to be the persons they are in front of us. But in closed films, we see the surface projection of a backstage "unity" of personality now underpinning a "theatrical" acting style that presents to us an anxious duplication of selves. Here, for Dyer, "it is the anguish of the powerfully oppressive nature of social roles that is articulated. Either the character is split between her/his inner self and outward appearance . . . or else two characters are shown to represent opposing facets of the same personality type" (102). It is possible to conceive a character "split" between an "inner" and "outer" self, or giving an "appearance," only if a deep "self" is taken as "true" and discernibly established as the basis of successive performances. Implicit in "theatrical" performance is the notion of a face being donned, a presentation being accepted as real in some circumstance that could seem unbelievable, and thus unsupported, in others.

In our simulacral culture, there persists as a riddling focus of concern the idea of the ineffably talented actor, the actor who might surpass the limitations of the star (even while being a star), a person whose capacities for camouflage and transformation are all developed to the point of mastery. This is the creature Craig Fischer has referred to—adducing the case of Dustin Hoffman—as a "consummate actor," a worker at what Dyer calls "polysemic" performance who "uses Method techniques to 'get lost' in a role" (2002, 83–84). The "polysemic performer" is a limiting case of the unitary actor, one who wears many masks—and often compromises a major star career in order to do so—but who is taken as a solitary presence behind the scenes. As Ratso Rizzo or as Raymond Babbitt, as Stanley Motss or as Willy Loman, Dustin Hoffman is uniformly perceivable as Dustin Hoffman, the "consummate actor" who is capable of twisting himself in as many bizarrely different directions. "When I watch *Rain Man,*" writes Fischer, "I never believe that Hoffman is an autistic person; rather, I am struck by how Hoffman creates a repertoire of gestures, tics, and vocal inflections that imitate the autistic experience and present Raymond as a believable character. The extradiegetic notion of Hoffman as a 'consummate actor' gives audiences an interpretive hook ('Wow, that guy can play anything!') that helps them make sense of his disparate roles and diverse career."

"That guy," note. Fischer notes a Martin Short impersonation of Hoffman on "SCTV." "I'm such a craftsman," says Short doing Hoffman doing Michael Dorsey doing Dorothy Michaels (from *Tootsie*). "I now understand what a woman feels" (2002, 83).

There are those who think that in many ways the signal "consummate actor" of our day is Johnny Depp, "a nice fellow who happens to be a great actor," as Mike Newell put it when filming *Donnie Brasco* with him, "a man unencumbered by ego, and increasingly confident of his gift for transforming himself into anything he wants to be" (Heard 2001, 68). And Newell is hardly the only observer who has concentrated on Depp's transformative capacity. "Depp brilliantly inhabits his character, down to the Boston accent, weasel mannerisms and various looks and posturings that evoke the '60s stoner, the '70s drug-dealing slickster with cool shades, and the '80s and '90s wreck rattled by addiction, poverty, desperation and fallout," says Doris Toumarkine about Depp's performance in *Blow* (*Film Journal International*). "Depp is a man who comes into sharp focus and, more important, attains full life only when he loses himself in a role," writes Richard Schickel (*Time*) about Johnny as "Donnie Brasco." Writing about *Dead Man,* Michael DeAngelis describes the "outsider" status that is essential to Depp's persona, suggesting that Johnny's appeal depends upon "ambiguities, contradictions, and mystery," upon his being portrayed "as an unanchored figure who belongs nowhere and is therefore wholly accessible to his audience" (2001, 293). For DeAngelis, Depp's career has implied a movement "beyond the sorts of traditional and stereotypical definitions of masculinity that might constrain virile young males to surmount the vicissitudes of woundings and maimings in order to preserve the impression that they are invulnerable" (2001, 293).

Mikita Brottman calls Depp a "watchful, secretive actor with an apparent taste for danger, duplicity and disguise," as well as a "pathological role-player—somebody who comes into sharp focus and attains full life only when he loses himself in a role" (Hunter 1999, 107), while for Brian Robb he is a "host of contradictions" (1996, 7) who has "sought refuge in oddball and freakish roles away from the mainstream as a way of avoiding potential failure" and whose "off-screen role echoes the film parts played by James Dean and Montgomery Clift" (11). Jason Clark of *Matinee Magazine* found Depp's portrayal of Edward Scissorhands an example of theatrical artistry: "Using elements of clowning, pantomime and sometimes silent comedy, Depp creates a childlike creation of epic proportion, yet gives it such a restrained, heartfelt slant *that he often disappears inside of it*" (emphasis added). Roger Ebert, too, cannot quite find Johnny: "Johnny Depp is an actor able to disappear into characters," says he of *Sleepy Hollow* and the luminous Ichabod Crane Depp manufactures there (Ebert 1999).

It must be said that the "invisibility of the actor" attributed to Depp in some criticism is entirely rhetorical, a matter for textual claim and therefore a feature of the attachment of persona to performer by publicity agencies divorced from the technical and personal production of character in which actors are contractually involved. While the idea that Johnny can disappear into a role—indeed, that he can disappear at all—and presumably reappear at will, is nothing if not the height of romance, and therefore exceedingly alluring to fans, adolescent and not, still there is something to be questioned in it. The appearance from nowhere, after all, links deeply to a viewer's excitement in witnessing it, rather as though the passion and desire of the viewer may have conjured the performance and the performer out of thin air. That Johnny may have "disappeared into" the performance imbues it with a kind of authenticity that is supreme, since apparently no extrinsic trace of him remains to margin the act, to modify it, to compromise or negate any aspect of it. The performance is purified exactly by the total immersion of the performer, the fact that no hint is accessible to an audience of the mechanism or the mechanic that lies under and behind.

Yet the critics and adorers observing Johnny "disappearing" into his roles do not actually know him outside the professional stance in and through which he makes a self available to them; and are therefore poorly positioned to determine whether or not an actual Johnny has disappeared before their eyes. "Johnny Depp disappearing into his roles" is therefore a critical construction, a particular framing of the "actor"—let us call him "Johnny"—behind the many characters we see onscreen, and a framing, to be sure, not available for underpinning every screen worker simulating a character. Underneath most screen characterizations, as critical and marketing discourse would have it, lurk actors who apparently fail to "disappear" inside their roles, people like Cary Grant, Robert De Niro, Julia Roberts, Gwyneth Paltrow, and Woody Allen. These are some of the star personae we expect to find again and again no matter what the role being performed. They are actors, in a sense, who *cannot possibly disappear,* or who, to be more precise and also bloodier, actually will disappear the moment they disappear. They have what Janet Staiger calls a "monopoly upon a personality" (Bordwell et al. 1985, 311). They have a predictable and recognizable value. The "disappearance" of a "disappearing actor" may be exclusively in the province of publicity. If not all actors disappear into their roles, still another possibility is that an actor who disappears isn't noticed and publicly reported: Rock Hudson is a nice example of an actor of whom the critical and marketing discourse never established a case for disappearance, and who, history has suggested, did virtually nothing else but disappear. Those who make the claim for Johnny's "disappearances," however, surely believe they are seeing *something* vanish, and we might ask what that something could be.

For chameleonic actors who "vanish" when they characterize, and equally for those who allegedly persist in shining through the parts they play, there is typically posited by publicity a unitary stable actor persona beneath the performance, one that perdures through time and is thought by the public to underpin the act. Whether through "vanishing into" a character (Depp) or standing identifiably nearby (De Niro), it is the backstage persona, an apparently underlying spirit and being, that achieves this underpinning—either disappearing or remaining discernible as the case may be. When critics imply that a disappearing actor disappears into his roles, they postulate a stable being who becomes systematically guised, unguised, and reguised in multiple ways through a career: one "true" face covered by a lot of masks (hence the polysemy invoked by Dyer and cited by Fischer)—in short, a somebody who exists, though we do not know him. Unlike John Wayne, who doesn't disappear because his characters are for the most part comparable from film to film and are therefore associated with him personally; or Jack Nicholson, who doesn't disappear because although his characters vary he obtrudes through all of them; the polysemic or "disappearing" actor is attributed with a fondness for—even an addiction to—disguise, a shapeshifter's drive to multiply the unity of self.

Although he "disappears," however, Depp is different.

Even if beneath the various screen characterizations he has adopted, Johnny can be thought a stable and single person adept at secrecy and camouflage, nevertheless that "deeper person" is not being offered unmediated to fans and viewers; but is being represented on the publicity stage by yet another being who is as polysemic as the surface performances are, a being, indeed, systematically created for us to appreciate in his role as "Johnny Depp giving polysemic performances onscreen." The "Johnny" beneath the many screen Johnnies is many Johnnies.

That construction, not nature, is the basis of an actor persona is shown in Haralovich's description of studio-made production stories that typically "gave the studio an opportunity to boast about its excellence ... [and] identified personnel and how they worked, discussing the filmmaking activities and atmosphere in some detail" (1999, 197).

Publicity gives us to believe in characteristics of the actor beneath the role he plays, for example, his stability or instability as an agent of unwavering, continuous being; his history of emotional involvement—his emotional career. But the era of which Haralovich writes, the 1940s, was not characterized as ours is by publicity *about publicity,* by open reference (such as we find in her critique itself) to publicity materials as such: scholars in 1945 did not write about the graphic composition of *Mildred Pierce* newspaper ads or describe, with this kind of astonishing clarity and illumination, the workings of the poster that were meeting the eye in the lobbies of theaters across the continent: "Poster ads transmitted the essential attributes of the film, generating viewer expectations and forming what Barbara Klinger has termed 'a tentative contract between producer and consumer.' Posters identified the genre of the film and placed its stars/characters at a point of narrative suspense. Poster graphics often linked head shots of stars/characters to each other and to a central narrative enigma through glances and tag lines" (Haralovich 1999, 197).

What Haralovich notes above merely happened. In this early era of "critical naiveté"—by which I mean not that no one had critical thoughts about the construction of the movie business, but only that critical thoughts of this kind were not, by and large, published—the backstage world was treated as real, and really unavailable except through the narrow, fortuitous aperture of publicity. Today it is shown as a construction (and publicity a constructive mechanism), quite as interesting in its own right as what we find onscreen. So, just as we may look at Depp's screen performances themselves, or at critical reviews of them, for insight about the Johnny behind the roles—"What would he have to be like in real life in order to give a performance like this?"—we may also find it profitable to examine the backstage constructions of Depp's "true" personality for insight about the Johnny behind that "Johnny."

Jason Clark, for instance, in recognizing the Johnny Depp who has an agent, who reads scripts, who is conveyed to the shooting location and costumed and made up for the camera as being a person "daring, intuitive and willing to take on a wide variety of roles despite his pretty looks and leading-man visage," hardly convinces the contemporary reader of his intimacy with Depp. That the variety of his roles is seen stereotypically as "wide," that Depp's looks are "pretty" though not "stunning" or "smooth" or "infectious" or anything else that hasn't been said a thousand times, that his is, of all things, a "leading-man visage" like that of Gable and Lancaster and Douglas and Ford, indeed, that his many roles are taken on because the actor-potentate is "willing" rather than "pecunious," all contribute to the pasteboard thinness of Clark's deftly made façade. Clark takes us "backstage," not backstage. In that very rarefied domain, he has Depp as a sensitive screen adventurer, whose Grail—the next great performance—is perpetually evading and alluring him and teasing him to try new things; John Wayne was presumably not "daring" or "intuitive"—his characters were.

Once the critical establishment has moved beyond the surface of the screen, there are only pragmatic limits to the denizens that can be envisaged there. Nor is there reason to suppose this subtle "backstage" world should be populated other than by the most bizarre and extreme of types, precisely the sorts who in the 1940s, 1950s, 1960s, 1970s, and 1980s adorned the screen itself. Depp, for instance, can be casual, even lascivious, instead of tautly daring: Ebert writes of his performance of Dean Corso in *The Ninth Gate* that it is "strong *if ultimately unaimed*" (Ebert 2000, emphasis added), implying that the actor, when we find him in his "private space" in our spyglass, can be relaxing his control without losing his power, can have presence without clear vector. So the "real" Johnny is both daring and unaimed.

Of the same performance, Elvis Mitchell wrote in the *New York Times,* "There's no leading man less interested in staying close to type than Mr. Depp." This is a veritable anatomy, suggesting that if Depp moves proteanly from type to type without being locked in any type, he does so because association with a particular type *does not interest him.* Indeed (presumably), of all actors one could imagine, Depp is *less interested than any* in associating with a type. Only a banana step away is the claim that he is afraid of being typified. While his characters may be types, Johnny playing them isn't. Johnny, in fact, isn't even interested in the sorts of types his characters are. Can this mean Johnny isn't even interested in his own characters? Dean Corso, after all, is certainly something of a type. He fetishizes first editions but never has his eye more than one step from a checkbook. He's a dealer. What could be more typical, at least in the age of bourgeois capitalism? But Johnny has *no interest* in staying close to type, as Dean Corso does. To travel from the character to the underspace in which he is performed by the actor—at least for Mr. Mitchell—is to experience desperate inversion.

But to go further, an apocrypha of backstage rumor, fiction, re-portage, and speculation has been gathered around Depp, all of which not only credits the view of him as an actor who longs for continuous reidentification and personal change but supports a view of his competence to hide himself successfully over and over in so many different kinds of roles. If he is both atypical and daring and aimless in his true self, he is also, like Lifton's young student after Hiroshima, always in search of a position, a home, a stance, an atti-tude, an orientation, a belief, a view, a room, a country, a way of life, a destination. To learn that his favorite book is *On the Road* is shock-ingly congruent, even epigrammatic since his "true" space is one that is open to continual movement, something like a road, or an ocean. He is a drifter, or a shark. We can know him as a Florida high school dropout, a thwarted musician (heard in *Chocolat*), the trasher of room 1410 at New York's Mark Hotel (because of "frustrations") in an event that "appears in every profile of Depp" (Heard 2001, 113, 115), the boy who had the tattoo WINONA FOREVER stitched into his arm and then, after disconnecting himself from Winona Ryder (offi-cially on June 21, 1993), had it copyedited to WINO FOREVER, a public activist, a devotee of Kerouac and in general a serious reader bent on choosing his movie projects on the basis of the scripts. All this data is, of course, typically romanticized by the adoring fans and critics who wish to make of Johnny an object upon which to fawn: a film script, for instance, will provide an indication of shooting logic and ex-pense, therefore of likely profit, and is both sensible and typical as a basis for actors choosing to do or not do films—Depp need not be configured as especially literary in order to be understood reading his script carefully; the Mark Hotel incident (amounting to a few thousand dollars of damage) was good publicity for the hotel but surely not the greatest act of vandalism ever to occur there; and the high school dropout moniker is a glory of what Goffman calls "bio-graphical reconstruction": there are thousands upon thousands of high school dropouts, but once one of them has become famous, it makes a certain amount of romantic sense to look back and identify the high school trouble as a leading factor that contributed to the stardom.

In his continual motion, Depp is a connoisseur of wines, or, as he puts it, a "cork dork" (Compton 2001, 149); a young man with a his-tory that vaguely resembles Don Juan's (though he doesn't interest himself in types) since he is a former lover of the "supersvelte supermodel" (as Richard Schickel puts it) Kate Moss, as well as of Ryder, Jennifer Grey, Sherilyn Fenn, and, if she can be believed, Tally Chanel, who claimed, "Our eyes locked, and he asked me to marry him" (Heard 2001, 60). He is known as the proprietor of The Viper Room on Sunset Boulevard (where, I am obliged to add—since mention of it is *de rigueur* in discussing this particular aspect of Depp's life—River Phoenix stumbled onto the sidewalk and died, a "poor, sweet hippie boy, just trying to buy himself some of that Depp out-law chic . . . [s]ome of that trailer-trash threat, some Cherokee-cheekboned blank-eyed cool" [Compton 2001, 149]). He was an actor "hard to work with" on "21 Jump Street," an assaulter of hotel secu-rity forces as well as a notoriously bad parker in Vancouver, a jay-walker in Beverly Hills (Heard 2001, 111–112), and in Chicago a peckish young man who would eat anything: "A FOX TV reporter tried to corner him for an impromptu interview. When she pointed her microphone in his direction, he leaned over and bit the end of it, saying, 'I don't think this thing is working'" (Heard 2001, 45–46). Yet to Winona Ryder, he was "really, really shy" and her parents, for-mer hippies, "loved him a lot" (Heard 2001, 61, 64).

Even backstage to co-workers he is a fount of charisma. "He's everything a star should be," said John Waters, on making *Cry-Baby*. "Working with him was almost as exciting as it must have been working with Johnny Hallyday in France in the beginning." He's at the same time a fount of humble professionalism, worrying about the scars he had to wear as Edward Scissorhands "not out of vanity, as was reported, but simply because they'd be distracting." Wearing a black rubber suit in 100 degree heat made urinating difficult so, consummate professional, he "curbed his coffee intake" (Heard 2001, 58, 68).

Another of the characterizations that have been superimposed on the "true" Johnny Depp, whoever he is, is the pouting ingrate. "An ungrateful Johnny Depp—who's made a fortune thanks to Holly-wood—has moved to France and turned his back on America," wrote the *National Enquirer,* April 13, 2001. "What's more, Depp is sinking to new depths by publicly blasting the country that's made possible his fabulous success. Taking aim at the United States, the outspoken star of the violent new movie *Blow* declared: 'It's madness there. When the horrors that happen in America, like little kids going to school with .22-caliber rifles and shooting their friends and teachers, killing people, isn't a rare occurrence anymore but happening all the time, anywhere is better than the U.S.'"—a portrait undercut October 8, 2001, when Depp told *Extra TV*, of the 9/11 tragedy, "I never felt more patriotic in my life until I saw that happen." The *Enquirer* went on, "The pouting performer adores Europe because it gives him more personal freedom. . . . The wealthy ingrate, who's learning to speak French, is living with girlfriend Vanessa Paradis and their daughter Lily Rose."

If an ingrate, also a gentleman. One night in London, after shooting *Sleepy Hollow*, Johnny was besieged: "He and Vanessa were having a quiet dinner in a London restaurant with a couple of friends to celebrate the pregnancy. Before long, photographers started peering in the window, looking for photo ops. . . . 'That angered me,' explained Depp. 'They were turning something sacred into a product. . . . I asked them nicely, Please, I can't be what you want me to be tonight—I can't be novelty boy, a product. Please leave me alone for just this one night'" (Heard 2001, 229). When they didn't oblige, he became a drooling beast, taking a three-foot piece of wood and attacking them with it. Later the young fellow with the "pretty looks and leading-man visage" reportedly said, "The beauty, the poetry of fear in their eyes, in their filthy, maggoty little faces was worth it" (229).

Johnny's punishment, if there has been one, is utter domestication: the same "drooling" Johnny is reported salaciously in the February 15, 2002, *People Online* as "facing diaper duty again" (he and Paradis had a son on April 17, 2002). Domestication, indeed, has been a flagrant theme of Depp's offstage persona construction since he began dating Paradis. The December 2000 edition of the Johnnydeppfan.com newsletter notes for its eager readers, among other items: images of "our favorite little family," a blurb to the effect that Vanessa is "Johnny's most beautiful girlfriend yet"; an affirmation from either Johnny or Vanessa, it's hard to tell, "I stopped looking for myself since I've found you, the best one in me actually is always you"; a taste of Johnny's ebullience after the birth of his daughter: "I feel like there was a fog in front of my eyes for 36 years. The second she was born, that fog just lifted"; Johnny's ostensibly newly adopted plebeian artistic taste as he experiences fatherhood—"I've been deeply influenced by my daughter," he tells *Star Magazine*. "I've watched every single Disney animated film, like probably 50 times, at least. And I like them. I love them. They're really great" (*Star*); and notice of Vanessa's new CD, where "You can also hear Lily-Rose babbling on one song." As the editor of the web-page says herself, "It's a wonder I didn't aspirate saliva and choke due to my sharp intake of breath when he came on the screen again. Sigh. End of Report. Sigh. Sigh. Sigh."

The "real" Johnny Depp behind the multiple screen characterizations, then, is—to put it mildly—confusing. He is ineffably inconsistent, shifting, migrating, developing, flippy, spontaneous, calculating, literate, punky, handsome and beastly, paternal and pretty, unaimed and destructive, wanton and frivolous, amorous and angry. In a London pub he pulled both ears—"very hard" (Heard 2001, 118)—of a descendant of Sir Robert Walpole, yet had once been "really courageous" and hard-working (we imagine, even noble) as he learned to imitate the movements of Chaplin and Keaton for *Benny & Joon* (Robb 1996, 87). Is he, then, if so mercurial in his "real" temperament, an actor who—as so many critical voices have persistently suggested—disappears?

As I write these pages, it is becoming a little fashionable for young male actors in the public eye to imagine themselves being invisible, to be sure. The pressure of the relentless publicity, public exposure, fan curiosity, and career-building is perhaps most acutely felt by those upon whom we fix our attention exactly as an ongoing requirement to be on show, a sense of gasping for air in an environment where every molecule in one's proximity is tagged, flagged, and bagged by the press, the internet interlopers, the vast audiences whose support is ultimately critical to continued success. Yet Leonardo DiCaprio seems to be replaying the little brother role from *What's Eating Gilbert Grape,* yearning to adapt and re-perform Depp's peculiar magic, when in the Sunday *New York Times Magazine* of November 24, 2002, he confesses to Marshall Sella how painful it is to be "suddenly defined in the media as a cutie-pie": "DiCaprio has resolved to become a cipher. 'Defining yourself to the public on a consistent basis is death to a performer,' he says. 'The more you define who you are personally, the less you're able to submerge into the characters you do. People are likely to think, Oh, I don't buy him in that role.' Accordingly, DiCaprio now strives to live below the media radar. He ruefully laughs about his 'strategy of not feeding the piranhas,' always adding that 'this experiment is a work in progress' (62). One must hide oneself to submerge, then. But if people cannot see one submerging, disappearing, how can one be thought to have disappeared?

DiCaprio's self-mystification is a clear-cut gaming strategy, however, while Depp's is considerably harder to recognize as such. There has never, for instance, been a period in Depp's career when he has willingly offered himself to the press in any detail or depth, when he has ever been so warmed by attention that he has needed a cooling respite. He is surely the cipher that Leonardo DiCaprio dreams of becoming but we are in no position to say that this is because he made a strategic decision, or because he took an agent's advice, or because he calculated an angle at which he could turn away from the scrutiny of his public. If he has done these things—and he may have—we cannot see him doing them, because unlike DiCaprio and other young actors, he does not give the interview in which he scoffs at stardom, complains about reporters, and articulates his plans to hide. He acts out positions (his, perhaps, but again, we cannot know) rather than defining them. He is generally silent. When he speaks up, he is often cryptic, as in his introduction to a small volume about *Blow* in which he offers an observation that is itself a mantra and also something of a challenge to our very attempt to grasp any meaning at all in his persona: "Among the many amazing wisdoms that George [Jung] so generously shared with me, there is one in particular that haunts my thoughts constantly: 'One is the number and two is the one.' The most frightening thought of all is that I'm pretty sure I know what he means" (Demme and Depp 2001, 9).

What can it mean if Johnny Depp *knows* what George Jung means?

To improvise upon Jean-Louis Richard's script for Truffaut's *Fahrenheit 451,* "In order to be lost, one must first be found." The idea that Johnny Depp is actually disappearing in his many screen roles is consistent with the logic—and dependent upon the belief—that there does exist a single authentic unitary Johnny who can be clearly identified and recognized *somewhere sometime by someone* even if he is nowhere to be seen in, for example, the likes of timid Edward Scissorhands, ballsy Donnie Brasco, quaint Ed Wood, adorable "Cry-Baby" Walker, or wholesome Gilbert Grape (cases, by the way, where the eponymousness of his character name leads to a condition wherein it is difficult even to isolate him as a subject of discourse, the very mention of his character name immediately diffusing into a reference to the film that contains and gives reference to that character). Even, and especially, when we cannot find him onscreen, or anywhere else, is our difficulty produced by his vanishing act?

It seems to me that publicity has made of Depp a protean movie star, perhaps the very first of the species distinctly so nameable. Offscreen, the Depp with whom we have been presented is inchoate, fluid, developing, never finished—in short, and once again!—*no thing*. Not particularly found, I would say, he cannot particularly become lost. On one hand, he is as much visible in his fullness onscreen as anywhere else. On the other, we see nothing of him there, but nothing of him backstage either. To discover the "real, real" Johnny Depp we must be willing to confront emptiness, to generalize to an experience that is backstage of the show business backstage, in the everyday world where we navigate to the box office to pay money to see his image and where, perhaps, in some real room next to a real street, he comes to stand beside us. A friend confided to me, with a mixture of excitement and embarrassment, that as she reached into her purse to find payment at a hairdresser in Los Angeles one day she looked up and suddenly he was standing next to her with his "magnificent hair": her vocal apparatus froze as he smiled into her face and walked away. Or perhaps, like us, he buys a ticket and sits in the dark at a theater—this is certainly the "Johnny Depp" we meet onscreen in Mika Kaurismäki's *L.A. Without a Map* (1998), watching Anouk Aimée onscreen while seated next to Anouk Aimée (watching herself)—and for him, as for us if we can just be willing really to trust what we see, the Johnny beneath the character does not exist. "You're saying you're not a fan of Johnny Depp?" Pam Grady asked him, and he responded, "I'm not a fan. I don't buy into him. He's overrated" (see Grady n.d.). The contrived polysemic "real" personality of Depp as actor beneath his roles is an interrogation of the star persona as we have come to know it. In his case the star behind the "star" behind the characters—that stable base upon which the publicity machine's "Johnny Depp" has been built—is neither visible nor knowable, by contrast with what Steven Cohan leads us to believe could have been said of Humphrey Bogart, an actor aligned with his performances whose "persona is a faithful copy of the original" (1997, 81).

Johnny's persona is no such faithful copy, because it is too variant, nor can we be sure there is a singular original. We are at an impassable distance from him, as is he and as is each one of us from ourselves. In that sense, he has become what Thierry Jousse defines as an *acteur,* a person who becomes impenetrable even as he seems to hand over his secret. He is ineffable, unknowable, exactly because instead of living in a backstage area to which, although we do not presently have it, *access is imaginable* (like, for instance, Brad Pitt in his East-meets-West fusion garden in the Hollywood Hills reported in the November 2001 issue of *House & Garden:* "If he weren't an actor, he says, he might have become a landscape architect"), Johnny inhabits a conceptual space that is utterly behind; behind the behind, as it were; beneath the beneath. That the "backstage Depp" so mawkishly reported is an ostensible construction makes possible our conception of an always unexperienced "Depp backstage of the backstage," a ghost with whom we can identify only with the least recognition. Perhaps the ghostliness of that ghost is what makes Depp's screen acting so sensitive, so simple, and so deeply touching.

BLanc

Interviewed in New York late in 1995, Jim Jarmusch shared with *Cahiers du cinéma* the reason he liked Johnny Depp. "He has a very fresh, very pure personality, a whiteness that makes you want to cover it with graffiti" (Saada 1996, 26). Notwithstanding the interest this comment bears toward a discussion of Jarmusch's *Dead Man,* to which we will come, it seems nonetheless a remarkable review of Depp as a figure of the screen. Surely the purity and fresh-ness are evident palpably, in the trademark wide-eyed stare, the relaxed posture of the lips that do not always have something to say, the unblemished complexion and innocent smile that the actor has carried with him beyond his adolescence. Yet, that whiteness . . .

Jarmusch's term—translated into the French as *blancheur*—has a twofold meaning, of course. It connotes at once all that we can mean in making reference to the fact that Depp's skin is white, and as well a *tabula rasa* innocence and cleanness, the quality of a slate that has never been marked or that has miraculously, after a life of many markings, been wiped clean.

The term "white" in racist Western culture has long been virtually synonymous with a condition of invisibility so pervasive and intense as to trump even application of the descriptor, "invisible" (see Foster 2002; Dyer 1997). To be white has been to hold and use power, especially the power of demonstration, and thus to evade the inspection of others in the depths of one's commitment to a process of inspection. Worth and Adair, for example, found in a study of black and white teenagers learning to use filmmaking equipment in Philadelphia that while "white teenagers or graduate students find the filmmaking activity an appropriate means of controlling images of distant and unusual places and events," and while "for the white groups we have studied, filmmaking activity is not inconsistent with the conquest of new territory, new people, and new ideas" (1972, 240–41)—yet "blacks prefer to *be* the image in front and . . . whites prefer to *manipulate* the image from the back. . . . Black groups tended to organize themselves around the activity in front of the camera" (244).

If to be white has been to control and define, how much more has this been the case for white males. There is, therefore, something deliciously contradictory in Jarmusch's observation that Johnny's whiteness is precisely what makes him vulnerable to inscription. While he has with his "purity" taunted Jarmusch's desire—the way a portrait of a little girl in white taunts the hero of Vonnegut's *The Sirens of Titan:*

> He . . . insisted that Constant admire a huge oil painting of a little girl holding the reins of a pure white pony. The little girl wore a white bonnet, a white, starched dress, white gloves, white socks, and white shoes.
>
> She was the cleanest, most frozen little girl that Malachi Constant had ever seen. There was a strange expression on her face, and Constant decided that she was worried about getting the least bit dirty.
>
> "Nice picture," said Constant.
>
> "Wouldn't it be too bad if she fell into a mud puddle?" said Rumfoord. (1971, 23)

—Johnny Depp has surely also, in the superiority of his whiteness, been a repository of desire himself, himself a marker of skins and surfaces that come into his dominating view. In *Dead Man* and other films, when Depp gazes into the camera, it is we who feel vulnerable to being marked by his look. Jarmusch, ironically, is represented in a photograph that accompanies publication of the interview that contains his comment: in the picture he is himself a taciturn and remote Great White Presence, his hair the color of snow, his long white hands balancing his long white face, his eyes averted.

I think Jarmusch not wrong, however. Depp certainly catches and holds our regard, and we do not stray from watching him move in his purity, attempting at his every gesture to reach out and contact him through an evaluative gesture of our own. That gesture is the avid reader's project of naming, characterizing, deciphering, and then forming the reality so revealed in a fixity of perduring presentation, exemplification, and fear. In the sense that he can typify whiteness par excellence, then (*The Brave* and *Pirates of the Caribbean* are exceptions to this rule), we never stop commenting upon—inscribing—Depp, or having the feeling of being subject to his evaluation. Each movement he makes seems to erase itself, leaving him perpetually open to new reading by us and new empowerment.

In Emir Kusturiça's *Arizona Dream,* for example, Depp plays Axel Blackmar, a fisherman working and living in New York. His cousin Paul (Vincent Gallo) one day comes to visit, "captures" him, tucks him into the back seat of his convertible, and drives him to Arizona to visit his uncle who has asked to see him. As they drive, we see Axel shifting in the seat and dozing. Paul is singing "Happiness Is a Warm Gun," from The Beatles' "White Album." The city swirls in multi-colored lights outside the car, then the Lincoln Tunnel, then the road. We take Depp to be an epitome of unwritten blankness in his sleep, and inscribe the twisting, visually warped, luminous world onto him as his dream. The Arizona dream of the film, then, thanks to Depp's innocence, is as much our own dream laid onto him, spread across his body and actions as so much graffiti.

Yet, too, always the dominance of his whiteness takes its place, so that he is never paralyzed, never out of touch with his motivations, never wondering what to do or how to do it. Even his solitary gaze into the lens is read by us as a knowing, perfectly evaluative gaze. He is an apprehender, and as such a model onscreen for the viewer who is watching him. When he does not know something, he is informed; we take him, indeed, to be an innocent abroad in all his films, suspecting that each screen moment brings him orientation, history, prospects. As we watch to understand the film, Depp watches to understand the diegetic world.

In *L.A. Without a Map* we discover him only a few times, finally, and climactically, watching an Anouk Aimée film at her side in a private showing, the completely absorbed, all-absorbing film viewer *inside* the film. He proceeds through his films, then, partly in order to see and understand, to be on the watch; and one reason Jarmusch may have felt the desire to *cover* him with graffiti is this, that Depp's absorption of the surround is relentless and the graffiti would have provided *Jarmusch* with some privacy.

There is a completely different sense in which Johnny is white, however, and in which inscriptions made upon him are important. For if whiteness suggests innocence and blankness, the quality of not-yet-having-been-written-upon, if whiteness is inscrutability, it specifically challenges the latent—perhaps not so latent—detective in every viewer, the systematic observer whose commitment it is to read the cinematic body. The detective, writes Tom Gunning, is "the exemplary fictional invention of modernity. The use of causal reasoning, penetration into the modern metropolis, exploitation of disguise and the blurry borders of personal and social identity, scrutiny of the smallest physical items and elements of everyday behaviour for the imprint of revelatory clues; the frequent use of technology for surveillance—all these traits mark the detective as a character who negotiates the modern environment with unique mastery" (2000, 94). Depp throws modernity in our faces.

And while it is of course fascinating that Depp himself plays a detective in many films, and began his career on "21 Jump Street" doing exactly that, he is still, and foremost, an object of detection for us. He is a principal feature of our modern cinematic environment; and, I would argue, he constitutes a kind of topological environment unto himself. His are certainly the most ostensible and beguiling examples of "disguise and the blurry borders of personal and social identity" to be found on the screen today.

In a thrilling discussion of Sherlock Holmes, Gunning elsewhere notes that the method of that quintessentially modern figure "opens onto a peculiarly modern world in which the forces of everyday life can mark people as deeply as an officially applied branding iron" (1995, 22). Indeed, claims he, contemporary urban circulation "marshals a range of factors which imprint the bodies of individuals with their own history." If screen performers are similarly marked in general, with their own biographies and with the scars of their own screen careers, it is fascinating to consider Jarmusch's contention that Depp is not; that he has managed, "with unique mastery," not only to detect the environment in which he has moved but more importantly to make himself invulnerable to detection there. That we may successfully inscribe him with graffiti suggests exactly that he has not yet been inscribed, regardless of the wealth of screen roles he has adopted and the plenitude of backstage lore about his "real" life.

Somehow for Jarmusch—and I believe for every Depp watcher—after all of what he has been through in life and pretended to go through onscreen, Johnny is still fresh, unknown, virginal. His every moment is one in which he awaits experience.

THE OUTSIDER

I guess I still feel a little bit outside it all . . . ish. I mean, not so much outside as just not inside.

Johnny Depp to Danny Leigh

When Jarmusch, speaking as a filmmaker, indicates a desire to cover Johnny with text, he is suggesting that he wants to socialize him, to render him both decodable and navigable. Already, without being written upon, his body is a text itself, a poem, a mystery, a metaphor, an epigraph inscribed in an untranslated and untranslatable set of glyphs. But Jarmusch is saying, in the plainest terms, that he wishes to imprint Johnny's pristine, untrammeled surface with his own configuration of a character, because Johnny Depp permits himself to move through a dense terrain in a quest for understanding while himself remaining open and unmarked in the process. He is in many ways, then, the epitome in contemporary culture of the nineteenth-century *flâneur*.

This cultural and personality type, intimated by Charles Baudelaire in his reflective essay on Constantine Guys, "Le Peintre de la vie moderne" (The painter of modern life) in 1863, had been described in more dramatic terms by Edgar Allan Poe (influenced by Baudelaire) in his story "The Man of the Crowd" (1839). "The film from the mental vision departs," wrote Poe, anticipating beautifully the luminous gaze of Depp onscreen, and also our gaze transfixed by his, "and the intellect, electrified, surpasses . . . its every-day condition. . . . I felt a calm but inquisitive interest in every thing" (1998, 84). Traveling away from the confines of the neighborhood in which he had been born and lived his entire life, and migrating into the press of social life in the streets of Paris—Gunning, in his analysis of Holmes, calls this a "thicket" provided by the "complex maze of urban circulation" (1995, 22)—the *flâneur* learned to take pleasure in the observation of strangers, the "reading" of the signs they would emit as to class and experience, feeling and attitude and alignment, history and anticipation of the future. Depp, for example, catching the spirit of the *flâneur* himself, "jumped at the chance" to do *From Hell* because, like a denizen of what Benjamin calls "the great period of *noctambulisme*" (1997, 50), "it meant I could talk to some of the great Ripper-ologists and *I got to wander through the area of Whitechapel at night. I loved that*" (www.tiscalo.co.uk; emphasis added). The *flâneur* is enabled to make the readings that give him pleasure by virtue of the newly designed citizen as signifier, emblem of a system of codes whereby aspects of the visible presentation of self are codified and utilized as a basis for retrieving information. It is precisely such a system of identification, now loosely but cannily employed by a population accustomed to rigorous coding and recording, that we employ when we "read" Johnny Depp's onscreen and offscreen behavior as indications of his "true" self.

The consideration of Depp in terms of the Parisian *flâneur* is by no means as arcane a project as it may seem. Not only does he, in his movement and ocularity onscreen, evince the half-sleepwalking, eager sentience of the man newly returned from long sickness, described by Baudelaire and Poe, the man who in his fever was, as François Truffaut supposes Jean Vigo to have been, "considerably more brilliant, more intense, and stronger" (1978, 28); not only does he seem to be browsing the neighborhoods of the narratives in which he is embedded; but as a citizen of the twenty-first century he has in fact transplanted himself to France, with the effect that, even as it contained Baudelaire's circuit and sparked Poe's lingering imagination, Paris is also the precinct of his own most urbane identifications, a city in which he can meet an interviewer "over a glass of Merlot in the loungy anteroom of a discreet hotel located on a small, snaking side street" (Kaylin 2003, 95). It is finally the music of Serge Gainsbourg and Jacques Dutronc that moves him, the comedic acting of both Louis de Funès—"the master of the instant. He occupies each moment in an absolutely magnificent way. His charisma is total"—and Jean Gabin in *La Traversée de Paris* that stimulates his memory and enthusiasm: "When they're on the screen together . . . it's too much. Too much" (Grassin 2003, 54).

"The more uncanny a big city becomes," writes Walter Benjamin in describing the *flâneur,* "the more knowledge of human nature—so it was thought—it takes to operate in it. In actuality, the intensified struggle for survival led an individual to make an imperious proclamation of his interests. When it is a matter of evaluating a person's behaviour, an intimate acquaintance with these interests will often be much more useful than an acquaintance with his personality" (40). By "interests," we may now understand not only business practice and ethical plans but philosophical commitment, political alignment, cultural predilection, and interactional orientation—all of which are taken to say less about personality than about an actor's intentions toward experience. DeAngelis comments, for example, on the way the

> 'deeper' sexual ambiguities of Depp's persona remain more susceptible to press speculations and inferences that sometimes appear to be contradictory—even when expressed by the same reporter. Noting, for example, that Depp's fans include "millions of teenage girls and gay men," one biographer describes the actor as "almost asexual in most of his films," then reverses himself to suggest that the actor's characterizations "rely as much on their feminine attributes for their success as they do on Depp's high cheekbones and classic good looks." (2001, 296–297, quoting Robb 1996, 7–8)

Flânerie is all around. Here, the notation by Brian Robb of Johnny Depp's "feminine attributes" and "high cheekbones and classic good looks" as accoutrements of the actor's success with characterizations is an example of the *flâneur*'s casual judgmentalism raised to the status of critical acumen; as, in its way, is DeAngelis's keen observation that in observing the way he does, Robb is being contradictory. The *flâneur*'s predisposition, in this example evidenced in critical practice but equally available in Depp's screen performances, is to regard the world as a way of decoding it: consider the deftness and rapidity of his assessments of human frailty and situational vulnerability as, in *Pirates of the Caribbean,* his Jack Sparrow contrives to manipulate and control situations. In *Fear and Loathing,* he is exclusively an observer, one whose impressions are filtered and sharpened through a narcotic lens. A prototype of the contemporary window-shopper or café denizen, the *flâneur* is a figure who experiences urban life as strange, in the particular sense that he is confronted over and over by types he must struggle to recognize since they have been moving in circles different than his own, populating a world that to him has always been outside his ken. The reading of the "interests" of unknown others cumulates as a social analysis, of the sort that Veblen entertained in examining conspicuous consumption (1908) and that C. Wright Mills had in mind when he wrote about status panic (1951, 254–258). Whole populations can be observed, catalogued according to taste and conciliation to trend, predicted, followed, measured, catalogued, and in this way known. Yet the desire to know the other who circulates secretly in the press of social life is exactly the impulse that fans and critics have allowed to flower in their address to Johnny Depp.

It was of course the Haussmannization of Paris around 1850 that made Baudelaire's *flâneur* possible at all, that massive project of urban development for "the advancement of the bourgeoisie's business interests" (Schivelbusch 1986, 181), first through the production of long straight avenues along which the eye could perambulate to the horizon (by means of the demolition of entire quartiers and "a general levelling of Paris, to eliminate the minor humps and hillocks which could play havoc with a road intersection or a long perspective" [Chapman and Chapman 157, 77–78, quoted in Schivelbusch 1986, 182]); and then, after 1852, through the opening of the first department store, itself a city within the city in which an end was put to the previous confrontation and conversation of buyer and salesperson by the omnipresence of the mute price tag and in which the customer's "panoramic eye was not dealing with landscapes or boulevards but with goods" (see Schivelbusch 1986, 188–193). As Shelley Rice notes, the optical experience is paramount in Haussmann's new Paris—Victor Fournel called it "Paris demain, Paris futur"—since the planner "was not content to let his monuments simply sit in the middle of space; each of his disengaged edifices was to be suitably set, like a jewel, in the crossroads of his networks of boulevards, which functioned as vistas—long-range visual perspectives. But this neoclassical idea begins its metamorphosis in Haussmann's Paris. . . . Vistas were sometimes lost by a pedestrian ambling down a street three miles long, who perceived as his primary reference only the endless avenues; but then a view might suddenly come into focus" (1997, 124). *Flânerie* is thus the beginning of a contemporary form of perception, and at the same time the origin of an experience of the everyday that is intensely perceptual, the street wanderer gaining his purchase on the city by means of the clues he can pick up by looking at it.

Our contemporary *flânerie* is movie-going. But although virtually all the characterizations we see onscreen are swiftly decoded and stored for future reference, the performances given by Depp challenge perception rigorously by referring exactly to no previously accepted codes, no stock characterizations, no articulations in the system of class or status displays. He is as though in search of identity.

In the context of the newly opened metropolis, the *flâneur* is a persistent innocent, always confronting strangers, always innocent to the motives of others, always caught in a state of wonder and confronted by a field of decodable information. Depp gives a sense of precisely this quality of curious innocence in his Ichabod Crane in *Sleepy Hollow,* in his Frederick Abberline in *From Hell,* in his Gene Watson in *Nick of Time,* and, relative to the manipulative others he must deal with throughout their diegeses, in his Dean Corso in *The Ninth Gate,* his Joe Pistone/Donnie Brasco in *Donnie Brasco,* and his Agent Sands in *Once Upon a Time in Mexico.* Schivelbusch reminds us that the nineteenth century's "preoccupation with the conquest and mastery of space and time had found its most general expression in the concept of circulation," an experience made possible by the new boulevards opened up by Haussmann, and that led to a world in which continuous movement among strangers made detection a central achievement of modern man. "If the *flâneur* is thus turned into an unwilling detective," writes Benjamin, "it does him a lot of good socially, for it accredits his idleness. He only seems to be indolent, for behind this indolence there is the watchfulness of an observer who does not take his eyes off a miscreant. Thus the detective . . . catches things in flight; this enables him to dream that he is like an artist" (1997, 40–41).

Gunning notes that Arthur Conan Doyle's model for the paradigmatic detective Holmes was Dr. Joseph Bell of Edinburgh, "who astonished students and patients with his ability not only to diagnose diseases from symptoms but also to read a person's occupation and background from details of body, gait, and clothing" (1995, 23). He quotes Bell: "Racial peculiarities, hereditary tricks of manner, accent, occupation or the want of it, education, environment of every kind, by their little trivial impressions gradually mold or carve the individual, and leave finger marks or chisel scores which the expert can detect" (23, from Sebeok 1983), and goes on to conclude, "This method of reading persons opens onto the new world of mobility and rapid circulation . . . in which signs of class and occupation have moved below the threshold of immediately recognized conventional signs to reach the level of unintentional—and often unrecognized—symptoms" (23). We live, and Johnny Depp's screen career is constructed, in that "new world of mobility and rapid circulation." As the *flâneur* is the prototype for contemporary urban man, we are each molded upon his form, and consequently bring a questioning expertise fascinated to decode "little trivial impressions" to each contemporary experience.

If our reading of the screen includes attention to the actors who populate it, our confrontation with Depp is a disarming and engaging one particularly because signs of his class, his attitude, and his social condition are particularly well masked, even effaced. He is thus a perfect mirror for the viewer, presenting nothing to look at but only the face of another person gazing out at the crowd, trying to fathom his circumstances. The more we look past the surface of his characterizations and fail to find a stable personality, biography, class identity, or career, the more we are confronted not with him, not with our social world, but with our own relentless project of searching and trying to identify: our detective predilection in the opened precincts of the new global "city."

But Benjamin warns, "No matter what trail the *flâneur* may follow, every one of them will lead him to a crime" (1997, 41). Depp, the object of our persistent *flânerie,* is frequently described by the press as an "outsider" or an "exile." Once suspended from school for "mooning a gym teacher," he introduced himself to Iggy Pop by saying, "Fuck you, fuck you, fuck you" (Zehme 1991, 34). By 14, he had "sworn off drugs forever" (34), a young man who had lived on the dark side and is therefore especially worth watching and deciphering. He believes—or believed in 1990—that "he was once Houdini" (75), and in general evinces "a lack of devotion to institutional authority, as evidenced by his reputation for being difficult or demanding on the set of '21 Jump Street,'" where he reportedly lit his underwear on fire, antagonized producers, and "threw a punch or two" (Rebello 1990, quoted in DeAngelis 2001, 295). The outsider is at once a relentless reader and a hard read—someone we do not know and accept as one of ourselves, a stranger worth examining, an object of intense speculation and observation; and someone who himself observes the world from outside, at pains to come to terms with it. The contemporary urban scene, especially in Los Angeles, is centered on mobility, for example, but Depp is a non-driver. Nonetheless, he is "even on foot . . . ever vigilant of traffic minutiae":

> "Your seat belt! Your seat belt!" he hollered into the snarl of Beverly Boulevard, where we trod along. Depp had spotted a man driving with his seat belt dragging out on the pavement and could not bear to think of the consequences. The startled driver now owes his life to Depp. Likewise, Depp spotted a woman driving with her door ajar. "Your door!" he yelled. "Your door is open!" No doubt, that very woman is now living a rich and productive life, thanks to the selfless instincts of a certain movie actor who is currently looking carefully for his next big project. (Zehme 1991, 32)

And, responding to Pam Grady's question of what the film would be like if someone made *Being Johnny Depp,* Depp invokes a textual problem familiar to the stranger: "Well, it wouldn't make any money at the box office. It would probably be very uncomfortable. It would probably be uncomfortable to watch. Certainly for me. Definitely for me. I don't know. *It would be an interesting read*" (Grady n.d.; emphasis added).

Depp's pain often seems linguistic, in fact, as though it is the fixing of experience in description and naming that constitute sacrilege for him. "The only thing I have a problem with is being labeled," he has told interviewers many times, in one way or another. He is beguiled to report that George Jung called him a "witch" (Leigh 2001, 1). Told that Mike Newell, the director of *Donnie Brasco,* described him as "someone you could take home to your mother," Depp says, "We all have to go out and peddle our asses, but those things are just sticky labels people use to sell you" (Leigh 2001, 2). To Michael Okwu he admitted such labeling isn't really his cup of tea: "I don't want to be caught up in the who's-who stuff . . . I don't want to play the game" and he is reported as never reading anything that's written about him, thus implicitly maintaining an enigmatic stance about his reading of, his response to, those labels. His performances are frequently taciturn, his dialogue frequently minimal, and when he uses language he uses it with precision: Craig Offman writes in www .salon.com about a twenty-minute battle Depp had with Holly George-Warren, the editor of *The Rolling Stone Book of the Beats,* about keeping a serial comma in an essay he wrote for her collection. And though he is not without opinions—"He wanted to go somewhere else. He was an amazing man," he says of Vincent Price (Grady n.d.); "What we should be asking is why kids need to anaesthetize themselves," he says about drugs (Leigh 2001, 1); "It's like joining a club, a clique just because everyone else is in it. You don't have any particular interest in it, and it has nothing to do with who you are as a person. You just join it because it's the thing to do," he says of the Hollywood machine—the positions he takes tend not to be definitive about the subtleties of his character, the delicacies of his position, the poetics or politics of his worldview in any more than a purely situational, momentary, reactive way. He is therefore modern in the vibrant yet always unsettling way of moving well beyond the stable identification, the deeply committed knowledge, the relationships, or the bonding characteristic of the settled community that the modern world eclipses.

LIGHT and Darkness

No feature has more stunned viewers than the watery, hungry, reassuring, unrested "almond brown" eyes that have "made Johnny Depp a gorgeous pouting icon" (FeatsPress). With Edward Scissorhands, for example, we have the feeling that it is by way of the eyes he is made utterly vulnerable, and that if the world displayed to him when he comes down from his castle is ultimately a painful panorama there is also nothing of it that he does not see. With Donnie Brasco we have the sense of an immensely articulate, nuanced power of observation, an acoustic and optical magnification that makes accessible the tiniest details of human performance and social organization; he is a Linnaeus. Pistone/Brasco's life is in continual jeopardy every moment of every day he works undercover; the success of our affiliation with him resides in his never failing to take note, never failing to be outside and yet connected through the powers of his observation. In *What's Eating Gilbert Grape,* his Gilbert has to "keep an eye" on the Grape family, his paternalistic surveillance interrupted only when a strange young woman comes driving down the road to lure him out of town. Distracting his eye, she enchants him; and the family he has been caring for begins to disintegrate. Dean Corso in *The Ninth Gate* has an educated eye, an eye that has studied the operation of the eye. When he reads illuminated manuscripts he scans them with a historically laminated vision, and it is through this vision and what is revealed to it that viewers are wedded to the story.

The observation of the world is only truly opened up to its full development when it is freed from dependence upon sunlight, and so it is hardly an accident that the *flâneur* makes most of his perambulations at night, benefited by the public illumination that first gas lamps, and later electricity, made possible. Benjamin rhapsodizes on Robert Louis Stevenson's rhapsody "on the rhythm with which lamplighters go through the streets and light one lantern after another" and then remarks, "At first this rhythm contrasted with the uniformity of the dusk, but now the contrast is with a brutal shock caused by the spectacle of entire cities suddenly being illuminated by electric light" (1997, 51). It is public illumination, indeed, which makes the act of observation stand out from its background in civil gesture, which facilitates the gaze and at the same time draws our attention to its centrality in social organization. The motion picture is a condensation and displacement—in Freudian terms, a dream-version—of nocturnal illumination in the bounded darkened space of the theater. The screen is an illuminated public space in which, *flâneurs* all, we can perambulate (thanks to the motion of the camera) in order to capture visions of the strange persons who inhabit those *quartiers* we did not know; for, after all, the cameraman's "est l'oeil qui doit 'voir' à la place du spectateur ce que le cineaste essaie de faire passer par l'action et les personages" [is the eye that must 'see' in the spectator's place that which the director makes happen in the action and the characters] (Courant 2002, 60).

Schivelbusch affirms that the theater had the greatest appetite for light in the nineteenth century (1995, 50). Film certainly had the greatest appetite in the twentieth. The screen is thus the repository of a collective optical trust, the topos of a systematic optical peregrination, as well as being the locus of a dramatic exposition in which vision and detection are taken as paramount. If we accept visions as replacement for the apotheosis of action that was our greatest achievement in the nineteenth century, still there is more to the optical intensification of experience produced in *flânerie* than mere erotic delight and aesthetic fulfillment. Gunning shows that the age of the *flâneur* was also one in which the circulation of the individual within the crowd was delimited, bounded, and finally fixed through a pervasive system of decoding, measurement, and reading embodied most formally in the practice of forensic photography. In the rogue's gallery, suitably organized, the body of the individual citizen becomes in itself "a sort of unwilled speech, an utterance whose code is in the possession of a figure of authority rather than controlled by its enunciator" (1995, 32); this "figure of authority" is a kind of watching, assessing, cataloguing *flâneur*. Thus, between the police agent and the shopper in the department store there is a difference only in the geography of their adventure.

What is now a basis for film casting was once essentially a procedure for criminal identification: measurements were taken of various parts of the face, compared, catalogued, and used as a basis for filing arrest photographs; so that ultimately descriptions from witnesses could make possible the retrieval of actual pictures of individuals who had formerly gone without this kind of stable public recognition, moved liberally without their features and gestures being fixed in a catalogue. Since the 1930s, the cataloguing of features and gestures has been a stable part of actor typification and recognition and one of the bases for actors' consistency in obtaining work. For instance, Danae Clark observes that in the heyday of the studio contract, the actor who refused to play the same part twice, who refused to resemble himself onscreen, was an offense to the moral code embodied by studio practice, a threat to studio hegemony, and a vulnerability to the smooth architecture of efficiency that studio filmmaking represented.

Depp is the antithesis of the typical obedient studio contract performer, an actor whose every gesture has been a break from the illusion of what Clark calls the unified persona. Further, he represents a return of the freely circulating individual in the context of an extremely repressive "society of the spectacle," where public illumination, the systematic development of the gaze, and the intensification of identificatory practice all tend toward the fixing of identity and the immobility of the individual. He is freely circulating, too, in an arena filled with serious and judgmental observers who would happily isolate, diagnose, and bound him. His very indefiniteness in the face of an articulate social mechanism for isolating, diagnosing, and bounding people reflects to us our propensities for using observation to police the social terrain, flies in the face of our technologically supported social strengths. We must remember that the vast potentialities for physical and social mobility that were made possible by technological expansion in the middle of the nineteenth and beginning of the twentieth centuries were also countered precisely by the social organization of the gaze, which led to a scheme in which psychology was rendered visible through gestural and vocal utterance, personality was rendered stable and recordable, character was made measurable and comparable, and motive was made calculable in advance. Depp flashes that dominating social gaze back at us, mockingly, and at the same time continues in his many characterizations—and, more importantly, in his offscreen elusiveness with reporters and biographers—to avoid the aggressive gaze of those who find him alluring, beautiful, mythic, enigmatic, bizarre, trendy, provocative, and ultimately criminal and who set themselves to knowing, and therefore debilitating, him.

For Johnny Depp is nothing if not elusive. What is amazing about him is how in a (cinematic) world so well illuminated and well examined he persists in being obscure. In a culture of pervasive *flânerie,* where on every front the stranger is being identified and transformed into knowledge, he remains not only a mystery but also a darkness. Indeed, in Robert Rodriguez's *Once Upon a Time in Mexico,* he has his eyes put out by a sadistic torturer, and spends the last part of the film wandering the streets behind a brave boy who leads him the way. The blood that flowed out of his eye sockets has dried on his cheeks, to create a bizarre and symmetrical sign, now black and unmistakable: the sign of two inverted hands, with fingers spread. The Johnny thus centralized by Rodriguez—and emphasized by the director in a portrait medium-shot that tails after the last of the end credits—is both sightless and visionary, however.* As a blind man he must stumble his way, grope in the black air for an angle at which to shoot his enemies. Here he is an ultimate confrontation and mockery of the cataloguing and dominating vision of the nineteenth century, a signpost to the dead end that positivism ultimately promises. And he can be seen as pointing the way toward the Emersonian skepticism that Stanley Cavell cherishes: what is this world? What are we in it? Yet at the same time, he manages in his sightlessness to have the most precise vision possible, his aim unhindered, his instincts sharpened, his orientation infallible although his energy is on

---

* This moment is something of an homage to Zatoichi the blind swordsman, who appears in films from 1962 onward, most recently embodied by Takeshi Kitano in *Zatôichi* (2003).

the wane. His battles take place in midday sunlight in order that the inordinate brightness may cue us to the depths of his deprivation and apotheosis.*

In a system controlled by opticality—that is, silence—Depp is typically the subject of a symphony of (almost always conflicting) rumor. In a universe where the stability of character is a requisite of bureaucratic functioning and a chief treasure of the new absolutist state, he clings with such delicious (and also nostalgic) tenuousness to each moment of experience, drifting from one attitude to its opposite, from one character to a completely unrelated other, from stance to stance as in a choreography. That he has migrated from Kentucky by way of Florida, by way of guitar music, by way of the fiction of Kerouac, by way of affiliation with Allen Ginsberg, by way of being a teen idol, by way of a calculated rudeness to photographers, by way of run-ins with the police in Canada and the United States, by way of indeterminacy about his sexuality, by way of sensitive masculinity, by way of numerous girlfriends, by way of frequent collaborations with Tim Burton (he has appeared in three Burton films, *Edward Scissorhands, Ed Wood, and Sleepy Hollow,* and will play Willy Wonka in a fourth, *Charlie and the Chocolate Factory*), by way of friendship with Marlon Brando or Tobey Maguire, by way of recurring irrational fears of the musical entertainer John Davidson (cured by the time Davidson joined him to shoot *Edward Scissorhands,* where Johnny found him "a really sweet guy" [Zehme 1991, 32]), by way of the drug scene on Sunset Boulevard where he came to own The Viper Room, by way of a wholesale rejection of increasingly violent American capitalist society—that, in short, we have some knowledge of the stations through which he has passed on his journey, tells us virtually nothing about the principles he stands for as an actor or filmmaker,

---

* The use of the eyes here instances, as well, a style David Bordwell calls "intensive continuity" that places "a greater constraint on actors' performances. . . . We lose what Charles Barr calls, in his fundamental essay on CinemaScope, graded emphasis. Eyes have always been central to Hollywood cinema, but usually they were accompanied by cues emanating from the body. Performers could express emotion through posture, stance, carriage, placement of arms, and even the angling of the feet" (2002, 25). With intensive continuity, "close-ups and singles make the shots very legible. Rapid editing obliges the viewer to assemble discrete pieces of information, and it sets a commanding pace: look away and you might miss a key point" (24). Ironically, in this film, Depp ends up missing all the key points while simultaneously missing none of them.

the vision he has of the social order, what in the world he finds beautiful, valuable, true.

This notwithstanding various "politically flavored" quotations attributed to him in the global press, the very globality of the venue itself an instigation to exactly the sort of follow-up disclaimer that both scrubs the persona and confounds a reading of the politics. Consider, for a neat example, that on September 4, 2003, the German magazine *Stern* quoted Depp as saying, "America is dumb, is something like a dumb puppy that has big teeth—that can bite and hurt you, aggressive." In the context of this statement, he mentioned the renaming of French fries to "freedom fries" in the House of Representatives' cafeteria on Capitol Hill. "Nothing made me happier than when I read that—grown men and grown women in positions of power in the United States government. I was ecstatic because they revealed themselves as idiots." This is, if hardly a philosophically rigorous position, surely a statement of attitude and perspective out of synch with the prevailing paranoia in post-9/11 American governmental circles, a statement, indeed, that in conjunction with Depp's having taken up residence in France can without difficulty be interpreted as critical of the America that had launched itself against Saddam Hussein and the civilians of Iraq. By the fifth of September, however, Yahoo! News was reporting that "actor Johnny Depp says he intended no 'anti-American sentiment' in comparing the nation to a dumb puppy and blamed news reports for misrepresenting his opinions." Depp "apologized to those 'who were offended, affected or hurt by this insanely twisted deformation of my words and intent.'" That *Stern*'s "deformation" was "twisted" seems plausible enough, indeed, in view of Depp's explication of what he apparently meant: "Taken in context, what I was saying was that, compared to Europe, America is a very young country and we are still growing as a nation. . . . I am an American. I love my country and have great hopes for it. It is for this reason that I speak candidly and sometimes critically about it." If Depp speaks openly about political agents, if he takes a position congruent with a political perspective, even if not expressed in the aptest language, he is still, ultimately, resolvable as a surface without perspective (like others in the public eye whose every burp is subjected to spin).

Aside from the fact that in a society of spectacles a character who is difficult to perceive has a certain capacity for revolt, however, what is the importance of the fact that Depp's screen presence is difficult, if at all possible, to know? Why should we care to recognize that for all the illumination available in our society, he persists in remaining a figure of darkness? I have suggested that the clearly identifiable individual is a product of the society of the *flâneur,* and of systematized social observation (policing); and that Depp's secrecy represents an undoing of the social structure that supports isolation through observation. Depp is no underground hero, however. More and more he stars in films by major filmmakers that are mass-marketed successfully. He is reported in large-circulation newspapers and magazines. While it is more than convenient to regard his elusiveness as a tease to provoke continuity of media focus, still we must wonder if he may not also be the harbinger of a new kind of social arrangement that dispenses with knowledge and information as mere remnants of an increasingly worthless nostalgic past. In the age of computer animation, gaming, virtual reality, and serial narrative, not to mention serial crime and mass production, the best function of knowledge is as material culture, objects to be possessed—and stored. The turn of the twenty-first century revealed a substantial ecological crisis, generally and in media culture. There is no spare storage room for all the mug shots of all the criminals, all of whose features have been measured and filed away. The filing cabinets are full. The computer memories are not expandable infinitely *at no cost.* While storage is reserved principally for the agencies of social order, there is decreasing space available to store information about narratives, characters, actors, historical figures—individuals long thought to be interesting in their own right for political or aesthetic reasons. The idea of the "person" can perhaps now be usefully severed from any particular biography and generalized to a type; ultimately, in dramatic renderings, it will matter little whether we have seen the previous installments of a serial, since the particularity of people and events will be washed away in the double enthusiasm of the ambiance and the form. Every scene sufficiently full of bizarre effects erases every previous such scene. It is the effects that are the star of the film, not the individuals who endure them (see Bordwell 2002). In the new Age of Patriotism, surveillance technology mimics action-film style and visual effects augment, then replace, vision.

Whether or not we can be said to *know* the stars we watch is, of course, a potent and troubling question. Their personae are typically open to our inspection while their offscreen day-to-day personalities are reserved; the "backstage" appearances we see on talk shows, in interviews, and so on, reveal still other constructions. This much is not news. But the typical star is a throwback to the age of *flânerie,* not a figure that resists it. However certain or stable our knowledge, it nevertheless consists in fixing an identity to an image. And if Benjamin is right that the *flâneur* always comes upon a crime, we need not imagine that he always and inevitably comes upon a criminal: crime can be implied by discreet and moral behavior, as its contradiction, perhaps as its artificial surface. When in the era of observation and recording the habit of discovering images of the stranger was codified, normalized, institutionalized in photographic record-keeping, what happened morally was the solidifying, the establishment, of fact-based identity in relation to appearance. The typical movie star of the Hollywood golden age is no less fixed in our perception, and resides with us as a kind of template of feeling, personality, ethical commitment, and interactional capacity—that "monopoly upon a personality" adduced by Staiger. Our "knowledge" of the star, then, functioned socially to create a moral beacon, a sign of class and cultivation. The consistency of the star persona, that depended upon repetitions of similar roles, was a necessity insofar as we were to record that persona and store the record; in short—if we were navigating socially, we needed the ability to set our sights and make identifications that stuck.

But Depp, conceivably the first movie star we will never quite know, shows what kind of narrative future is available to us once the precise rendering of personality and character are abandoned for movement, pulsion, effect, and scene. Whereas Bogart, Bacall, Lancaster, Douglas, Garbo, Davis, Bergman, and Grant were in need of a stable cinematic ground against which to be known as stars, Depp's floating persona can function extraordinarily well against a fast-paced effect-filled background where it is never possible to get a good look at him, or to come to terms with what one has seen. To repeat, I do not suggest that we can really *know* a star from the screen work we see; only that the illusion of *knowing* was systematically produced for the viewer in studio publicity machinery from the 1940s onward. The contemporary publicity machine is producing of Johnny Depp a colossal riddle, largely, perhaps, because the riddle is a perfect center in a film for viewing, in which an audience's memory, feeling, analysis, and understanding are outmoded.

The blockbuster effects movie is different in kind from the extravaganza of the studio heyday, in which delicacy viewers and fans could be fascinated by the "auxiliary dramas" fostered by rumors of offscreen romance between the stars, or by "accounts of fabulous extravagance and ingenuity: 35,000 extras, real cream baths on the sets, multi-million-dollar location shooting ruined by hurricanes, dangerous stunt work actually performed by the hero or heroine" (Staiger in Bordwell et al. 1985, 87).

The blockbuster effects movie—*Die Another Day* (2002) is as good an example as any—requires that the production expense not sit statically onscreen to be assimilated through the ogling view, but instead race across the screen, itself the central protagonist of the film. The actors must be a forgettable backdrop against which the special effects can be featured optimally, and indeed each effect must race away to be followed by its grander, more galvanizing successor. Nor, for its success to be ideal in the eyes of the producer, should the film as a whole linger in the appreciation of the audience. With conglomerate financing, global marketing, and synergistic deployment of resources, no one filmic experience should be so all-consuming as to block audiences from immediately acting upon a hunger to see still more. Multiplex theaters reach their true potential when customers spend the entire day there, eating all their meals in the refreshment complex and shuttling from one screening to another. The now widely publicized film festival is a model for this kind of behavior, usually arranged for publicity so as to show international stars themselves appearing to flit from film to film to film. Until Johnny Depp, this form has had no stars. Principal players, yes, to be sure. Schwarzenegger is not an effects star, but an action star (or was, since now he has taken quite another role in our social life), and action film is the last gasp of traditional cinema. In effects cinema, the audience is hungrier than ever before, because totally unsatisfied and incapable, in fact, of experiencing satisfaction. We must imagine, then, a cinema in which knowledge of the star—the fixing of identity—is only a debilitating factor; in which a subtle taste of the star is all we ultimately want. And not even a taste: an opinion about the taste. After the movie, we are still fit and ready to consume, indeed hungrier than before: we rush on to other films, magazine interviews about the making of the film we have just seen, plastic toys based on figures from the film (the Edward Scissorhands doll), posters, Internet chats, baseball caps, milkshakes in specially designed drinking cups, and above all, rumors: rumors about the making of the picture, rumors about the working relationship between Johnny Depp and Roman Polanski, Johnny Depp and John Waters, Johnny Depp and Tim Burton, Johnny Depp and Orlando Bloom, Johnny Depp and Hollywood . . .

All Depp's screen appearances have been experiments in this direction, steps toward a cinema of the absolutely presentable. For an especially interesting example, consider *Finding Neverland,* in which his James M. Barrie is a shifting surface of playful forms, a kind of mirror reflecting flickering light like the mirror representing Tinkerbell in *Peter Pan,* achieving an absolute presentability aimed at adults and children with equal directness. He sparkles as its luminary body, the new form of film star for the twenty-first century, each moment of his presence onscreen enlivened by that presence yet promising no future but the hunger to recapture. Dean, Bogart, Brando—all these are personalities seized and offered by the cinema. Depp is entirely an image, changing with every frame and therefore unspooling in his manifestation at 24 fps. Depp is film itself.

INTERLUDE

How am I writing about film, and how am I finding Johnny Depp on the screen? In a voice and with a manner that is consistent with the biography of my own thought, to be sure, in all its precarious turnings and spontaneous attachments to, its windings upon, the thought of others who wrote about other experiences and instigations, who never had a thought of Johnny Depp. And then, more particularly, with something of the kind of attention that was committed by Roland Barthes when he looked at photographs.

Writing about the photograph, that frozen wafer that reflects the conjunction of reality and art, Roland Barthes distinguished two elements or dimensions. The first, he wrote, "has the extension of a field, which I perceive quite familiarly as a consequence of my knowledge, my culture" (1981, 26). This he called the *studium,* which can be interpreted from the Latin as "appreciation" or "taste" but which, when I read Barthes, I choose to conceive as a route, since by means of the studium the eye is led to perambulate through the image in a set of directions according to which the received culture is once again explored and renewed. Through the *studium* we recognize, place, locate in a narrative continuity, evaluate, evade, and exchange the image itself in a system whereby knowledge, mapping, dramaturgy, status allocation, the attribution of self, and class position are made accessible as referents of language in visible—that is, photographable—manifestations. It is through the *studium* of the image that it bears an ontological reference to a real scene, a geography, a world.

The second attribute or dimension of photographs for Barthes was the *punctum,* the point, which he called "that accident which pricks me (but also bruises me, is poignant to me)" (27).

For me in my time, the *punctum* is an obstruction of route and routine, precisely in the sense that when I encounter it my eye is stopped in its peregrination, is derailed, is thrown into the pure experience of gazing and meditating without gaining the benefit of an accretion of knowledge. The *punctum* is the locus of mystery, or the unknown, the consequential, the disordered, the oneiric, all of what is essentially lovely about experience without at all contributing to our ability to use it. If the *studium* is about knowledge, the *punctum* is about understanding. The *studium,* writes Barthes, "is that very wide field of unconcerned desire, of various interest, of inconsequential taste: *I like / I don't like*" (27). But the *punctum* is a "detail" that "rises from the scene, shoots out of it like an arrow, and pierces me" (26). Barthes concludes that "to give examples of *punctum* is, in a certain fashion, to *give myself up*" (43). An example that I will give: in the advertising poster for Jim Jarmusch's *Dead Man,* we are confronted with an immense photograph of Johnny staring out at us. The *punctum* is his left eye, which seems to envelop us and attend to our every feeling of fascination with him. Because he sees us seeing him, he is there, and the photograph is more than a photographic surface. In *L.A. Without a Map,* Mika Kaurismaki plays with this *punctum,* replicating the photograph as a cinematic shot and allowing Johnny to move his eyes around, and even off, the screen.

In cinema, it seems to me, the equivalent of Barthes's *studium* is a superimposition of fields, including such laminations as the narrative, the performance, the ontological reflection of a prior and organized world, and the language of genre. To the extent that a viewer is equipped to place a film in a context of historical production, a socioeconomic and cultural dimension of organization and control, or an aesthetic domain, the film can be known as a "statement" or an "indication about," a "reflection" or an "imagination of," some identifiable action, either real or else based on a transformation of reality according to any one of a cluster of widely shared and relatively limited formulae such as "dream of" or "memory of," "feeling of," "intimation of," and so on. When we appreciate the *studium* we come to say, "this is what happened in such and such a film." Whether we address the work on the diegetic or the metadiegetic level, we nevertheless scan it for meaning, assemble the clues we find, and render some articulation that takes account of the field of our experience as a function of the field of our knowledge. The *studium* of a film, in short, is the thing we are talking about most of the time when we refer to the film at all—everything that begins at the beginning and ends at the end.

But the *punctum,* once again, even as we notice it and attempt to speak, is already a self-identification, both striking out at us and forcing us to admit something of ourselves. The *punctum* of a film is some variously defined element—a scene, a moment, a word, a prop, a character; it seems to me it can be literally anything—that insists upon its presence though it has nothing to do with completing the *studium.* Barthes suggests that a photograph could be speckled with *puncta* and surely a film can be, too.

Consider, for three simple examples, Hitchcock's *Shadow of a Doubt* (1943), Ford's *Stagecoach* (1939), and Godard's *Contempt* (1964). One of the *puncta* in Hitchcock's *Shadow of a Doubt* (and one that in a different light I have written about at length elsewhere [see Pomerance 2002]) is a waitress in a bar who occupies a scene that could have been set virtually anywhere else to the same overall narrative effect. For a moment, in this girl's eyes, we see a craven appetite to possess a ring, and from this dull gleam we can surmise something about every other central character in the film. A *punctum* in John Ford's *Stagecoach* is Andy Devine's hysterical voice. His is a character neither masculine nor feminine, but both; midway between what John Wayne represents and what Claire Trevor does. A *punctum* in Godard's *Contempt* is the curious resemblance of Brigitte Bardot, in certain scenes, to a large cat. As she paces the rooftop of the Mediterranean villa, with the line of the sea stretching turquoise behind her, she exudes an animal magnetism that we can retroactively, reflexively, attach to Jack Palance, that we can search for hopelessly in Michel Piccoli, and that we can be stymied to comprehend the absence of, in Fritz Lang. It is a mistake to think of Barthes's *punctum* as a solitary item, a flaw or deflection, a misalignment or exaggeration for effect, since in the end it is not by accident that it resides in the image. Similarly, in cinema, where one finds an element that stands out from the perceptual range of the film itself—I would prefer to think of such a thing as a *point of view*—one can have a clue to a reinterpretation of the entire work, a reinterpretation, at least, insofar as it requires an interpretation that does not exclude it as purposeless decoration. Let me very briefly reconsider the three examples I gave above, since it is through an examination of *puncta* that I hope to show what it is Johnny Depp brings to the films in which we find him.

Shadow of a Doubt is, on the surface, the story of a nefarious man who visits, disrupts, and almost destroys his sister's family in order to save himself from the police. The complication of the plot is an infatuation of sorts experienced by his niece—who goes by the same name as he does, Charlie—a girl who, because she takes such an interest in the details of her uncle's life, comes to know more about him than he would wish anyone to know and thereby becomes a liability. He tries (and fails) to kill her. He has made an effort to purchase her loyalty by offering her an emerald ring, a ring she chooses to return to him by way of dramatizing a rejection based on what she has come to suspect—this event taking place one evening in the 'Til Two bar under the eyes of a girl who is serving at tables, who knows the young protagonist from school but whose social class is decidedly inferior. What this young waitress represents in terms of class position, lack of access to resources without the step of marriage, and desire, resonates for us to some extent in the portraits of all the other women in the film save Charlie, and offers some keen insight—at the particular moment when Charlie is discovering for the first time her uncle's craven nature—into the role of marriage in America at this time (1943) in saving women from needful positions such as the waitress occupies by trapping them at home. Briefly: our profoundest understanding of Charlie's mother's condition—and thus, of Charlie's—is by linking her with this sad waitress, *rather than by giving only a surface reading that would isolate the waitress in a class of her own.* Charlie is not above the waitress; they are one; because the waitress, trapped in her class and cupidity, is the mother, trapped in her marriage. The resolution of the film is that Charlie marries the very detective who has tracked her uncle—a resolution that has little to do with crime but much to do with women's position in American culture and the institutionalized means of rationalizing and resolving that position. And while an emerald ring can be returned to a problematic uncle virtually anywhere (in a garden, in a kitchen, while walking down a street); and a conversation between a girl and her uncle, in which she comes to see what he really is, can happen anywhere as well (in a garden, in a kitchen, while walking down a street); only in the presence of a figure such as this waitress can young Charlie's options as a woman be spelled out plainly to our view. The film is not about Uncle Charlie or about the ring; it is about young Charlie and what it is for her, at this time and in this family and in this place, to be a girl. The waitress is her mirror opposite and her secret self.

Stagecoach recounts the story of a lawbreaker brought to an exquisitely humanitarian justice after a journey in which the social values and mores of his traveling companions are brought into critical relief. In the stagecoach trundling across the West is to be found—as numerous critics have observed (see, for example, Grant 2003)—a microcosm of the American social fabric, the educated and uneducated, the principled and unprincipled, the dignified and undignified, the rich and not so rich, the vulnerable and invulnerable. What, however, are we to make of the two men driving the coach, Sheriff Curly Wilcox (George Bancroft) with his steely gaze, and his deputy, Buck (Andy Devine), rotund, emotional, and saddled with a fractured voice that skips uncontrolled into broken treble cascades? Is he not in some sense the quintessence of the feminized male, and are not the two drivers of the coach therefore somehow married in their commitment to one another and their job? Had Devine not been cast in this role the film would have lost a useful framing device, which it now possesses thanks to his inescapable vocality. John Wayne's sophisticated and dominating, but deeply civil, masculinity as the Ringo Kid, along with all the other postures of masculinity we see (from the dissipated Dr. Josiah Boone [Thomas Mitchell] to the oily Hatfield [John Carradine] to the timorous Samuel Peacock [Donald Meek] and the aloof and prudish Henry Gatewood [Berton Churchill]) is recast in its relation to the naturalized, taken-for-granted, everyday softness and receptivity of the masculinity of Devine.

Contempt is a dramatization of the fundamental antinomies of social existence, art and commerce, love and bureaucracy, the transcendental and the quotidian, convicted passion and spontaneous need, and existence and reflection, all in the context of the production of a film version of Homer's *Odyssey* by an aging German filmmaker, Fritz Lang (Lang) working with a neurotic writer (Piccoli), a sullen actress (Bardot), and a tempestuous American producer (Palance). While the sound track is full of lengthy philosophical ruminations, the eye is relentlessly confronted with visions of the matter-of-fact. But in the middle of all this, Bardot paces back and forth on the roof of a Mediterranean seaside villa in a bathrobe, her gait the gait—and her posture the posture—of a proud jungle cat. What is contributed to the film by this intrusion of the animal (a particular animal, to be sure, the safety of which this actress has devoted her off-camera life to protecting), except a denial of civilization, a hunger for passion, a direct caress of the light of the sun? This *point of view,* as I would call it—meaning not the point from which a view is taken but the view as a point of concentration of narrative energy and focal intensity—this point of view notifies us that the film is human, that all film is human. Human: living, fleshly, animal. Indeed, the point of view reveals a secret that the narrative field is designed to cover. The narrative field in itself leads us to believe the film is a mechanism for unveiling, unfurling, unraveling, and producing the event of itself. But the point of view, the cinematic punctum, acknowledges (suddenly) that it is need that produces art, not a system. The system organizes the production, shapes it, but it is need that brings art into being and that leaks through in the moment of the point of view. To invoke the need directly it is necessary to show the animalism, the passion, as though it has inhabited the scenario. Lang as Godard's "director" may pontificate about this need; Piccoli as the "writer" may pace back and forth trying to articulate it; and Palance as the "producer" may whine and harangue; but Bardot is the embodiment of need, is need itself on legs.

All this by way of suggesting that the *point of view,* the *view-point,* is an essential element of film. And it is surely essential for coming to an understanding of the film of Johnny Depp, there being inevitably something in each film that springs out at us, something that is not a concern of the story or even of the story-of-the-story but that prods us, announces itself unmistakably as poignant. What one might call the "details" of a film or of a performance are nothing so much as the constituent parts of the image that we can read as intelligible because of our knowledge of what it refers to. The *view-point* is not, then, in that particular sense, a detail at all, because all the details are integrated into the fabric of the film. It is something that rends detail, breaks through, provokes, initiates a revolution.

⁌⧉⧉⁍

It is my way of apprehending the films I write about to consider them as narrative fields and view-points. So it is that a cinematic moment will suddenly leap up toward me with the force of a central and urgent manifestation. The ostensible plot of a film is a mere formula in which I must locate myself, but not a tool for grasping the significance of what is onscreen. I would go so far as to say the story is the arrangement, a specific one of many possible perturbations in the narrative field, which makes the view-points possible.

Just as Andy Devine's whining voice constitutes a view-point of *Stagecoach,* Bardot's pacing a view-point of *Contempt,* and the waitress's dull gaze a view-point of *Shadow of a Doubt,* so in the field of *Once Upon a Time in Mexico* is the equivocal blindness of Depp an iconic feature that steps out of the frame to provoke and riddle our attention. It is as though the entire story, such as it is, has been recounted in order to make possible the removal of Agent Sands's eyes. In *A Nightmare on Elm Street* Glen Lantz evinces a solipsistic, almost masturbatory yearning to withdraw from the objective social world into a bubble of inner fantasy. The sense of that character as inhabiting himself, rather than the scene of his friends' agonies, is a major view-point of the film and the central view-point of the Depp performance. In *The Astronaut's Wife,* the perturbing moment is Spencer Armacost's meeting outside his space capsule with the force from the beyond, a meeting we are put in position to observe and, indeed, experience.

One of the chilling moments in *Pirates of the Caribbean: Curse of the Black Pearl* is borrowed from *The Sea Hawk* and does not contain Johnny directly onscreen. The pirates of the Black Pearl are secretly boarding the British navy ship by moonlight, emerging out of the water, snaking up the anchor ropes, and becoming invisible for a moment whenever a beam of moonlight strikes them. With knives clenched in their grimacing teeth, eyes blazing blue, these blue men emerge not so much from the sea as from the oceanic depths of our unconscious, hell-bent, unstoppable, sliding up into the ship like so many eels, and the shafts of green-blue moonlight, more than a mere source of illumination for them, constitute the domain in which they exist and move. Suddenly we can be aware, if we allow ourselves to be, that Captain Jack Sparrow is in fact a creature of this domain, that he is made of moonlight. Thus the purely Apollonian critiques of Depp's characterization in this film—that he is randy and stupored with liquor, that he is foppish, that he is slovenly and out of control—all stemming from a conviction that he should be purposeful and accomplished, aggressive, brutal, the quintessence of "hard" masculinity, fail to grasp the shadow side of the actor and the enshadowed quality of the character he has built. The rope ascent scene is a vital clue not merely to the pirates but also to the true nature of the film, and of Johnny's presence within it.

ॐ ॐ

Mary Ann Doane writes of Freud's "screen memories" as being

> characterized by their intensity; they are, in Freud's words, recollected "*too* clearly." What is lost in meaning is gained in affective force. For these memories fasten on the trivial, the indifferent, and ultimately strike us as hollow or empty. In this respect the screen memory is deceptive, for it is above all a displacement—both temporally and semantically. The trivial, the indifferent, the contingent come to act as a veil, covering over significance; "an unsuspected wealth of meaning lies concealed behind their apparent innocence." The detail—that which stands out in a scene—becomes a *screen.* (2002, 166)

Am I in this project bent on choosing for my subjects of concentration precisely the trivial, indifferent, contingent moments and materials in Johnny Depp's films so as to screen from myself, and encourage others to screen as well, the true significance of his performances and the films that contain them? Is the view-point I am suggesting we hunt for, derived from Barthes's *punctum,* nothing but an "apparently innocent" deflection from a "wealth of meaning" at which we will now be certain not to arrive?

We should remember that in writing about "screen memories" in *Beyond the Pleasure Principle,* Freud was careful to say that the world surrounding the perceptive individual is "charged with the most powerful energies." He was not devoting himself to an analysis of the experience of viewing film, but in that experience, are we not similarly confronted with "an external world charged with the most powerful energies"? Consciousness, wrote Freud, "would be killed by the stimulation emanating from these [energies] if it were not provided with a protective *shield against stimuli*" (Freud quoted in Schivelbusch 1986, 166). The screen memory, the *punctum,* helps ensure that once one has seen a fact that is startling enough, one no longer has an eye for certain impressions (Schivelbusch 1986, 165), one is safeguarded from the onslaught of the sensible. While such a system can produce distraction, precisely by substituting the contingent for the meaningful, as Doane would have it, the perceiver must always guard against deflation of what may be truly meaningful by a socially and politically controlled system that establishes a hegemonic "meaning" in order to safeguard and protect certain limited vested interests not principally his own. The question as to whether the *apparently* contingent perceptual object is contingent, trivial, and indifferent in truth is more vexing.

I have tried to ask myself, in watching Johnny Depp's films, whether in fact the view-points that strike me as valid and imminent might not function well as the bases for setting out a meaning that diffuses itself through an entire film. Further, if such a meaning can be found—that *Donnie Brasco*, for example, is about performance, not police work or organized crime—perhaps what has earlier been thought "meaningful" suddenly reduces itself to contingency. I take the central thrust of Doane's argument to raise precisely such a consideration, to suggest a play between meaning and contingency that can be stimulating to the viewer rather than limiting, encouragingly provisional rather than stifling and definitive.

In the modern age, writes Benjamin, "a touch of the finger now sufficed to fix an event for an unlimited period of time" (quoted in Doane 2002, 151). The "touch" Benjamin is referring to is the one involved in the operation of an electric switch, in the case of Depp in the key moments of his films that I focus on here the switch that controls the operation of a movie camera, or the mouse that controls a computerized edit to place a sequence narratively. The view-point, then, is made possible by the broad technology that enables the structuring of moments. While it is certainly possible to regret the fragmentation of time that cinema makes possible, to advocate the cherishing of a more continuous sense of historical time such as is foundational to printed literature, the challenge facing us now, I believe, is to find in cinema some means of address and acknowledgment, some hopeful openness to the full experience of sensation as a basis for contemporary meaning. As long as films are with us, so will we be fascinated by the power of moments. One of the aspects of Depp that is most enchanting is his capacity to fill the moment, to center screen moments more pregnantly and more troublingly than other actors do.

Perhaps that is why some of the most charged performances he has given onscreen are the briefest: for instance, his appearance in Richard Martini's *Cannes Man*, where the camera interrupts him meditating with Jim Jarmusch and with a scowl he tells us to go away. In *The Railway Journey,* Schivelbusch writes about "panoramic perception," the experience of seeing the world from a moving railway carriage that transformed the consciousness of the nineteenth century. Movies, too, roll through time, and have the inexorableness in their motion of the hurtling train. To race past Depp kneeling on the grass in his meditations is to be caught and stunned—as one is thrown forcefully forward—by a figure at the wayside caught in another time.

JOHNNY DEPP STARTS HERE

GILBERT

Gilbert Grape. A formal boy, not a Gil. A boy with dignity, good posture, a moral sense, a backbone. A boy who makes no superfluous gesture, his smile when he offers it always genuine because he comprehends—indeed, is capable of comprehending—no irony. His long red hair—red: it is really orange, the color of rusted farm machinery—is immaculately clean, although it is true we never see him cleaning it. (Depp dyed his hair "red like one of his childhood friends and [had] his teeth bonded and then chipped out." "I remember kids growing up, how their teeth always looked chipped," he says. "Gilbert wouldn't have the money to fix them, and he wouldn't have cared" [De Vries 1993].) He works as a delivery boy and grocer's assistant at Lamson's store, always in an apron that is spotless and white, unstained by work or accident. The floors of the store are wooden—sixty years old and soft as chamois. He sweeps them in the afternoon, patiently, steadily, and almost no one walks the aisles to interrupt him since Lamson's is the country store of yore, and on the outskirts of town is a spanking new Foodland with music and air conditioning and a tank full of lobsters here in the heart of Texas. Lamson's is the kind of store where the owner (Tim Green) has steadfastly refused to increase the price of pickles, and, indeed, we see the pickles, bottle upon bottle, tantalizing yellowy green and glowing, waiting upon the shelf for some customer to desire them as much as we do.

Briefly to interpose what virtually every reader of these pages will already know: Foodland represents not only the new and contemporary world, but a universe of speed, detachment, well-accounted profiteering, rationalization, and consumer manipulation, one in which customers buying food have precisely the experience of noticing that the cash register tapes detail each and every item they have bought and that these items are now registered to their checking account number or credit card number in the institutional computer. Lamson's is an outgrowth of quite another social scheme. Customers come back again and again and are known personally to the owners, who work in their own store and do not obsess with accounting their customers' purchases instead of showing concern to keep their customers stocked and satisfied. This is the universe of the small business, all but effaced by the end of the twentieth century by conglomerates (like Foodland). Mr. Lamson's jars of pickles are arranged to be stared at, certainly, but the pattern of social activity in a store such as his gives real reason for believing people will stare at them—in the sense that shoppers will spend time on the premises, share a story or two, stand and have a thought. Foodland represents a waystation in a social world where mobility is the central organizing principle; Lamson's bespeaks the small town that has a rich, indeterminate past and a future that always resembles the present.

So full of love is Gilbert Grape that when his mentally challenged younger brother (Leonardo DiCaprio) climbs the town water tower, perhaps to the threat of his young life, Gilbert has no hesitation, no embarrassment, no shame borrowing the police chief's megaphone and singing, in front of the assembled townsfolk, a song from childhood, "I know a boy whose name is Arnie . . ." to lure the boy down. Gilbert does not make love so much as tumble into sex, responding to stimulus the way a flower does, instantly, fully, passively. While he is the center of a film, he is not the center of a story but only its motor. In the simplest possible way he has a sense of dignity, of honor—not pride. His close friend, the town mortician's son Bobby McBurney

(Crispin Glover), admits that when he and his father prepare bodies for funeral they sometimes make jokes about them. After Gilbert's mother dies, rather than consign her to the funeral parlor, he makes a pyre of the farmhouse in which he has spent his youth and sends her up in flames.

What's Eating Gilbert Grape is a study of boyhood, a study of the rural environment, and a study of cinematic color. It is not by accident that we see the pickle jars piled up in Lamson's grocery, or watch Gilbert's rusty hair juxtaposed against the vanilla ice cream his long-time paramour, Mrs. Carver (Mary Steenburgen), fingers into his mouth while he is unloading the groceries he has delivered to her, or note the brazen red decorations of Foodland. There are, indeed, two color schemes in this film—it was one of the last cinematographic undertakings of the master of color, Sven Nykvist—one the bucolic, eroded, softened palette of the small town gone to seed (modeled in a way on the work of William Eggleston); the other the flamboyant, ridiculous, saturated, and completely artificial palette of the commercial (read urban) scene. Through the way the film is colored alone, we are able to see that it contains a portrait of rural life seen from the perspective of quite another world.

Writing of the production in urban centers of a mass media image of the small town, Arthur Vidich and Joseph Bensman argue that "the mass media frequently present rural life in idyllic terms . . . the image of the cracker barrel, the virtues of life close to soil and stream and of healthy, simple, family living" (1960, 104). They note further that "romanticization" of rural life

> reflects the need of the urban dweller to conceive of rural life as
> simpler and freer from the complexities, tensions and anxieties
> which he faces in his own world. Rural life is thus conceived as
> a counterimage which highlights his own situation. However,
> when presented to the rural resident, it serves as an image
> which enables the rural dweller to form symbolic and ideologi-
> cal resistance to urban society. (106)

The idealization of this romantic view is a postcard vision of bucolic, untrammeled, ostensibly authentic agrarian life featuring a pre-industrial environment architected out of wood, not iron; long-standing and diffuse communal relations; virtuous politics and peaceable territoriality; and an abiding mistrust of the city and all the city stands for—all of which is to say, a pastoral utopia of high moral standards where favor goes to a practical, "natural" turn of mind.

This romantic pictorialization of the small town is constructed, in its purest form, in line with Farm Security Administration photographers' perspective on America, in a 1.33:1 or 5:4 pictorial ratio, using a 50 mm. lens. This lens most closely approximates the minimized distortion of normal, unmediated vision (where mediation = urbanization) and the aesthetic form of classical—which is to say, pastoral—art. The color palette emphasizes the contrast between the ruddiness of flesh tones and the green of nature (as can be found in, say, William Holman Hunt), an aspect most easily rendered on film by using filtered tungsten-balanced negative stock with exceptionally fine grain in an outdoor setting in the "magical" hour between 5 and 7:30 or 8:00 on summer evenings. This is "L'heure fauve" of Baudelaire. Rusted metal picks up a magnificent depth of color, the green of grass seems to radiate against people's flesh, weathered old painted wooden storefronts take on a pastel candy quality. As for dramatizing such a tableau, it is typically convenient to soften social interaction and speech by scripting for a southern drawl, by reducing comment in general so as to produce a kind of "natural" taciturnity among characters whose relations are presumably long-lived and thoroughly established, therefore not in need of a great deal of navigational chatter. (Hitchcock reflects these conventions of dramatization in the cropduster sequence of *North by Northwest*.)

What is systematically rejected, typically, in the bucolic portrait of small-town life I am describing, rejected as hopelessly and despicably urban and futurist, is contrivance, mass experience, mass production, self-consciousness, verbosity and prolixity of expression, pose, sham, and artificial illumination. The country is the place of lanterns and oil lamps, fluorescent ceiling lights retained from World War II era use; not floodlights and LCDs. The country is the place of spontaneity and ingenuousness, not of performance and method, or rapid social and conversational mobility. Needless to say, the American country town is also the homestead of solid Christian virtue, not a mixing pot of racial and ethnic minorities whose polyglot culture comes from an inestimable distance: that is, from some "city" over the horizon. Wickedness is hardly absent in rural life, but it is "natural" in the sense of being longstanding, hereditary, and familiar, the excess of sentiment or the unfortunate lack of it, not technocratic bedevilment: it is Boo Radley (Robert Duvall) in *To Kill a Mocking-*

bird; it is the Wicked Witch of the West, not the charlatan Wizard (Oz, we must remember, is one of the first great cinematic cities). Once again: this archaic view of the pastoral scene, this "country life," is an urban construction: a view from afar.

Lasse Hallström's *What's Eating Gilbert Grape* is just such a portrait as I am describing, bucolic in setting yet urban in point of view. The material of the film is less a narrative than a catalogue of typical small-town events meticulously described. Central to our attention is the family of the deceased Albert Grape, who live on a farm just outside the sleepy town of Endora (Texas). Larry, the eldest son, having left home, we are left to consider the relationships and circumstances of Gilbert (Johnny Depp), a youth in his early twenties, the "man of the family"; his mother, Bonnie (Darlene Cates), who used to be the belle of the town when she was in high school but who, after her husband committed suicide, more or less kept her place, in the sense that she lived a life of extraordinary stability and immobility, gaining more than four hundred pounds and becoming all but attached to the sofa in front of her television. Around her, Gilbert and his siblings, Amy (Laura Harrington), Ellen (Mary Kate Schellhardt), and Arnie (DiCaprio), rush and circle like piglets around a sow. Amy is sedate, servile, domestic, wise; Ellen is resentful and trapped, high-strung, incapable of keeping order; Arnie, rambunctious and dependent, is about to turn eighteen with the mind of a ten-year-old; Gilbert is at the end of his tether. An eastern girl named Becky (Juliette Lewis), driving westward in an Airstream with her grandmother (Penelope Branning), stops in town for a few days and befriends Arnie and the confused Gilbert, who falls in love with her. When his mother dies and the family is broken up, he and Arnie eventually ride off with Becky and her grandmother, happy to leave the confines of Endora and to be heading for a new life.

While the film is full of "event"—Arnie climbing up the perilous water tower and being put in jail; Burger Barn coming to town; Gilbert accidentally leaving Arnie in the bathtub overnight while he trysts with Becky; Arnie's tumultuous birthday party; Bonnie's demise—still, the central happening around which the film is constructed is a mythic event not extremely predictable in all small towns, although to be sure it is often enough depicted as being common in portraits of the rural made by people who do not live in small towns, namely, the young man's departure for another, typically urban, way of life. For, as much as the film illustrates for us Gilbert's

too-comfortable, even suffocating, placement in Endora—his clois-
tering friendships, his desperate sexuality, his entrapping family history, his uncertain and improbable future in the town Endora must
surely become as Foodland and Burger Barn reconfigure it—still
every thread of the tale leads to the moment of what is designed to
seem like freedom when, Becky and her grandmother having returned after a year's absence to trek westward again, Gilbert and
Arnie hop into the Airstream and become nomads themselves. From
sedate and comprehensible small-town Gilbert, then, our protagonist becomes a mysterious wanderer, a lover, and even—because it
seems clear enough that after Becky and Gilbert are united surely
Arnie will be their "child"—a father.

The myth played out here, then, is that the boy must be taken out
of the country. The agrarian life, which depends upon male fortitude
even as much as upon female wisdom, and surely upon the labor of
both, cannot sustain the boy, at least not the boy who is central and
heroic in film. Not the boy, and not the man who wishes he still were
one. Gilbert's buddy, Tucker Van Dyke (John C. Reilly), must give up
being a handyman and opt for a career managing the Burger Barn—
he urbanizes himself. Mr. Carver (Kevin Tighe) drowns in his children's swimming "pool." If the agrarian and the urban are central to
this film, however, neither of these conditions is explicitly amenable
to visual presentation in and of itself. A shot of the bucolic farm at
sunset, for example, will be indistinguishable from a photograph of
same, framed and hanging in a Soho gallery or spread across a poster
flying over Santa Monica Boulevard. Some device must be used to
construct the agrarian ethos onscreen, in order that a topos can be
established for Gilbert Grape to depart.

With this problem in mind, I would like to look at three small
scenes and the way in which they can be said to "interact." But in
order to make my purpose transparent, I must first say something
about the way in which I am *not* viewing Johnny Depp in this, and
other, films, the need to make such a statement recurring again and
again as I tackle this performer, quite as though the very act of looking at him persists in requiring constant reexamination and a new
approach. There is in narrative cinema a logic of characterization,
infallible and dramaturgical. Every character is caught in the warp
and woof of a narrative weave that implicates and displays every
other character, and the minute a line of dialogue is uttered it renders accessible to the audience a particular character among other

characters at a moment in narrative time. This moment implies other moments. It implies a history, some of which may be extradiegetical (is likely to be, indeed)—the time before the moment we are perceiving, a chain of moments situated socially and historically and leading, with some calculable inevitability, to this moment. And it implies a future of moments that flow forth and outward from this moment, implications, destinations, conclusions, developments, forthcomings, unfoldings, truthtellings, fabrications. Acted screen moments are, in this way, existential. In the particular sense in which I am now speaking, Gilbert Grape is Johnny Depp caught and manifested in a certain masquerade that extends itself through time in relation to the masquerades of other actors "being" his sisters, his friends, his brother, his mother, his townsfolk, and so on. To be interested in Depp in *What's Eating Gilbert Grape* can be to express an interest in his grounding as he constructs the role of Gilbert, an interest that culminates, one could say, in some fascination for (and belief in the plausibility of) Gilbert. To extend this a little, such a view of Depp and of Gilbert can be seen to lead to an interest in the story of the film. Gilbert has an affair with Betty Carver, and then leaves her and falls in love with Becky: that sort of thing. There is a line running from Depp outward to the character and the character's world, and in looking at the actor in this context one must finally examine his creation, the character.

I am not really interested in Johnny Depp as the portrayer of this Gilbert, principally because I am not really interested in this Gilbert, in the fullness of his story. I might argue, indeed, that none of us caught up with Johnny Depp are interested fully in this Gilbert, and that to be caught up with Johnny Depp is precisely to be disengaged from Gilbert Grape and other characters he plays. But Gilbert, at any rate, is not exactly what this text is about. (Yet we cannot escape from him.)

Just as there is a Gilbert who may or may not seduce our investment, there is a biographical Johnny, a biological, historical, practical, embodied, and largely unseen absolute "Johnny," who had girlfriends, now has a wife and two children, lives in France, takes acting jobs like playing Gilbert Grape, smokes cigarettes, had a long history of scrapping with paparazzi and reporters, and has a filmography to his credit. This Johnny is conventionally taken to reside under, or behind, the Gilbert we see onscreen and occasionally, perhaps, to leak through him—although it can be admitted our ability to discern these moments of leakage is suspect and open to much questioning, since the leakage will have many of the characteristics of the performance through which it "appears" and is thus ultimately indiscriminable. But we can believe in a backstage Johnny, and be fascinated by his many adventures, his narrow escapes from the law and from embarrassment, his press releases, his fan clubs. Instead of moving from Johnny outward to Gilbert, then, we can move from Gilbert inward to Johnny, along the same line as before.

I am not really interested in this Johnny, either.

It is, first, only the screen Johnny I am captivated by (although that screen may sometimes be the surface of a newspaper page). But it is the image of the public Johnny, the momentary construction, I want to know about. The construction that appears and flashes by, not the actual person who works to play the roles. I am not doing biography. Yet at the same time as it would vitiate my interest to have it pulled back into a study of the man himself, it would confound my interest to have it invested in the peregrinations of his characters. Just as I don't care, in short, who Johnny slept with while filming *Gilbert Grape,* I don't care what Gilbert Grape does or does not do with Becky. I am not doing plot analysis. The Johnny I find onscreen is biographically real, however, and also working to figure in a plot.

And that is why it is possible for me to expend my fascination completely on a single scene, or a triad of scenes, scenes that might shed some light on the way a film works in its completeness but which, nevertheless, hold my fascination quite securely in themselves. In order to be interested in these scenes, in this film and the others I shall write about, it must not be required that they seem important in the diegesis; or that the backscreen Johnny leak through them. What is at the center of my vision, then, is just the configuration of Johnny onscreen as a kind of glyph in and of itself. There are moments in which we cannot avoid deeply looking, or block the effect of that looking on our thoughts, feelings, and abilities to understand film, life, experience. Without emphasis on biography or the story, then:

The first scene: Gilbert is having a chat with Tucker on the veranda in the afternoon. We see them in medium—and then in long—shot. They sit side by side, Gilbert on the far left of the screen, Tucker beside him in the center, hardly moving. Behind, some of the Grape yard stretches back to a row of trees, and then a field and the horizon under a cloudless overcast sky. Just previously, Bonnie Grape had a temper tantrum at dinner because Arnie, out of control, was taunted by Gilbert. Pounding on the table, Bonnie causes the entire room to shake, as though struck by thunderbolts from Thor. So it is that Gilbert travels secretly into the basement with Tucker and a load of two-by-fours, to put additional support under the floor. But the basement is not a happy place for Gilbert, and we soon learn why. His father hanged himself there. Tucker recalls this sad and important fact for the first time, educating the viewer. Now, outside later, he is showing sensitivity to his friend. That is what is happening in the scene and why, *in terms of the unwinding of the plot.* Let us call that the unwinching mechanism of the scene.

There is then the matter of what the scene looks like, a principal matter since in motion pictures there is a vision to be seen and it is, conceivably at least, more than a mere illustration of what is said on the sound track.

Earlier in the film, we have been shown, somewhat systematically, Nykvist's capabilities at color composition—"Nykvist tames colors as a lion tamer does his royal beasts," claims John Simon (2003). He demonstrates in the shots inside the Grape house, for instance, and in the shots in Lamson's grocery, and in the shots in the town square when Arnie is climbing the tower, and in the shots of Gilbert and Arnie driving Becky and her bicycle out of town to the grandmother's camping site, that he is adept at the use of color contrast. In the opening landscape shots of the town, for instance, a cadmium yellow newspaper box stands on wet pavement outside the gray Ramp Café; at ENDOra OF THE LINE Drugs, the red brick façade contrasts with the green striped awnings; a turquoise sign counterbalances against a concrete gray patio with ruddy picnic benches at Dairy Dreme; in Lamson's the dark green Comet cleanser cans and flamboyant orange Tide boxes and bright green pickle jars and Gilbert with his dark orange hair are all electric against the dirty white walls and hanging fluorescent fixtures. But in the scene I am describing between Gilbert and Tucker, all the colors blend and merge in a suffusion of soft warm light. It is mid- to late afternoon and the sun is reddening, this visible in the grass behind the boys and in the ruddiness of their complexions. Gilbert, enshadowed, wears blue jeans with a green striped shirt over a white T-shirt (this heightening Depp's swarthiness), and over these a fawn colored denim jacket. His garb suggests a natural, chthonic world. Tucker has an ochre T-shirt roughly the color of Gilbert's jacket under a faded blue denim jacket, dark green pants, and a bright green base-ball cap in his hand. His clothing, as well as his orientation, is slightly more commercial and urban, more imported. When Tucker says he is sorry about Gilbert's dad and is told, "Don't worry about it. It's okay," we cut to a long shot in which the corner of the house, with the two boys, is visible at left in a cave of shadow, two yellow metallic chairs, unoccupied, waiting for conversationalists on the porch. The wind is blowing through the trees, there is no motion in the long dark recently ploughed field at the back, and Tucker's beat-up white and red Chevrolet pick-up truck waits tranquilly in the sunlight beside the boys.

This is a scene of deeply feelingful bonding between two young men, a moment of contemplation between them. Everything we see in the picture seems to have been there for a very long time. Neither boy makes movement as though to get up and leave, or as though to adjust himself, or as though to be expressive. They merely sit, the way the truck sits, the way the field rests behind the trees and the house sits on the ground with its yellow metal chairs peacefully wait-ing. What is invoked here is stasis, reflection, tradition, orientation, and resolution. If Tucker is on the verge of moving on and away from this world, Gilbert here seems not to be, and is therefore vulnerable to Becky's influence later on; yet even in his vulnerability to urban influence, Tucker is still a country boy, one who fits perfectly with the place. The vision is of a coherent utopic zone where nature exerts a centripetal force upon everyone and every object, eroding them, harmonizing them, approximating them to one another.

The urban vision of country life, however, requires that the small town be understood as a place to leave. "The currents of American energy moved around and beyond the small towns, leaving them iso-lated, demoralized, with their young people leaving them behind like abandoned ghost towns," writes Max Lerner, from whose perspec-tive "America was formed in its present mold in the process of city building, and it is still true—even in the era of the suburban revolu-tion—that wherever American places are being shaped anew the new forms irrepressibly move toward becoming cities" (1957, 149, 155).

If the motivation for Gilbert's departure is to be Becky, and if Becky is to remain a benevolent force, it is necessary that he be aligned with her in such a way that with no urging on her part he can bring him-self to be ready to leave Endora in order to follow her. She cannot frown upon the town. And Becky is the only possible motive: that the single greatest bond holding him in place in Endora—his mother's house with his mother in it—is to disappear, is hardly a sufficient reason for Gilbert to leave, as we can understand if we consider the contrasting case of the much less lovable, manipulative Betty Carver. She is clearly an urban personality "vacationing" in the small town for the duration of her marriage, which ends abruptly with her husband's fatal heart attack. Immediately—indeed, while still in possession of the rented limousine from the funeral—she makes arrangements to head out of town. Gilbert's ties to Endora are more perduring and more rooted in history than Betty's, and so only a force such as Becky can move him. But Becky's view of town life contrasts with that of the typical urban personality. Rather than simultaneously admiring and undercutting rural life, rather than romanticizing, she accepts Endora and everyone in the Grape family for what they most simply are, good people caught in hard circumstances. Gilbert is not to be seduced, then. Yet for the film to round through his coming of age, he must leave with her. How is the affiliation formed, that will lead Gilbert to think it natural for him to be at Becky's side?

The second scene: Late one night at Becky's pondside campsite, Gilbert holds her in his arms and whispers, "I got nowhere to go." She is wearing a dark red sweater, and he is still in his fawn jacket. We cut to an extreme long shot of the pond, with the tiny campfire visible on the far bank. The sky is red, like Becky's sweater, and is reflected in the pond. The fawn of the jacket has become the color of a tree lit by the fire. He tells her the story of his life and we watch as she listens, her lips matching her sweater, the orange fire light cast up into her face. "She used to be so pretty," says Gilbert of his mother. "She was so pretty and so . . . fun." The firelight on his face is the same color as his flaming hair, against the darkness. In the silences between Gilbert's words we hear the fire crackling. They kiss and lie together in the orange light, Becky with her short dark hair and light body, Gilbert with his soft intentful face and long hair. Now, in a shot taken from above them, we see the two faces locked in a kiss as they lie upon the orange grass, their orange faces lost together. Their genders meld, their identities meld, their discreetness disappears upon the fiery grass. Indeed, even the color of the film—as we have known it—disappears, since the scene and the culminating shot are like a black-and-white composition shot through a red filter.

Suddenly it is morning, we are looking from a distance, the light is blue and starched clean, the moment is sealed.

The third scene: Gilbert and Becky have slept side by side and are waking in the blue light of morning. We continue to look down. On the lush green grass a sleeping bag is opened beneath them, the black-and-red-check interior lining beneath Gilbert's back. Becky lies partially on top of him, her pink face near his pink face, her pink hand touching his neck. There are three compositional linkages positioned in vertical laminations in this shot. At the bottom (furthest from our eyes) is the ground, Endora, linking to Gilbert's fawn-colored jacket. Connected with this linkage is the tranquil relaxation, the familiar and situated ease, with which he rests, eyes closed, as they nestle. On top is Becky's red sweater, linking with her red lips and the red of the sleeping bag that she has shared with him. And in the middle of these two linkages, both of which are established through color, is the physical connection established by her hand on his neck and his hand circling her shoulder. Becky, then, is of herself (top) and of Gilbert (middle). Gilbert is of Becky (middle) and of Endora (bottom). As, in the next shot, they rise, he moves up with her and away from the ground, as though to take up a new status and alignment in life. Without dialogue, without gesture, and simply through compositional effect, he has moved over to her, and it has become logical that her moves will be his.

In all three of these sequences, the narrative work is being done by the cinematography—the lens, the light, the film stock, the camera position and focus. What is quintessential is that Gilbert not commit actions, since the plot requires a vital action to be committed upon him. Signal in the development of the film, then, is Johnny Depp's poise, since in all the shots I have described above the slightest untoward move on his part could distract the viewer from the composition, and it is the composition that is striking the mood and articulating the meaning.

Regardless of Johnny Depp's biography, then, and regardless of the history and intentionality of Gilbert Grape, we must appreciate that here and in every other scene where he appears he is constrained to be part of the vision onscreen, a figuration in the frame. He is a pictorial element, not merely in the essential sense, that is, that as a film actor his image is part of the construction of the frame, but in the sense that the "pictorial element" is what we see in him, the way he is pictured. Every film actor is a pictorial element, but Depp is actually pictured as one. In other words, the pictorial effect to which he contributes is not marred or displaced by narrative action (Gilbert's history); the action is *what is pictorialized*. In the third scene, the positions and the change of position *are* the action and they are also the picture. And in this scene Gilbert functions to hold our eye inside this particular frame, to dispel any thoughts of other places and other possibilities. One could say the frame traps him, but in the veranda scene the frame is the agrarian world of his childhood, since with Tucker he is sitting on the veranda of the Grape farmhouse. The picture onscreen, then, shows unmistakably Gilbert's condition in Endora; the frame *is* Endora, and Gilbert is harmoniously locked there. In the campfire scene the frame is the bond between Gilbert and Becky, their indiscriminability one from the other, their unification and identity. In the awakening scene, the frame is the renovation of Gilbert's alignment toward Becky and his small-town world. Another way to see the first two scenes in terms of the third: In the first we establish the connection between Gilbert and Endora that lies at the base of (on the ground in) the morning scene. In the campfire scene we establish the link between Gilbert and Becky that occupies the middle layer of the morning scene. While the third scene could be played dramatically without the two others, what they contribute is a depth of focus to Gilbert in the morning scene, a sense of his groundedness (derived from his moment of talking with Tucker), a sense of his love (derived from the merger in the night campfire scene), and finally a sense that he can move (upward, toward the future but at the same time toward us) as he joins with Becky.

The design of *What's Eating Gilbert Grape* puts forward two complementary and quite different visions of Endora as a static community in a time of cultural change. Through the characterization of Arnie, the town is configured as something of a trap, since, like Oliver Sacks's ticquer, he is at the center, without cessation, of "an excess of nervous energy, and a great production and extravagance of strange motions and notions: tics, jerks, mannerisms, grimaces, noises, curses, involuntary imitations and compulsions of all sorts, with an odd elfin humour and a tendency to antic and outlandish kinds of play" (1985, 87). Arnie seems like a spirit who cannot escape from the confines of his recalcitrant body, and in that, something of a prisoner inside the sharp, perduring control of the town as moral force. Every time he tries to climb the water tower the police come to the scene; every time he disappears from home all his siblings rush out on an anxious hunt for him. His every discomfiture is felt as an attack by his empathetic, all-embracing mother, from whose nourishing body and presence he seems not yet to have been separated.

But in the characterization of Gilbert, Endora is less trap than picture, the stasis being embodied in the principle of composition and the conceit of the discerning artist's vision. From this abstract and arbitrary point of reference both the boy and his surround are intelligibly, transcendentally *seen*. Here lies the basis for the astonishing tranquility of Depp's performance, a quality that is diffused through the entire film—while his facial expressions vary, he typically holds himself perfectly still within shots. The stasis is turned to playful self-parody at a moment when, trying to seduce him in her kitchen, Betty Carver receives a telephone call from her husband at the office. She insists that Gilbert take the phone and while he is sheepishly talking to the husband she creeps up, ducks under his delivery boy's apron, and begins to fellate him. Now he must wriggle away from the pleasurable *position* she is providing in order to remain composed in his conversation, and here we see him torn between wanting to stand still and needing to escape. In a way, this battle between Gilbert's feeling and his moral sense reflects the sociological and dramatic tension in the film.

A concluding comment about Gilbert's voyage: While in conventional portraits of small-town life it is typically the fate of the boy to leave rural life behind, in the case of Gilbert Grape the movement away from the town is modulated by two important forces. The first is Becky's love not only for Gilbert but also for his entire family, and the place in which they live. She does not enter Endora as a critical and alienated urban force, and it is not as an outsider that she returns to gather Gilbert and Arnie and carry them away. The second is the perduring sense of memory that is Gilbert's throughout the film— memory for his mother as a young woman, memory for his father, memory for Endora as it used to be before Lamson's was threatened by Foodland and before Tucker was ready to sell himself to the Burger Barn. Whenever in a screen composition Gilbert is visually here, he is unmistakably also *there*, in an eternal past that he carries with him. Depp made the film in part because he "saw similarities between the character's fictional life and his own small-town upbringing" (De Vries 1993). He told Jamie Diamond of *Cosmopolitan* that the film "struck some old memory chords." Becky is not stealing him for another kind of world, then; and he has the past inside him as he goes off with her—the past impersonated by Arnie, to be sure, yet also contained and revived by the tranquillity in his soul. With the Grape homestead gone, and the frames of this film as well, it will fall to Gilbert and Becky to enshrine together a new spirit of (cinematic) place.

spencer

On Monday, the thirteenth of April, 1970, at five minutes and thirty-one seconds after ten o'clock in the evening, Eastern Standard Time, one of the two oxygen tanks on the command module of the National Aeronautics and Space Administration's *Apollo 13* burst, an event that is described by Henry S. F. Cooper, Jr., the chronicler of the voyage, as having the effect of "spewing into space three hundred pounds of liquid oxygen, which meant the loss of half the craft's supply of this element for generating electricity and water. The oxygen came out in one big blob, and in gravityless space it formed a gaseous sphere that expanded rapidly; the sunlight made it glow. In ten minutes, it was thirty miles in diameter" (1973, 4–5). Personnel at NASA immediately began to misinterpret the glowing blob they saw on their screens: "After two successful lunar landings, which had been preceded by two Apollo flights around the moon, no one at the Space Center was thinking in terms of accidents" (5). The personnel on board that craft, Captain James A. Lovell, Jr., of the U. S. Navy, and his two civilian companions, John L. Swigert, Jr., and Fred W. Haise, Jr., came soon to learn that there was a distinct possibility they would never return to earth alive. For something just over four days they lingered on the fringe of space, making repairs to their craft as directed by frantic and inventive engineers in Houston (and as depicted in Ron Howard's *Apollo 13* [1995]), until at seven minutes and forty-one seconds after one o'clock of the afternoon of Friday, April 17, they safely returned.

Cooper, whose text is a terse and evocative masterpiece of narrative utterly absent the romantic, dramatizing touch, describes a moment on the *Iwo Jima,* an aircraft carrier that picked them up in the mid-Pacific, which is to say, on the dark side of earth, "away from the sun" (191):

> After a short welcoming ceremony, Haise told the ship's captain that it was nice to be warm again, and Swigert said, "It was so damn cold." This was uncharacteristic talk for an astronaut, and a few weeks later, after he had had time to think things over in the warmth of the South Pacific and then Houston, Swigert was to deny ever having been particularly uncomfortable in the spacecraft. Haise would later liken the discomfort to that on a camping trip through the north woods without adequate clothing. Yet the frogmen who met them commented that they could still feel the chill of space through the command module's open hatch. (199)

Since the *Apollo 13* mission is one of the space disasters from which survivors returned to tell the story, it provides a clue as to the subjective experience of space under harrowing conditions, a far from romanticized view not readily available from typical fictional and journalistic accounts of space missions, nor from the tragic catastrophes that befell the space shuttle *Challenger* at 11:39:13 A.M. E.S.T. on January 28, 1986, and the space shuttle *Columbia* at a few minutes after 9:00 A.M. E.S.T. on February 1, 2003, during both of which events all the humans on board lost their lives. For it is, after all, our imagination of space that engages our attention with such events in the first place, that enchants us, and that mobilizes mankind to the kind of exploration the *Apollo 13, Challenger,* and *Columbia* missions so painfully epitomized. The "chill of space" that the Navy frogmen could "still feel" inside the *Apollo* command module, as it bobbed in the Pacific, and the extraordinary envelope of darkness that engulfed the astronauts as they waited to descend, with hopes that the jury-rigged systems NASA's engineers had thought up for them to build out of materials lying at hand would turn out to work properly and prevent them from being burned to a crisp when they entered earth's atmosphere, constitute together a magnificent and deeply horrifying vision of what it is like out there, beyond our boundaries, beyond our civilization, beyond our ken. "Up in the spacecraft," writes Cooper (191), "the planet on which the astronauts were about to land had virtually vanished."

Similarly catastrophic and frightening is the pivotal moment in Rand Ravich's *The Astronaut's Wife* (1999), when Commander Spencer Armacost (Johnny Depp) and his partner, Captain Alex Streck (Nick Cassavetes), raptly engaged in some routine extra-vehicular activity during a typical manned space mission, suddenly and inexplicably lose radio contact with Earth for two minutes. When Armacost and Streck return, apparently sound of mind and body, they are subjected to a round of examinations and press conferences, but too soon afterward Streck suffers what seems a massive heart attack and dies. Then, at his wake, his wife commits suicide by electrifying herself in a bathroom. Armacost leaves NASA with his wife, Jillian (Charlize Theron), for a high-ranking executive position in New York, where he will assist in the execution of a special twin-pilot fighter plane. Here, at the welcoming party in his honor, he takes her aside and, in a lovemaking scene that involves the participation of the camera, impregnates her. But in the days that follow, Jillian begins to find her husband cold, strange, impenetrable, withdrawn, as seems expectable of an ambitious young man suddenly put on the pathway to wealth, fame, and corporate success but at the same time in a way that is inexplicable, unresolved, mortifying. One day she is accosted by Sherman Reese (Joe Morton), a man who had worked on the NASA mission and who is convinced that a close analysis of the retrieved command module audio tape of the two-minute broadcast silence reveals not just the voices of Spencer Armacost and Alex Streck but a third—and unidentifiable—signal. This tape, he insists, is being suppressed by NASA, as he himself was suppressed in his efforts to study it. He is convinced, moreover—in a way that eventually produces Jillian's, and also our own, conviction—that an extraterrestrial presence was up there with Spencer and Alex; that it encountered them; that this encounter was the true cause of Alex's death; and that the presence in some way entered Spencer and remained inside him, using him as a vehicle for journeying to, and subsequently

insinuating itself among the population of, Earth. While Jillian manages in the end to put an end to the aggressions of the creature that
has become her husband, she does not prevent the birth of what turn
out to be twins, happy young boys who hold out the dream of being
pilots when they grow up.

Surely the most remarkable scene in this film, indeed one of the
most remarkable scenes of Johnny Depp onscreen, occupies itself
with the two minutes of radio silence that terrify the engineers at
NASA. As Reese by posthumous videotape persuades Jillian to consider what may have happened during the problematic interval,
Ravich's camera brings us alongside Armacost and Streck's capsule in
deep space as they proceed with routine extravehicular repairs. We
see Depp in his full spacesuit, brilliant silver against the blackness of
deep space. Suddenly he looks up, directly into the camera. His eyes
widen inside his helmet. He has seen something, something hideous
and terrifying and overwhelming, that is swiftly approaching him—
because now as the camera dollies forward we see his eyes become
orifices, his personality open receptively and vulnerably through his
face. We swoop forward, impersonating the "thing," whatever it is,
move through Spencer's face plate, and enter him through his pupil
in a hungry flash.* When he is beyond the range of NASA's meticulous and orderly control, this scene seems to suggest, Armacost,
which is to say Depp, belongs exclusively and entirely to us, the
viewers who are ravenous for him and who long to enter his private
world. Here, NASA is the rationalized bureaucracy of political and
social control, managing the mapped circulation of persons and experiences through a normative order, a system of moral codification
and relentless global surveillance. This is the global social stage. But
in deep space, for two minutes, Johnny is out of the spotlight and
available to the invisible, yet carnal, presence of the unsocialized
alien that truly wants him. Each viewer is that alien.

Alien emplacement is the theme here. Yi-Fu Tuan writes, describing experiential perspective, that "the mind discerns geometric de-
signs and principles of spatial organization in the environment"
(1977, 16). Further, "Human beings not only discern geometric pat-

---

* A similar moment of alien invasion involving the iris and a solitary moment in
   outer space occurs with the astronaut Patrick Ross (Justin Lazard) in Peter
   Medak's *Species II* (1998); but the choreography of the camera is radically different, and we do not follow the alien inside its host.

terns in nature and create abstract spaces in the mind, they also try
to embody their feelings, images, and thoughts in tangible material. The result is sculptural and architectural space" (17). This is
possible, writes Tuan, because "place is a type of object. Places
and objects define space, giving it a geometric personality" (17). For
Ravich, the alien form is the quintessence of space, which is to say, a
complete absence of definition. In order to have form, it emplaces itself in Armacost/Depp, in effect becoming the astronaut/actor. But
the strategy of the mise-en-scène is to have us accompany the alien
on its journey of definition, so that we, too, enter Johnny and reside
within him for the duration of the film. Place has heat, while space
does not; and just as the navy frogmen could feel the "chill of space"
inside the Apollo 13 capsule when they popped its hatch, Jillian Armacost senses the "warmth" of the newly defined alien presence inside her "husband," even at the same time as she senses, too, a curious
social chill (produced by the fact that if the alien has devoured
Spencer's memory and knows Jillian, still Jillian does not know the
alien).

It has, of course, become entirely conventional, from at least a
commercial journalistic point of view, to think of Johnny Depp as
something of an alien himself. Hilary De Vries passes along the story
that his forearms are covered with scars from self-inflicted knife
wounds. Jamie Diamond reports that he asks a restaurant waitress to
give him "everything. Can you satisfy my every desire?" and that he
doesn't "feel part of anything." To Chris Heath of *Details* magazine
he reported, "I can remember being so happy [as a youth] that I made
noises." Flying to Vancouver to work on "21 Jump Street," he suddenly announced, for no particular reason at all, "I fuck animals."
Yet it is in an entirely less naughty, and thus less intrinsically orderly,
sense that Ravich's film *alienates* Depp. For here he is no mere embodiment of our secret desires, our repressions, conveniently mate-
rialized for the superior voice to denigrate and tame. He is suddenly,
now, from the outside, an intruder, one who does not belong in any
sense of what the word "belong" can mean on earth. He occupies
place without permitting that he himself should be occupied in turn.

As she begins to suspect the truth about the man she is living
with, Jillian must face, at the same time, *her* past—which is to say her
story as it has been told explicitly in this film. Now it can be apparent to her—and to us as we, perhaps far too easily (since, from her
perspective, we are aliens, too), sympathize—that when Spencer

impregnated her at the celebration in New York, he wasn't Spencer at all. He wasn't the person initially identified for us as Spencer, identified, indeed, only in one shot as beneath a blanket he permitted her gaily to use her mouth upon his genitals; and then echoed for us in a telephone conversation with her as in his capsule he moved further and further from Florida, from North America, from Earth. We may recollect with a shudder the rather curious copulation scene at the party in New York, in which Spencer, a little inebriated and heady with joy at his new executive position, takes Jillian aside in the huge executive lobby where his business partners are chatting and celebrating, holds her against a wood-paneled pillar, lifts her dress, and slowly enters her. But as he moves inside her, the camera itself slides through a 90-degree tilt, turning the pillar into a floor, turning standing Jillian into prone Jillian, and turning Spencer's upright, desperate, yearning position into an utterly controlling and assured one where he is, and has, all power. Now she is pinned, and his sperm will inexorably find its way inside her. Although we saw this clearly at the time, it is only in retrospect that we grasp the significance. While during its occurrence onscreen the viewer is positioned to find this scene pleasurable—"positioned" narratively much in the way that Jillian is "positioned" by the camera—a second sight of it, in memory, reveals that the pleasure was itself an intoxication, its purpose to dull response and resistance. That his thrusts brought her a magnification of promise and hunger prevented her from wishing for their termination, from acting to expel him before it was too late.

In 1972 a television film called *The Astronaut,* written by Harve Bennett and Robert Biheller and directed by Robert Michael Lewis, told a similar story. Not far into the future the American television-watching public witnesses the first astronaut to set foot on Mars, Colonel Brice Randolph (Monte Markham). When he returns he is lionized. But it soon becomes clear that Randolph in fact died on Mars—an event mission controllers foresaw, putting up a false image on television so as to minimize panic. The returning "astronaut" was a surgically altered double, Eddie Reese (Monte Markham), a man who convinces everyone except Gail Randolph (Susan Clark), the wife of the original astronaut, who after sleeping with him begins to suspect something is different. *The Astronaut* and *The Astronaut's Wife* are companion pieces, essays on male sexuality (both modeled on Gene Fowler Jr.'s *I Married a Monster from Outer Space* [1958], in which Gloria Talbott played the violated wife and Tom Tryon her alienated husband). In the Lewis made-for-TV film, a replacement male is designed through a medical process, but a process insufficiently thorough: specifically, the subtle innuendo of the film suggests that the penis and lovemaking technique of the "actor/astronaut" were neglected by those who perpetrated the scam. Male genitality, indeed, was not the open secret in 1972 it had become by 1999. Masculinity depended culturally on the exercise of certain social controls, upon a style of speaking, a postural attitude, a bodily form, a kind of knowledge and intent. A pervasive homophobia forbade discussion or representation of actual male genitality as characteristic of masculinity. The wife could admit that she discerned "something," and that she discerned it in the bedroom; but could not say what her "something" was.

In the Ravich film, by contrast, the sexuality of the "astronaut/ actor" Spencer Armacost is considerably more overt—"You like peaches?" he asks his wife at the beginning of the film, when she has crawled between his legs. "Well, isn't that a peach?"—but his body does not require replacement, since the alien merely enters him. In other words, both Gail Randolph and Jillian Armacost are examined in their respective films as women capable of knowing, and therefore recognizing, the telltale penises of their mates; but unlike Gail, who surely experiences invidiousness, Jillian is in the invidious position of *not* cohabiting with a different male body. Her awakening can therefore come only as a result of receiving a message—a badly recorded message, to boot—via video. Her sexual response and sensitivity having been duped by the alien's method of invasion, the stimulus that can inform her must come from the next best thing to sexual experience, the mass media.

In *The Astronaut's Wife,* the alien has no place before he finds Spencer, and henceforward Spencer's body becomes the geometric, social, conceptual, and diegetic home of the alien. Before that alien embodiment, then, the body of Armacost/Depp is a space, not a place. Surely it is the place of Armacost, and yet before the moment of his surrender in space, a moment that comes earlier in the film than our awareness of it, we hardly know Spencer at all; he is the archetypical generic astronaut, a pilot with a military body and a rule-oriented mind. Not so much a character as a bureaucratic cipher, then, Spencer is a space waiting to be turned into a place. The alien is the first personality (that we can tell) he has had. But what is curious about this for viewers astonished by the screen work of Johnny Depp is precisely that the camera allows those viewers to become that personality by invading him through his eye. Before our invasion of him, he is only an attractive shell.

That we do not know the Johnny beneath the Johnny we see, then, is both a foregone conclusion and a premise of this alarming film. He is a cold configuration waiting for the warmth of characterization, affiliation, invasion, imagination. But if we in our passionate viewership constitute the alien in this film, the force that creeps into him and voyages to earth, then it must also be true that before he came along in his shiny but penetrable suit we were condemned to passively anticipate him, lost in space. For us, as well as for the characters in this film, *The Astronaut's Wife* is a significant voyage. And, as Carl Sagan wrote, "When you pack your bags for a big trip, you never know what's in store for you" (1994, 215).

HImseLF

An actor who capitalizes on his given being may manage to appear as a candid non-actor, thus achieving a second state of innocence. He is both the player and the instrument.

Kracauer, "Remarks on the Actor"

As Carl Sagan once wrote, "When you pack your bags for a big trip, you never know what's in store for you" (1994, 215). The artist and filmmaker Terry Gilliam having been obsessed for years with the idea of making a film of Cervantes's *Don Quixote,* and a suitably munificent producer having turned up in France, he finds himself in pre-production in Spain with a team of highly energized, not to say nervous, colleagues and somewhat dismayed to discover that the actors' contracts have not been carefully written in such a way as to guarantee their presence for rehearsal. Particularly difficult to pin down are the French actor Jean Rochefort, who is to play the errant knight, and Johnny Depp, who will play Toby Grossini, a contemporary advertising executive who, according to the plot Gilliam has worked out with his writer, travels backward through time and finds himself trapped in the body of Sancho Panza. Keith Fulton and Louis Pepe's *Lost in La Mancha* (2002) is the tale of the making of Gilliam's *Don Quixote,* laced through with hand-held shots of production meetings, location hunts, costume fittings, and telephone calls as well as second unit footage of what scant rehearsals were possible in the very limited time the actors could find with one another, and the escapade of shooting the film under the worst imaginable conditions. Depp's role in this film is at once small and enormous, as befits an actor of almost mystical status.

"Well . . . here's an actor," says Gilliam on his telephone to someone we never meet, rambling around his well-lit production office and shot in extreme close-up. "Here's an actor. Here's an actor." The camera moves a little to the left and the rather lithe body of Johnny Depp is seen leaning forward over a table, scanning a wall full of Polaroids. "Oh, there's Bob Hoskins. And Ian Holm . . ." Johnny has a very delicate voice, and a way of speaking that is neither affirmative nor interrogative but something in between. His eyes are very large, sweet, throbbing, and his hair comes down to his ass. There is a thick patch of long white hair mixed in with the dark hair. He is wearing denim. "Yes, yes," he says articulately. He is not clean-shaven. He smiles a little, and shakes hands, and is utterly sweet and unassuming. Then, as quickly as he came, he is gone.

What can we take as treasure from this short, first encounter, pirates of consciousness that we are? Johnny is as much a movie fan as we are, certainly, a fellow who gets excited to recognize pictures of Bob Hoskins and Ian Holm. If he likes the idea of going to the movies, is he conscious of that pleasure when the camera is turned on him? Does he experience himself making these things that he imagines himself liking to watch? (In fact, as we may know, he does not like going to movies, does not go to movies very much at all.) Does he feel a sensation in the process of making that he can recognize, that he can impute to other actors such as the ones who are pictured on Gilliam's wall? Now, here, in fact, staring at these Polaroids, he is nothing if not involved in the process of movie-making. Does he stand back in his moment of recognition and admiration to see himself as an actor engaged in a moment of recognition and admiration? All this, notwithstanding the question of whether the scene we have just watched was scripted in the first place. Did they do this in several takes? The documentary style of production leads us to read the scene as unitary and singular, as having been produced using a camera out of a singular spate of untransformed social activity that took place in Spain on a particular date. Is it that, or is the question even worth asking, since we have no way of ever truly knowing the answer?

Now Monsieur Rochefort has arrived. He has spent the past seven months teaching himself to speak English in order to work in this production. A man of great gentleness and modesty, as well as the living embodiment of Don Quixote de la Mancha, he stands with twinkling eyes while the costume designer tries out pieces of painted cardboard and metal on his head and shoulders. Then we see him working with Depp, saying lines over and over. As Rochefort speaks, the camera cuts to Depp watching him, his eyes enormous, ravenous, his lips open in a delighted smile. Although they appear to stand no more than six feet apart in the same room, we never see Rochefort and Depp in a single shot together at this point, and we are led to wonder about the division between them signaled by the intercutting between one-shots. Do they find one another impenetrably strange? Are they friends who have no need to speak? Is our sensation correct, that the matching shot of Johnny watching as Rochefort speaks is not quite perfectly aligned? Is Johnny in fact in another place at another time, the filmmaker only contriving to convince us—perhaps to convince himself—that his two principal actors have found one another? Depp and Rochefort both seem to find Gilliam hilarious, charming, bizarre, inspiring, confusing, delightful, incomprehensible.

In a scene in the desert, Johnny as Toby/Sancho is locked by the neck to a team of convicts in mobile wooden stocks and all of them are scuttling along the dusty ground late in the afternoon like some many-jointed giant armadillo, while Don Quixote comes upon them on his horse Rosinante. Rochefort is an expert horseman, tall and fluid in the saddle. Johnny has dirt on his face and is cursing, along with the other prisoners. Suddenly jets from a nearby air force base launch into an air defense protocol, their engines roaring across the sky. The action is stopped and all the actors look up in disbelief, along with Gilliam and his entire crew. The jets keep flying for what seems like hours, tipping their wings ("because Johnny Depp was there," claimed Gilliam. "There's a movie star! Hey, Johnny!" [Sterritt and Brottman 2004, 213]). Rochefort has back pain and is helped off his horse. He must sit for almost an hour before he can walk to his limousine.

The next day a sudden rain shower becomes a vast torrent. The equipment is tied down, but begins to float away in an impromptu river, a river brown as toads. The production is closed down for a few days. Rochefort's pain is worse. Johnny is calm, meditative, chuckling amicably, his long hair a kind of flag in the bristling wind.

Sancho's horse is found weeks ahead of shooting and patiently trained by an assistant director for a scene where, vaguely reprising a horse in a celebrated scene in Preston Sturges's *The Lady Eve* (1941), he will walk behind Johnny, nudging him forward by pushing on Johnny's bum. The horse, as much as any other actor we meet in this film, is extremely diligent. When the time comes actually to shoot the scene, however, the horse becomes abashed in Johnny's presence. Although Johnny is patient, if not exceptionally friendly to the beast, the horse doesn't respond properly even when prodded from behind. He turns to the side and won't push Johnny an inch. (Perhaps he senses that Johnny does not like to be pushed.) To invent a screen moment now that the horse has balked, Johnny has to pretend to yank a huge fish out of a stream and do battle with it. He becomes very involved. "Here, you fucker. Here, you fucker!" For a moment it becomes strikingly clear that Johnny is actually attempting to communicate with the fish—which is a prop; that he has invested the object with personality and will, and that he is attempting to link his own spirit with it through the purity of his expression. Several dozen local financiers, who have put up millions for Gilliam, have been bussed to the location to watch the filming of this great moment from several yards away. They seem enchanted to be near Johnny Depp, who seems entirely unaware that they are present, the prop fish possessing more reality for him.

Now, Rochefort's back having worsened, he has flown to consult with his doctors in Paris. One senses trouble, the word "doctor" coupled with the word "Paris" somehow instantly suggesting the phrase "interminable delay." One sees his jet moving away into the sky, turning, vanishing.

Information flows in that they are doing tests, that he will be gone several days before returning. "Doctors," "Paris," "tests." Gilliam arranges to shoot other material. Rochefort's doctor indicates that it will be at least ten days. Depp has apparently left the shoot, since we see him no more. Where did he go? More important: *when* did he go, since we did not see his departure, did not feel the slow, twisting, inexorable pain as he walked away? In what way is he "not here" after all? Is he in his hotel, nearby, not on the location? Is he in a nearby town? Is he just off-camera? Is he halfway around the world? Somehow it is this last, yet we imagine him hopping on a plane and flying back the moment it is announced Rochefort has returned. We imagine him getting out of a limo and waving and rejoining his friends, who have been standing in Spain waiting for him. But there is no hint of him. There is the memory, but no trace.

There is the memory, but no trace of Johnny at all.

It is announced that Gilliam, Depp, and Rochefort were financed originally as "principals to the production," which means that if any one of them is replaced all the financing must be rearranged from the beginning. Considerable murmuring. News comes that Rochefort will not in fact be able to return, that he has a slipped disk. The completion guarantor cannot find a way to ensure finishing funds, or to be certain that he will not himself be liable for the costs incurred so far. The sets and costumes are packed away, and the production breaks up. As Ronald Davis puts it in *The Glamour Factory,* "The teamwork and support system that had existed over the course of filming, the bonds that had grown as a result of the pressures, intensity, and mutual objectives, dissipated almost overnight" (1993, 256–257). The warehouse that was rented and converted to a soundstage is converted to a warehouse again. It is all over.

This film gives a beautifully evocative picture of what might be called the minimalism of film performance, by which I mean performance as pure construction. So much of the popular mythology of filmmaking centers on the idea of film production as a conspiracy, an extended conversation between celebrated individuals acting in their secret capacity as collaborators and friends, in which they share anecdotes about real estate and good wine, about restaurants, about their favorite hotels, and in which they encourage and assist one another in externalizing some shaped excrescence of feeling and form that becomes garbed as the performance. According to this myth, what we could expect to find backstage of a production—in just such a place as this film reveals to us—is private conversation, private feeling, emotions that actors would not wish to make public and over which they would labor to stretch a totally false public relations skin. We would expect to find actors complaining about other actors behind their backs, bad-mouthing people all round, in general acting like overpaid and overpampered prima donnas. We would expect to find exasperated directors and producers, neverendingly astonished by the self-centered self-indulgence of the overpaid, overpampered prima donna actors. We would expect to see actors chatting with one another like the best and oldest of friends, flaunting in front of our hungry but trespassing gaze exactly the warm closeness we would like to fantasize is our own to enjoy, but that we too sadly recognize is not ours at all. Jean Rochefort hugging Johnny—as we would like to be hugging Johnny! Rochefort hugging Johnny instead of standing six feet away, regarding him with warmth, even adoring him like a fan, speaking his lines over and over.

Indeed, not only does Jean Rochefort not hug Johnny, he does not seem to know Johnny. He does not appear, even now and even here, to have been introduced to Johnny. His enunciation has the perfectly honest, palpable, warmth of the man stepping up to a bank teller, a man without familiarity and friendship but with an ultimate purity of feeling and purpose. The two play scenes together, helping one another move through the lines as gracefully as any two persons might help each other step through snowdrifts to reach a curb. What Johnny brings to the set from wherever he lives—we do not know exactly where he comes from but it is somewhere in France, he simply appears, and then disappears—is his presence, literally. He appears in a room, and can thus be photographed. When asked to slip the wooden stocks over his head, he fits himself into them and moves exactly as he is told to move, while the camera catches him in close-up saying what the script calls for him to say. When the take is over he stands patiently, without opinions, without expressive freight, without the ballast of excessive energy that needs venting or displacement. He is driven to locations, he is posed in front of the camera, he is fed dialogue to speak, he is fitted with costumes. Three local Spanish gentlemen take their shirts off and get photographed with a wide-angle lens from ground level; they are giants who stomp across the countryside. One of them is to bend down, gather Johnny up in his fingers, and pop Johnny into his mouth. The camera pretends it is Johnny, the man walks up, grins, bends over, lifts his fingers into his mouth as if to deposit the tasty morsel that is Johnny, and smiles as he swallows.

If the conspiracy theory has filmmakers as controllers of their destiny, minimalist theory suggests a fulsome and utter passivity, the actor merely existing in the domain of character and the character laid upon him like a coat. It is not what he does that transforms him in film; it is what is done to him before the lens. In *Lost in La Mancha,* the steady ruination of Gilliam's project (a diegesis that also links him to Quixote) makes it seem that the entire production is a helpless passive entity being affected by the whims of unseen Fate. Yet there is no particular reason for believing filmmaking really happens this way; that of all pockets of genuine warmth and feeling in the social universe absolutely none of them should be found in such working environments as are constituted by film shoots such as this. That we do not see Johnny soothing Rochefort does not mean anything as to whether or not it happened, since no film can show all of everything. That we do not see the horse nudge Johnny from behind tells us nothing about the horse. But we are left with the palpable thing itself, the story of the making of a story, as though stories are exceptionally difficult—or exceptionally interesting—to make, and as though the making of a story, in all its glory and peril, constitutes the basis for the kind of story that is truly important to tell.

One occupational hardship for actors, then: that they may be in a position to be picky about the roles they will play does not free them from the obligation to say yes to some scripts, does not liberate them from finding themselves backstage. Once they are in a working situation, their capital includes not only the backlog of work they have done but also the backlog of commentary to be found in the working community about them as workers. All such commentary is part of a diegesis about diegesis, a storytelling about storytelling, rendered in a style and in practical terms the relative formality or informality of which has no consequence upon the casting of the actor who is affected. Whether the storytelling is accomplished through anecdotes at a bar or swimming pool or through the production of a film like *8½,* or *Day for Night,* or *Lost in La Mancha,* it will not be in the power of the actor to cast himself as a conspirator or a minimalist. That decision will rest with those who script, cast, and produce the accounting. And clearly both structural myths exist to substantiate the formation of the actor's diegetic character. Whether, as in *Day for Night,* the actors are shown to love and cherish one another while working, even to admit that they need love, that they say, "Love me," "I love you," "I really love you"—in short, that they inhabit a conspiracy from which the audience is coolly excluded—or whether, as in *Lost in La Mancha*, they appear unlinked, unaware that they are in the presence of fatality, grief, loss, is not an existential matter but an element of film style.

Three Johnnies of *Lost in La Mancha* meet us at one and the same time. One of them, an actor named Johnny Depp, who has let his hair grow and has dressed in denim today, who smokes Gauloises nonstop, whose speech when we hear it is very articulate and sweet and restrained, is shown by his directors—Fulton and Pepe—to relate superficially and without emotional or historical connections to the co-workers to whose company he has contracted himself, these co-workers including Jean Rochefort. A second Johnny, the actor employed by Terry Gilliam, is obedient, professional, respectful, amicable, and sweetly unapproachable because fastidiously polite. Of the third, the Johnny Depp who is playing these Johnny Depps, we can surmise only that he traveled back in time to a period in Spain, when a movie was being made about a man who traveled back in time to a period in Spain. The more we watch him, the more we cannot tell how much we do not know.

Depp doesn't look as much like a movie star as a guy who might be mistaken for a movie star.

Rob Blackwelder, "Deppth Perception"

Cannes Man: the title of a film and the title of a nonentity. The film, by Richard Martini, recounts an escapade late in the life of the fabled Hollywood producer/shyster Sy Lerner (Seymour Cassel), in which, to win a substantial bet, he converts a "nobody," Frank Rhinoslavsky (Francesco Quinn), into Frank Rhino, the most celebrated figure at the Cannes Film Festival, all within a week. He does this by craftily projecting into his conversations, into other people's gossip, and therefore into the industry's belief, the fantasy of a $25 million dollar production based on a "Hemingway-like, Faulkneresque" script written by Rhino; this film-within-the-film is called *Cannes Man* (pronounced *Con-Man,* under which moniker, in fact, the DVD was re-released). And indeed, as it turns out in the finale, in order to save his life Lerner really does have to make *Cannes Man* and the *Cannes Man* we have been watching is (of course) none other than that film. In order to swing industry opinion to his aid in this elaborate fabrication, Lerner requires that attached to his "project" be some authentic names, and we see him working on the likes of James Brolin, Dennis Hopper, Menachem Golan, Julian Lennon, Benicio Del Toro, Harvey Weinstein, and Treat Williams. But the most golden apple on the tree is Johnny Depp.

Johnny is quietly meditating, cross-legged on the ground, with Jim Jarmusch. Surrounding the two are a bevy of morose-looking guards, of whom Lerner must beg permission to speak with Johnny. "Just for a minute, it's okay," Johnny says. Jarmusch is irritated to have his meditative balloon punctured, but Johnny happily coos, "We're up there. We're above you." Soon enough he is happily dickering about points, rights, sequels, television, and who will direct, this last because Lerner has offered the film to Jarmusch in order to include him in the conversation—"What, did you just come here to talk to *Johnny Depp?*"—and Johnny suddenly has ideas that he might like to direct as well. "Of course you are a director, too," says Jarmusch. "No, no. I'm not *really* a director," Johnny demurs. Frank Rhino walks up to be introduced, immediately sits down next to Johnny, and wraps his arm around him. Johnny squirms. He and Jarmusch pick up margaritas to substitute for the meditation, and light cigarettes together. Johnny offers Rhino a cigarette and is more than dismayed to learn the "writer" doesn't smoke. He convinces him it's religious, meditative, and puts a cigarette in Frank's mouth, flicking open his lighter with great professionalism only to discover that the cigarette is backward.

As the conceit of *Cannes Man* is that a producer is "putting together a picture deal" amid the hustle and bustle of the Cannes Festival, it is a necessity of the plot that the landscape be thickly populated by financiers, stars, and "lesser" movie actors "desperate to further their careers." The Hollywood movie world, here depicted, at least that portion of it inhabited by actors, has grown since the days of *The Bad and the Beautiful* (1950) to seem unfictionalizable—metafictional—so that the only way to "represent" stars or actors onscreen is to have actual stars and actors play "themselves." The audience is presumably now unwilling to believe in a "famous internationally celebrated movie star" with a name they cannot recognize on the marquees of theaters that visible festivalgoers at Cannes visit in "everyday life." Thus it is that the celebrities in this film must operate doubly, as Kracauer suggests, each being both player and instrument (1960, 95). Benicio Del Toro, for example, a little eager at the breakfast table with some of his cohorts from *The Usual Suspects,* is both the actor Del Toro contracted to play a scene in *Cannes Man,* and his public persona, recognizable to the audience as the star they have seen fulfilling contracts in other movies, the "famous" Benicio Del Toro. And this is the case with all the celebrities. To the extent that they are visible to us as famous celebrities and public personae, of course, they are commodities being marketed, even as the professional actors who go public in these personae are marketers of these same commodities. The "walk-on" performances they contribute to *Cannes Man* are advertisements for themselves as potential players in films in general, just exactly as the walk-on behavior they disport in the city of Cannes during the festival is an advertisement as well. The walk-ons of *Cannes Man* are not structurally different from the walk-ons that professional actors/festivalgoers "do" in the guise of "simply being at" the festival.

The implicit suggestion of the film is that in the city of Cannes, during the festival each spring, stars and actors are in fact present explicitly to market themselves and thus inhabit the scene exactly as commodities, which is to say, as performances of *themselves.* These self-performers are, however, the actors beneath the "celebrities" we see onscreen in this film, since the technique of the filmmaker was to shoot during the actual 1995 Cannes Festival using actual festivalgoer performers in walk-on performances of festivalgoer performers meeting, confabulating, and negotiating to get contracts with the best possible return. To whatever degree Jon Cryer or Benicio Del Toro, for example, may emerge from their hotel rooms and do "walk-ons" (self-promotions) in the guise of "Jon Cryer" or "Benicio Del Toro" (openly and yet not overtly looking for work), in *Cannes Man* they are filmed doing this, in the process becoming the onscreen "Jon Cryer" or "Benicio Del Toro" plainly looking for work (since the fiction erases the modesty), and the venue of this search, the Cannes Festival, is at once not only the location in which Martini's movie is being made but the setting in which his movie story is taking place. One distinct possibility not to be let out of sight is that beneath, behind, or nearby those masked celebrities are the actors wearing the masks, people entirely unknown to and unseen by us, who bought tickets, flew to France, and occupy hotel rooms when they are not "on display" as actors who presumably occupy hotel rooms. That is, they are notably available for shooting this film even as they disport themselves as notably available for shooting films. *Cannes Man* is thus populated by actors pretending to be themselves pretending to be themselves. All this pretense makes for a certain discernible self-consciousness, and we have a distinct sense of them not only exuding personality and feeling but also being sharply aware of the presence and positioning of a camera to which they can play. There is thus something distinctly artificial about the star performances here, since the performers seem to know they are performing; yet are existing in a "backstage" world where performances are being traded and not explicitly given *as such*. While it is impossible to negotiate at Cannes, apparently, without conning people, without putting on a show of some kind, and thus without giving some kind of performance, nevertheless the performances people give (on camera) are not "on-camera performances" and we are to take these performers merely as their normal, everyday, off-camera, "naturally stagey" selves. For a very similarly structured, but entirely contrasting, portrait of wheeling and dealing at Cannes, one may turn to Henry Jaglom's *Festival in Cannes* (2001), where there is a sense that stars, producers, and actors sometimes lead real lives—this suggestion, of course, entirely fabricated but in a process that permits and encourages a different kind of acting style.

What is interesting about all this is that Johnny Depp doesn't fit the picture at all and it is his failure to fit that is illuminating, even shocking. When we see him, we have the distinct impression that, although he is aware there is a camera present, first, he doesn't deeply care; secondly, he doesn't have a clue as to why; and thirdly, he is beyond any sensibility that could inform him as to what is going on around him. He is entirely unconscious of himself as a celebrity whom we might wish to see, whom a cameraman might wish to photograph, ensconced as he is in a private and transubstantial domain. How is this accomplished?

While actors in character for the camera typically do not look into the lens (even being understood, when they do, as having been separated from us by the "apparatus"), they do maintain a partial "turnout" that is negotiated as much by the camera placement as by their own stance; and in that sense, the form of film remains theatrical. The camera slices into interpostural alignments between characters so as to permit the viewer to occupy a position on the inside; the

camera observes from outside the boundaries of the situation characters who recognize themselves as such, and therefore as observable,
as prone to the curiosity of the Other. Further, the lens, when it presents itself, is sufficiently familiar—not only to the actor but also to
the character—to be invisible. But in the meditation sequence between Jarmusch and Depp, Depp acts as though the camera and its
presence are distinctly notable, distinctly strange; as though he is in
no particular way worth paying attention to and, therefore, as
though he is surprised and even taken aback, distracted, a little irritated, by the camera's attention; as though the interpostural alignment he is effecting with his friend Jarmusch is a private, even religious, one, something not to be interfered with. Added to this is
the positioning of the camera between Jarmusch and Depp, looking
down on them as they sit cross-legged on the grass. It doesn't quite
relax enough to join them, and so it doesn't indicate inclusion, and
thus implies precisely the examination Johnny seems to find so
outrageously incomprehensible. As the camera shoots Johnny from
over his shoulder, the slightly intrusive camera angle and Johnny's
marked diffidence combine to give the impression he is aware of the
camera's presence only as an unfriendly (but tolerable) interruption.

He can be taken, therefore, as entirely "innocent" of his own
performance exactly in the sense that he is retaining his status as
Johnny Depp the sometime-performer-now-caught-inopportunely-
in-privacy; unknowing about the circumstances that are framing his
action as performance; and deeply concentrating on his existential
sense of self in the moment. Ironically, we meet him in a scene where
he is presumably meditating, bringing himself to a level of consciousness where he has no sense of himself being utilized by others,
couldn't care about mundane goings-on, and is beyond any sensibility that could inform him as to what is transpiring around him in
everyday terms. Then, bizarrely, almost hilariously (except that his
sincerity forbids the exploitation implicit in our laughter), in the
middle of this scene, he is able, in an instant, to dive into the arcane
details of negotiating a picture deal without losing his tone, his quality of suspension, his distance, his immense consciousness (as op-
posed to self-consciousness), even batting issues back and forth with
Jim Jarmusch, who has fallen out of his meditative stance and, irritated, is being "Jim Jarmusch pretending to be Jim Jarmusch." Even
here, by the way, Depp is seen from the outside, from above, as
though the negotiation is a necessary pain inflicted upon a moment

thoroughly cleansed of cinematic presence. The impression we have with Depp, then, is that while all the other celebrities are "really" there, he, for one, is *really* there.

This *real* impression he manages to give frequently onscreen, very frequently. And it is one of the agencies of his charm. Near the end of the film, "Frank Rhino" must evaporate. To signal that our schlemiel-turned-writer has fallen from grace, Martini engages him in another conversation with Johnny and has Johnny, of all people, turn away from him and have him escorted out of the scene. Once you have been dismissed by someone as *real* as this, you really are "nothing."

RAOUL

A remarkable scene near the beginning of Terry Gilliam's bizarre and oneiric *Fear and Loathing in Las Vegas:*

On the empty highway between Los Angeles and Las Vegas, "somewhere near Barstow," Raoul Duke (an exceedingly wired Johnny Depp, with a cigarette holder that seems to be cemented to his teeth) and his attorney Dr. Gonzo (a porcine never-sober Benicio Del Toro) are screaming along in a flame red Chevrolet convertible whose trunk, as Hunter S. Thompson writes in the book of which this film is in many ways an extraordinarily faithful rendition, "looked like a mobile police narcotics lab. We had two bags of grass, seventy-five pellets of mescaline, five sheets of high-powered blotter acid, a salt shaker half full of cocaine, and a whole galaxy of multi-colored uppers, downers, screamers, laughers . . . and also a quart of tequila, a quart of rum, a case of Budweiser, a pint of raw ether and two dozen amyls" (1971, 4), every last molecule of which one or the other of these Knights of the Shining Countenance proceeds during this film to consume. On the radio, a woman is smugly announcing, ". . . report says illegal drugs killed a hundred and sixty American GIs last year, forty of them in Vietnam."

At the side of the road stands a hitchhiker (a somewhat etiolated, very blond, long-haired Tobey Maguire), a boy innocent enough actually to exclaim when they stop for him, "Hot damn! I never rode in a convertible before!" "Get in!" says Raoul, with a too-delirious eagerness, photographed in extreme wide angle to suggest from the boy's perspective his grinning face looming like the Cheshire Cat's.

We cut to the kid in the center of the back seat, pressing against the backrest with pasty-faced trepidation. "How long," muses Duke to himself, "before one of us starts raving and jabbering at this boy? What will he think then? This same lonely desert was the last known home of the Manson family. Would he make that grim connection?" He quickly turns and stares into the kid's face:

RAOUL: There's one thing you should probably understand. *Can you hear me?* (He hops into the back seat and puts his arm around the kid.) I want you to have all the background. This is a very ominous assignment.
(Gonzo loses control of the car and it swerves madly, the boy trying to climb out at the same time. Raoul has his arm around the kid's neck. [To himself:]) Our vibrations were getting nasty. Was there no communication in this car? (He is whispering into the kid's ear, holding him with both hands. The kid giggles.) Had we deteriorated to the level of dumb beasts?

Raoul introduces his attorney—"probably Samoan—are you prejudiced?" (KID [as Raoul pats his cheek]: "Hell no")—and offers the stunned boy first beer, then ether. It is suddenly transparently clear that the hitchhiker is no longer happy to have taken this hitch.

Gonzo has a vicious hallucination and pulls the car over in a cloud of dust. He is having tremors, bleating like a stuck pig. Raoul pops an amyl under his nose, then takes one himself, flopping back against the boy like a pillow, his arm affectionately around the boy's shoulder. The boy's brow is covered with sweat, rigid and white with terror. He believes himself to be in the presence of all that is unsettling, all that is powerful, all that is incalculably—and therefore frighteningly—attractive and repulsive at the same time, a serpent with a cigarette holder in its jaw, a spirit that seems hardwired to some vast dynamo, and a mind exploding with thoughts of the sanctum of forbidden delights. Gonzo starts up about killing someone, pulls a gun out of a paper bag, and waves it in the air, and the boy flies out of the car and tears down the road, yelling, "Don't worry about me," frightened half out of his mind.

But here is what is remarkable: watching this, not only the boy but we too have been put uptight. While our easy identification with the innocent boy and his concomitant withdrawal from the unmitigated and shapeless zaniness of Raoul and Gonzo are necessities of the filmic architecture—we must come to understand the acutely perceptive alienation of the form of journalism Raoul Duke (personifying Hunter S. Thompson himself) is practicing on this journey, and seeing him as something of a monster assists us in grasping the irony of his own scathing analysis of the monstrosity of American culture at the end of the Vietnam War—nevertheless it is possible to sense a certain delicious appropriateness in the casting here, an alien presence, as it were, beneath the personification of Raoul Duke that we are watching. If the hitchhiker seems petrified of Raoul, yet also stunned, lolling too easily in his fondling—yet also needling—caresses, how is it that the viewer has so pungent a suspicion that the Johnny Depp behind Raoul has a similarly precarious hold on himself and the situation? For it is unmistakable: just as Raoul seems teetering on the lip of sociability with the innocent boy, unable to be certain he can sustain warmth, affection, intelligence, aspiration, curiosity, or delight before tumbling into an abysm of despair and horror, unable to guarantee his reserve in the moment so that the experience can be preserved from rupture; so Depp himself strikes us as continually threatening the integrity of the motion picture in which all this is happening, balanced insecurely between the effortless performance and the open presentation of catastrophe.

(In 2003, he would reprise this teetering balance, this daring filibuster, in *Pirates of the Caribbean: Curse of the Black Pearl,* the story of a nineteenth-century social critic just as *Fear and Loathing* is the story of a twentieth-century seafarer who is too far from the sea.)

Two aspects of Depp's performance of Duke are salient. He musters a concentration toward, and conviction in, the ephemeral qualities of the moment, seeming to explode with sensibility and engagement even as, utilizing the script by Gilliam, Tony Grisoni, Tod Davies, and Alex Cox, he illuminates his response from a vast and articulate schema of political, economic, and cultural analysis. He can be said to be fully alive in the moment, fully synchronizing his musculature and vocality with the intentionality and indication embedded in his dialogue. Throughout the film, indeed, Johnny's Raoul is lavishly expressive without ever being decorative or even emphatic. Of course, the genuineness and repleteness of his momentary responses is systematically camouflaged by the overriding ongoing dramaturgical conceit of the film, namely, that the wild pharmacopia in the trunk of the red convertible is relentlessly passing into the bloodstreams of Raoul and Gonzo: Depp's responses as Duke are therefore entirely dismissable as random pharmacological side-effects. ("The cocaine he was 'snorting,'" said Terry Gilliam, "was powdered milk. By the end of [the picture] he had so much milk in his lungs he could breast feed the crew" ["Bravo! Profile"].) To put this more graphically: we may be led to concentrate so furiously on Johnny as centerpiece of the events he inhabits that we do not appreciate the relationship between his actions and those events, what Goffman (1974, 379) calls "the meld of what the current scene brings to him and what he brings to it."

With the boy in the car, for example, Raoul's actions appear overwhelming, but this is because they are shot by a camera that duplicates the boy's perspective on him. To use Raoul as a mirror for the uptightness of the youth as a representative of fundamentalist culture is to recognize that culture, and see that Raoul is exaggerated because of a prevailing value structure of self-abasement (that the boy exemplifies) that is threatened by his liberty. Similarly, in the hotel scenes in Las Vegas, to take Raoul as overexpressive or hyperbolic in tone is to accept the bland and repressive logic of institutionalized hospitality and take seriously the overriding importance of public decorum. To acquiesce less is to see Raoul with less exaggeration, to understand that he is attempting to plummet to the psychosocial nexus in the American—especially the Western American—heart.

If it is characterized by a special pungency of emotion, Depp's performance here is also notable because it spectacularly lacks sustainment, the capacity to extend the sense of involvement over time. For most of us most of the time, experience leaves traces that linger varyingly and take the form of afterimages, afterthoughts, aftertastes, or aftereffects. These traces are not specifically memories (since memory is also an experience subject to boundings) but attributes of the experiential boundary, residues that dissipate or dissolve and contribute to the effect of experience being more than momentary. The specific experience that memory is a memory of, in other words, has a lingering quality of sorts. When we close a door, we experience a brief awareness that a door that had been open is now closed, and that awareness, that second "closing," is a trace. But in *Fear and Loathing in Las Vegas* Johnny Depp gives to his sensations of the moment a specific and brutal curtailment, energized by an incalculably flexible and desperately hungry motility that makes radical change—of position, of reaction, of ideation, of posture, of mode of intoxication—an ongoing normality. "Keep moving," as Thompson put it (17). As much as he invests himself wholly in experiencing the moment, then, he does not extend his experience, savor it, reflect upon it by and large, investigate or develop it. He therefore continually is. The performance of Duke is relentlessly existential. As Depp described "the way [Thompson] thinks": "You can actually see the wheels turning and see the ideas coming. That was really the key for me because he is thinking constantly, there are no lulls, and he is very quick-witted" (Heard 2001, 187).

The Duke that Depp becomes is unpredictable, and in a way unmemorable (confounding some viewers, I believe, who are not attuned to the exquisite difference between this performance of Johnny's and others). Since his behavior is entirely animal, while his analysis is deeply philosophical, he represents an inherent, even blinding, contradiction. We surf through the movie with him, yet when it is done we are left with only the scantiest traces of what he has been before our eyes. For this reason it is true, exactly as Duke puts it, that it is "impossible to walk in this muck. No footing at all." The Las Vegas that is the screen domain of this film brings to him a non-stop phantasmagoria provoking, teasing, obliterating, then re-creating, affronting, and also surrendering to his language. "It was time," he offers, "for an agonizing reappraisal of the whole scene," but what a scene: "The place fairly reeked of high grade formica and plastic palm trees." The ability to detect displaces the ability to navigate and control; seeing is all. "Ether," he muses: "You can actually watch yourself behaving in this terrible way—but you can't control it. Ether is the perfect drug for Las Vegas."

Here we find two vital clues. The first is the importance of watching. Johnny courses through the narrative in a pair of amber-tinted goggles, his eyes agog. This is not because he is astonished or alarmed by what he sees, so much as because he seems to feel powerless to digest the enormity of it. Like grain in the craw of a Périgord duck, the world has been crammed into him, by way of the eyes. (As in *The Astronaut's Wife*, his eyes are portals for reception.) The ability he describes (about ether) to watch oneself, yet not to control oneself, suggests the ascendance of sight and awareness over tactility and manipulation—a cinematic program. The second clue: on this "perfect drug for Las Vegas" (which is the putative site of the American Dream), one watches *oneself*. The self-reflexivity without analysis suggests the importance of the subjective point of view for grasping experience and gaining an informational hold. Duke is a journalist. More than questing for the American Dream he has given himself over to the project of writing out that quest, seeing it in all its painful nuances. He writes and speaks out a litmus test for the American condition from the point of view of the litmus paper. Goffman writes: "If the onlookers laugh when the clown suddenly finds himself falling like a stone it is because they had all along been projecting their musculature and sensibilities sympathetically into his walk and now find that their leaning into his anticipated conduct, into the anticipated guidedness of his doings, their framed prediction of what is to come, is disordered. In this sense watching is doing" (381). Indeed, "Watching as doing" might be called the standard journalistic posture. But for Depp in *Fear and Loathing, doing is watching*. It is through investment in the drugs that represent his world, through devouring that world, that Depp as Duke anticipates having the perspective required to relate us to ourselves. Since he understands only by participating, since he apprehends structure only by living it, he must at one and the same time *be* the story and contrive to report it:

> The only way to prepare for a trip like this, I felt, was to dress up like human peacocks and get crazy, then screech off across the desert and *cover the story*. Never lose sight of the primary responsibility.
>
> But what *was* the story? Nobody had bothered to say. So we would have to drum it up on our own. Free Enterprise. The

American Dream. Horatio Alger gone mad on drugs in Las Vegas. Do it *now:* pure Gonzo journalism. (Thompson 1971, 12)

What may cause anxiety about his performance here, then, is that he is more fully committed to moments emotionally than our civilization permits—we literally will not and do not "project our musculature and sensibilities sympathetically into his walk"; that in this flamboyance he is so scathingly true to the scene he reports — "This is not a good town for psychedelic drugs"; that no moment of Johnny's profound involvement is extended or linked to the moments that follow, so that he seems to hop like a jackrabbit from riposte to riposte; and that his method of observation is so involving as to forego any hope of what we would deem worthy (that is, safe) objective distance. He is in it: too much in it. As we read in the book version and Depp openly demonstrates onscreen: "My body felt like I'd just been wired into a 220 volt socket" (132). Nothing can be hidden from him. The world is in that drugstore in the trunk of his car, and he is going to try all of it—perhaps all of it at once.

All this seems implicit enough in the scene with the hitchhiker, and not so much about Raoul Duke as about Johnny Depp. Whether or not he has the vast experience with drugs his publicity has consistently suggested—he is "what GQ delicately termed 'the philosopher king of the stoners,'" writes one journalist (De Vries 1993); and "It would be difficult to argue that I was anti-drugs. I'm for, ah . . . being smart about the subject," says the "philosopher king" himself (Leigh 2001)—he manages to strike us as a young man who would boldly take all those drugs only because they were there to be taken. He seems to have the energy to flip on a dime from experience to experience, thought to thought, without leaving a wake. Above all, he strikes us as being so extremely sensitive that experience of any kind will utterly penetrate him, and that he seeks the penetrating experience: the extremity of Duke's responses, gestures, and provocations is thus readable as a natural expression of Johnny's intrinsic openness to feeling and expansive passion, the openness that makes him complain as he is interviewed about *Chocolat,* "We close ourselves off and we live in these little worlds that are comfortable and safe. It's routine and boring and filled with fear and guilt and it's no good, you know? It's no good for you" (Okwu 2000). All this directly contradicts the tenets of rationalism: the willingness to forego, indeed negate, some experiences in order to dwell analytically on others for the ultimate purpose of gaining mastery: thus reflection; the will-

ingness to suspend or dilute intensity of experience in order to preserve the ability to steer the ship; the self-ostracism from the body, in
order to elude the seductions of the flesh and more easily find the
reins of manipulation. Instead, to show us what we have become, he
gives in to those seductions, refuses to dilute his experience, does not
dwell upon a thought in order to master a situation. He becomes
something of a leaf blowing in the wind.

Raoul, Again

B ut we may ourselves seek mastery, measurement, exclusion.
We may approach Johnny Depp from a rational perspective,
with a desire to estimate him. Thus, we may seek to know
what is this "America" of the American Dream, in order to know
who is this Johnny inside the Raoul Duke bravely seeking it in order
to expose it to the light of day. It is certainly a dream, and a culture—
as Duke points out in the film—where one learns to be disappointed.

A fully-fledged American capitalist aristocracy was in place by
the turn of the twentieth century, and included such luminary rare
birds as John Jacob Astor the financier, George Pullman the railway baron, J. Pierpont Morgan the banker, Henry Ford, Cornelius
Vanderbilt, Milton S. Hershey, F. W. Woolworth, and Louis Comfort
Tiffany. By World War I, American economic culture was centered
on mass production, particularly on the department store in which
through national chains millions of units of relatively inexpensive
items could be sold at a low per-unit price in such a way that vast

fortunes were agglomerated. The Second World War drew manufacturing up to new levels of productivity and profit, with the result that when the 1940s were ending, vast supplies of consumable materials in which labor had already been invested rested in warehouses waiting to be bought. Unbridled and unprecedented consumption was required, and the advertising world as we know it came into existence to produce and drive the ceaseless hunger that was a hallmark of consumerist culture. Since the early 1950s, America had sustained a complex and frenzied devotion to material wealth—its excesses, its broad diffusion across a wide geographical and sociological landscape—and in particular to two products that by 1960 were so numerous and so pervasive in their distribution and influence they had become, everywhere but in conditions of the extremest poverty, imperceptible and central elements of the American background: locomotion and drugs. One transformed the settings in which the social body acted; the other transformed the social body that acted in those settings.

Many sorts of things moved, of course, and much production was associated not only with what would be moved but with what might move it or the means by which this could happen systematically. Locomotion meant: packaging and packaged goods, a system of agricultural production linking growers and consumers who were separated by great distances, thus mobile refrigeration; automobiles, railway cars, airplanes, and the infrastructures for keeping these maintained; the idea of taking a vacation and the tourism business, including airline, railway, and bus reservations systems; clothing and accoutrements associated with movement, such as cruise wear, safari gear, sportswear, and portable irons, toothbrushes, and radios, not to mention luggage and a repertory of ideas about the exotic; publishing, broadcasting, motion picture production and exhibition, and all other forms of the transportation of ideas, influence, mythologies, and images from point to point; the traffic system for regulating vehicular and pedestrian movement; the legal system with its local traffic rules or its national rules for taxation upon goods and services moving across borders; the police, immigration, and customs systems for handling transportational infractions; the educational system for organizing the movement of thought through people's minds locally and nationally; advertising as a system for routinely creating, disseminating, and promoting the impulse to move physically, socially, intellectually, and economically; not to mention oil, gasoline, and diesel fuel production and the making, transportation, and selling of any fuel at all for making any vehicle at all move either empty or full of cargo; the interstate road and bridge system, a vast web of engineering accomplishment and financial investment; a widely diffused empire of hotels, motels, and restaurants catering to the hospitality of people distanced from their homes. America was a world on the go. Locomotion meant a culture devoted to what Schivelbusch called "panoramic perception" (1986), yet less as the specialized experience he described (that flowed from the unique event of a railway voyage) than as an experience so quotidian and routine as to be virtually imperceptible: there came to be no other kinds of perception. The landscape was a territory to move through, not a perspective in its own right. "Keep moving." What it was to see the world pass through the windows of a railway carriage in the nineteenth century came to be the experience of seeing an action movie late in the twentieth.

And drugs set the body in motion within itself. Three kinds of drugs developed systematically in the national marketplace during the twentieth century. First, over-the-counter (though not always the drugstore counter), soft, chemical treatments like herbal tonics and headache remedies, vitamins, cold and influenza medications, caffeine, sugar, vanilla, coca, and nicotine each infiltrated the national diet as staple and as decoration. I will never forget a sickening black licorice-flavored concoction I was force-fed for digestive troubles; an apricot-flavored delight that was purported to heighten my vitamin A and D; and the omnipresent, bland, horrifyingly metalic cod liver oil, balm for anything and everything. This is not to mention mustard plasters, balsam inhalations, baths in a soothing solution of cornstarch for chicken pox and sunburn. A cup of coffee and a doughnut were, in the 1920s and onward, *the* democratic breakfast for the urban worker, and a delight for virtually anyone: "We've stopped for a light snack," says a genteel character in *Homer Price,* a staple of children's literature from the early 1940s onward. "Some doughnuts and coffee would be simply marvelous" (McCloskey 1976, 54). In Sturges's *Sullivan's Travels* (1941), a diner operator in rural California gives Veronica Lake and Joel McCrea coffee and doughnuts (caffeine, gluten, and sugar) for free, an ultimate signal of kindliness, charity, and democratic brotherly feeling.

Secondly, medicinal preparations were, and have continued to be, a commercialized extension of the medical practitioner's knowledge: painkillers and tranquilizers like paregoric (for migraine), morphine, and codeine; soporifics, vasodilators, barbiturates, corti-costeroids, antidepressants, antibiotics, anticoagulants, stimulants, muscle relaxants, stool softeners; hormones like insulin and epineph-rine; antioxidants, ace inhibitors, and Beta-blockers; statins; the vast and always expanding pharmacopia of "wonder" drugs to which only shamans—certified and not—had legal access.

Then, so-called "hard" or "street" drugs included substances against the circulation of which august laws had been enacted, since that circulation and the usage it led to had not been institutionalized (regardless of how powerful or even beneficial was the effect of using them): marijuana, lysergic acid diethylamide, mescaline, Ec-stasy, cocaine, heroin, opium, ether, amyl nitrate, to name some. And the drug business was anything but frivolous to those involved in it. As Thompson's Raoul notes, "One of the things you learn, after years of dealing with drug people, is that *everything* is serious. You can turn your back on a person, but never turn your back on a drug—especially when it's waving a razor-sharp hunting knife in your eyes" (56).

Alcohol, too, was restricted in public. Just as the American public, through its pious devotion to locomotion, was caught up in an un-ending shift of position, an ongoing caravan, a trek that could never discover a home (symbolized with gentility at the end of *What's Eat-ing Gilbert Grape*), so was that public ineffably, and always, high, stoned on sugar and Demerol, caffeine and LSD, amyls and ether and Benzedrine and Coca-Cola, a six-pack of Budweiser and a couple dozen reefers mixed with Marlboros and Ecstasy, Chardonnay from California, hits of epinephrine, laxatives and diet pills and sleeping pills and pep-me-ups, or two hours' worth of Bloody Marys swal-lowed "for the V-8 nutritional content" (104). Everybody was al-ways taking into themselves a pleasurable intoxicant that would change them inside; and going somewhere that would put a new background behind them, at least for the night.

To be stoned on the reservoirs of a personal pharmacy, indeed, while noodling around in a monstrous convertible—"Everything was automatic. I could sit in the red-leather driver's seat and make every inch of the car *jump*, by touching the proper buttons. It was a wonderful machine. Ten grand worth of gimmicks and high-priced Special Effects. The rear-windows leaped up with a touch, like frogs in a dynamite pond" (104)—was, by the late twentieth century, the epitome of the American Dream. And the Dream's hub, the whirling cacophony in the center of the film, is the National Attorneys' Conference on Narcotics and Dangerous Drugs, an event toward which Raoul and Gonzo aim themselves, and from which they retreat, in a gleaming white Cadillac, and one, as well, that Raoul and Gonzo plan to observe and report from the most sympathetic possible point of view: "Some of the mescaline pellets had disintegrated into a reddish-brown powder, but I counted about thirty-five or forty still intact. . . . Not enough for anything serious, but a careful rationing of the mescaline would probably get us through the four-day Drug Conference" (100). For observational purposes, indeed, mescaline was ideal, "a sensual/surface drug that exaggerates reality, instead of altering it" (143).

In a culture so pervasively devoted to the consumption of drugs legal and illegal, toxic and non-toxic, pharmacological and nutritional, listening to sententious policemen rant at such a conference while being stoned on mescaline constitutes an extreme form of piety. So, too, does the continually wandering, gliding, swooping quality of the narrative, which moves with unrelentingly jerky insistence toward a realization, a clarity, a truth that seems always to beckon from just over the horizon. Experience and reflection are mobile: "You can always see the wheels turning . . ."

Finally, the film gives an exquisitely disorganized, quintessentially messy rendition of the ravaged state of Duke's consciousness by the end of the conference weekend, a consciousness projected and mirrored in his hotel room—

> There was evidence in this room of excessive consumption of almost every type of drug known to civilized man since 1544 A.D. It could only be explained as a *montage,* a sort of exaggerated medical exhibit, put together very carefully to show what might happen if twenty-two serious drug felons—each with a *different* addiction—were penned up together in the same room for five days and nights, without relief. (188)

The *"montage,"* in fact, is an apt description of the film itself, and Depp's performance handily conveys the sense of an "exaggerated medical exhibit": intelligence, hopelessness, incisiveness, eagerness, experimentation, motility, and freedom from the encumbrance of nostalgia, wedded to what American society could envisage only as a pathological lack of respect for authority and a diabolical disregard for bourgeois conventionality and taste. Depp went so far in his commitment to idiosyncrasy and personal autonomy, indeed, as to hurl even Thompson's critique back in his face: "ugly, screwy, flashy," the journalist had faxed about the costume, and Depp responded, "Doctor, Too late" (Heard 2001, 191); but he went on to say something profoundly passionate and mysterious and true: "I am an actor and can only do what I can do. I am NOT and CANNOT be you. But I can come pretty fucking close, and will. This is *my* work!!!" (192). It is in his manner of "coming close" that Depp is astonishing. We can say that he never entirely becomes his character, and we can surmise— but only surmise—that he never stops being himself. Yet, as we know nothing in the end about Depp, it is left to us to imagine his position in a strange space between the actor and his role, a space always changing its shape and luminosity and thus never for a moment becoming absolutely fixed or bounded or clear or, for that matter, old.

DON JUAN

It was like a long, spectral Arabian dream in the afternoon in another life—Ali Baba and the alleys and the courtesans.

Jack Kerouac, *On the Road*

In Jeremy Leven's rather bizarre *Don Juan DeMarco* (1995), Johnny DeMarco, a young New Yorker claiming to be, dressing and speaking in the garb and language of, and in general demanding that others acknowledge him as Don Juan (Depp), is contemplating suicide on top of a building (beneath a huge billboard that says, "The Beaches of Canary Islands SPAIN Unlock the Mysteries"). Bereft of his adored and beautiful Doña Ana, he finds life not worth living. He is talked off his ledge by a canny but burned-out psychiatrist (Marlon Brando), who, riding up to greet him in a cherry-picker crane, and claiming to be none other than Don Octavio de Flores, embraces him like a long-lost brother and fellow master of the ways of the world, and says to him, "You are *the* Don Juan? . . . You must not forget, my friend, that the power of your love, the power of love of Don Juan is eternal and will not be denied." As a matter of honor, the youth commits himself to Don Octavio's care in an oasis retreat of sorts: a clinic where the staff are eager, indeed too eager, to drug him into submission. The psychiatrist's "real" name—that is, the name by which he is known by his somewhat bloodthirsty colleagues—is Dr. Jack Mickler. Mickler and Don Juan spend their days confabulating. To Mickler's quiet suggestion that many might think the identity of Don Juan a delusion, the poetic youth parries gracefully that it is surely Don Octavio's delusion that he is a psychiatrist.

As long as he engages with Dr. Mickler in "therapeutic" discussions, Don Juan is saved from the drugs that will erase his memory, and thus his self—as long as, Sheherezade-like, he can continue the tale in which he comes slowly to reveal the story of his life, a grand and romantic fable told onscreen in flashback as the content of a film-within-the-film narrated by Don Juan and watched by the viewer-psychiatrist and an audience of psychiatrist-viewers at the same time. This inner story, set in what looks very much like the artificially dusty, sun-baked world of Walt Disney's 1958 production *The Nine Lives of Elfego Baca,* has Don Juan falling madly in love with the twenty-three-year-old Doña Julia (Talisa Soto), the "faithful and devoted wife of Don Alfonzo" and, given her husband's middle age, a young woman who "would have been better served by two men of twenty-five." To the perplexed but increasingly engaged (and middle-aged) Mickler, Don Juan tells the story of his consummation with Doña Julia, and concludes: "There are only four questions of value in life: What is sacred? Of what is the spirit made? What is worth living for? And what is worth dying for? The answer to each is the same. Only love. Doña Julia was my first love." But when Don Alfonzo comes upon his wife with her young lover, the girl suddenly vanishes from the boy's life, never to be seen again. Soon after, he suffers the death of his father at the hands of the villainous Alfonzo, upon whom he exacts a bittersweet revenge. As his grief-stricken mother prepares to take herself off to a nunnery, Don Juan swears on his father's dying breath to roam the world in search of love and, to please his mother, sails off to safety.

But his ship is manned by scoundrels who sell him into slavery in "an obscure sultanate." So it is that, in the middle of this entirely phantasmagorical film, which is—true to its phantasmagorical hero—at one and the same time entirely playful and entirely serious (about matters of genuine philosophical interest such as being faithful to one's fantasies and being conscientious in love), we find the hero, who has clearly been hiding inside the identity of Don Juan, now re-trapped in, of all places, a Sultan's harem. In the company of the Sultan's eunuch, he marches down a shady colonnade in delicate slippers, royal blue pantaloons of gauze, and swaths of a gilded scarlet veil that covers his head and lower face. As he puts it himself in voiceover, "My mask had been replaced by a mask of another sort." Seen from the point of view of Western conventions, which is the point of view from which Don Juan has cast and costumed and scripted himself, it is a mask that obscures, instead of accentuating, his masculinity, this in order that he may be secretly escorted by the eunuch to the rosy, ephemeral chamber of the Sultana Gulbeyaz (Jo Champa), where, as she undresses him, he "began to develop a theory why he had been bought." If in her carnal desire Gulbeyaz is as plain and direct as Don Juan has ever been with any woman, he can only demur: "But I still loved Doña Julia . . . I cannot go on living knowing that I defile the memory of the woman who brought my manhood alive and made it sing." On the other hand, as he discovers, perhaps giving himself to the Sultana is not as difficult as all that. We see him fall—quite without pain—into her delectable power, then watch as he is carefully secreted away in the evening in the Sultan's harem, with "God's canvas" of fifteen hundred nubile girls frolicking in a swimming pool among potted palms.

For two long years—a screen dissolve of two brief seconds—the lovemaking continues until one day the Sultan comes upon him in his concubine outfit. Smiling at his coy beauty, winking with lust, the plump little potentate whispers secret instructions to the eunuch, whereupon in a flash we see Don Juan aboard a ship, sailing away, the black mask upon his eyes again: "Oh well, all good things must come to an end . . . I had learned to love in a thousand ways, each one a lesson in the soul of a woman." He may be beloved of women, then, and womanly, but not so womanly as to desire men, or to permit himself to be desired. Cutting back to Mickler's office (where this narrative is being spun out) we see the doctor, looking just a little nauseated, asking if this could be continued tomorrow. Mickler is as plump as the Sultan, of course, and is himself the "sultan" of the psychotherapeutic bracketing tale. Yet as much as Don Juan's crafty Sheherezade narrates toward extensivity, continuity, and the suspended conclusion—for without suspension, the conclusion can only bring the pharmacopia that will dissolve his belief and fantasy life—so, too, the psychiatrist-ruler is so sated and overwhelmed by the tale he himself opts to put off its denouement into an ever-receding, always alluring, future.

Indeed, who is the performer dressing in the concubine's veil: is it DeMarco or Don Juan?* The vocalization of the narration here is Don Juan's; but is not DeMarco putting the vocalization on? Given that both the concubine and Don Juan are being put on by DeMarco, why, we may wonder, does DeMarco require to put on a Don Juan who puts on the concubine? Another way to phrase this: if DeMarco wishes to put on the concubine, why must he put on Don Juan first? Even Don Juan's rarefaction and effeteness, the sophistication and the polish, the poetry of the lothario—those characteristics that make him beloved of women, and thus, in a way, womanly—are part of DeMarco's careful performance.

It is worth considering the self-disclosure of DeMarco/Don Juan's narrative, the Sheherezade he has been forced to become as its narrator, since the story he tells Mickler becomes an incarnation of the story of his telling it, a full-fledged embedding, just as in *The Arabian Nights*. The story of the Sultan Shahriar and his concubine Sheherezade is that of a brutal monarch who insists every night that he be told a story by one of the girls of his harem, and as soon as the tale is done he orders her beheaded. In order to save her life, the clever Sheherezade, when it comes to be her turn, concocts a tale of the most wondrous elaboration, which continues night after night with embeddings following upon embeddings, for a thousand and one nights. Indeed, it is only because of our predispositions about gender display (of the sort Johnny Depp is here both catering to and

---

* It is surely as possible, by adopting a less traditional point of view about masculinity, to think the concubine's garb is the outfit that reveals DeMarco's true masculinity, and that Don Juan is his obscuring face.

dislodging) that we might have reason to see Don Juan's narrated concubine as different in kind from DeMarco's narrative Don Juan. In the story-within-the-story, just as Don Juan admits in his voice-over, his mask is replaced by a veil, but still his face is covered. How almondine, how penetrating, are the concubine's eyes as they peer out from above that veil! How graceful is the concubine's form! It is entirely impossible in watching this sequence to be oblivious of the fact, always entirely present yet often itself entirely disguised through Depp's career, that he is, if anything, pretty.

In the way that the nameless harem girl he seems to be in this inner tale hides from the potential wrath of the Sultan each night, Don Juan hides each night from the potential judgment of Dr. Mickler and his colleagues by spinning out his autobiographical story. And to the degree that the tale of Sheherezade is taken as a model for the story of Don Juan DeMarco and Dr. Mickler, Depp's Don Juan must be seen, on some level, not as a lothario but as a scheming princess. In the inner tale, it is not the Sultana Gulbeyaz who is the ultimate audience, after all, but her husband, the potent Sultan—a male figure who in certain respects mirrors Brando's Mickler. Gulbeyaz, indeed, is a co-conspirator with the incognito Don Juan: both have long dark hair and similar facial features, both are involved in maintaining Don Juan's presence in the harem and keeping his identity secret. As Gulbeyaz is a woman playing a trick on an all-powerful male in order to save her life—at least her sex life—so, at least in the architecture of the narrative, is Don Juan feminized, and Depp with him.

In fact, to the degree that the Sultan is a marker for Mickler, so, too, is Mickler a marker for the audience watching the film, an all-powerful controlling force before whom actors spin out their tales with extensivity, continuity, and the suspended conclusion in order that their futures may be ensured and their fates put off. Don Juan's lovemaking is masculine, but his narration about it, to Mickler and to us, is feminine. Thus, in the tale-within-the-tale, we can hardly be surprised or disoriented—as surprised and disoriented, for instance, as he declares himself to be—to find him in drag. And when the camera tilts up his body, from the arch little slippers to the provocative pantaloons to the daunting veil and the covered face to the penetrable eyes, we think at once two contradictory things: first, how will he survive this? Yet also, how appropriate he seems; how unproblematic survival in fact will be for this creature whose beauty is so powerful and so compelling. When at the climax of the little inner story the Sultan finally appears, a sexual bonding is suggested that will be both possible and perilous; perilous because the Sultan will know in an instant that he has been deceived, and will surely become an agent of death, but also possible because Don Juan—that is, Johnny—makes such a beautiful young girl.

Also to be entertained, of course, is the fantasy that the Sultan knows very well who is under that veil, and that Don Juan knows (or is at least on the verge of knowing) that he knows, and that still other delights are in store. If the Sultan can be presumed to know already what is going on, and to be homosexual, then Don Juan—that is, Johnny—makes such a beautiful young lover. Either way, he is not in truth the womanizer he pretends to be. And when at inner story's end he makes the declaration, "I had learned to love in a thousand ways, each one a lesson in the soul of a woman," we can find two quite contradictory, and yet unconflicting, ways to understand him. As a womanizer—that is, as the personification of the surface mask he has been putting forward to the world—he has learned how to make love to a thousand women. He has learned something of the extreme variation of female presence and desire. As a princess or concubine—a male entirely at home collaborating with a princess or hiding himself in a harem with concubines—he has seen a thousand sides of the feminine self. Also: the feminine self is truly his. A thousand women have taught him his womanhood. One is reminded of Michael Dorsey's (Dustin Hoffman) concluding confession to Julie (Jessica Lange) in *Tootsie* (1985): "I was a better man with you as a woman than I ever was with anybody as a man." But in *Tootsie,* after his gender masquerade (in the service of bringing home a paycheck as an actor who has made so many enemies he can't get work as himself) is done, Dorsey returns to the home turf of his masculinity. In *Don Juan DeMarco,* as he laces on his mask and sails away, the Latin "lover" merely moves out of a narrative construction into the (still narrative) world where he has been concocting it, still a powerless concubine spieling to save his life in the presence of a now-exhausted, bored, too-knowledgeable man. (For Dr. Mickler has come to the end of his own tether and is ready not only to retire from professional life but to give up hope.)

Feminization is certainly a recurring theme in Johnny Depp's work onscreen. From the oddly eccentric and delicate Edward Scissorhands to the distinctively effete Ichabod Crane, from the prettified Wade "Cry-Baby" Walker to the prostitute in Julian Schnabel's

Before Night Falls, not to mention Ed Wood, he has provided a range of what might be called "sensitive" characterizations, ones in which his character's capacity includes, notably, to feel sensation, and to revel in the pleasure of that feeling. These performances have been balanced by what might be called "extremes of masculinity," to wit, the desperate Dean Corso in *The Ninth Gate,* the Machiavellian protagonist/trickster in *Donnie Brasco,* and so on. Between these types, one might position Raoul Duke in *Fear and Loathing:* a personage trapped in the sensorial whirl of an extended hallucination but evoking incessantly the dominating energy of an active agent who penetrates the scene in which he is caught.

In *Don Juan DeMarco,* the rhetoric of gender is embodied through degrees of masquerade, the male being configured as a reduction, even a denudation, and the female being elaborated as painted and decorated mask. Gulbeyaz and the girls of the harem typify, by extrematizing, femaleness through make-up, costume, and the construction of surface. Mickler, exploding out of his lounge suits, unconcealable in his bulk and honesty, typifies masculinity. Though Don Juan affiliates with Mickler, both out of respect and out of powerlessness, he constructs himself as a female character (it is Johnny DeMarco who constructs himself as male). The floor-length flowing black cape, the sombrero, the mask, the rose he dangles and leaves with his lovers—all these are elements of embellishment. The facial hair is a kind of make-up. So, too, is the notably concocted "Spanish" accent, exaggerated and hollow when he pronounces the name of his beloved "Doh-nah Hool-yah." While the decorous dressing, choreographic body movement, flamboyance of gesture and elocution are all configured within the overall narrative as symbolizing a gracile European masculinity of an age gone by, the patriarchal masculinity of a romantic age of chivalry and heroism in which such heroes as Don Juan might really have lived to duel at swords, make love to a thousand women, and swoon at sunset, an age that might at least have been the screen world of the 1920s and silent film, still, in contrast to Mickler's matter-of-factness and bluntness it is difficult to read Don Juan as anything but effete, which is to say, in terms of that patriarchal world, hypercivilized and feminized.

And if inside Mickler's stodgy masculinity there reposes the spirit of exactly such a feelingful, demonstrative being as Don Juan seems to be, if because of this affinity Mickler is to be believed susceptible to the charms of Don Juan and the bearer of some kind of fraternal feeling, still it may be too much of a leap for the chauvinist audience to tell itself that inside the male performance as we know it, the performance apotheosized by Mickler, is the tenderer presence of a woman. Thus, in front of others (Mickler's colleagues, who stand in for the audience), DeMarco's therapeutic bond to Mickler (DeMarco's ability to claim that Mickler has cured him) must exemplify a male-to-male relationship. That is why, in the climactic moment of Don Juan's incarceration, as he brings himself to the staff table for a hearing with a judge (a critical viewer), he appears without mask, without costume, without Spanish accent, without affectation. To convince this pillar of the bourgeois community—by which must be understood, in this still-patriarchal day and age, a man who would have no truck with the idea that every man is most truly a woman— Don Juan must just be nothing but a boy from Brooklyn, tell the story of his life in the simplest, most journalistic terms. In this scene, the staff of the clinic are seated at the table, and aghast at what they detect to be the duplicity of the patient. Especially aghast, of course, is Bob Dishy as clinic director Dr. Paul Showalter, himself the leading promoter of drug therapy and long-time institutionalization for DeMarco. But the judge believes Johnny and sets him free. Patiently observing the proceedings, from a seat in the rear, is the ever-attentive Mickler. At film's end, we see him fly off with his wife and Don Juan to take up residence "forever" on a deserted island, where Don Juan can find Doña Ana (Géraldine Pailhas), the lost love of his life, and where Mickler and his wife can waltz off into the always-promising sunset.

Has the masculinized Mickler been seduced, however, by the feminized Don Juan, the womanizer inside whom there resides a female spirit? Or has he bonded with a masculinized boy who lurks still deeper inside that spirit enacting and mobilizing it throughout the film? Or is an even more original, poetic, feminine spirit hiding still deeper inside that boy? We never find explicit answers to these questions. But as he dances off under the final credit roll, Mickler is noticeably graceful and mannered, even delicate.* He seems to be Don Octavio de Flores once again, and perhaps this is his true self after all.

---

* This dance, indeed, is carefully choreographed to be a reprise of the one performed by Brando with Talia Shire, as Don Corleone gives his daughter away in marriage in *The Godfather* (1972).

Unavoidable in response to Depp's performance in this film, both as Johnny and as Don Juan and as the delicious concubine, are two considerations. First, far from seeming a young man exquisitely suited to playing a girl; that is, far from raising the thought of gender transgressiveness or arbitration through a not-so-subtle suggestion that his masculinity is purely performative, what I think he leaves us with is the suspicion that masculinity does not exist, even in masquerade. If a theory of gender performativity would suggest a gender identity that is completely laid on, constructed, without verifiable basis in substance; yet still that thin identity is essentially derived as binary; and even if one is but gendered in surface, as it were, there are a limited number of clearly discernible models from which performances can be made. Depp here, however, seems not only arbitrary and performed, but also never quite "male" and never quite "female." In the opening sequence of the film he lures from her table in an exclusive hotel a beautiful woman who is waiting for a man; making love to her in a room upstairs he seems to produce an orgasm that is operatic, indeed coloratura—"I wonder, does a Stradivarius violin feel the same rapture as the violinist when he coaxes a single perfect note from its heart?"—but the sound recording of the woman's vocal release is synchronized with the utter silence of his movement as seen from above (that is, a position in which we cannot see his mouth). The sound we are hearing, then, is also the sound of him. By contrast: when as the Sultan's concubine he is shuffling down the colonnade with the eunuch, he is a little bow-legged and he moves with a trace of the Chaplinesque wiggle we saw displayed by his character Sam in Jeremiah Chechik's *Benny & Joon*. There are many other examples in *Don Juan* of Depp's gender equivocation. In short, he is a principal agent for a gender that is not only cultural and arbitrary but also, even in the glory of its performance, indeterminate.

And indeed, anyone in the film whose gender seems more than indeterminate—the staff at the psychiatric facility; Don Juan's many lovers; even his fabled Doña Ana—seems utterly fake. As Mickler's wife, Faye Dunaway is gaunt, uncertain, meditative, playful, anything but seductive in a traditional "feminine" way, and so she is believable as real, real because indeterminate. Part of Dunaway's reality, too, is her systematic avoidance of the attempt to express reality, to project; and so she seems utterly human. "Early on," she writes,

"Bill Alfred gave me as a motto 'Silence, Exile, and Cunning,' from James Joyce's *Portrait of the Artist as a Young Man*. I took it as my motto then and still hold fast to it today. I have given it to my friend Johnny Depp too, and we both live by it. It's meant to be the credo of an actor. It's the only way you can survive. Silence, exile, and cunning" (Dunaway 1995, 225).

Secondly, the episode in the Sultanate invokes the theme of Orientalism. For it is surely not out of Arabic history and experience, politics, sensibility, or sociolegal understanding that the Sultan, the Sultana, the eunuch, or the harem have been created. Products of the Western imagination, to be sure, are the idea of the lusty dusky wife, writhing in her Eastern silks; or the image of the perverse Sultan, fatuous in his eagerness for pleasure of any variety while at the same time controlling vast and uncountable sums—sums, presumably, not only of rubies and dinari but also of sexual cupidity, corporeal desire, and capacity for physical abuse. In such a portrait it is not difficult to recognize the condition described by Edward Said: "The Orient idioms became frequent, and these idioms took firm hold in European discourse. Beneath the idioms there was a layer of doctrine about the Orient; this doctrine was fashioned out of the experiences of many Europeans, all of them converging upon such essential aspects of the Orient as the Oriental character, Oriental despotism, Oriental sensuality, and the like" (1979, 203).

But to go so far as to conclude, with Said, that in watching such a sequence as this any viewer might become "consequently a racist, an imperialist, and almost totally ethnocentric" (204) is a hermeneutic indulgence, an excess if not political than philosophical. This is because of the distinctively fabular and distancing nature of the sequence, and indeed of the film—the sense we have engaging with this material that it is at one and the same time a trap for our illusion and imagination and an insubstantiality, a dream. Some would claim, "a dream, indeed!," protesting that if the Orient of the despot and the sensualist is a dream it is only or principally an Orientalist's "dream," that it is nothing but a product of the machinery of the Western cultural imagination, which is a mainstay and underpinning of the imperialist project. As experienced by the sleeper, a dream is far less coherent, far more engaging, than the most hegemonic cultural project. Cultural constructions are, in a way, the abstraction and generalization of myths and repressions through a fixing and focusing social organization and technology. Yet the dream itself is also pure poeisis, born, to be sure, of cultural arrangement as much as of personal affect and memory; but developed in a nonlinear, unproductive, unalloyable form. The dream does not inform and educate; it mystifies and makes us wonder. It is clear in *Don Juan DeMarco* not that the Sultanate is narratively real, and is thus born in a reality and directed toward a reality, but that the Sultanate is *only* narratively real, that it constitutes a domain locatable nowhere but in the ethereal territory that is the imagination of an imagination's imagination (for the Don Juan who invokes it is a figment of the mind of a young man who is himself the figment of a filmmaker's mind). The Sultanate is a parody of the Orientalist's projection critiqued by Said and a parody, to go further, positioned on the softest of groundings—hyperfiction. Exactly as Depp's gender is indeterminate therein, so is his ethnicity.

And it is vital to the project of the film itself that such a gauziness and ephemerality characterize the slave boy here, since he must in the end be established most clearly as an invention-within-an-invention, a fabrication made up by a fabrication, Don Juan DeMarco. Don Juan is a fabrication, to be sure, that we choose to accept and reside with, through the agency of Mickler, our bureaucratic, scientific, rational, and discursive alter ego. It is, in the end, our awareness of Mickler's awareness and Johnny DeMarco's awareness that fictionalization is going on that keeps the film from becoming a slide into psychosis.

A word about a word. After Don Juan leaves his mother, it is not merely to a Sultanate that he is brought but an "obscure" Sultanate. This suggests, of course, darkness, the darkness of duskiness and otherness, but also the darkness of dream and intimation. Yet even more precisely, the obscurity of the obscure Sultanate aligns it with the dark room, not only the unconscious but the *camera obscura,* the locus of shadows. And exactly as the Sultan is obscure, being a subject of the camera, so is the Don Juan who "remembers" him, and the Mickler to whom he is giving the tale. Don Juan DeMarco is thus not only a lover and delusionary, he is a filmmaker; and if the Sultanate sequence is a film within this film, Johnny Depp as a slave boy is its star. The esotericism of the Arab, his enormous appeal to the Western imagination, is shared by the Hollywood star. Among other things, Orientalism is glamour.

Donnie (Joe)

We meet Donnie Brasco and get close to him, indeed fear for his life, before we learn that he does not exist.

Ostensibly, Mike Newell's *Donnie Brasco* (1997) is a film about an undercover sting operation aimed at the arrest of certain members of New York crime "families." Central to "Operation Donnie Brasco" is the placement within the close precincts of such a "family," specifically in a bond of trust with the key lieutenant Benjamin "Lefty" Ruggerio (Al Pacino), of FBI Special Agent Joseph Pistone (Depp) who is pretending to be a fence and low-caliber hood named "Donnie Brasco." We see Donnie meet Lefty in a bar, befriend him by revealing professional knowledge about jewels that surpasses Lefty's, and systematically allow Lefty to take him under his wing and bring him into alliance with his friends and business partners who are engaged in graft, theft, and murder. Retreating at night to his hotel room, Pistone makes reports. As his bond with Lefty becomes closer and more emotional, Donnie's activities are made more vulnerable to compromise by the intrusion of inept FBI handlers from D.C. who wish to take over supervision of the case. In the end, he is rescued from his performance just in time, receiving a medal while his wife, Maggie (Anne Heche), whose fear and frustration at his long absences from real family life have led her to the brink of divorce, obediently watches.

Any discussion of the film per se would have to say much more about the delicious turns of the plot, the astonishing performance by Pacino as a thug who never quite had the chance to climb, and the use of music, editing, and mise-en-scène to establish the drama of mafia life and Donnie's precarious existence within it. But in order to understand Depp's involvement here on more than the surface level, we must see that *Donnie Brasco* is not really a film about the mafia and an FBI operation to nab mobsters. One particular scene, to which I have alluded, is illustrative of a theme that runs deeper and more engagingly in this film.

Lefty, his boss Dominick "Sonny Black" Napolitano (Michael Madsen), Donnie, and some others are going out to dine together at a Japanese restaurant. In the foyer, the host calmly asks the gentlemen to remove their shoes. Meekly, they all comply—except for Donnie, who gruffly refuses. Again and again, in broken English, the Japanese host repeats that it is necessary that shoes be removed. The other boys in the gang cannot understand Donnie's reticence, and they goad him. He claims that his father was killed in Okinawa defending the United States from just such people as this, and accuses them now of coming over here and dictating to Americans. As his wrath boils, the ire of his friends is ignited and they attack the host, pushing him into the bathroom where Donnie finally joins in the beating. The man is left bleeding and unconscious on the floor as Donnie and his friends make their way out into the night. We cut to Donnie later on, despondent in his room, withdrawing a tape recorder from his boot and holding it in his palm as it replays the victim's cries and groans. In a beautiful shot with a rotating camera, the tape recorder in Donnie's hand seems to slowly twist (into a knot) as he listens to the brutality that is the outcome of his performing.

A thematically similar scene takes place later, when Donnie is with Lefty and the boys in Miami. Retreating from the action to a motel where he is to meet his FBI contacts, he has a few moments to catch his breath. As he lies back on a couch with a cold beer can pressed to his temples, a young agent who has been transcribing the Brasco tapes asks what "Forget about it" means: "Everybody's always saying 'Forget about it.'" Here Donnie launches into the linguistic analysis I describe in the first part of this book, demonstrating the subtle pronunciational, situational, and metalinguistic nuances that color the phrase and lend it meaning.

Such sequences as these have no place in a traditional crime film. That the criminals might visit a restaurant is logical, to be sure; even that one of them, a traitor to the cause, might be wearing a "wire";

even that in order to disguise his true status as a mobile microphone placement he might be forced to beat up someone who threatens to engineer the revelation of the microphone. All this is *de rigueur* for any film about the mafia. But not Donnie's artfully scripted explanation to his mobster friends, nor the invocation of his "dead father." In a crime film, action is the subject of the camera. But here, what is central is appearance. More important in the structure of this scene than the violence committed upon the restaurant host is Donnie's clearly demonstrated need not merely to resist the man's attempts to convince him he should remove his shoes, but also to have (and show us) a rationale for such resistance that can be presented openly to his friends. The scene indexes a range of "proper" behaviors: the "proper" behavior of a man joining his friends out for an evening; the "proper" behavior of gentlemen acquiescing to the cultural dictate that they should remove their shoes; and the "proper" behavior, the etiquette, of a mobster in the company of other mobsters, who does not under any circumstances wear a microphone to assist the FBI or in any other way compromise their privacy. Here, however, Donnie is committing a *faux pas* (as Sonny and the boys would have it), not merely insulting the host (and thus compromising *their* performance as proper gentlemen out for a sociable meal) but also insulting the men who are with him by ruining what is in fact truly their social event. He is doing this in order to cover yet a greater—indeed, for him a lethal—insult: that he is not who he claims to be and is recording their every word.

Central to the scene as performed by Pistone as Brasco (and, thus, by Depp as Pistone) is Brasco's ruination of the dining experience by puncturing civil decorum (this decorum constituting for the Mafiosi a covering mask to hide their own subterranean activities and motives). And the explanation about the father is to cover that insult, to give Brasco a legitimate reason, in Sonny's eyes, for being angry about being asked to remove his shoes. The dynamic of the scene is Brasco's unavoidable production of an insult (unfamiliar with Japanese restaurants, perhaps; or at least unprepared for what would happen in this one, he did not take pains ahead of time to *avoid* putting surveillance equipment in a shoe that would have to be removed), an insult, further, that could ultimately ruin his performance if his dining companions choose not to humor him (gentlemen in this gang go out of their way not to offer one another insults of the sort he is now offering). For Brasco here, not to provide a cover story is to risk severe consequences—to be thought, perhaps, a man who is not everything he is pretending to be: a true member of the gang has, under normal circumstances, couth. For a person like Donnie in a circumstance like this a suspicious thought—on, say, Lefty's part—can be the beginning of a disaster. Indeed, we are shown Lefty watching Donnie throughout the episode: watching with great care and precision but also with great tact and delicacy. He, too, must not offer insult.

Now, while the mafia films of Scorsese and Coppola are anthropologies, detailing the ceremonial structure of events, the nature of statuses, and the power relations in such localized communities as we see depicted in *Donnie Brasco,* the latter film is instead arranged so as to convey the dynamic and strategic pitfalls that threaten someone who is *not* a bona fide member of such a community but who is pretending to be one. In that sense, the film could have been set in any community (all communities require socialization and performance) but by telling this particular story Newell can raise the stakes on Pistone's performance of Brasco; here, treason—inauthentic performance—is cause for instant elimination. The scene in the Japanese restaurant is specifically *not* a cultural description of proper hoodlum etiquette; it is a dynamic exploration of what can go wrong for Donnie, what is likely to go wrong, and what he must do on the spur of the moment to head misfortune off at the pass. As such, the scene requires etiquette, but is not *about* the structure and delicacy of that etiquette in itself. It is a scene in which we see a tour de force of improvisation—improvisation *in extremis,* indeed, since it leads to sincere brutality. And the scene itself is in the film specifically to make possible a display of this improvisation.

Suggested here, somewhat obliquely, is the possibility that all these boys are putting on performances of the sort that occupies Donnie's attention; that any one of them might have a lot to lose because of some as-yet-undetected problem that is hidden—but not in a boot. Reality—negotiated and interactional social life—is little more than a complex arrangement of such performances as this. Yet Donnie is giving a different kind of performance entirely. We are not seeing Donnie performing as Donnie; we are seeing Joe Pistone performing as Donnie, a fact sometimes hard to remember since the scenes of Joe returning to his home in New Jersey, sneaking into his wife's bed in the middle of the night, and leaving before dawn are placed with such dexterity and sparseness in the film we never find broken—or lose—the engaged commitment that has been fostered in us—and fostered in Lefty and his gang as well—that Donnie is nobody but Donnie, day and night.

The Japanese restaurant scene is about the difficulty, and cost, of an actor's maintenance of performance under debilitating conditions. It suggests something about commitment to role and to the business of sustaining role, and a great deal about the need to stand a performance on a material ground that can hardly be accurately predicted in advance. If it is a scene about performance in everyday life—behaving "nicely" when one goes out for dinner—it is also about staging an artificial role; therefore both "performance" and performance, both social life as viewed through the metaphor of the stage and actual stage business. Joe Pistone is engaged in stage business when he mounts Donnie Brasco; and this Donnie must be a Donnie who can be engaged in the performance of everyday life as other gang members would be, when he makes excuses for not taking off his shoes. Actors, then, must play characters who act.

(That, of course, is what Al Pacino and Johnny Depp are both doing in this film, Pacino the more silently since Lefty is not an FBI agent pretending to be a hood, even though his every move is being watched by his superiors.)

The film, then, is about acting, not crime, and the Miami motel room linguistic analysis scene is nothing less than a visit backstage of the staged stage (the stage on which Pistone has Donnie performing), where some novices get to study with the master by examining his method of reading the script. "Show us how many ways there are to read this line," they may as well be saying. And as Pistone, affectionately putting on and taking off Brasco just for them, Depp does. But is it not remarkable in a way that in this film about classical acting, the star should be none other than Johnny Depp, the actor so many viewers and critics believe is simply made by the bizarreness of his roles? In the Miami motel room scene—a scene, by the way, so dependent on nuances of vocalization it is impossible to render it properly on the page—we see Depp's Pistone as a profoundly accomplished technical actor, one who has a keen ear and a precise sense of timing. To recall, or re-view, the Japanese restaurant scene in light of this scene is to see a masterful performance, produced out of thin air by an actor (Pistone) who could have had no warning he would need to produce it. In many Japanese restaurants, after all, hosts are quite willing to abide stodgy Western customers who wish to retain their shoes; who could have predicted the neurotic obsessiveness of this particular man, or his adamance, as it may also be, in the face of Donnie's open insult? Depp's genius is to convey the sense of Pistone's sudden improvisation.

Often in matters of performance production, an issue of central strain is the maintenance of coherence in the face of what might be understood as centrifugal pressures threatening to lead to fragmentation, puncturing, or invidious contexting. To understand performance, given such possibilities, is to see the opportunities for disrupting it. Every performance is to some degree the defense against such disruption that concerted energies, or merely everyday contingencies, can provide. Briefly to reconsider the two scenes I have mentioned as shields: in the Japanese restaurant, inadvertent collision with a highly ritualized personality puts Brasco in the position of having to "make a scene," since for purely technical reasons there is no way he can actually remove his boots without his performance coming completely undone. (And what is fragile is not only his performance here, tonight, in this place; but also the coherence and continuity of his performance earlier, in every scene these men have met him in.) Every performance involves itself, after all, with structuring dissimulations in an ongoing way and with a view to incorporating—overtly or not—some accounts that can cover what is happening and other accounts that can explain unpredictable twists, adaptations, and muffings. But a secret "wire" is no muffing. Given the extreme confidentiality, not to say unholy secrecy, about all aspects of the relationships shared by men such as these mobsters, no account is imaginable that could explain how one of them could be at one and the same time both legitimate as a member of the secret society and at the other a wearer of recording equipment that could make possible a public legal record of private conversations. Nor is one always and inevitably in a position to predict in advance which restaurant one's colleagues will bring one to. So Brasco's predicament is caused by a contradiction between the flow of the narrative in which he has embedded himself (the future thrust upon him by his friends because of their decision to eat sushi) and the repertory of accounts available to someone playing in this company. Therefore, that Pistone's "Brasco" is susceptible to such easy destruction is a fate no actor playing a role could negotiate any better than he spontaneously does in this scene, inventing a story, to be sure, that includes patriotism, filial loyalty, enemies, and the male preserve of war—exactly such themes as Sonny and his friends would appreciate.

The "forget about it" scene is yet another sketch of an actor's vulnerabilities, this time a little slyer. While Brasco's happy mutterings to his young colleagues are little more than an easy affirmation of his skill—acoustic, vocal, mnemonic, linguistic—the telltale markers in this scene are the facial and vocal expressions of the friends who are so curious about mafia lingo. Their cultural distance from it; their innocent giggling as they try to imitate Donnie like so many avid groupies; their apparent inability to appreciate the delicacy of the work he is doing (as evidenced by the delicacy of the renditions he is providing for them, even as he nurses a migraine and tries to treat himself to a backstage break), all suggest rather forcefully how dependent this star is on those in the wings who support his performance and also how unprepared these supporters are to lend real support. They cling to him from beneath and from the sides as mere impressions of extrinsic support; and their behavior and naive admiration—that is, their lack of blasé comprehension—blatantly signal, if not to us then surely to Pistone, how vulnerable he is while running their game. In truth these agents, or others exactly like them, are soon to be responsible for a colossal goof-up that almost rings the curtain down on the Brasco skit—this is the provision of the yacht from the Abscam affair, a utility that could be available only to government agents, put forward as a venue Donnie could reasonably have access to because of his personal mob connections.

Still another interesting moment of vulnerability for Donnie occurs without warning at the Miami airport, when a U.S. Attorney heading home on business comes across him by accident. In Donnie's Hawaiian shirt, Pistone is confabulating with Sonny Black when a voice comes from behind: "Joe? Joe Pistone? Remember me? Southern District?" Under Sonny's eyes he lands a powerful right on the man's jaw, dropping him to the ground. "What're you doin'?" says Sonny. "Grabbed my cock," says Donnie, walking away briskly. "Fuck'n degenerate bastard. What a sick fuck. Grabbed my cock."

To his confederate, Richie Gazzo (Rocco Sisto), an FBI informer who has been working in Florida for some time, as they ride the escalator out of the building, he says, "Get me on the next flight back." And when Richie, nothing if not an incompetent, says, "Yes, Joe," he becomes vicious. "You call me Joe again, I'll cut off your tongue. Piece of shit."

In this invidious contexting we see a simple demonstration of how simple role conflict—a normal aspect of everyday life in our highly mobile society, with its demands upon individuals to act in a number of often incompatible capacities and wearing often incomparable faces in front of different audiences at different times—can escalate into performance crisis. Typically, as we interact in social situations, the identities, attitudes, and alignments we put forward as sincerely meant are taken by others with a certain flexible seriousness, since the others who are watching us are themselves obliged to manifest multiple performances. As Susan Sontag writes, in her essay "On Style," "The human will is capable of an indefinite number of stances" (1966, 32). When my doctor takes my blood pressure during a routine office visit, for example, I enact the role of the compliant and attentive patient; yet he is hardly so nonplussed when I break from this performance to gasp at his flashy new palm pilot and ask where he got it that he can't smile proudly and tell me. If he is less likely than I am, for dramaturgical reasons connected with his professional status, to break from performance, he is not altogether unable to do so, and his ability to accept my breakout is linked to his awareness, and mine, that circumstances can just as easily disrupt his performance—a bevy of fire engines screaming by on the street outside, for example. In all this, the fragility and flexibility of performance is a guarantee of tolerance on both sides, since every performer knows himself and all other performers to be vulnerable to "normal" perturbations in the foundational circumstances upon which a performance must stand. In cat-and-mouse games, however—and the relationship between mafia criminals in New York and the Federal Bureau of Investigation is certainly a cat-and-mouse game—the rules of engagement are considerably stricter, since on both sides of every encounter, every moment constitutes a possible occasion for the penetration of one's proximate space by life-threatening forces (see Goffman 1971). Here, the very fact of performance evaporates to reveal a commitment to self and others as being sincerely engaged in whatever is done. Just as the FBI agents are hardly mounting their dangerous and expensive routine only in order to discover that Lefty Ruggerio is merely playing at being a thug, so Lefty and his associates are not willing to learn out of their association with Donnie Brasco that he is in truth a federal agent and not the collaborator they take him to be. Pistone's performance as Brasco must therefore be played out on a knife's edge, each step being of necessity a construction vulnerable to interference that can be lethal.

Nor is an actor's ability to sustain a performance in front of an audience dependent only on variables local to a scene. Vital also are the actions of supporting players; the knowledge and preparation of those hidden in the wings; and the nature and origin of costume, prop, or script elements in current employ. The characterization must have a suitable emotional tone and reflex sensibility, a feelingfulness, which can be utterly at odds with what the actor considers to be natural or appropriate to his backstage "real" persona. To put this most extremely, actors who portray frightening and vicious killers onscreen (the chilling Henry Silva, for example, in *The Manchurian Candidate* [1962]) need not in "real life" be frightening or vicious; may be (as I discovered) kindly, civil, genteel, and good-natured backstage or off-camera. From his wife's responses to him, it is evident to us that Joe Pistone is nothing at all like Donnie Brasco; and yet, through the duration of his performance, which is in fact going on much longer than she would wish (although, ironically, just long enough to occupy the center of this film), he is becoming steadily less like "himself" and more like the character he is playing. Joe Pistone, in short, is a method actor. While we may have good reason for wishing to interpret Johnny Depp in the same way, of him we have no evidence.

One of the obstructions to the coherence of "Brasco," then, is the pressure put upon Pistone by his wife—at a geographical remove, her potential to disrupt his performance played out entirely from "offstage"—whenever he speaks to her secretly on the telephone or drops home for a quick visit, pressure entirely understandable in objective terms while at the same time constituting an irritant for the viewer, who is identifying with the actor's travails, not the wife's—all this notwithstanding that, of course, this "wife" is yet another actor. This in two senses: she is Anne Heche pretending to be Maggie Pistone; but also, as Pistone's wife, she is devoted to putting up the image of the happily married mother of his daughters in the face of growing fears that she is losing him either to his job or to the people he is meeting while doing it.

I want to suggest briefly two other significant sources of vulnerability for Pistone, since these bracket the performance as a structured entity, and since they are responsible for our greatest moments of empathetic engagement. The first is Pistone's relation with his FBI superiors, specifically Dean Blandford (Gerry Becker). The second is his friendship with Lefty Ruggerio, the man he is working hard to finger.

Blandford is a paragon of the sniveling bureaucrat, a man whose power masks his ineffectuality and incompetence. He thus represents the limiting case of the unhelpful producer, whose actions cannot possibly be predicted to support an actor's performance. In the Miami motel safe room, Joe reports a connection with a boss named Santo Traficante; Traficante would like to be able to go out for a day on a yacht. If they can get a suitable vessel, they can possibly get Donnie close to the man. But Blandford balks at springing for the $6,000 it will take to rent the boat, notwithstanding the fact that Traficante is the "boss of Florida"—in short, a "catch" of inestimable proportions. Blandford also refuses to tolerate the street language that comes out of Pistone's mouth as he continues to play out Donnie backstage: "We're going to have to wash your mouth out, bud. I'm a Mormon, mister. Now, clean it up." Then it becomes apparent he has made arrangements for Joe to be equipped with malfunctioning tape equipment. When one of the agents complains amicably about the quality of the tapes, Joe grabs the machine, smashes it against the wall, gives Blandford a look that could kill, and leaves the room. "We're getting what we want," Blandford says softly. "Fuck him."

The agency for which Pistone is working is represented in the film as being ill-equipped to support the rigorous sort of performance he is capable of giving, and the tension between his devotion as a performer and the agency's systematic casualness—exemplified by Blandford's hesitations and Gazzo's stupidity—is shown as the source of a major performance vulnerability. A second source is a tension within Pistone, caused by the fact that he has allowed himself to identify with Lefty Ruggerio, the man he is in place to catch. The social proximity that is the keystone of Pistone's performance, after all, cuts two ways: he comes close enough to get information reserved for intimates only, and he at the same time develops the affections and sensitivities one comes to have for one's friends. He goes to Lefty's apartment for Christmas dinner, becomes concerned about Lefty's heroin-using son, is himself transformed into the dutiful son/apprentice Lefty has not yet had, and learns so much from Lefty's generous teaching that he wants to save money (earned on a gig arranged by Lefty) to give to Lefty so that he can buy the yacht of his dreams and sail away from this sordid life. As played by Pacino, Lefty is capable of murder, to be sure, but is essentially a Beat philosopher, witty, somewhat sensitive, extremely loyal. Donnie knows that when the jig is up Lefty will most certainly be executed by his own superiors for taking him on as protégé: "Donnie Brasco—he's a friend of mine," runs the first mantra of kinship, soon to be followed by "Donnie—he's a friend of ours." If he can manage to get Lefty the cash and persuade him to just fly off, possibly he can save the old man's life. Persuasion isn't Donnie's strong suit, however. Lefty keeps his place in the hierarchy, Donnie is ultimately revealed as an agent in disguise, and Lefty walks off to his own execution at film's end. But the viewer is smitten with the fear that Donnie's personal loyalty to Lefty will outstrip his self-consciousness as a performer in character; and that he will make a slip. Our need to feel that Pistone is a feelingful human being is dramatized through the opportunity afforded us to identify with Donnie's friendship with Lefty. He must experience performance vulnerability in order for us to continue to like him.

Then, finally, it is worth noting what is remarkable about Depp's performance in this film, namely, that while in fact he presents to us nothing but Joe Pistone, from start to finish, he does this in such a way as to convince us, most of the time and also most profoundly, that we are in the presence of Donnie Brasco, a Donnie Brasco, indeed, who is nothing at all. What Pistone does to Lefty Ruggerio, in short, Depp does to the viewer. Yet, just as he allows us to meet and be close to Donnie, he shows us that Donnie is being put on. "Donnie" is at once the novice entering the gang of professionals and meriting our sympathy for his youth, his innocence, his desire, his sincerity, and his ambition; and a creation of a professional outsider using the mask of "novice" as a cover for his uninvited intervention. But Depp has us precisely balanced on the edge between watching the novice and watching the outsider, watching "Donnie" and watching "Joe." Which one is it that we feel close to, worried about, eager for? He manages, then, to confound us as we identify with the role, much as Pistone's wife claims she is increasingly confounded herself. The performance gives a tremendously ingratiating and absorbing sense of realism—all Pistone's efforts to muster an act seem to be Donnie's efforts to muster merit. The harder Pistone works, directly in front of our eyes, the more he disappears for us and the airy creature he is building takes on proportion, gravity, and pulse.

At the conclusion of the film, once the operation has been wound up, there is cause for happiness, since everything Pistone was working to achieve is now securely in the bag. But the moment is cold, bureaucratic, deeply depressing. Watching Joe Pistone being photographed with his award feels like attending Donnie Brasco's funeral—even this a deft fabrication and hook for our sentiment, since the Donnie Brasco we and Lefty came to love and adopt never lived for a moment and was never, though we could not take our eyes off him, there.

GLen

G len Lantz in Wes Craven's *A Nightmare on Elm Street* (1984) is a cardboard figure seen against a cardboard ground, that of the suburban culture of a cadre of high school students, longtime friends and make-out partners, who are being tormented by an invisible and seemingly all-powerful force from The Beyond. The Force is Freddy Kreuger, the ghost of a dead child-killer, who torments the children of the people who burned him alive by inhabiting their dreams, especially dreams set in boiler rooms, gardens, and other closeted spaces. While the kids giggle in the bedroom of some of their parents, who are away for the weekend, or walk down the corridors of the high school, or go for a late evening stroll in the too-quiet neighborhood, they are prone to being sucked into another dimension by this bloodthirsty, hideous zombie-beast/killer who dispatches them in what seems to be a ravenous gulp and spits back their blood for all to see and be mortified by. The action of the film is a simple repetition of this mantra, proceeding through the members of the group with tedious (and pornographic) persistence, until only one is left alive, but as a figure in the "carpet" of this action Glen stands out as bizarre and interesting.

He is, from the moment we meet him in this, Johnny Depp's first film, and also throughout the action until the moment of his own horrible death, hardly other than a purely oneiric being, caught, as it were, between the quotidian world of well-socialized middle-class children playing "grown-up" in their bourgeois parents' constraining environment and the poetic, distorted, revolutionary world of fictions, inventions, aspirations, and feelings. Glen is a dreamer, to be sure, and also something of a dream.

In our first glimpse of him, he is tall and slender, not muscular—sensual rather than active. Wes Craven admits he had not been particularly interested in casting him, until his adolescent daughter went gaga, raving about Johnny as a "fox" (Heard 2001, 15). His medium length hair is cut in Romanesque, statuary style, and he sports a baby blue angora sweater, soft and receding, alluring and perfectly unprotective. He moves with grace and speaks softly, saying relatively little. His aquiline looks, his dark skin, the radiant blue sweater, the slender delicacy of his posture—all these suggest distance, emotiveness, poetry. We discover that while Rod (Jsu Garcia [as Nick Corri]) and Tina (Amanda Wyss) engage in sex, Glen listens, his huge eyes imagining the scene and at the same time seeming to transcend it, as though he is not quite awake to his own awkward position as a sexual being ritually excluded from the sexual action. "Morality sucks," says he, turning over and going to sleep. He is ostensibly talking about his girlfriend, Nancy (Heather Langenkamp), who won't put out before marriage; but just as much he is referring to himself.

The condition of not being awake recurs in *Nightmare* in a disturbing way, since it is while people dream that ghostly Freddy seizes and captures them into his hideous "world."

What Glen Lantz is not awake to is a central issue in this film. Most curiously, he has difficulty staying awake at all, frequently dropping off into a daydream or a doze, or being caught by his friends in a state of slumber. Nancy, for instance, has become terrified to fall asleep, convinced that the ghostly serial killer will capture her the moment she slips out of waking life. Yet her need for sleep has become overwhelming. She makes a bargain with Glen to sit by the side of her bed and to awaken her if she screams; it is only with the security of his calm presence by her bedside that she feels the confidence to depart from waking life. Indeed, she falls into precisely the sort of chilling nightmare she feared, walking the empty streets to her father's jail (he is the local police constable), where Rod lies in his cell, arrested for murdering Tina. We too are invited into this nightmare—it becomes a film-within-the-film—crawling out the window with her and walking terrified down the empty sidewalks in the darkness of night, with sure conviction a murderer is lying in wait. At the jail window she peers down to see Rod sleeping and Freddy slinking into his cell. As in this dream she screams for Glen, whose promise to watch over her has not produced his actual presence there, Freddy comes after her. Soon we are jolted out of the film-within-the-film back to Nancy's bedroom, where she is jerking hysterically in her bed. But Glen, his innocent promises abandoned in his oneiric nature, has fallen asleep at his post!

Together, and awake now, they run to the jail, insisting that something is wrong in Rod's cell. The father and his assistant resist their pleas to look in on Rod. When finally all of them do, the boy has been strung up by a bedsheet.

Glen's death scene is particularly gory. He tells his mother he is going to stay up to watch Miss Nude America on television. "How can you listen to your stereo and watch television at the same time? You won't hear what she says," says the ditzy mother (Sandy Lipton). "I don't care what she says," says the predictable teenage boy. He's flaked on his bed, the television propped on his thighs, headphones in place over his ears, and he's as asleep as asleep can be. Suddenly Freddy's razor-fingered hands reach up from the bed and draw him down into the mattress, quite as swiftly as though he were being devoured by a crocodile while floating on the surface of the Zambesi. The torso clad in a football jersey, the headphone, the legs in their sweat pants—it's all sucked under with a single yelp. Then, as though every adolescent in the universe has contributed to its strength, a massive gusher of blood erupts from the bed, rises up to the ceiling, and creates an inverted pool, dark, crimson, swirling over the bed. The scene was filmed with a rotating set, like the "You're All the World to Me" routine in *Royal Wedding* (1951). Depp, offered a stunt stand-in, begged to film the scene himself (Heard 2001, 18).

We might ask what is brought to the gentle character of Glen Lantz by the casting of Johnny Depp, even though this very early performance by the actor onscreen hardly makes *Nightmare* a "Johnny Depp" vehicle except to those who treasure every moment of his virtual presence. Yet a reflection on the screen performance of sleep may inform us about the particular character and flavor brought to Glen Lantz by Depp's engagement.

The act of sleeping, like the act of orgasm, the act of tasting food, the act of thought, the act of remembrance or recollection, and, indeed, the act of knowledge, constitutes an activity that is entirely encased in subjectivity. Only an offset indexical trace is provided to the objective observer, and thus to the screen viewer, to indicate its operative presence. It can be said that cinematic sleeping is pure performance in the specific sense of being an act without inner reality; it differs from running, for example, which can be produced as a simulacrum only by an actor who is exerting himself (even on a treadmill). Purely subjective activities are those to which the bounding proprieties of play may conveniently attach themselves. In *Artists and Models* (1955), for example, the poverty-stricken Jerry Lewis shares with his poverty-stricken roommate, Dean Martin, an invisible "meal": they do play-eating, play-tasting the play-food on actually empty plates. In *When Harry Met Sally* (1989), Meg Ryan famously broadcasts a play orgasm. Spy and adventure films are full of moments when protagonists pretend to think in order to gain time. And detective films almost always contain a central moment when the sleuth pretends to know more than he does in order to gain knowledge—often precisely the knowledge he is openly claiming (falsely) to have. There is, finally, hardly a one of us who has never pretended to be asleep. All these play behaviors replicate pure subjectivities. It is exactly the pretense at sleep that Depp is engaged in as Glen Lantz, since the exigencies of film production forbid an actor actually to doze during the making of a take—a very costly process that may have to be repeated numerous times with precisely the same act timed and spaced out in the same way, a trick hard to perform when one is not in conscious control of one's body.

Therefore, *A Nightmare on Elm Street,* organized in many ways around a character who is sleeping or who falls asleep inopportunely, is not only a film about *cauchemar* but also one about subjectivity and its inaccessibility. The theme of the film, in fact, is specifically that Freddy Krueger (Robert Englund), a once-murdered child killer who lived in the same neighborhood as his present-day victims, remains to take vengeance on the community that spurned and neglected him exactly by attempting to inhabit the dreams of its young citizens, by working to penetrate to the core of their subjective experiences. In order to appreciate the appearances of Freddy, it is necessary that we, too, give ourselves to make that penetration, that we agree to acknowledge Freddy as an internal beast, a corpular figment of the imagination, and that we agree to visit the dreamspaces where he roams. We must transcend Glen and his friends, indeed, at least insofar as they exist for us embodied as the actors in this cast, since they do not experience their own subjectivity as we must in order for the film to work. We must see not only what the dreamers dream, but also the dreamers dreaming it, so that the panic of their situations is registered by way of the grimaces on their faces— grimaces they do not see. For his part, Glen, though he sleeps, does not dream, and we never get inside him. Our artful alienation from Depp has thus been present through his entire screen career.

What, now, is it about Johnny Depp that makes him so believable— and believable he must be, above everything else, given that he is acting out a lie—as a boy who is sleeping? In Kusturiça's *Arizona Dream* (1993) and in *Donnie Brasco,* he apparently has an orgasm, and yet there is something too swift, too unsavored, too expeditious, too prodigiously purposive (in the Keynesian sense) about it for us to think the act wholly believable. In *Edward Scissorhands* he tries desperately to eat, but is more believable as a person engaged in trying than as a person engaging an appetite; when he cannot quite manage the food with his scissorhands, neither he nor we are profoundly disappointed. In *Blow,* in *Sleepy Hollow,* and in *From Hell* he is apparently engaged in the subjective act of thinking, and yet in all three films there is a perduring quality of anticipation that takes precedence over cogitation; less than deducing and calculating, he is waiting for something to happen, to reveal itself. What he displays is not intelligence exactly, but patience. So, if subjective experience seems so alien to him, what leads us to believe he could really be sleeping?

I think there are two contradictory and fascinating answers. First, we do not believe Johnny as Glen is sleeping; we suspect exactly that he is pretending to sleep, this because we wish it to be so. The player who gives pretense of sleeping must end his game, and thus his pleasure, by "waking up." And in order to sustain his performance, he must continue it regardless of the distraction from without. The pleasure for the visitor in coming upon such a player is exactly that he can approximate, observe, fantasize interacting with, and even perhaps, delicately, touch the sleeper without apparently being detected. If the sleeper is only a "sleeper," by the way, the visitor to the bedside can imagine that he is himself imagined by the one on the bed, sensed, engaged with, but all in a way that can never announce itself and therefore that need never require the visitor's admission or acknowledgment. The eroticism of the moment is entirely a shared secret that neither party need admit it is sharing. The "sleeper" is not so much a passive and exploited object manipulated by the visitor, as an active and calculating subject who positions himself as a "passive."

Depp has a sculptural form, especially in this film. He epitomizes the human being as described by Justice Holmes: "The soul, having studied the [body] of which it finds itself proprietor, thinks, after a time, it knows it pretty well. But there is this difference between its view and that of a person looking at us:—we look from within, and see nothing but the mould formed by the elements in which we are incased; other observers look from without, and see us as living statues" (1892, 190). The smoothness of his skin, the proportions of his limbs, are all, in *Nightmare,* as if from Donatello. But in order to be beautiful, the sculpture must be sleeping, passive to our tactile regard. That is why the sleeping marble inspires even more than the waking model. As much as Depp is ideal as a sculptural form, it is also true that making him into such a form is a subtle and powerful way of handling Depp, since that form will make it possible for us to admire him in ways that are out of the question when he seems to be able to acknowledge. To see oneself being seen is a source of power; at one point in the film, Glen counsels Nancy to turn her back on Freddy, a gesture that will remove all power from the wraith. Freddy's power, anyone's power, partly resides in the ability to see people seeing him. (All this notwithstanding the fact that every screen character is asleep, that not a single one actually acknowledges our view; yet the opened eyes of those who are "awake" incite and invoke the viewer, even as they make viewing possible for the characters.) "The artist looks only from without," writes Holmes; Depp makes every one of his viewers an artist.

The second reason Depp's sleeping works is perhaps less fantastic. Although a character's seeing (access to sight) is another subjective experience intangible to the cinematic viewer, still we approach it tangentially through the organs of sight that are extremely visible, especially in close-ups. The character with small eyes, or with eyes spaced too widely apart, is easily read as unperceptive. But Depp has enormous and apparently penetrating eyes. While Glen seems very young and innocent, in other words, his gaze suggests a voracious appetite for experience gorging itself on the world. (One always has this sense of visual hunger, watching Depp.) Having used those eyes relentlessly, he is tired. So the sleep we see is the precise analogue of the ocular activity that punctuates the role.*

Johnny's sleep frees us from the power of the gaze that it is relieving. As he recuperates, we can be freed from the captivity we experience, figuratively, in his stare. His stare, of course, is the screen itself (on the gazing screen, see Dixon 1995). When he sleeps, the screen seems momentarily to disappear and we can breathe. Only a figure who uses the gaze as powerfully as he does can make possible the release we obtain when he shuts his eyes.

AXEL

There is a strangely revealing moment early in Emir Kusturiça's *Arizona Dream* (1993). Axel Blackmar (Depp), an erstwhile and meditative employee of the New York City Department of Fisheries, has been lured by his cousin Paul (Vincent Gallo) to drive to Arizona, where their Uncle Leo (Jerry Lewis) is

---

* A particularly engaging and beautiful portrait of a character experiencing vision as wearying is provided in Wim Wenders's *Until the End of the World* (1991).

about to be married (to Millie [Paula Porizkova], a girl young enough, and apparently attractive enough, to be sleeping with Axel instead), and one evening he is sitting with Leo in Leo's pink stucco house watching home movies of himself as a child, his now-deceased parents, and Uncle Leo. Like every other moment in this somewhat hysterical and very moving film (a film touched by what Andrew Horton has called "holy madness" [2002]), this moment is complex and problematic. Axel's parents, it turns out, are dead because Leo killed them—that is, because he was driving the vehicle in which they died. Filled with remorse and a sense of fraternal duty, Leo has taken the young boy under his wing to raise as his own son; and now he wishes Axel to take a job in his Cadillac dealership as a way of passing him a future career. Like a son, though he is not one, Axel is resistant, and has a need for a certain distance from his uncle even though, at the same time, he can never get the memory of the smell of Leo's shaving lotion, from the childhood days of the home movie, out of his mind. Improbably, however—but also with extreme aptness—Leo is Jerry Lewis, and if in his present-day incarnation, storming around the house in an unfitted pink tuxedo and bellowing commands at all and sundry, he seems the epitome of the bourgeois businessman, here in the home movies he is the quintessence of the physical comedian, aping for the camera, pantomiming, dancing in the glorious black-and-white silence that flickers on the screen.

Axel is exhausted, vitiated from his long ride from New York. Leo has obviously been hoping for this moment of reunification for a long time. The two sit side by side in silence, absorbed by what's on the screen; and we hear Axel's voiceover telling us about his childhood as, along with the two men, we watch the movie-within-the-film. Is it the home movie itself that is capturing them? Or the memories welling up inside, which the home movie is triggering? It is clearly evident as we see Axel's and Leo's faces that they are captivated in the presence of these images; but it is equally evident that we are captivated, too—not only by the home movie but also by Kusturiça's moment, which gathers Leo and Axel for us to watch as they watch. We may ask the same questions of our own involvement as we ask about theirs. Is it what's onscreen that is holding us in a freeze? Or is it what we are remembering of our past that the screen is bringing forward in a spasm of light?

But in the middle of this event, the screen "Leo" does something particularly goofy and clownish, and the watching Axel explodes into laughter. At this instant, we are treated to a medium close-up of Johnny laughing, with the black-and-white screen light flickering on his face and his eyes wide open grasping every nuance of the memory from the mnemonic clues spread across the frame of the image. There is something about Johnny's laugh . . .

It is as though the fiction of the filming has been punctured for a moment, and Johnny, not Axel, is present to us. He is present with, of course, two Jerry Lewises, the first sitting silently—even critically—beside him, watching every gesture of his doppelgänger onscreen, both an engaged Leo and an evaluative Jerry; and the second up there in black and white, the professional jester (even if he makes money selling cars), both a professional Jerry and an engaged amateur Leo. It is also as though if Axel is present with Leo, then Johnny is present with Jerry; indeed, Leo is sitting next to Axel/Johnny and they are both watching Jerry: Jerry as Leo, to be sure, but a Leo acting in a particularly "Jerry" way. And in a flash it is clear that if the Johnny who is laughing is a big Jerry Lewis fan, has been utterly captured by this "Jerry" screen moment, it is also true that, regardless of what the script calls for in terms of Axel's "absorption" with what's on-screen, Johnny, too, is absorbed and has let the absorption leak into his performance. It is in the way the laughter erupts out of him without warning, as though while thinking of what Axel should do next he has suddenly become distracted by the weightlessness of the real moment.

Johnny's is a beautifully modulated, subtle, polite, charming, and innocent laugh. It seems a perfect sign of an untainted, unselfconscious responsiveness, an openness unaffected by learning, experience, canniness, wariness, intuitiveness, or any bent toward exploitation. (The same innocence characterizes his sense of outrage in a television documentary ["Bravo! Documentary"]: to the impertinent question of an inquisitive reporter, upon seeing him with Vanessa Paradis, as to whether or not they are going to get married, he sharply replies, "Are you going to change your underwear tomorrow?") I have heard Roy Orbison described as such an innocent, as such a presence. Johnny's laugh in this moment certainly shocks like a phrase in a Roy Orbison song. When, suddenly, the home movie ends and the scene draws to a close, we feel the grating termination of this innocence, the brutality of the end of Axel's childhood (which is also Johnny's childhood), the crushing pressures ready to impinge upon him in adulthood. Indeed, the film inexorably progresses with Leo's incitements to him; with him taking a job at the dealership; with him meeting Elaine and Grace Stalker (Faye Dunaway, Lili Taylor), moving into their farmhouse, sleeping with Elaine while being in love with Grace, trying to satisfy Elaine by fabricating an airplane for her out of sticks and bicycle parts, running out helpless in the rain too late to stop Grace from shooting herself in the head—in short, growing up. All this brutal maturity is possible, in a way, because of that innocent, genuine laugh.

It is not as though Johnny Depp's smiling face is a rarity. In virtually all his film parts, and in virtually all his publicity photographs and public appearances, Depp provides smiling moments to his many fans and observers, yet it is hardly a natural smile we see. Briefly with Lewis, in front of Lewis, and for Kusturiça, he seems to let down his masks to permit a direct response. Two responses are possible for us—and at once. We may interpret this as Axel having an unguarded moment; and such an interpretation prepares us for the difficulties and pains he will encounter in the future when exactly such unguardedness as this becomes an impossibility for him. And we may see Johnny leaking through Axel, sharing with us a moment of abandon in the presence of the pure comedy we see onscreen. (In *Benny & Joon,* Depp will himself do this kind of comedy, taking off Chaplin and Keaton.)

In *Arizona Dream* there are further moments of striking genuineness and innocence, quite different from this one. In one, Paul is giving a much-anticipated stand-up comedy performance in a talent contest at a local bar. His routine—utterly unappreciated by the audience (in what is a comic turn itself)—is a pantomime version of Cary Grant's performance in the celebrated cornfield scene from Alfred Hitchcock's *North by Northwest* (1959). Along with Elaine and Grace, Axel is seated at a table in the audience raptly watching. Gallo's performance in this sequence, some of it unintended, incorporates an astoundingly accurate rendition of some of Hitchcock's shots, including one of Cary Grant merely standing at the roadside doing nothing for about six seconds; a sense of agony when the cornstalk props turn out to be improperly placed on the stage; a sense of frustration and humiliation at the boorishness of an audience insufficiently familiar with the Hitchcock to appreciate his skill; and a preposterous lack of self-critique in this frustration, as though everyone really should know every shot of any film Paul happens to adore and people who don't really are boors. He is outraged when the judges terminate his performance early and force him offstage before he finishes the Hitchcock sequence—in this outrage becoming a target of laughter for any observer who, like the judges, does not happen to share his predilections. Yet at the same time the scene is deeply moving, even troubling, for those of us who recognize both the Hitchcock and what Paul is trying—so brilliantly—to do. During his performance, Axel is one of these appreciative few, and he bursts into unaffected and genuine laughter. Here, however, we do not get the sense of Depp's naked vulnerability to the moment (and to us).

It seems more as if Axel is laughing than as if Johnny is. In the earlier scene of the home movie, it was a filmic image that had captured both Axel and Johnny—something that could capture anyone watching, and indeed, something just as filmic as the image that *is* capturing us as we watch the scene. Because of the filmic quality of the home movie, in other words, and the general availability of film, Axel is approximated in his viewing to those of us watching him watching. To the extent that the target of his gaze is not just Uncle Leo, however, but Jerry Lewis, Axel the character is himself converted to the actor playing him. At the moment when, watching the home movie, we suddenly realize it is not Leo we are watching but Jerry Lewis "being" Leo, we also suddenly realize it is not Axel laughing at all this but Johnny Depp "being" Axel. In the talent contest scene, however, the target of the gaze is a performance *with only a filmic reference,* a reference in a film that watchers in the scene are not directly and presently watching (even though excerpts of the Hitchcock are cut in for *us*). Indeed, as a performance at all, and as a stand-up comedy performance in particular, it is, to put it mildly, bizarre—thus the jury's disaffection for it. The performance is the more distanced from us, just as it is from those in the bar watching it, exactly because of its generic strangeness.

The generic strangeness obliquely raises for consideration the importance of translation as a structural element in Depp's screen presentation. What, after all, should make Paul's performance strange? It is, like all performances, a translation. Paul is translating Cary Grant's Roger O. Thornhill. Leo Sweetie was pretending onscreen to be a comedian very much like Jerry Lewis. But as Leo Sweetie *is* Jerry Lewis, his pretense is perfect, so much so that he temporarily vanishes. Thus it is that Axel can be enthralled by the verisimilitude of Leo's "Jerry" act. When the act reaches its apotheosis and only Jerry remains, Axel, too, must temporarily disappear, since if Leo was in Arizona Jerry is not. In Paul's case a perfect performance is impossible, *and Paul knows it.* What is hilarious about his routine is that he bravely struggles toward a complete translation of the completely untranslatable Hitchcock scene, even in the face of the impossibility he recognizes. What is remarkable and strange about the home movie scene is that Leo Sweetie (in Lewis's astonishing performance) seems unaware of how perfect his screen performance *can* be: in short, Leo does not know that he is Jerry. And neither—until the home movie unspools—does Axel or Johnny. It is as though Johnny realizes suddenly, and with immense delight, that the Jerry Lewis who is playing Uncle Leo *is also Jerry Lewis!*

Although he is a young actor of considerable talent, Vincent Gallo does not have the performing reputation of Jerry Lewis. So we remain at a further distance as he performs, and can presume that the Johnny Depp beneath Axel does, too. Further supporting this distance is the rivalry between Paul and Axel (exemplified by their spat early in the picture when Paul tries to persuade Axel to come to Arizona with him), and their generally aggressive young male banter throughout the film. More: while Axel is interested in women, airplanes, and direct experience, Paul is interested in movies and, it seems, in movies alone, sitting up late at night with Elaine's huskies cuddling around him speaking John Cazale's lines from *The Godfather, Part II* (1974) word for word as he watches it on television. If Paul is funny he is also strange. If Leo is strange, however, he is also funny!

In short, the bar scene includes what we might call in-character laughter from Axel; just as the home movies scene contains out-of-character laughter from Depp—this judgment possible only insofar as we can imagine a "Depp" relatively less present in the Axel who is with Paul than he is directly with the home movie, a "Depp," for instance, who is more a Jerry Lewis fan than a Vincent Gallo fan. That the two young men—Depp and Gallo—are about the same age, while Depp is young enough to be Lewis's child, assists us in framing these possible offscreen relations. The home movies scene is shocking in its directness of presentation of Depp, and coming early in the film it disaligns us with the conventions of narrative cinema. The vulnerability and genuineness in the bar scene are ostensibly performed, and appertain to the character, not the actor.

A further moment of "screen genuineness" occurs as Grace is playing Russian roulette with Axel in a moment of drunken despair. She makes him promise that he must go through with the game no matter what, and in what seems a moment of reckless innocence, he agrees. Picking up the gun, huge for his slender hand, he spins the barrel, puts it to his head. A shot from above shows him with the barrel beneath his chin. In a close shot he pulls the trigger. Nothing. He gives a quick thought and pulls it again. Nothing. Again—nothing. And again and again. Grace knocks the gun away. "You have to play by the rules." They tumble to the floor and kiss. Here, the innocence of Axel is dramatized through Grace's response to him, first egging him on but then penetrating with her knowing gaze the mask of innocence this innocent is wearing. Once it is clear he is not in his depths a suicidal type (as she clearly is), his life must be spared. What is shocking about the scene is that Grace knows Axel's innocence before he does.

In innocence is the capacity for transformation. The film concludes with an Eskimo sequence, photographed in the tundra. Axel and Leo are side by side in mukluks, chatting (in no known tongue) about a flatfish they hold between them and that finally elevates itself and flies away, this entire scene occurring some time after Leo's death and "flight" to heaven in an airborne ambulance. The conversation is, in effect, Axel's "Arizona dream," although it is shot entirely without the standard conventionalities for narrative dream sequences and seems scarcely more dreamlike than anything else in the film. But the strange and incomprehensible "language" Axel and Leo are speaking dominates here (covered with English subtitles). When "Leo" speaks, it is evidently Jerry speaking in his stead, doing his fractured language routine of great repute. But what is it we hear when "Axel" answers him? Axel, to be sure, responding to the Leo he loves and regrets losing—but also Johnny, trying to be a little like the Jerry Lewis he has had the opportunity to meet and work with in making this film. And Jerry is responding to him, as though he is in truth not only Axel's diegetic but also Johnny's metaphorical uncle, as though Johnny is kin.

WILLIam

The eagle never lost so much time as when he submitted to learn from the crow.

A timid, somewhat brittle-looking white man in spectacles, William Blake (Depp) rides on a train west from Cleveland to the town of Machine, across Indian country, to take up a promised position as clerk in an industrial concern. He is something of an innocent, a "naïve young guy who's trying to get his life together," according to Depp (Goodall 1999, 193); his train ride seems to last forever. (He is on the train. Fade. He is on the train. Fade. He is on the train. Fade. He is on the train. Fade . . .) When he arrives in Machine he learns without delay that the position he had been promised, for which he has traveled across America, was given to someone else almost a year ago. He insists on seeing the owner, Dickinson (Robert Mitchum), who, icily smoking a cheroot, throws him out of his office at riflepoint (silently reprising a scene he played with John Wayne in Howard Hawks's *El Dorado* [1967]). Disconsolate, he wanders the mucky streets. Here he encounters a prostitute, Thel (Mili Avatal), who has been roughly thrown out of a saloon. She brings him home to her hotel room, where they tenderly make love. As they rest, the door is thrown open and her fiancé, Charlie (Gabriel Byrne), strides in. On the spot he shoots the unfaithful Thel dead, his bullet passing clean through her and into William's chest. William shoots him and flees into the night on the dead man's horse. He enters the wilderness. In a state of collapse, he is discovered by an obese Indian named Nobody (Gary Farmer) who leads him through the forests away from the society of white men and away from a posse of hired killers who, on orders from Dickinson (who owns virtually everything in Machine and who is, as it turns out, the dead man's father), seek to bring him down and collect the bounty on his head.

But Nobody lacks the medicine to cure William's wound, and is soon enough assured that his companion is on the road to death. The further they ride into the woods, the more William, slumping on his horse, weakens. Riding together through the splendid wilderness, Nobody and William form a strange bond, since the Indian is familiar with the works of the British poet after whom the "fucking white man" has been named; and the white man, for his part, is lost at this distance from European civilization unless he has his guide. Slowly, however, he loses not only his capacity to sustain life but also his affiliation to European culture. He becomes more a part of the horse he is riding, even as his body tends to collapse in the act of his riding it. At one point he drops to the ground over the body of a felled fawn, embracing it, rubbing its blood upon his face as a ritual mask. The white men these two wanderer-brothers encounter in their travels— camping robbers, the cruel posse, a pair of marshals, a racist who runs a trading post (and offers smallpox-infected blankets, ideal for Indians)—are of progressively less concern to them, seem, indeed, mere phantasms from a remote and barbaric culture. Nobody and William approach the Great Lake. Nobody puts William in a ceremonial canoe and sets him off on his endless journey.

Jim Jarmusch's *Dead Man* (1995) is a film in which Depp must be multiply transformed. His hypercivilized effeminacy becomes a dignified, even regal, masculinity. I do not precisely agree with the astute reading of Michael DeAngelis: "Throughout the narrative, the figure of William Blake maintains an 'outsider' status that sets him apart from the prevailing corrupt practices sanctioned by white men" (2001, 290). "Prevailing corrupt practices" are widely diffused in a culture, through the hegemony; any "innocent" rider on a white man's train is party to those practices, this fact noted by Jarmusch when he has the train move slowly past the site of a massacre apparently perpetrated upon whites by Indians and shows Blake's inclusion among the presumptuous white passengers through his sudden fear, which mirrors theirs. But Blake's whiteness does ultimately dissolve in the relation with Nobody, so that finally, if never an Indian at birth, he is an Indian in death, and he is the hero, suitably reborn, of one version of what Leslie Fiedler calls "the Western story in archetypal form," in which a transplanted WASP confronting a "radically alien other" in the wilderness is led to metamorphose into "something neither White nor Red (sometimes by adoption, sometimes by sheer emulation, but *never* by actual miscegenation)," to fall "not merely out of Europe, but out of the Europeanized West, into an aboriginal and archaic America" (Fiedler 1969, 24–25). William's active stance to both society and his own career position is modified into a receptive, beatific passivity, a merging with all things. And his dependence on human relations, the sociality of his identity, is changed through his dialogue with Nobody into a solitary strength, a personhood, in which he recognizes the idiosyncrasy of his relation to the world, that each man is in nature, that nature speaks to each man.

All this happens in a way that is distinctively reflective, or doubled, since the black-and-white cinematography by Robby Müller gives an incessantly pictorial, even photographic, rendition of this western world. As Benjamin says of the adept of the nineteenth-century panoramas, "The city dweller, whose political superiority over the country is expressed in many ways in the course of the century, attempts to introduce the countryside into the city. In the panoramas the city dilates to become landscape" (1986, 150), so with Jarmusch in his figuration of this film, in which the "dilation" is produced through the exegetical gesture of William's voyage. Each image is both its narrative content and a photographic record and display of this content; our attention is continually moving from the events to the way the events look, here captured with a magnificent luminosity reminiscent of the stunning work of James Wong Howe in, say, *The Outrage* (1964). The world represented, even at its most Europeanized, has been tamed only in a rudimentary, haphazard, arbitrary way, and so the film feels rough and often harsh. There is an insistent presence of cruelty and crime: from the begrimed, and somewhat dopey, engineer (Crispin Glover) stepping back to visit the train passengers in the opening sequence, through the explicit rudeness of Dickinson's clerk (John Hurt) as he attempts to dismiss William, through Dickinson's icy and inhospitable glare, through Charlie Dickinson's rude interruption of the lovers in the hotel room, the shooting, the flight into the woods, the casual makeshift medicine of Nobody, the ugliness of the posse trailing William and the coldbloodedness of its leader, Cole Wilson (Lance Henriksen) (named for the slimy gunfighter played by Jack Palance in *Shane* [1953]). "One can feel obliged to look at photographs that record great cruelties and crimes," writes Susan Sontag: "One should feel obliged to think about what it means to look at them, about the capacity actually to assimilate what they show. . . . All images that display the violation of an attractive body are, to a certain degree, pornographic. But images of the repulsive can also allure" (2003, 95). The film moves from the social to the existential, reflecting the two profundities of Johnny Depp's personality, the two poles that co-exist in a curious tension—his keen and delicate sociability and his Beat loneliness.

It is uniformly social sensitivity, after all, not brutality or savagery in his personality, that leads Depp into rough encounters with the press, with the media, with the police. He does not lash out because he has been subjected to overwhelming natural force, but he becomes irate and often bellicose when people treat him without respect, when interviewers take the liberty of forgoing civil etiquette, when his privacy is invaded. Rather than being coarse in his social relations, he is exceptionally polite, even mannered, taking offense at the predicament of being trapped in a world where most of the people he must encounter know no such courtesies. Indeed, the media environment is as rude and inhospitable a world as can be imagined, with the press of deadlines and the search for the spectacular image or story continually seeming to justify the sort of behavior on writers' and reporters' part that could never pass in civilized society. There is a presumption, for instance, that because stars get paid a lot of money they should feel obliged to reveal everything about themselves to the curious multitudes; that they have made a Faustian deal in exchange for their high salaries to relinquish the rights to privacy of person (person, not territory) that are common in Western society. Depp is very sensitive to this issue, and becomes violent when invaded. In that sense, he is profoundly civil and European, the perfect embodiment of what Nobody scathingly labels the "fucking white man."

Yet at the same time he conveys the impression of having a Beat soul, treating the experience of the moment fully and passionately and detaching it from its problematic embedding in historical narrative; moving forward with openness and sensitivity, with immense drive to get beyond the present, yet without hope; attaching himself to music and the poetic; disregarding bourgeois conventionalities. Even a cursory glance at his film roles in chronological order shows this willingness, even urgent need, to move musically forward always into new territories, without regard for the limits of convention or the dictates of the past. It makes sense that it is Johnny, of all possible actors, who, when William Blake, informed by Nobody that they are being followed, desperately asks, "What should we do?" is given to hear his guide scornfully reply, "The eagle never lost so much time as when he submitted to learn from the crow." (Make your own mind up; you must live with your own mind.)

Dead Man is a poem to the dualism that locks European and native cultures, etiquette and nature, investment and existentialism, capital and tranquillity, murder and music. Johnny Depp has a foot in each of these cultures, and in that respect, centered exclusively on his performance—a performance that is also, as the film progresses, more and more the absence of performance—*Dead Man* is itself a doubling. A doubling that is not, to be sure, an allegory, that mode which, for Gunning, is "willing to court the artificiality that foregrounds significance over depiction" (2000, 27)—but instead a twofold vision, a vision in two directions, a history of the future. On old Dickinson's wall, as he stands pointing his shotgun at the timorous William, is a portrait of himself standing and pointing his shotgun at the portraitist. Here Robert Mitchum, in his final screen performance, is used to epitomize the same two worlds, the brutal exigency of capitalist civilization as reflected in the style of the portrait and the tradition of portraiture; and the poetic, charged, existential uncertainty embodied in the man's powerful living stance. Mitchum bequeaths his legacy to Depp in this scene, in this moment, and, indeed, beneath this canvas. And Jarmusch bequeaths us a vision of ourselves as both agents of the cinematic gesture and witnesses of the dramatic moment.

For double the vision my Eyes do see,
And a double vision is always with me.
                                        William Blake (1802)

EDWARD, GEORGE, JACK, AND BON BON

C omplaining about Ang Lee's "laborious" *Hulk,* David Denby mutters, "Without some sort of pop madness roiling around in the basement of the material—some kind of lawless impulse—a monster movie has very little reason to exist. If a man who turns into a behemoth isn't a metaphor for forbidden human desires, then what does he represent?" (2003a, 84). Setting aside the lawlessness of the monster, or at least his penchant for loitering outside the precincts of civilization as we know it, we might wonder at Denby's thoroughly capitalist reading of the monster film (by which I would include the monster character in the ordinary film). What, after all, but loyalty to capitalism might guide a filmmaker's obsession toward human desire in particular, and forbidden desire at that, as though the yearning *to have* (even to have experience, to have connection), even rendered utterly inappropriate through some process of hideous transformation, really were at the center of the universe?

For Leslie Fiedler, however, the monster, at least the Freak, is

> one of us, the human child of human parents, however altered
> by forces we do not quite understand into something mythic
> and mysterious. . . . Only the true Freak challenges the conven-
> tional boundaries between male and female, sexed and sexless,
> animal and human, large and small, self and other, and conse-
> quently between reality and illusion, experience and fantasy,
> fact and myth. (1978, 24)

In this way, the image of the monster becomes nothing other than an
image of our "secret self," the "I" we have not managed to recognize
and acknowledge as our own. Monstrosity is about being, not having; about knowing, not using; about wondering, not wanting. And
what we see projected onscreen in monster movies is not a semblance
of what we most long to possess as much as a semblance of who we
truly, yet unadmittedly, are.

With Scissors for Hands

Edward Scissorhands's monstrosity is only partly suggested by his
name. He is fitted, to be sure, with slashing, swiping, jabbing, prick-
ing, blades for fingers, long delicate blades, swishing gleaming blades
(reminding us, at moments, of the blade/hands of Freddy Kreuger).
Does he not reflect to us, then, precisely the prodigious difficulty of
having and holding, a kind of capitalist *cauchemar?* He suggests the
ending, the denial, of all we do with our hands that shapes, models,
caresses, senses, and probes the world. Imagine him trying to pick his
nose. Imagine him trying to caress a piece of silk. Imagine him attempting the kind of dexterity that might lead to an oil painting, a
manuscript, masturbation. How, indeed, *does* Edward Scissorhands
masturbate, except not at all? How does he experience any of the
pleasures of the hand? More pressing for him—as we are shown: how
does he manage to sleep on a waterbed? And how does he relieve
himself? Of how he eats we are given some obtuse description in a
scene of family awkwardness at the dinner table, and it seems he eats
little—so there is nothing strange about the fact that he is rather
lithe, and his face seems hollow. Like Hamlet, perhaps, he "eats the
air, promise-crammed." He is also the child of a departed, well-
meaning father left to wander the world gone corrupt.

And what of his mind? What does Edward think about, and how, if, as Frank R. Wilson suggests, "the hand speaks to the brain as surely as the brain speaks to the hand" in an arrangement whereby "the more one looks, the more it appears that the revolutionary hand-brain marriage qualifies as one of *the* defining and unifying themes of human paleoanthropology, of developmental and cognitive psychology, and of behavioral neuroscience" (1998, 291). Edward can surely slash and stab, bisect, and therefore dismember and disassemble, and even articulate (in the original Latin sense of dividing into sections [Wilson 1998, 182]), even if he is not especially *articulate:* i.e., fluent, intelligible, eloquent. But can he use those metal devices to feel, can he hold? Ownership is about grasping, holding, seizing, doling out, in general using the fingers to bring wealth into the palm of the hand. But Edward is without palms. So the image of him draws to our minds the idea of the end of capitalism, the end of ownership, the idea of a state of affairs in which possessing, holding, clenching, retaining, are all quite impossible and indeed undesirable. We see that Edward becomes an artist, a coiffeur's coiffeur. He heralds an age (a Platonic utopia) when artistry is a supreme accomplishment, holding the place in human affairs that possession holds today.

But more than this, with his pouting mouth and innocent, wide-open eyes that seem to query all things—what Jim Jarmusch has called "amazing" eyes (Goodall 1999, 194)—he suggests a human being terrified to desire (not a monster of desire). Desire brings only trouble, as does approaching any person too closely. His monstrosity lies precisely in revealing to us our inescapable dangerousness, that we embrace the world only with peril. If we must remain detached, at a distance, we may fall into the horrid loneliness of lacking and always desiring the human touch; and it is the prospect of this fall that he makes apparent by his good-natured, sweet-mannered, yet utterly hopeless attempts to be fully human.

All this is only part of what is frightening about Edward to those who contemplate him. Even darker and more chilling are his origins. For he began in, and grew in, and inhabited, a remote corner of the world, high on a hill and yet not beyond the boundaries of human perception—a hill at the end of the street, as it were. Behind a great wall, beyond a great garden, he was made. The inventor who made him had at his disposal a grinding, shuffling, groaning apparatus (the music of Danny Elfman is instrumental in establishing the acoustic properties of the inventor's domain and, thus, the charming horror of the film)—nothing, that is, like a biology—and Edward was there put together from parts, slowly, inexorably, musically in a systematic involvement that turned and turned not unlike a waltz. Far below were the lights of human civilization. But the inventor died before finishing his work. Always with Edward Scissorhands, then, one has the sense of an alarming and deeply penetrating subjunctivity, that he *would have been otherwise*. No matter what he is, no matter what presence speaks to any situation, there is a distant prospect, a horizon of possibility, lingering in our consciousness and yet unmanifested. There is an ultimate condition that could not have been realized, and yet was planned. Edward has therefore fallen, and indicates to us all our fallen state, our Lack, if you will.

In watching Johnny Depp performing Edward, then, we have the sense of someone gently, even casually, articulating a distance from the everyday; a remoteness he both strives to overcome and must resign himself to; a knowledge of inconceivable non-existence of the embrace; a gentleness born of the self-knowledge that he is too swiftly and too easily a killer. More: the world is something he must always stand outside, a space in which no objectivity is possible since objects, things, are those that offer resistance to the hands (Ortega). As Cassiel (Otto Sander) says in Wenders's *Faraway, So Close!* (1993), "Only the things we can touch truly exist for us." So for Edward, what he sees is perilously close to illusion. And he warns us of our own vulnerability in this regard, our inability to know because of our own inability to touch comprehensively, purely, enough. His pure subjectivity and his material poverty render him incessantly subject to human kindness, human deceit, human violence, and human definition, since without hands he cannot even spell himself. He becomes the object of love, and the film of his story becomes a love story, because in the face of all this, nothing else is possible.

With a Million-Dollar Smile

Money, writes Sartre, "is less a possession in itself than an instrument for possessing. That is why, except in most unusual cases of avarice, money is effaced before its possibility for purchase; it is evanescent, it is made to unveil the object, the concrete thing; money has only a transitive being" (1956, 143).

At a climactic moment in Ted Demme's *Blow* (2001), George Jung (Depp) and his partner, Diego Delgado (Jordi Mollà), have struck a deal with the head of the Colombian drug cartel, Pablo Escobar (Cliff Curtis), to distribute his cocaine in the United States. This marks the beginning of the American cocaine wave of the 1970s and 1980s (the film is something of a history of that wave). We cut from the three men smiling their new affiliation and mutual regard at Escobar's farm in Medellín—with Diego letting out a whoop of anticipation—to a montage of rapidly flipping slides, each showing George and Diego shaking hands with a new business partner. There is a rapid pulsing drumbeat on the sound track, underpinning Manfred Mann's Earth Band's performance of Bruce Springsteen's "Blinded by the Light," and the slides flip along keeping pace with this rhythm, moments passing rapidly into history with smiles and long hair, garish clothing and lit-up faces, all the angles of bravado, ignorance, youth, power, and lust jangling and juxtaposing to create a feeling of exhilaration. As the music fades we see George lying on the floor of Diego's house, sunlight streaming in, and a sea of paper money swirling around him as he flicks bills up into the air as if they were so much cotton fluff.

In a rapid cut we find ourselves dollying backward as George trucks through the house with a huge cardboard box full of money. "Where do I put it?" he asks, with the most casual, even innocent, matter-of-factness. Diego directs him here and there, and what we see as he moves methodically around is that every room of the place is filled with boxes piled almost to the ceiling. Indeed, because we are dollying backward, we concentrate on Depp's face as he scans territory we cannot see, and gradually, as we move, piles of boxes enter the frame at right and left, embodying the object of his now-lapsed sight. The room becomes fuller and fuller of boxed money the more he searches, and each moment of the journey constitutes for us an aggrandizement, even an acceleration, of our wonder at the amount of money already there. The two men are arguing, as George keeps walking, about whether they have just finished counting three million or two million five. "Weigh it," says Diego, "Three million is sixty pounds, two point five is fifty." George, however, is still casting his eyes around the hallways, where there is nothing but money piled in boxes. "Fuck it," says he, "two-five is fine with me." (There is so much money that half a million dollars has become nothing.) And then goofily, with a hopeless look that says there is just no place here, anywhere, for this box of bills, "We gotta get a new boat."

Roughly estimating that any one of these banker's boxes contains about half a million dollars, we can see that George is traipsing around looking for a spot among about a hundred million or more tax-free American dollars. Given that he started out as a working-class nobody from Boston, and that the drug business more or less fell into his lap, that his successes to this point have been spontaneous and inexplicable, almost as magical as they are enormous, and that if he is now experiencing virtually unimaginable power he is also unable to predict its continuance or ensure it against interruption by the forces of authority, George's matter-of-fact, unpretentious, low-key attitude in this scene, the simplicity of his predicament trying to find space for a box, and the mechanical quality of his marching and looking, all testify to a humble, passionately realistic and existential, even Beat approach to life. This is no gloating, bubbling, arrogant Scrooge McDuck beadily gazing at every gold coin in the sky-high piles of coins that fill his abode in the 1950s Disney comic version of cupidinous wealth.

There is a generous hopelessness that Johnny Depp brings to this scene, and to this entire film. He is always willing to do what he is asked to do, yet never with any feeling of certainty as to what the outcome will be. His performance is therefore momentary, in the precise sense that each moment is experienced to its fullness without regard to strategic planning or the limiting degradations of memory. He lives in the present, entirely. When, just earlier, one of Diego's compadres in Miami, to whom George has traveled in order to do Diego the favor of picking up a cocaine load, puts his pistol in George's mouth in order to make clear that he has to be paid within a matter of days, Johnny's reaction is splendidly uncalculating, unneurotic, even hilarious: he merely senses the gun, and responds as well as he can with this item in his mouth to the questions that are fired at him. A conversation, after all, is a conversation; questions demand answers. In the same delightfully perfunctory way, he is now, in Diego's house, searching for a place to put a box full of cash; and whether or not he is short by five hundred thousand dollars, whether tomorrow he will wake up just a little less rich than he planned, is entirely immaterial in the face of the overriding fact that there is no more room here for anything. In this acting is also an echo of the kind of elegant physical comedy (Keaton, Chaplin) he much admires—the actor has a simple physical problem to solve: talking with a gun barrel between his lips; carrying a heavy box of money around and looking for a place to put it down; and nothing outside of solving that problem is of any real concern.

By the end of this roller coaster of a film, George has lost everything and also been arrested, convicted, and imprisoned with a long sentence. His wife has left him, and his daughter, the only thing in life that he cares about, has rejected him and made a life of her own. But one day she comes to visit him in prison. They embrace in the garden, where he works every day. They talk. He tells her how much he loves her, and she looks at him tenderly, her eyes full of compassion and understanding. As he hugs her, however, the camera suddenly rotates and we see that she is eleven years old. Then, slowly, she fades into the air. He has been imagining all this. The guard brings him back to his cell. A closing title card indicates that George's sentence will end in 2015 and that his daughter has, to this date, never visited him at all. In this last scene, all the tenderness of fatherly love and loss is etched on Johnny's face, the eyes always on the verge of crying but holding back tears, the face a mask of resigned calmness as he gives the garden a last look and retires to his cell. Again, each aspect of the performance is centered on a physical task firmly settled in a present moment—weeding, looking up, speaking, touching, embracing, realizing, breathing in the empty space, responding to the guard's call, walking through the gateway toward his cell. We sense that the sentence is being lived out one day—indeed, one moment—at a time, without memory of the days gone by, without regard to the number of days remaining. We, indeed, cannot be presumed to possess such a balance for traveling only in the present; we need to see this moment in a greater context, to be able to use this moment as a springboard toward a trajectory. It is therefore for us, not for the story, that the information is provided as to when he will be released. For George at this moment—for Johnny—there is nothing that can be imagined as "2015."

Presence is transitory and provisional, even as it is the only source of true and penetrating experience. The conundrum of experience, its distinctness from and opposition to nature, perduration, memory, and the eternal is nicely typified in François Truffaut's *Baisers volés* (*Stolen Kisses,* 1968) by a climactic encounter between the heroine, Christine Darbon (Claude Jade), and a strange man in a trench coat who has been following her throughout the film and finally walks up to speak to her while she is sitting on a bench with her lover, Antoine

Doinel (Jean-Pierre Léaud). "J'ai découvert," says he, "que la vie est dégoutante. Le monde est provisionel. Moi, je suis définitif." * While Antoine is certainly ebullient, spontaneous, unpredictable, adventurous, even ridiculous, and therefore a persisting harbinger of acute experience, this stranger, who promises to transcend the moments of the everyday, is monotonous, tedious, virtually unperceivable in his flatness. Because direct experience is transitory, too, one never possesses it, never quite settles into it, never learns it well enough to master a situation. Therefore there is no moment of supreme poise, and every instant is pure exactly because it is replaced. The movement of Johnny Depp circulating through the house in *Blow*, at each instant searching for a place to put his box of money yet not finding one and so being forced to move on, is beautiful because of the simplicity with which it exemplifies presence. There is a sense in which all his performances onscreen are composed of such moments, chained together.

In cinema, presence has two reflections, movement and feeling, and because he manifests movement and feeling so profoundly, Johnny Depp is the most profoundly cinematic actor of our time. Movement, first, is an inherent quality of cinema itself, and to this extent the search for a spot to plant the money is a quintessentially cinematic event. As Siegfried Kracauer notes, movement is a "cinematic subject par excellence" (1960, 42). He typifies three great types of screen movement, the chase, the dance, and nascent motion (42–45). All these figure broadly and persuasively in Depp's performance style but are essential to his configuration of George Jung in *Blow*. All the film is a chase, in that George is running after the phantom of success and wealth (by way of the drug trade) and also in that with increasing perspicacity and doggedness, agents of the FBI are running after him. In the scene I have been discussing, there is a curious and attractive—although quiet—desperation on his face, it apparently being the case that he must find a repository for his cash soon, very soon, within moments. The money, now fluid, must solidify into an edifice by being made part of the architectural structure of boxes that is contained in the space of the house. Indeed, with a swift dissolve, we learn that George and Diego have decided to bank in the same Panamanian institution that guards Noriega's funds, and after

---

* "I have discovered that life is disgusting. The world is temporary. I, on the other hand, am definitive."

we see trolleys of cash being wheeled into the bank's vault we are witness as the two get passbooks to their accounts. Nor has the money come to rest, indeed. It will turn out many of George's problems in life stem from the fact that Noriega's bank is far from safe.

Depp never ceases to dance, to move rhythmically and sensually onscreen. The montage sequence in which still photographs of him shaking hands with business partners speed along to "Blinded by the Light" is only an open declaration that his every pose can be animated and set to a beat. There is a dancer's poise as he walks through the house with his money, his head turning from side to side, his voice conversing with Diego in the other room while he keeps to the beat of his footsteps. Watching his moves onscreen, one senses he is singing as he acts.

Nascent movement is "movement as contrasted with motionless-ness" (Kracauer 1960, 44), highlighting and abstracting cinema's ability to move. This is evident in the editing of the photomontage, where the flickering images suddenly freeze on a musical downbeat, only to begin moving again. Given Depp as the principal subject of these photographs, however, what is called up by this technique is the alteration between his dancing and his still image, between the intensely evocative look of his person in close-ups, in still shots, in poster images, in publicity photographs, and the ongoingness of his proceeding through narrative action. For every viewer of Depp, in a way that could not have been possible with Bogart, Garfield, Valentino, Grant, his presence in cinema is an alteration between the unfolding presentness—the dance—onscreen and a substantial reservoir of posed images in the domain of publicity. This was especially notable with Jarmusch's *Dead Man,* where the image of Johnny's face smeared with fawn's blood and staring into the lens, in a large number of differently designed publicity posters, could alternate for viewers with the scene in the film where he makes himself up this way, self-consciously, a little timidly, wonderingly. In the sequence I have been discussing in *Blow* there is a similar, and provocative, alteration between the confidence we see in the glowing George in the slides and the jazzy yet modest purposiveness as, down to earth with the money itself, he hunts to get it out of his hands.

In his movement, and therefore in his continuing yet also fleeting presence, Depp here gratifies "the isolated individual [viewer]'s longings" by urging him to recall "the nineteenth-century *flâneur* (with whom he has otherwise little in common) in his susceptibility to the transient real-life phenomena that crowd the screen. According to the testimony available it is their flux which affects him most strongly" (Kracauer 1960, 170). In a continuing way in film after film, yet typically and paradigmatically as he cannot find a home for his box of bills, Depp stimulates our senses and provides us with what Kracauer calls "stuff for dreaming."

It is in our dream life that vision is *felt,* that all appearances are *emotional.* Movies convey images as e-motional, as derived from motion, and as replacements—because equivalents—for motion. Schivelbusch's "panoramic perception" is a swell of emotion, and at the same time a loss of the bounded, static, under-stood vision. Being motile, our feeling in the present is also both hope and memory; and it is the motility that links where we were to where we hope to be as we observe each from where we are (this is Freud's formula for the dream). The second reflection of cinema, feeling, is another inducement to presence, and what *Blow* allows us to see articulated about Depp's performance is its intense commitment to emotion, yet also, and precisely, emotion *now.* His screen moments are therefore the opposite of moments in action cinema, which must inexorably produce a thrust of attention and a straining to resolution that can be usefully obstructed in order to create tension in the viewer. Depp precisely does *not* create tension, because as with dreams his moments efface one another and absorb us entirely in their expansiveness. We are not led to anticipate. Watching Johnny Depp onscreen is a hopeless experience.

With a Poem

Speaking of an unresolved plan of Francis Ford Coppola's to film Jack Kerouac's legendary classic *On the Road* with himself in the lead, Johnny Depp made an admission to Christopher Heard that may stand as an epigraph for all his film roles: "I was excited as hell to talk about *On the Road* as a movie but at the same time the idea made me queasy. The idea that I would be embodying that character . . . I wanted badly to do it, but I wasn't sure I wanted to do it" (Heard 2001, 139). Far beyond ambivalence, however, this posture in Depp is positively beatific, since at every moment he exemplifies both the zeal for involvement in his action and the wonder, self-examination, profound religious commitment of doubt that riddles like a plague of butterflies and brings the greatest certainty. It is the existential trembling, and we see it always onscreen with him, and at each moment he is wondering how to move on, and how to stay, so that he urges himself forward but also stands in the light, a glorious light that is light for moving in. "Nothing human was foreign to him," Stella Adler said of Marlon Brando (quoted in Halberstam 1993, 270). She did not know Johnny Depp, of whom this is also true.

Toward the end of Chuck Workman's *The Source* (1999), we are in a bar, very late (as it feels), but no one is there in the camera's territory but he. His back is to us; he faces a shiny cash register. Slowly he turns away from the bar, where a glass of whiskey quiet as a doe waits for him, and speaks to us of "Belief and Instructions for the Writing of Prose" by Jack Kerouac. He hasn't been eating, there's no food, and there's no one in the bar, it's the end of the afternoon, the red hour, but he's put on a little weight, and his hair is light red and was just sleeping, but his voice is the gentle voice of the world, it doesn't interrupt, it doesn't announce, and he stands still and recites. "Six, blow as hard as you want to blow." He's wearing a black and red lumberjack shirt over a red checked shirt, and in his right hand he's got a cigarette lit between the second and third fingers, just waiting there, but with the thumb and third finger of his left hand, at the bottom of the screen, nervously but quietly he's turning the cigarette around and around and around—it's a log in the river of his palm—turning it as though working out the combination of a safe, and his voice is not too loud. He's not going anywhere, simply and perfectly framed, but his voice is going, and it's not so much the words we hear as his voice speaking the words, even slurring the words. He's tired, he's been up all night slamming and gulping in the whole world, racing to every flicker of the world, he's been traveling, but now he's telling of all his travels. There is also an interview Jack Kerouac gave on television to Steve Allen, who is playing the piano as he asks the questions, and he asks, Steve Allen asks, "How long did it take you to write *On the Road*?" and hard-chinned Kerouac actually says, "Three weeks," and Allen asks, "How long were you *on* the road?" and Kerouac says, "Seven years." "Seven years, and you wrote it in three weeks!" says Allen, "I was on the road for three weeks and to write it, it took me seven years." Three weeks.

Now Johnny has moved left to the other side of the room, and he's wearing a tan jacket from the late 1940s, with wide rich lapels under which you could hide a horse, and his eyes are brown as a chestnut horse, and he's reading to us from *On the Road,* when Dean Moriarty meets the tenorman, whose "big brown eyes were concerned with sadness, and the singing of songs slowly and with long, thoughtful pauses" (Kerouac 1991, 199), and who drinks in all the pit and prune juice of the world, and there's something about Johnny's voice, because it's all his voice, he's not moving but his voice is moving, he's only walking back and forth and the camera is tracking him, but he's looking at us, straight into the lens, and the lighting is exquisite in the particular, almost Cézanne-like, way it calculates and balances all things, negates all things, so that nothing is left but Johnny's voice, not even the words, and there's something unadorned and moist—from the lakes—in his voice. That voice is not an activist voice, not a political voice, but the voice of those "ornery loners fending off absorption into mainstream culture while paving the way for larger, more explosive movements to come," as one critic puts it, and in producing that voice for us to hear in *The Source,* Depp is sharing "aspects of the Beat-hipster sensibility" (Sterritt 1999). That voice is concentrating not on the words but on the feeling of the desire to speak what is being said, the feeling of the need to recount, so that Dean Moriarty doesn't come out sounding like the center of the thing, and the tenorman doesn't come out sounding like the center of the thing, and Sal Paradise, who's telling us all this, and who is most certainly Johnny, doesn't come out sounding like the center of the thing, but the world is the center of the thing. This is a beautiful reading, because he's keeping his gestures out of it, he's looking straight into the lens, except once when he drops his eyes and you're suddenly conscious that he's got eyes, real eyes, that have to blink, and he blinks, and he's talking into the lens, that reflecting ear, and we are trapped like light in the chamber of his voice. Because it's everything and it's anything.

Then he reads about how he held her and should have kissed her and the thighs, the essence is in the thighs, and he cannot speak of this essence, but it happened, and she was, but now it's gone, but he is still with it, he's gone, he's gone into it and with it, and he says it's from the "Baudelaire Poems" by Jack Kerouac and he walks off.

It is all about the complete presence that is also not committed, not locked, but always hungry and moving on, he's always "gotta go and never stop going till we get there" (Kerouac 1991, 240), so that one knows him and yet never ceases wondering about him, even though he's so familiar, like a sandwich, as though he has put down a worn and well-known (and slightly old) suitcase (a satchel), but his voice goes on with the conviction that it must populate his breath, on across all of the roles that depict all of the people in the world, because there is so much to tell and to show, so many gestures, so many poses, so many costumes, so much light, so many places to stand, so many kisses, so many arguments, so much to understand and to gaze at and to look through, and, as it was for Sal Paradise, for Johnny "the road is life" (212).

He is speaking to us but he is looking through us because we must be understood but there is so much more to understand (and we are obstructions to that understanding). He is decidedly inarticulate, not as though he is Dean Moriarty but as though he has spent his time drinking in Dean Moriarty, his own Dean Moriarty, or as though he's bypassed Dean Moriarty to become Sal Paradise, who digs and is dug, who is stunned to hear Dean Moriarty tell of meeting someone who "could talk all night . . . , only thing is he doesn't bother with talking, ah, man, the things, the things I could—I wish—oh, yes. Let's go, let's not stop—go now! Yes!" (Kerouac 1991, 201). He's not trying, that's for sure, he's just standing and talking to us of this thing and everything, of here and everywhere, with a voice that points at nothing and everything, and huge brown eyes that do not leave us except to drop and blink, and for just a moment, a long moment, he could say, except he doesn't say,

> I had reached a point of ecstasy that I always wanted to reach, which was the complete step across chronological time into timeless shadows, and wonderment in the bleakness of the mortal realm, and the sensation of death kicking at my heels to move on, with a phantom dogging its own heels, and myself hurrying to a plank where all the angels dove off and flew into the holy void of uncreated emptiness, the potent and inconceivable radiancies shining in bright Mind Essence, innumerable lotus-lands falling open in the magic mothswarm of heaven (173)

but he doesn't say this, he doesn't say any of this. Maybe he's dreaming he'll get to the end of America. There'd be nowhere to go but back.

In every Johnny Depp performance there is a moment when he is the prototypical "Beat disciple" (Zehme 1991, 34), when he is separated from the script, when he is there as a person searching and investigating and peering at the lens in order to find us, to know us, to look through us, by way of which peregrination he will come to know himself, to be able to say, "I had found the teachers, the sound-track and the proper motivation for my life. Kerouac's train-of-thought writing style gave great inspiration for a train-of-thought existence—for better or for worse. The idea to live day to day in a 'true pedestrian' way, to keep walking, moving forward, no matter what. A sanctified juggernaut" (Depp 1999, 70)—and be detected in this devotion not by virtue of what could be watched but by virtue of what could be heard, because the sound of his voice triumphs over the meaning of his words. He becomes at this moment, and then at every moment, a singer, or a surfer, an initiate into the "mysteries of all things considered Outside" (70). The words of his scripts are an ocean and he rides them. He reveals himself in *The Source* because *On the Road* is his favorite book, the book he said was "life-changing for me" (70), and Kerouac is the voice that made him listen to voices, yet now he has become Kerouac, or even fully Johnny Depp, which for him is more imperative. In this imperative moment we know that there is mortality and distance, that we are apart, the face on the screen no different from faces peering in at the window, faces at the fish market, faces in the classroom, every face unknowable and unapproachable and yet always journeying, as we are journeying to know every face in the world, all the faces together, which are our own face.

The explosive spontaneity, the dissipation and dissolution, the on-going suspension of the present moment, a moment continually re-solving itself both forward and backward, are caught and tamed, frozen and given room to fly, in the vocal spasms of Jack Kerouac's Dean Moriarty that punctuate Sal Paradise's experience of him and of life in *On the Road,* Dean Moriarty saying, "Yes, Yass. Yass. Yes!" saying, "Oh me, oh my, but—," saying "If—," saying everything and saying the nothing that is also everything. In *The Source* it is evident Johnny is not Dean Moriarty, he is Sal, the one who is following Dean. "Yes!" someone is calling to Johnny, but Johnny is watching and going, holding his cigarette and turning it, watching and know-ing, singing of all things. If he emphasized what he said, he would be telling an event, an event from which we were excluded, and so the experience would hold us outside and apart. But as it is, we are there with him in the narrative space, and that drink is waiting on the bar. Because he is telling and we are listening, it is the conjunction be-tween his voice and our ears that comes alive in many-dimensional multi-colored tremulous form, as I am telling you this, knowing that you are there, and that if I speak it on and on I can reach the end, where we will be together, with no more land.

With a Posture

If the Depp screen performance is relentlessly existential, it is also in part an entrapment. We choose to be what we are because of the limitations of our situation. How easy it is to read Depp's performance of the transvestite Bon Bon in Julian Schnabel's *Before Night Falls* (2000) in terms of willfulness. The character is a male who takes delirious pleasure in pretending to be female; the actor playing the character takes pleasure in the license afforded him by the film to experiment with disporting himself inside this character. Schnabel commented, indeed, in a Bravo! documentary about Johnny, on how much delight he took in being able to shoot right up Johnny's ass, thus lending further weight to the argument that the Bon Bon role is expressive (for both the character and the actor).

But Schnabel goes to lengths to show that the prison in which Bon Bon lives is a brutal place, that the inhabitants are poor and destitute, and that they are all under the control of a vicious and cold-hearted lieutenant (also played, in a scene near the Bon Bon scene, by Depp). Bon Bon is everything of masculinity that the lieutenant is not, flamboyant, hungry, intimidated, poisonous. To credit Bon Bon's open homosexual availability to desire is surely to neglect the plight of a pretty male in a situation of brutalizing close confinement. It is possible, then, to read each nuance of the construction of this "femininity" as an expression of the performer's existential problem. While we never meet the Bon Bon inside Bon Bon, we can as easily surmise a desperate fear and loneliness as a sexual cupidity and urge to transgress. Far from throwing "normality" in the face of the male establishment, Bon Bon may be adapting in the only reasonable way to circumstances that are totally disempowering; and each aspect we see of the characterization is a testament to those circumstances.

And it is clear when we meet the lieutenant that there is a too-strong resemblance. Just as much as we can detect Johnny Depp behind both characterizations, we can suspect a kinship between Bon Bon and the lieutenant, as though the "woman" represents everything the lieutenant is hiding to the exact degree that the lieutenant represents everything Bon Bon cannot bring himself to be. Interviewing Arenas the poet (Javier Bardem), the lieutenant is fantasized by his victim as having a magnificent hard-on through the entire scene. Outside in the yard, Bon Bon is metaphorically leaning over with her ass in the air, waiting to receive that hard-on, or some other. (In fact the enlarged rectum is used by Bon Bon for smuggling—among other things, Arenas's manuscript.) Exactly as the pervasive homophobia of the culture and the institution prevent the lieutenant from openly expressing his homoerotic desire (so that, by inversion, he becomes a torturer), it prevents Bon Bon from being able to bend over without first dressing up as what all the other inmates regard, and accept, as a gender clown.

One interesting side effect of Depp's performance as Bon Bon (a performance, by the way, for which, according to Schnabel, "he wouldn't let me pay for anything. . . . He just worked for free and said, 'Just put it on the screen'" ["Bravo! Profile"]), specifically a side effect of the high quality of his costume and make-up job, and a side effect that is quite distinct from the appearance of the actor in drag in *Ed Wood,* is his disturbing verisimilitude as a woman; and the freedom this has given many who see the movie to admit openly how attractive Depp can be. The twin performances as Bon Bon and the lieutenant thus illustrate the pervasive homophobia of our own culture most strikingly, revealing how masculine Depp can seem in uniform with an erection straining inside his pants (to match the thick pistol he forces into the poet's mouth), yet also, and under protection of this umbrella, how alluringly feminine he can seem in drag (when he really tries). We can admit that he is pretty in one scene as long as we are able to admit in another that he is really tough. At the same time as we are perceiving Johnny Depp in this mutually reinforcing dualism, however, we are also perceiving the characters, and so the film is about our ability to enjoy Bon Bon as long as we can also enjoy the lieutenant just as much as it is about our twofold ability to enjoy Johnny in the roles. Johnny's sexuality (which was a topic of more mystery when he was younger [see DeAngelis 2001]) is of far less interest in this context than the dualism possible in our estimation of him; our ability to love both the passive softness and the military toughness at once. It is as though Jack Smith has entered the Reaganite world of male hard bodies.

If, however, Bon Bon is softened by circumstance, and his every gesture an enunciation of his existential condition; so, too, must the lieutenant be brutalized in the same way, and must each of his gestures be an indication of his own plight. Two masculinities compete against one another, and yet also enlighten one another. Because the

Bon Bon sequence is close to the lieutenant sequence in this film, it becomes possible for us to see the prison, Bon Bon's environment, as a socializing force upon the lieutenant's masculinity. The ability to display one's erection as an impudent symbol of crass power is no more inherent in males than the ability to sell kisses for cigarettes in the courtyard. It is the culture and the institution that has made of both these men what they are, and we can profit by reading their actions as indices of their conditions, of what Henry James called "the whole envelope of circumstance."

cap'n jack (four preludes)

"Nobody looks better in rags."

John Waters on Johnny Depp

1

To fans addicted to Johnny Depp's "beauty," "youthfulness," and "romantic allure," Gore Verbinski's *Pirates of the Caribbean: Curse of the Black Pearl* may seem something of a tumble, not to say a wholesale fall from grace, and his dissolute, utterly dissipated—while still inexcusably young—Captain Jack Sparrow a sad excuse for a dashing pirate. No Errol Flynn this, at any rate, although one can see that at no moment is the actor beneath Cap'n Jack unconscious of the legacy of Errol Flynn. The apocrypha about this performance, based, to be sure, on comments from the actor and also hurled into print in virtual synchronization with the first screening, was that Depp had concocted Cap'n Jack from five sources, with a possible sixth, U.S. Federal Inmate 19225-004, also known as George Jung, never mentioned even though Johnny Depp describes him as a man with "the weathered, broken, damaged soul of a pirate who'd seen too many days at sea" (Demme and Depp 2001, 8). The five: the witticism of Shane MacGowan of The Pogues; the nonchalance of Muhammad Ali; Peter Ustinov's outrageous vocalism in Robert Stevenson's *Blackbeard's Ghost;* the Tuareg custom of putting black shadows around their eyes, "as if they've seen a lot" (Grassin 2003, 52); and the aloofness of Keith Richards ("He's my god"). In October 2003, in fact, the *New York Post* reported Richards gifting Depp with one of his guitars. "When I decided to do the movie I started thinking about pirates of the 17th and 18th centuries. It came to me that the modern-day equivalent is a rock-and-roll star," Depp told *Playboy.* "I wanted to take the spirit of Keith, the beautiful, laid-back confidence," and, "he is kind of a pirate" (Weinraub 2004, 65).

At the same time as we disesteem this pirate manqué, the Johnny lurking inside him may also seem a sad excuse for a radiant movie star. Has Depp abdicated his throne? Is Orlando Bloom as Will Turner the princeling come of age, and has Depp's glowing form taken on a tarnish? As Sparrow, neither quite effeminate, nor quite inebriated, nor quite a fop, yet in a way all three (while at the same time being none of them, but instead a meticulous parodist taking pot shots at all three), he stumbles through scene after scene, performing, as the *New Yorker* had it, "on his own wavelength" (Denby 2003b, 94), defeating his enemies more by accident than through skill, and failing grandly to win the heart of the beautiful girl (Keira Knightley) whose eyes instead shine for the dashing and beautiful (and hardly middle-aged) Turner. It seems altogether Bloom's picture when looked at in this way. His is the noble brow, his the climactic kiss and athletic prowess, the optimistic courage, and the vulnerability in the face of the three evils of the film: the evil of the black pirates led by Barbossa (Geoffrey Rush), the evil of the colonial forces led by Commodore Norrington (Jack Davenport), the evil of the slimy colonial bureaucracy led by Colonel Weatherby Swann (Jonathan Pryce), all of these villains, to be sure, dutifully bewigged or bejeweled, besatined or befuddled (for this is a loving mockery of pirate pictures and there are few moments in which we are not led to laugh).

But although the action is set in the sparkling Caribbean, where the seas glitter like sheets of turquoise and the palm trees shudder nobly in the breeze; although there are glorious galleons with sails bravely unfurled; although there are explosions, hangings, bewitchings by moonlight, and pirate treasure to catch our gaze, in truth there is nothing to look at in *Pirates* but Johnny; Johnny at the top of his mizzen mast spying the vast sea, Johnny dropping an eye to the deck where a leak has sprung, sliding down to bail hopelessly with a broken bucket; Johnny entering the harbor of Port Royal on the yardarm of a ship slowly sinking as he steps off it; Johnny sparring loquaciously with Orlando in a smithy's shop; Johnny winking, Johnny blinking, Johnny in a cell unable to convince the gaoler's dog to fetch him the key; Johnny corrupt, Johnny duplicitous, Johnny adorable, Johnny melodious, Johnny in a vertiginous dance where, like a puppet dangling from a madman's strings, he seems at each moment on the verge of toppling over and also on the verge of flying. At the end, when he presumes to imagine Knightley infatuated with him when she has no interest in him whatever, and slurs in his extremely awkward—and therefore hilarious—Cockney, "It wouldn't have worked out between us, m'dear," what's amusing is his goofy conceit, his air of masculine pride, since this is clearly a male from the castle of whose masculinity all the tapestries have been torn. It was always Orlando, from the moment of his first entrance, who captivated the maiden's heart here, always and only Orlando who had what maidens hunger for, and it was always Johnny who idiotically failed to notice this fact, know himself, understand his situation. By the gift of some grace, some animal instinct, he is of, and in, the world without really comprehending it.

(Sleeping Dancer . . .)

2

So it is that this film can be seen to purport and herald a new era for Johnny Depp, one in which he is, finally, and as though long-promised and long-expected, the proud proprietor of a much-accepted career; not only a star but a middle-class hero. The Hollywood publicity machine has crowned him and, indeed, he has crowned himself a little. "I just had a feeling that kiddies would like him and that it wouldn't just be like a kiddie character; the average Joe could like him and the heaviest of intellectuals could like him," he told *Esquire* (Richardson 2004, 99). "*Pirates of the Caribbean* has made you one of the hottest stars in town," cooed *Playboy* (Weinraub 2004, 59), that sensual bastion of the middle classes. Even the pretentious culture critics of the weekend supplements lost their reserve: "He is one of the most beautiful creatures you will ever see, with skin like maple butter, cheekbones you could spelunk in, and bottomless dark eyes," rhapsodizes a newspaper that should know its maple, the *Globe and Mail* (Schneller 2004, R2). And he was nominated for an Academy Award, a source of immense speculation among his fans and watchers who wondered whether he would, in fact, show for the show. "Red-carpet watchers saw a whole new Johnny Depp," wrote one reviewer:

> The famously scruffy Oscar nominee was surprisingly clean-shaven and especially dapper in a Gucci tuxedo. Gone were the tangled locks, replaced with a new do by Laurent D. of L.A.'s Privé Salon. The look "was going back to glamour but with an edge," says Laurent, who clipped Depp's hair just hours before the Oscars at the actor's Hollywood Hills home. There they spoke French, drank wine and listened to jazz as Depp's girlfriend, French pop singer Vanessa Paradis, 31, and their kids Lily-Rose, 4, and Jack, 23 months, wandered about. (Tauber et al. 2004, 85)

Pirates, indeed, saw Depp "adjusting to being recognized by a whole new demographic," as one reporter has it. "After being around for so long . . . all these kids were going to see the movie and I was just really touched, you know . . . Like, when you come out on the street and meet little kids and they go, 'Oh man, you're Captain Jack Sparrow!'" (Giantis 2004).

The era of *Pirates* is also one in which Johnny's youthful screen exuberance is finally surpassed by a younger actor, one in which he becomes the older male to whom the romantic lead looks up as a brother, father, uncle, teacher—which is to say, an elegant failure. But since the "elegant failure," Cap'n Jack, moves through filmic space with genius and embellishment, he is less a secondary role than a triumph of screen acting. So powerful is Depp's rendition of Sparrow's dilapidation, so frightfully disorganized is the performance, we can be led to imagine that Johnny, in truth, not Jack, is the one falling into disrepair. So perfectly unbalanced are Sparrow's gait and gaze we can imagine it is Johnny, in truth, who has lost his form. But in *Pirates of the Caribbean,* Johnny is at the very top of his form. Indeed there is not one moment when we can be sure of his sobriety, his sexuality, his mental competence, his memory, his fidelity, or his *bona fides* as a pirate or as an actor; perhaps he has pirated this pirate. "That's the worst pirate I've ever seen," Commodore Norrington keeps saying, a fan if not of pirates then at least (in a postmodern fantasy) of pirate movies, since he by his tone makes it clear that he means by "worst" not "most nefarious" but "most poorly turned out."

There is a wonderfully comedic, and also revealing, moment: as the fair maiden Elizabeth Swann's would-be lover, Norrington would revile it; but as the narrative plant whose estimations of Jack guide our own apperceptions, and whose disappointment in Jack's incapacities to perform as a true pirate should, incite our tickled affiliation with the film, Norrington, if he could but watch, would be smugly satisfied. Sparrow has been marooned with Elizabeth on an archetypical deserted island, an island, it bears saying, so perfectly archetypical it might have been ordered by catalog. It is one of those luscious utopian havens, warmed by a balmy breeze, shaded by arching and magnificent palm trees, cloaked in sand as white as diamonds, lapped by water the color of emeralds. No one else is around—not for hundreds if not thousands of miles. Jack drags her among the palms to a particular spot, sloppily digs in the sand to reveal a trap door, lifts it, drunkenly reaches in, and hoists out—a private stash of rum. So *that's* what you were doing here when everyone thought you were imprisoned, says she—spending three days lying on the beach drinking rum!

"Welcome to the Caribbean, Love," chimes he.

Much is connoted here. For contemporary viewers, one particularly vivid and delicious dream of boundless pleasure involves lying around on a pristine Caribbean beach with no distraction but a bottle of rum; in this light, Captain Jack becomes nothing but a pathetic middle-class contemporary tourist, thus a postmodern buffoon near and dear to the hearts of bourgeois viewers. Also, to the extent that we can make this reading we can realize that this particular visualization of a "typical" Caribbean island reflects and engenders our bourgeois fantasies for a Caribbean of fabled romantic pirate myths celebrated by Hollywood cinema from the 1930s onward while at the same time existing as nothing other than a setting, an abstraction by exploitation, for which we see alluring commercials on television and the continuing replication of which we tolerate and expect in motion pictures. The bourgeois vacationer stoned out of his mind on rum, with his girl in his arms, gaping at the waters rushing into the white beach, is nothing other than the "pirate" whom Depp is depicting in this film. Or: the middle-class bourgeois film buff's wildest dream is nothing but a pirate dream in the purest sense, by which I mean to suggest a program of invasion, dispossession, and reappropriation. We pirate our way through the narrative. Yet at the same time the film can be a different kind of pirate dream, one by which a wholesale rejection of stolid civilized bourgeois values, the sort of values Commodore Norrington represents, can be achieved in fantasy by the viewer as prelude to a recalculation of ethical, aesthetic, political, and social value. An optimistic flag to fly, to be sure. The fantasy of overturning the economy, just as Cap'n Jack and his maties on the Black Pearl are wont to do, can be sweetly terminated in the convenient reestablishment of bourgeois stance and value that comes with leaving the theater.

Whose island, we must ultimately choose to know, is Jack horsing around on? And I mean by this not Jack the diegetic figment, the man Elizabeth runs from and Barbossa would like to skewer, the man who turns Norrington's stomach, not that Jack. But the Jack who is Verbinski's game marker, linchpin of a narrative that is screened for profit, the Jack who smiles at us from the posters, aware of his audience. That Jack, after all, is a colonizer on that island, a colonizer of our joy and belief, even if he is also a reveler. Because Verbinski has him committed to landing there, slogging around that soil, the camera crew is obliged to follow, and so he is quasidiegetic, half in and half out of the story, with one foot in the sand that Elizabeth also steps through and another foot in a cinematic frame. For it cannot be doubted, as we watch *Curse of the Black Pearl,* that as much as the actors who are playing them, the characters themselves know they are in a film and have conspired, artfully, to take over this tropical paradise to make it our screen.

(Welcome to the Caribbean . . .)

3

Although Will Turner (Orlando Bloom) buys our allegiance by siding with Jack Sparrow; although he supports Jack, assists Jack, adores

Jack, and in the end accepts Jack, still he will never quite be Jack. He will be a proper lover for Elizabeth; and then her proper husband, much as Norrington would fain have been. But Jack is a man—or even, as Trinculo has Caliban, a fish—who, if Elizabeth had been mad enough to stay with him, would have lingered on the beach all day drinking rum. No laws of the monarchy and no codes of men would have barred him from totally pleasuring himself on every draught of every breeze, every thrust and parry with a sword (he fights, indeed, with a smile on his face), every opportunity to engage in badinage with stupid soldiers or to catch a girl giving him the eye. Through Cap'n Jack, Depp brings Dean Moriarty (back) to life, Will Turner his dutiful and adoring Sal Paradise. Cap'n Jack is a sprite of the present, hopping, joking, plotting, moving ever forward, without the least regard for that vesicle of feeling, that bubble, he calls himself. His braided goatee, his many scarves and earrings, his tricorner hat—all these seem to have blown through the air and landed upon him by accident. He is whatever the moment makes of him.

A startling example: the plot of this film, such as it is—and this is not a film one watches because of a plot—turns on the conceit that the former crew who sailed under Jack Sparrow mutinied and marooned him, but then fell under a curse that makes them transmogrify into ghostly and immortal phantoms by moonlight. Jack's quest with Will is to release that curse, get his crew back from the insidious pretender Barbossa, and once again sail the silvery seas. As the two struggle with the mutinous pirates in a secret cavern on Far Tortuga, swashbuckling in and out of patches of moonlight, with the pirates seeming all-too-human and then suddenly becoming phantasmagorical and then taking on human form again depending on what light they are in at any given instant, there comes a moment when Jack himself slides into a puddle of moonlight *and dissolves*. He stops and holds up a hand in surprise, for this is the first time he realizes that he, too, has been cursed and that in moonlight he is nothing but air and bones. But quickly, then, he steps onward, his silly smile still pasted irreverently on his face. What does it matter to him, after all, if he is a wraith or a scallywag, if only there is enough rum, and enough adventure, and an audience to watch him guzzle the first and delight in the second?

To put this more explicitly: Here Depp presents his frame and form entirely without regard to dressing. All the elaborately constructed performance we overtly see in *Pirates*—the rings, the braids, the hissing, the Cockney, the whispers, the winking, the postures, the gestures—wash away in the moonlight like so much publicity dross from a Hollywood marketing campaign. The real Jack is something more sylphlike, more haunting, more mercurial, more enterprising. The gregarious and bizarre characterization that enchants us is nothing but a package to safeguard something lunar and lost.

Now in the moonlight, suddenly, and stripped of the performance that has been a mere contraption, Depp seems what Sartre would have called "a work of pure imagination" in which "slow, lazy, sulky, the facts adapt themselves to the rigour of the order I wish to give them" (1964, 13). As he is invisible and we must conceive him, he becomes profoundly intimate, indeed a piece of our own dream-work. That is all, of course, a screen character can ever be; and so he is perfectly authentic in the moment of his invisibility, the moment when we digest and re-form him. What a stroke of genius on Verbinski's part to see through Johnny Depp. Yet what a stroke of genius on Johnny Depp's part to dress himself in such a bangled character, so that invisibility would so manifestly become him.

(Air and Bones . . .)

4

In this film, perhaps more explicitly or ineluctably than in his other screen performances, Depp appears to inhabit not scenes but single shots. That is: of far greater importance than the flow of his being through the narrative is the sparkle of his presence in particular moments. Kracauer cites René Clair's comment that screen actors "have to atomize their role in the process of acting" (Clair 1951, 87, quoted in Kracauer 1960, 95), this requirement stemming from the fragmented process of filming that leads the integrity of the performance as a narrative whole to reside in the hands of the editor and director, among others. But the characterization must have a momentary integrity. Indeed, that is its primary requirement, since our belief at each instant must be won anew and is the building block of the continuum of presentation that subtends the fiction.*

* The movie camera witnesses what happens before it, and provides a record, frame by frame, of that continuous momentary witnessing. In this respect the camera is related to early systems for assessing and ascertaining claims to knowledge. See Steven Shapin, *A Social History of Truth: Civility and Science in Seventeenth-Century England* (Chicago: University of Chicago Press, 1994). I am grateful to John Morgan for bringing this to my attention.

Further, although it should seem to the viewer that the character's momentary being is diffused and extended spatially and temporally through the permeable boundaries of the moment, into a mobile coherence we take to be the character's "life," nevertheless this impression must be deposited with the viewer on the basis of scanty observations. As Kracauer puts it: "The film actor's performance, then, is true to the medium only if it does not assume the airs of a self-sufficient achievement but impresses us as an incident—one of many possible incidents—of his character's unstaged material existence. Only then is the life he renders truly cinematic" (95).

Jack Sparrow, to be successful, must be entirely incidental as he appears. He must seem to exist fully—that is, beyond the frame of the diegesis—and without consequence as he scoops up a purse of coins on the dock at Port Royal, unseen by the harbormaster; as he admires the swords Will Turner has fashioned while the blacksmith is asleep; as he stares wide-eyed and astonished into the face of Barbossa's monkey, who has been named after him and stares right back with all the authority of a proper doppelgänger. Each of these moments, further, must significantly fail to contain or delimit Jack. He seems to leap and leak out of posture and instant in exactly the way that Depp onscreen often seems to leap and leak out of his clothes, quite as though his energies, shapelessly unfurling, make him ecstatic—make him linger beside himself: some presence that is entirely facial and postural moves forward to greet the viewer's apprehension, as though the moving body onscreen were but a shell to mock at the prospect of containing it.

But in this particular narrative, Jack is also, as I said earlier, indiscriminably foppy, fruity, and soused, which is to say, spontaneous, emotive, affective, and effusive in manner regardless of proprieties and circumstances. He is erotically stimulated by practically anyone (yet by no one quite as much as himself, which is why, I think, he is so amusing and also so intoxicating), and incapable of sustained rational commitment to everyday (read, bourgeois) values. That he might do battle for King and Country is inconceivable. His foppiness, his fruitiness, and his drunkenness—all three both hilarious and endearing and outrageous—constitute therefore the essence of piracy since they underscore a rebellious, insubordinate, impious way of committing the everyday business of life. Bourgeois proprieties, indeed, which scorn and refuse piracy—which seek to hang the pirate

from his own yardarm—are exactly the sober opposites of these characteristics: respectfulness, heterosexual (that is, brutal) manliness,
and sanity. Bourgeois values preexist and perdure beyond moments.
If the characters in this film are all searching for some magical IT (as
Kerouac has it), Captain Jack alone has found IT and is reveling in IT,
now, and now, and now, and now, but with no memory and no hope.
He has no "proper" foundation in time. In this way is his piracy en-
nobled and also glamorized, his freedom of expression a living poetry, his every gesture idyllic.

   If piracy, as epitomized here by Depp's Jack Sparrow, is a devotion
to the momentary life, the atomic life; and if film acting is of necessity the same; if impressing us with incident each of the actor's moments is nevertheless discrete; then piracy is ultimately cinematic,
and Jack Sparrow is a quintessential film performance (all this regardless of the apparent triviality of the plot and action of this film).
Nor is Depp himself foppish, fruity, and scandalously stupefied as
he does this enacting. The construction of an emotive pretext for
Sparrow, his flighty personality, his brutalized past, which makes
possible a momentary (pirate's) existence without calling up (self-
reflexively for us) film acting and the necessities of filmmaking, is
an entirely sober, responsible, and brilliant stratagem of Depp's. By
doing Sparrow this way, he can make of him a mirror to reflect all
his previous roles *as such,* to indicate not precisely what he has played
onscreen but the fact of his having played it there, the screened quality of the performances he gives. A line quoted by Kracauer from
Freud's sometime disciple Hans Sachs, who along with Karl Abraham had vigorously proposed a film about psychoanalysis that Freud
refused to approve (see Gifford 2004), virtually describes Jack Sparrow: "He requests the film actor to advance the narrative by embodying 'such psychic events as are before or beyond speech . . . above
all those . . . unnoticed ineptitudes of behavior described by Freud
as symptomatic actions'" (Kracauer 1960, 95). Our first glimpse of
Sparrow, after all, shows him discovering that his ship is sinking, in
short, being inept. At the end of the film there is ineptness again, yet
whose? as he explains to Elizabeth, yielding her to the young man
she has no intention of giving up for anyone, that it "would never have
worked out between us, m'dear." She, however, already knows—and
had no thought of anything working out in the first place. Is Sparrow
inept, for not realizing he never had a chance? Or are we inept, for

not being able to relinquish the thought of Depp as lover—not being able to unify Depp and Sparrow, since it is evident Sparrow could never have been anybody's lover, so precariously balanced is he upon the breeze of the instant, so proud is he of having gained this pinnacle of buffoonery.

Or is he being not a buffoon but a philosopher? Is he saying that if she may have fooled Will Turner, and the audience, into thinking of her as a young lady susceptible to the salty perfumes of the pirate, he has seen through her charade? He has seen her feeling for propriety, her ultimate commitment to the world he forsakes. He has seen that for all her infatuations, the pirate's life has none of the comforts she needs and believes she deserves. If in Minnelli's *The Pirate,* a swashbuckling privateer can metamorphose into a bourgeois princeling (Walter Slezak) for the purposes of disowning his past; here, on the contrary, Elizabeth's princely father (Pryce) is anything but a lapsed pirate, and she is therefore anything but a girl with piracy in her blood. (More interesting is Orlando Bloom's Turner, who as a boy was coddled by pirates and then abandoned, so that Elizabeth, a naive girl at the time, could adopt him and, by degrees, bring him into domesticated life.)

Jack Sparrow may very well be mouthing all this. But Johnny Depp is speaking. And what he must mean, by contrast with what Sparrow means, is intended only for the audience, who share his domain but are unknown and undreamed by this pirate. All our pretenses at adoring what is onscreen have been caught for what they are, self-serving and delusional. In fact, "it would never work out between us," not because Depp is less than Bloom the apple of our eye but because we aren't sufficiently committed to the piracy that is screen acting to acknowledge him for what he truly is. Our bourgeois rationale, in the end, is the orderly story. (In *Finding Neverland,* dressed *as* a genteel pirate, Johnny demonstrates this.) What Johnny does is acceptable to us only, and fully, when it serves the tale, that moral resolution utterly compatible with sense as we know it. His play, his fire, his passion, his process—that through his breath he chains moments together for us—all that is quite beyond our love. Whose fate, then, Johnny Depp's or his viewer's, has the greater loneliness?

(Now, and Now, and Now, and Now . . .)

Raphael

La fidelité c'est vivre comme si le temps n'existait pas. (Loyalty is living as though time didn't exist.)

Godard, *Masculine/Feminine*

Johnny Depp's first and, to this date, only directorial effort in film, *The Brave*, presents the last seven days in the life of Raphael, a young Native American living "at the end of the line," with his wife and two children in a shantytown. The brother of a suicide and an unemployed ex-convict who is virtually unemployable in racist White America, he resorts to making a contract with McCarthy, a wheelchair-bound overweight hypernarcissistic snuff-meister (Marlon Brando), whereby after a period of one week he will present himself to be tortured to death in exchange for the sum of $50,000. The cash brings him agonies as much as boons. Both his wife, Rita (Elpidia Carillo), and the local priest, Father Stratton (Clarence Williams III), are convinced he got it by illegal means and is on his way back to prison. His children are delighted with the toys he buys them, yet also terrified they will lose their father. A former partner in crime, Luis (Luis Guzmán), wants his cut, and attacks Rita in order to impress upon Raphael how serious he is in this desire. The situation is darkened by the news that real estate developers are moving in to raze the shantytown; after he is gone, Raphael's family will be homeless and will need every penny of the money he is giving his life to earn for them. In the end, he takes confession in order to put himself in a position to beg the priest to see to it that his family actually gets the cash; there is no one else he can trust. But the priest refuses, saying his vows forbid him to assist in a suicide. Finally, having attacked and killed McCarthy's insidious lieutenant, Larry (Marshall Bell), then having bathed himself in the river and been helped into a meditative trance by the medicine dance of his father (Floyd "Red Crow" Westerman), Raphael wakes to his last morning, kisses his sleeping children, leaves his sleeping wife her cup of coffee, and walks away to his death. On the way he meets the priest, who accepts the money out of his hand. In a montage sequence we see Raphael proceeding into the urban warehouse where his torturers wait, intercut with bulldozers demolishing the shantytown and a close shot of the priest removing his collar and throwing it away.

The Brave is clearly an allegorical film, telling not only the story of Raphael (Heb. = "God heals") and his family and neighbors but also of man's existential predicament facing a certain death and most particularly the ugly and intolerable conditions facing American Natives, who can be said to be in a position of complete insufficiency. Like Raphael, they must prostitute themselves to European Man, give their lives away for the perverse pleasures of debilitated, incessantly insatiable, violent, and racist Whites—or at least rich Whites. Raphael's inability to go for help to any person or any institution—"You think maybe the Government will help?!" he says snidely to the priest—his persistent good faith in the face of a despicable culture that reviles him, his unadorned and straightforward manner of addressing people and situations, his great physical beauty, his uprightness and honesty, mobilize sympathy not only for his personal plight but for the plight of everyone who is disenfranchised in this capitalist proto-utopia. When in the final shot we see the freight elevator doors close on him—like the giant maw of some gargantuan mechanical beast—as he prepares to descend to McCarthy's torture chamber, we understand that no solution presents itself to ameliorate the conditions of a young man who must sacrifice himself in order to give his family a chance in life; and who must become a mendicant even to find help in arranging to leave a meager inheritance. The Church, the State—all must be abandoned in order that a relatively paltry sum can be passed to a woman and children who would have no life without it. We are led to a moral outrage for a society that so brutally abandons those it has the power to exploit.

There is one more metaphor invoked by the film, more troubling than all the others in its way of implicating us. Raphael also represents the screen figuration in general, manipulated and ultimately disfigured and terminated for the viewing pleasure of powerful aliens who have no shred of concern for anything but their own pleasure. McCarthy's self-justification for entering the diabolical contract with Raphael is simply that watching someone experiencing terrible pain and death ennobles the soul, prepares one to withstand the terror of death when it comes; and is therefore a useful and morally acceptable act. While it is clear from the disorganized expressions on his face and the glaucous passivity in his dead eyes that McCarthy anticipates taking some definitive carnal pleasure in watching the beautiful Raphael writhe, he makes no open reference to the erotic as part of his schema of involvement although even the erotic, it is true, might bring some nobility to his rationale. Nor need we admit the pleasure of our gaze, confronted as director Depp ensures we will be by visions of bare-chested, long-haired, and exquisitely lit Raphael scarred and even hideously bloodied: bloodied first by Larry, who punctures his hand with a poker, and then by the life fluid of Luis, whom he brutally murders in vengeance. It does not hurt to watch pain on the screen or elsewhere. Certainly the imagination is assaulted (McCarthy is paying good money in order that his may be, just as we have in watching the film), but the body is not ravaged, the nerves not frayed, one's life chances not diminished by being presented with the spectacle of someone else's excruciating demise. If anything, a vision of the pain of others is comforting, reassuring us that we are not suffering as, in "Neither a Victim Nor an Executioner," Elie Wiesel wrote many years ago. In an extraordinarily apathetic world, one needs to witness suffering in order to feel anything.

In Depp's performance is an affecting quality of youthfulness. To be sure, he seems virtually always young onscreen, if not callow then genuinely innocent. The performer, after all, is working for the first time with a director who has never before directed performers. So he is forced to be utterly self-reliant. We see the strain and grace of this as he makes his entrances and exits, as he strides to the bus stop to travel into the nearby city where his "new job" is, as he fondles the hair of his children or his wife. Far from interrupting the performance, this youthfulness lends it an aura of purity and reality, rendering Raphael completely convincing in his fear at the fact of self-sacrifice. In one long scene, he cajoles Frankie, his son (Cody Lightning), to leave his play den (long established in an abandoned oil tank) and go with him into the city. On the way he assures the frightened child that he is not going back to prison again. And he explains that if ever he is not around, Frankie, a boy of about ten years, must be the man of the house. As the two sit by the side of the road in identical postures, they are little other than a pair of boys, the one a little larger and older than the other. Raphael himself had to become the "man of the house" without first having lived an adult life. When they get to town they burst into the grocery market, dashing and screaming around with the shopping cart like characters in a cartoon, a pair of puppies in paradise. Frankie is as taciturn and beautiful as Raphael, as purposive, as simple and direct and pure; but when he goes to sleep, his thumb is in his mouth.

Frankie has broken his arm and is in a cast that keeps the limb bent at the elbow in a shape at once a little strange and a little noticeable. As he and his father walk along the road from the shantytown to the bus stop, there is a very brief moment of astonishing purity on the screen—a moment that clarifies this entire film and all the acting on-screen of Johnny Depp. After they have taken several steps, we see Raphael move his arm down to his side and take note, suddenly, that until this gesture he has had it lifted at an angle precisely matching the angle that the cast forces Frankie's arm to take. More than just an unconscious posture of the father character to make his own experience equivalent to his son's, to match himself against the son and thus give up his seniority and his power; it is a posture of the actor, to join in, to make himself experience what his colleague in front of the camera is experiencing as he is constrained to walk this way. But it is hardly a signal. Raphael is not making meaning for Frankie; Depp is not making a statement to Cody Lightning to say, "I am with you." It is presemiotic, a use of the body and not the mind. The actor is sharing his colleague's experience, directly and out of his bodily feeling of the moment. Quickly, before anyone could read this as "significant," Depp moves his arm.

In the arm posture, and the fluid movement that dissipates it, then, are passionate warmth and sensitivity, directness and simplicity, humility and conviviality, all at once. And of course, Depp as Raphael becomes through this moment nothing but a child of his time. The killing of Raphael, perpetrated in this film not only by the pervert intellectual but by the entirety of European culture, is a child murder; and part of a systematic extermination. What appeals to me about this tiny movement is its charming grace and honesty, its generosity, and above all its brevity. Depp does not build theatrical performances, arching and then climaxing through the long structure of a film. He acts in moments, he seems to manifest himself in moments, not only politically alive but also musical. Performance for him is a dance, a ceremony, and touches the real.

MOrT

In a mid-twentieth-century contribution to the journal *College English,* Walker Gibson makes a distinction between authors and speakers. If, as for Gibson, the "real reader" of a text is one "upon whose crossed knee rests the open volume," we may surmise that the "real author," these days, is one beneath whose fingertips lay the keys of a keyboard. Next to him is, perhaps, a mug of steaming coffee. On the floor is a dozing dog. A fire burns nearby in a fireplace. Bookshelves behind him are filled with volumes, several shelves being dedicated to his own publications that are present, like tiny armies of clones, in multiple copies that gleam side by side in delicious commercial copiousness. This writer takes breaks to go to the bathroom; tries to get enough protein every day; pays taxes; even buys other people's books once in a while (especially, I might add, if he is busy writing a manuscript about Johnny Depp!). By contrast, what Gibson calls the "speaker" is a being "made of language alone, and his entire self lies on the page before us in evidence."

In *Frame Analysis,* Goffman usefully compares Gibson's "author" and "speaker" to the actor and character we find in stage work. And surely we can make the same connection between the actor Johnny Depp and the various characters he portrays onscreen: this is a distinction I have been implying here throughout. Everywhere we see performance we imply an actor, as real as any viewer in any audience, mobilized behind (or underneath) it. Yet the author/speaker distinction in writing is one relatively few people think or write about, most readers being satisfied most of the time to accept as the author of the words they are following the sitter who was photographed for the image on the back cover. There is still another way in which that distinction can come into play in terms of the act of writing, however.

The act of writing requires a certain collimation of attention (the collimator was a mechanical device, invented by Dr. Harold Johns, for sharply focusing the beam of a cobalt bomb onto a very localized portion of the body). Involved here are a concentration of earnestness upon a relatively minuscule portion of a statement or argument, since at any moment only a word or a phrase is being written (that must fit nicely into a larger field); a fondness, even penchant, for grammatical correctness and utility and syntactic flow; a vision of the reader, indeed of a specific reader worth tickling, massaging, leading, cajoling, and joining in discourse, and whose attention, like a living being itself, breathes with the text always vulnerable to falling away, blacking out, forgetting, yet also capable of being reminded and seduced again. The writer, in constructing, molding, and engendering the speaker, is aware, too, of harmony and timbre, of beat, of the logical necessity of filling in the holes he dug a moment before. Every step makes a depression in the ground, and so without intending to dig one digs perforce, sometimes with more force than is commensurate with a nice flat surface crossing which no unsuspecting traveler may stumble.

These and many other demands fall upon the writer as he works, so that in sum it may be said he mobilizes a number of capabilities and strengths, tastes, sensitivities, intentions, and memory traces—not to mention any one of a number of possible vocabularies. The sentence I just wrote, for example, is *one* way my meaning could be said, but there are other ways. The writer, then, is wrapped up in writing to such a degree that efforts are required of the mind, the body, the memory, the repository of aesthetic judgment (the soul?). The writer is, indeed, so wrapped up that he becomes professionally distinct from the person who has other jobs to do at other times. So many potential problems confront him in the middle of a sentence that going off and boiling a kettle of water is literally out of the question. He must dampen his hunger for a sandwich, or else weave it into a sentence in a way that makes sense as he goes. If the phone rings or the email in-basket chimes he must not just move himself away from his prose to respond to the outside world but jump, rather like an electron, and then, somehow, jump back again right into the same position from which he took off, if this is possible at all. We will never really know if it is possible, but such jumping must be done. And imagine if a rap comes upon a door.

Mort Rainey in David Koepp's *Secret Window* (2004) is a writer with a block. (In popular depictions—and this one originates in Stephen King—every bona fide writer must have his writer's block.) His wife has left him for another man, her dog, cozy at his feet as he tries to write, is pleasant but insufficient company, and he is spending far too much time sleeping. The housecleaner keeps moving his treasured personal fetishes (key pieces of paper, for instance) around and he finds himself suddenly beset as well by the unwelcome attentions of virulently angry good ol' boy, John Shooter (John Turturro), who is convinced Mort has plagiarized from him. Very little more needs to be said about the story of this film in order to convey the central and fascinating problem it poses, precisely and especially in moments where Mort, confronting the bellicose Shooter, pleads, affirms, and screams that he knows nothing about this so-called intellectual theft. We are, perhaps, not surprised to find that Shooter commits a great deal of violence, beginning with the murder of the dog and proceeding through arson, two other murders, and defacement of property. What is surprising in a particular way, however, is the climax of the film, in which we learn the secret that—to churlishly give it away—Mort Rainey *is* John Shooter, surprising because it reveals something more than the plot intends. The film is content to leave us with the knowledge that our sleepy, even cuddly hero is schizophrenic (terrifyingly so). But invoked here, well beyond Rainey in the face of Shooter, is the relation not only between the author and speaker of a particular text (in this particular case, a published story by Mort [or by Shooter] called "The Secret Window") but also between the person who becomes an author when he works and the author that person becomes.

A writer does not write while he is sleeping any more than a brick-layer lays bricks. When he talks about writing, thinks about writing, or dreams about writing he is operating outside of the activity that, in performance, demands his loyalties and considerations. In the act of writing one participates in a practice of becoming, of transform-ing, putting on the cloak of the author as one sits to one's task to make the speaker who will exist on the page. When one's work—fiction, prose, poetry, lyrics, whatever—is overwhelmingly demand-ing of all one's energies and strengths, the transition out of everyday life into authorial status can be a marked and intensive transition, so intensive that interruption can be more than merely disturbing. Mort Rainey, as played by Depp, is precisely an author disturbed in this way. To disclaim him as simply schizophrenic, as the script makes bold to do and as audiences follow along obediently to con-firm, is thus to accomplish at once, and also: first the downgrading of Rainey as a writer into someone whose professional work does *not* sufficiently and overwhelmingly engage him, and secondly, the obliteration of the author/speaker dichotomy, and thus, writing prac-tice in general, in the name of a hollow psychiatric diagnosis. I would argue that Depp's Mort is not a schizophrenic at all. He is any normal author, so deeply involved when he is caught up in the practice of writing that there is scant—or no—relation between the self he has become and the self he left behind in the everyday world. Then he is the author lost (happily, productively lost) in his work, and in his text, and so, in the text of his work. He is the author who has so fully become a "speaker" that a wholesale leap in consciousness has been effected. But Mort has a writer's block and is not working. The speaker he becomes, or has become, is alien to him.

To go a step further: it is imperative in all successful texts that the speaker, residing wholly and only on the page, should have no aware-ness of a dimension that cannot be represented in that plane. Speak-ers do not know of the existence of the authors who are making them speak, if those authors have given themselves over entirely to the process of "speaking." In film, because things must be visible, char-acters may present themselves face to face and yet be incapable of interpenetration. In *Secret Window,* there is no avenue by means of which Mort Rainey and John Shooter can understand one another's existence, and all their interaction must take place by virtue of simplistic, perfunctory dialogue and contest. Shooter is, or was, Rainey's speaker. Rainey was Shooter's author. To be more surgical: Shooter was the speaker Rainey became when he was "on the page." Rainey was the author who ultimately became Shooter. This film allows us to see the two independently of one another—and, in a wonderful and complex sequence, actually together onscreen and moving across the visual axis many times—finally positing that Shooter does away with Rainey and takes his place in the world. The narrative voice destroys the author and outlives him. So it is, of course, when an author actually dies but his books remain in print.*

What Depp manages to do here is to lead us to be convinced of two contradictory realities with equal ferocity and commitment. We believe Shooter and Rainey are two persons (through most of the film), indeed, two very different persons who are so unlike in their comportment, their educational background, their sensibility, and their etiquette that they would reasonably be expected to have nothing whatever to do with one another. Then, too, we believe that they are two aspects of one person, and that Rainey can be replaced by Shooter. In order to sway us down these two opposing paths, Depp manages to manipulate not only his displays of feeling and intelligence but also his physical appearance, advancing from a dozy, rumpled, utterly withdrawn depressive huddled on his beat-up old couch to a lithe, languorous, insidious, and vicious murderer.

Given that *Secret Window* is, in the end, a Hollywood film—and one based on a piece of writing by one of the most commercial and commercialized writers ever to work in America—it is hardly illuminating to invoke as illumination Foucault's assertion that the "coming into being of the notion of 'author' constitutes the privileged moment of *individualization* in the history of ideas" (101), since nothing but individualization is of any particular interest to Hollywood. Perhaps this film is, in the Foucauldian sense, an epitome of Hollywood production. But given that individualization, I have tried here to raise an even more troubling question. If Beckett could put it this way: "'What does it matter who is speaking,' someone said, 'what does it matter who is speaking'" (quoted in Foucault 1984, 101), we

---

* This is written one day after the death of Depp's friend Marlon Brando. Eighty at the end of his life, he is eulogized in the press as Stanley Kowalski or Terry Malloy, both created when he was in his twenties and yet, apparently as figures, immortal.

might consider that Depp's startling performance in this film raises the question, "How can we know who is speaking?" The answer, for readers and for filmgoers, is often easier than it is for the writers they read and the actors they watch. Implicit in *Secret Window* is a treatise on Depp's own view of his own performance, on how he can be certain of the authorship of the moments that get constructed onscreen with his image. He makes them, to be sure; but who is this "he" who is embedded in the making? To take a Method point of view: the more thoroughly Depp, or any actor, invests himself in the character he is playing, the less is he aware that he is playing a character. What I have argued is that this is not so much because he merges with the character as because his attentions are diverted entirely away from everyday business to the business of maintaining—satisfying the absorbing requirements of—the staged fiction.

When he is not in role, the qualities of the performance have no import for the actor and he is at a complete remove. To find one's character standing in the doorway, then, with a grimace on his face, is rather akin to walking into a screening room and seeing one's rushes on the screen. Depp avers that he does not see his films, and one thing, at least, he could mean by this claim (that startles some who hear it) is that he is emotionally and methodologically blind to the figure who stares out at him in the darkness. To understand that character he has to become him again, and in becoming Mort Rainey Johnny Depp must obliterate Johnny Depp.

DEPP THEORY

THE THEORETICAL RESPONSE

What if we argue that the history of visual art since the seventeenth century has been a rhythmic alternation between the enunciation of the desire to see and the enunciation of the logic of sight? What if we find in it a constant repetition of the pleasure of looking interrupted by the divagations of theory? If the pleasure of looking is mysterious, esoteric, implicit, profound, pulsive, centrifugal, and anarchic, surely the theory that explains the vision is rational, exoteric, explicit, superficial, harmonic, centripetal, and also monarchic, in the sense that it posits some supreme logical center around which the act of seeing is organized according to broad, general principles that can be applied across eras and populations regardless of the exigencies of local experience. Perhaps, indeed, every art form that has been terminated in the exhaustion and exhaustiveness of theory has either sprung up again renewed and renovated or made way for a new glowing form that has galvanized viewers to new plateaus of excitement and fervor, and then, in its turn, been exploited by theory for its own drier and relentless ends. What if we look at theory and spectacle as exhaustions of one another?

In 1839, for example, just at the time that photography was invented (through the work in France and England of Daguerre and Fox Talbot) and made public, there sprang up a tremendous and widespread excitement about it, catalogued in T. H. Maurisset's lithograph, "La Daguerreotypomanie" [Daguerreotypomania]. Here, while Louis Jacques Mandé Daguerre dozes blissfully in a cloud of its steam, a locomotive engine tugs a train on each flatcar of which a huge camera is positioned. Thousands curl through the picture to line up at studios, others dance in merry circles around the camera's lens. Photography can go everywhere, this seems to say; everyone is ready and eager for it. Photography will unify the classes, banish labor, bring on the pleasure of affiliation and pose, of realization and illumination. And at the same time as this, Paul Delaroche was bold enough to say, "From this day on, painting is dead" (quoted in Jay 1994, 136). Such theorization as this was an immediate response to the perturbations that had been produced in the field of the visible by the camera, as though without such an idea of summary and dismissal, such a pronouncement, it would have been (morally) impossible to see the daguerreotype at all. The daguerreotype and the excitement it produced in the optical field, and the idea that this very excitement was related to painting as its successor and terminator, went together.

In his essay on the dialectic of enlightenment, Martin Jay describes many aspects of the fraught and vibrant relationship between vision and theory in the context of new inventions, quoting, for example, Noël Burch: "From Daguerre's Diorama to Edison's first Kinetophonograph, each state of the pre-history of the cinema was intended by its initiators—and seen by its publicists—as representatives of their class, as another step taken toward the 're-creation' of reality, towards a 'perfect illusion' of the perceptual world." The stunning visions Daguerre and Edison produced, then, were "steps" in a kind of phenomenology. So it is worth asking, in response to the early viewer's eager and confused "What is it?," could not theory rush to offer an explanation of photography, a rationale, a purpose, and a program? If it was a "re-creation of reality" one could certainly, without too much trouble, find reality in it. This was a superior response to "merely" being stunned speechless (although, as we shall see, being stunned speechless, by the end of the nineteenth century, had again come into vogue).

If in 1839 the public was aflame with excitement about what the black box and the lens could do with light, already by 1859, a mere twenty years after the camera had been invented and had drawn such crowds to line up before itself, Charles Baudelaire was already moaning about photography. "Where one should see nothing but Beauty," he wrote in "The Modern Public and Photography," as celebrated and arrogant a critique as one will find of an art form that had become extraordinarily popular, "(I mean in a beautiful painting, and you can easily guess what is in my mind), our public looks only for Truth. The people . . . judge, in stages, analytically" (1983–85, 151–152). The ability to discover the everyday in the photograph has supplanted wonder, awe, sweetness, and light. Here Baudelaire proposes three tenets. First, the camera is a teacher. The verisimilitude characteristic of photography has transplanted itself unhappily into the world of high art, replacing the fruits of the artist's imagination with the all-too-real quotidian world that art should properly be trying to escape. "Since Photography gives us every guarantee of exactitude that we could desire," Baudelaire writes snidely, "then Photography and Art are the same thing" (152). (Soon later, to be sure, Baudelaire will change his mind about this "exact" reality and about art's relation to it; but for now he is deprecating of the camera's ability to realize actual life.)

Secondly, he makes the presumption, and quite casually, as though it needed no justification or preparation, that the reader is penetrating, that is, a person attempting to "guess" what is in the writer's mind—"I mean in a beautiful painting, and you can easily guess what is in my mind." Similarly, we can presume, the viewer attempts to guess what is in the mind of the photographic artist. Comment about art can and should be about that *trace* of art that resides within the mind. Baudelaire, in other words, is here writing not about art itself but about the idea of art: he is theorizing. Thirdly, he imagines a viewer who perceives analytically and in stages; who is himself, then, a theorist when he sees; and it is with only this viewer in mind that he frames his criticism. The proper viewer does not see all in a flash, or engorge himself with what he sees; but patiently and methodically chews and digests it in a systematic way.

Although Baudelaire is willing to admit that "the desire to astonish and to be astonished is very proper" (152), he seems obliged to leap immediately to the conclusion that "the whole question . . . is to know by what processes you wish to create or to feel wonder. Because the Beautiful is *always* wonderful, it would be absurd to suppose that what is wonderful is *always* beautiful." He imagines to himself a public bent on "wondering" what beauty is—in short, cogitating about it. At the same time this public is apparently "singularly incapable of feeling the happiness of dreaming or of marveling" (152). In a way, we can see Freud migrating after this idea at least in his impulse to inquire after, and ultimately map, dreams.

Nor is the Baudelairean approach at all out of fashion, it seems. On July 7, 2003, telling a CBC radio broadcaster about his "favorite" piece of classical music, the author and critic David Frum felt compelled to begin with an apology, to the effect that he was a man who was not very sophisticated, a person who loved music "less for what it is in itself than for its associations." Why, we may ask, if a critical theoretical approach to experience is not valorized above the experience it approaches, could it have seemed necessary to this critic to apologize for loving music because of what it brings to mind? Why admire sophistication, that ability to listen to music "for itself," which is to say, in the context of the history of musical form? And indeed, why entirely obscure the vital question of what music—or, for that matter, visual art—truly is, "in itself"? It is hardly, "in itself," a self-reflexive and sophisticated critical metadiegesis, a guidebook, a view or account subject to rational discursion. Frum would seem to consider art "in itself" to be rarefied and ideological, above the common experience in which it calls up vulgar daydreams. Though he does not know enough about music to enjoy it "for itself" (read, as he properly should), he must sadly content himself with merely making associations. But it is association that has given art its power, surely. In a photograph by Jacques Henri Lartigue reproduced by Gunning (2001, 97), we see "Ma Nounou Dudu" in 1904, a rotund little woman in a white apron and black dress, in the garden of Lartigue's house, staring up into the trees at a huge ball hovering in the air. How did the ball get there—did Dudu toss it up? Will it ever fall? Does anything ever fall, in truth? How can we wait in expectation and at the same time resign ourselves to the permanence of its elevation? And what is all this if not appreciation through association, the very approach that brings Frum to the brink of apology?

Photography had been the absolute harbinger of modernity, even more than gas and electricity, which ended the night; since it provided so intense and complex a sensation of the momentary quality of experience. Indeed, the "moment" as we know it flows directly from the modernism of the nineteenth century, in which the supremest qualities of energy and drive, of direction and purpose, of taste and movement, of grace and freedom, were apotheosized in the frozen temporal fragment, Marey's chronophotograph, or, the "photographic frame as point" (Doane 2002, 215). "What is at stake in instantaneous photography," writes Doane, "is the sharpness and precision associated with the point" (215). Yet sharpness and precision operate as contradictory impulses: the former draws out a viewer's sense of amazement at the experience of optical clarity, stilling the vision with a tranquil field of mysterious detail; the latter offers itself as a tool for establishing correspondence between the image and the world, a measure and a standard. Optical sharpness is a feature of the visual spectacle; optical precision is more theoretical, having to do with the utility of the seen scene. Now the photograph's impetuosity and responsiveness, its loyalty to verisimilitude and its suppleness of use, which had once impressed everyone, were held against it as productive of "mere" reality, a "truth" all too quotidian and mechanical. Implicit in Baudelaire's critical appreciation, then, is the conviction that *the everyday world* should if possible be transcended; and that true art, namely painting, had been able to achieve that transcendence, doing what photography could not: it could reach beyond the moment to the everlasting verities and forms. Photography was, and would always be, trapped by its own miserable ontology.

If, as Marshall Berman has suggested, Baudelaire was a "first modernist"; and if he was the first critic of photography, formally speaking; he was also, by virtue of the critique he made, photography's first critical theorist. And implicit in his claim that photography gives us only the truth is an extensive articulation of thought about what the camera does and what it presumably should do; what vision can, and ought to, be; what constitutes art and what the merely humdrum record of quotidian life.

But it is exactly such a humdrum record Baudelaire himself is soon later to celebrate as the substance of modernism, in his "The Painter of Modern Life." Writing about the work of Constantin Guys, he is stunned by the painter's ability to capture "the amazing harmony of life in capital cities," to delight "in universal life." Berman is saddened to "turn to Guys's slick renderings of the 'beautiful people' and their world," there seeing "only an array of dashing costumes, filled by lifeless mannequins with empty faces" (1988, 136). For the confident Berman, to be sure, this art "resembles nothing so much as Bonwit's or Bloomingdale's ads," and Baudelaire, raving about it, was only "writing advertising copy" without even getting paid for it. What Guys had in Baudelaire's estimation, however, that made him utterly remarkable as a man of his time, was the ability to snatch at the moving array of life and represent it in its spirit and its motion. In this seizure, he resembled the detective described later by Walter Benjamin: "He develops forms of reaction that are in keeping with the pace of a big city. He catches things in flight; this enables him to dream that he is like an artist. Everyone praises the swift crayon of the graphic artist. Balzac claims that artistry as such is tied to a quick grasp" (1997, 41).

This detective is something like a camera himself—Tom Gunning has movingly described the way in which detection as a nineteenth century profession relied heavily upon the development of descriptive photography (1995)—snatching at the visible facts made palpable upon the rapidly circulating bodies in the city and rendering these facts as the "amazing harmony of life."

But, then, what is it that can be said to resemble the figure described by Balzac in *Séraphita,* who possesses "a quick look whose perceptions in rapid succession placed the most antithetical landscapes of the earth at the disposal of the imagination" (Benjamin 1997, 41 n. 13), so much as the movie camera? When we see film, which is the manifold image, what kind of imagination do we use? We may try to link the images with the world as we know it, or take pleasure in the connection within the frame, or in the chain of linked frames, between moments and objects that when placed together create what Burke called a "perspective by incongruity."

Prototypical in Baudelaire, and implicit in both Berman and Benjamin, is a particular way of looking at visual art and the visually accessible surface of the world in general, what I am here calling a "theoretical" approach. While this approach is informative, it is different in every way from the excitement and rapture experienced by those who gaze at Dudu's ball lingering through all time outside the pull of gravity. If Baudelaire was one of the first to employ such a theoretical approach, he was also committed to penetration and breadth, on one hand linking his observations to a notional structure of everyday life and on the other avoiding being trapped by a pleasure of the gaze that could blind him to its meaning. Another way of putting this, and one that will nicely focus my present concern with Johnny Depp, is that for Baudelaire and his students the gaze was essentially about meaning, rather than sensation. And to collapse this idea even further, I would say that for Baudelaire images actually *had* meaning. It is not a large step from here to suggest that the theoretical approach to visual life precludes one's looking at anything if one does not have a reason for doing so, if the looking does not add in some way to knowledge. Vision, considered this way, is ultimately scientific. Tom Wolfe is invoking this kind of vision in *The Painted Word* when he suggests that for modernist critics, in order to look, one needed a theory. For Christian Metz, indeed, by 1974, all this is explicit: the cinema "is apparently a kind of language" (40).

Now, what the theory of the visual accomplishes for those of us who are actually caught in the experience of looking is an absorption of our sensibilities into a systematic and wholesale negation, which is collected and summed as the theorized world. And what is negated by this world, in a word? Spectacle. In "Le Peintre de la vie moderne," for example, Baudelaire says of Ingres that his portraiture "imposed a preconceived ideal upon the sitter" (Rosenblum 1985, 34); in other words, the painter had arrived at the point in the development of his vision where in order to see his sitter, he needed a theory. He was, although Baudelaire did not say this, a kind of "photographic" painter—"photographic" in Baudelaire's sense of truthful. Just after the invention of photography, theorists were differentiating between the painting of Delacroix and Ingres as being "on the one hand, a swirl of impetuous brush strokes that dissolves the identity of individual forms in a turbulent and nearly illegible drama of color and energy; on the other, a crystalline compilation of quotations from Greek and Roman art, exquisitely and deliberately delineated with cameolike precision on a painted surface of enameled smoothness" (43). The painting of Delacroix was thrilling.

Theory extracts, disembodies, and repositions experience as logic, rendering it utile for navigation, influence, and commercialization. An image can be commercialized as in Berman, where the very invocation of the Bonwit's or Bloomingdale's ad in fact creates the ad, even though the image is powerful in its own right. Or it can be commercialized by an approach such as I am taking, carefully lacing it into a scheme even for the denudation of the critical process that is its commercialization. The theory of the visual, most importantly, requires that we should speak of what we have seen, that we should affix our memory of it to a matrix of sources, locations, purposes, strategies.

I have not, in fact (as I hope in a moment to show), run far from Johnny Depp. Let me give a particular and shocking—because very current—example before returning to him. While I am writing these paragraphs, I happen to look up from my keyboard to a television monitor in which I see Marcello Mastroianni, by now quite an old man, running along a beach. There are many people; there are horses. Children are grasping black ropes and going up into the air, that is, out of frame. Suddenly in an extreme long shot I see an immense black pustule floating up into a blue blue sky near the sea, children dangling from long black tendrils dripping from its bottom; all this observed by a white stallion standing very close to me. Well, my mind immediately leaps into action to produce a theory of this image. What am I seeing? What is this? What is this thing in the sky, who these children, who Mastroianni, what the meaning of this white stallion? In what kind of world is this happening? How could this happen? What will be the outcome of the happening? In the next shot Mastroianni is waking up in a sweat. Was all of this a dream, or is he waking up days later? If a dream, was it only a dream? Whose dream—his? Mine (for surely, now that I recognize it as a dream, it has become my dream)? And what is a dream? And so on. (The film is *Everybody's Fine* [*Stamo tutti bene* (1990)] by Giuseppe Tornatore.) Do these questions help me understand the meaning of the image? Now I look up again and I am looking down at Mastroianni's hand as it twirls his fork in a bowl of spaghetti alla marinara, around and around and around and around.

As a student, and sometime producer, of "literature," I am certainly aware that there is a character in this film and that something is happening to him. But in order to see the black balloon ascending in front of the white horse, need I be aware of symbolic theory? And, indeed, is it truly important that I withdraw myself from contemplation of the beauty of the beach scene—not from understanding of the beauty, or exploration of the beauty, but from *contemplation* of the beauty—in order to be affiliated with, and then affixed to, the character as an agent of the story's rationale? Ultimately, once we commit ourselves to theory, we are committed to the story, even when films are not narrative. We are committed to binding our vision of temporal form into a rational system: the narrative, the subject, the genre, the technique, the politique, the inherent schism of reception. But none of this has anything to do with the fact that now Mastroianni has had a heart attack, is lying in a hospital bed surrounded by relatives. The camera comes in for a close-up of his face and I notice that his mustache is my late father's mustache. Indeed, it is my own. His mustache is my own, and I am my late father, but none of this need mean anything at all. To be is not necessarily to mean.

Abraham Kaplan once spoke (in class) of the alternation between the creative and the critical moment, using as exemplification the first stanzas of Genesis. There, God repeatedly makes and stands back to see what He has made (and finds it good). Are not visual experience and theory, what we could call "direct" and "mediated" vision, perhaps alternating in the same way? The theory of the visual not only produces the need to speak—or write—of what one has seen; but also an intense hunger to abjure this speaking and this writing; the seeds of its own destruction, in order that one can taste again, create again, live again. Finally, after understanding the drama, we are left with a yearning to experience the dramatic again. Perhaps the reason people try to see films they have seen again, by returning to the theater or acquiring the video or DVD, is to escape from the rationale that brings excessive explanation, to escape from the genre, the director, the stars, the story, and the social, psychological, and cultural implications and get back to the image. If the world of theory is a relentless and surgical argument, the vision is always unitary and whole, intrinsic and timeless even in its rhythmic advance. May we not alternate between this argument and this unity?

So one can imagine that out of visions theory produces both texts and hungers. The end of theorization is the desire to see, and the end of discourse is silence. What I would like to propose is that in the sense that the theory of the visual ultimately produces a rejection of the rational, we can understand the rapture of the gaze not only as the motive for theory but also as a response to it. Thus, the earliest cinematography, described by Gunning and Goudreault as the "cinema of attractions" and characterized by the Lumières' *Eiffel Tower* or *Moving Sidewalk* or *Baby's Breakfast,* while it can certainly be seen from Gunning's prescient point of view as "looking forward to" a "cinema of narrative integration"—that is to say, an increasingly theoretical cinema—may just as well have been a response to the hunger for vision that followed the intense theorization of photography that had occurred by 1859, and that was, indeed, already turning itself into a hunger for the visible. Just as at the end of the nineteenth century, photography, which had been a wonder, a revelation, and a form of magic, was already relegated to the trash heap of theory, was already well enough understood to theorists (such as Baudelaire and Oliver Wendell Holmes), so, too, was it reborn in amateur instantaneous photography, such as the picture of the Nounou Dudu.

Theory is narrative, in the specific sense that it provides an explanation based on a syntactically arranged chain of propositions, in the sense that it explicates a reality by opening it to a purposeful view, in the sense that it eschews both the aggrandizement of a moment and the grandeur of a perspective in favor of a rationality that puts both time and place in order. The order that contains time and space is paramount over the rhythmic effect and the point of view per se. Gunning's "cinema of narrative integration," which began largely with D. W. Griffith, is a theoretical cinema, one that organizes sensations and feelings in terms of an overriding system of knowledge and revelation. Writing of Griffith's filmmaking around 1908–1909, Gunning notes that "the key transformation in film's relation to theater during this period derives less from the new theatrical models on which the films drew . . . than a new attitude to the act of storytelling" (1994, 38). Earlier filmmakers were much less interested in stories (theories of the world). "Méliès," writes Gunning, "has declared that the narrative line of his films was little more than a pretext, the very last element of a film that he considered, subordinated to concerns about costuming, staging, and the creation of novel 'tricks.'" Further, "A complete and coherent story was of such little interest to the first filmmakers that adaptations of famous plays frequently consisted only of 'peak moments' from stage productions"; indeed, often "telling a complete and coherent story was . . . secondary to the effect of film tricks or the thrill of a famous moment" (39).

I take Gunning's central proposition about the history of film to be that narrative integration follows upon a period of the "cinema of attractions," a cinema loaded with what could be fabulous to the eye: costuming, staging, "novel tricks," whatever might constitute for the avid viewer the "thrill of a moment." Gunning does not go so far as to suggest what seems possible to me, namely, that the "cinema of attractions" is not only an antecedent of the kind of narrative development one begins to find in Griffith but also a reaction to something—well, two somethings—that came before. One of these somethings, I believe, was the conversion of photography from what I would call an attraction to what I would call a theoretical substance. Ortega writes that surrealism takes place in the mind of the observer; he implies that it is a theoretical act of vision. And photography in the nineteenth century had proceeded toward the surreal, occasioning a criticism based not on what the camera could show but on the relation between images and mental (read, cultural) life. In such a criticism, the thrill of vision is always deprecated in favor of sophistication of analysis. Meaning is mined.

But also, photography was anticipating the cinema of attractions more directly through the amateur instantaneous photography of the 1880s, one interesting instance in which the result of rationalization is the birth of a new process, a new excitement: "the startling nature of these new instantaneous images, freezing the movements of the world in previously unseen phases, gave the amateur a sense of discovery," writes Gunning (2001, 73); yet, at the same time, he admits that "these nearly comical images also carried connotations of scientific investigation and demonstration" (73). Scientific investigation and demonstration, while holding an attraction and a sensual delight for some, are often rationalized as systematic, institutionalized (the scientific appropriation of photography in criminal identification, discussed above [see Gunning 1995]), and objective. Besides Lartigue's "Ma Nounou Dudu" Gunning reproduces a Lumière instantaneous photo "suspending a bather upside down twixt sea and sky" (2001, 90). At a lake, a man has run off a dock and turned a somersault into the water, but the camera has caught him in mid-air, and upside-down, his feet pointing up into the air and his lips pursed in unending anticipation (this body a perfect representation in itself of the stunning visual form). Thus, art forms can oscillate between the exciting and the comprehensible, the attractive and the expository, the engagement of spectacle and the withdrawal of theory. In developing a theoretical approach, what matures is the faculty of reason alone. Emotional response, sensuality, aspiration, sensitivity are all dulled in order for this "maturation" to take place.

By the late 1830s, as Delaroche proclaimed, painting was "dead" and audiences needed a way to see again. By the late 1860s, surely the 1880s, much of photography was dead, too, and the way was open for what amateurs would do and for the cinema of attractions. Peter Greenaway suggested (perhaps a little presumptuously) on the BBC, July 6, 2003, that as of December 1983 motion pictures were dead, replaced by the remote control; although the rebirth of the cinema of attractions as the cinema of spectacle leaves reason to suspect that cinema may be reinventing itself as it goes.

There is reason, the cinema of spectacle seems to show, to pay close attention to the visually thrilling for its own sake. When we see attraction in cinema only as a harbinger of the all-important narrative that is inevitably to follow—both the diegetical story and the metadiegetical criticism of society per se in terms of the story—we attend to it but only superficially, as though its import inheres almost exclusively in what will be born from it. But the idea that a cinema of attractions was needed after the collapse of photography into theory is useful in that it invites an exclusive concentration on the allure of the screen for its own sake; and in that it directs us, at the beginning of the twenty-first century (the third century of cinema), to find a new value in the *purely sensational,* which may now be considered outside the pervasive armature of narrative that has cloistered it for almost a hundred years.

Most of the spectacle that has received attention—critical attention, scholarly attention, and popular attention—has been associated with technology: lens, camera, digital and other devices that have made possible new and exciting virtual realities, new editing forms, new kinds of screen color, new pyrotechnics, new visual composites, and so on. This is the blockbuster action cinema that, in 2003 at least, composed out of motion itself the central thrills in such films as *Terminator 3, Hulk, 28 Days Later, Lara Croft: Tomb Raider, 2 Fast 2 Furious, Bad Boys II, Spy Kids 2: 3D, X2,* and so on, and the blockbuster effect cinema, where the excitement inheres in the bizarreness of what can be seen: *Pirates of the Caribbean: Curse of the Black Pearl, The Matrix* trilogy, *The Lord of the Rings* trilogy, *Spider-Man, Spider-Man 2, Hellboy,* and others. All these films, to be sure, offer "eye candy" in the context of stories that are palpably thin; they are films the visual experience of which overwashes the attempt to theorize them. But very little attention has been paid to screen performance itself as an inherently experiential—nontheoretical—element of cinema.

While Richard De Cordova had once emphasized that the star emerged after, and not as part of, the early cinema where the apparatus of projection itself attracted attention, he came to aver that "the individual star has an undeniable specificity. The star's physical image is distinguishable from that of all other stars; the circulation of that image takes a historically specific course" (2001, 9). If the historical and aesthetic individuality of the star functions inside the theory of the narrative, however, it could do so only by reduction, dilution, in order that the tale could be generalized. My argument is that the star transcended the narrative, the expository stream, precisely as a trace of allure and mystery. What the earliest stars such as Charlie Chaplin and Mary Pickford share with Johnny Depp is a tendency to linger as discretely desirable individualities, objects of wonder, in the face of the flattening—because revealing—stories in which they are paid for embedding themselves.

It is in this context that I propose the kind of consideration of Johnny Depp that I have begun in these pages. What the new technology of attractions is to the conventional twentieth-century filmmaking mode, Johnny Depp's screen presence is to that of the movie stars of old. He brings glamour back to screen performance in a way that other actors of his generation have failed to do. For Tom Cruise it has been necessary to invoke romance (which is already a theory); for Brad Pitt, a masculinity; for Edward Norton, a self-consciousness; for Matt Damon, a charm (which is a sociability). But Depp, taken altogether, has avoided invocation. When we look at him we know that he is something to look at, and that through looking we will not succeed in coming to know.

THE PURELY SENSATIONAL JOHNNY DEPP

Johnny Depp is a pure sensation, something that is accessible to us long before the entrenching postulations of theory give it a name and suggest an angle from which it can be seen to best advantage. As a presence, he leaps off the screen to tangle with our sensibilities, our anxieties, our deepest feelings. Critics and fans alike speak of how beautiful he is. A colleague of mine who has met him attests, "In person *he is even more beautiful*." Easily, yet confoundingly, we begin to relegate his films and his performances to the popular, the kitschy. He raises a specific anxiety, for the theorist, attendant upon coming to terms with one's pleasure without being able to formulate a coherent explanation for it. That there is no particular program or coherence to the chain of roles he selects has driven some observers to extremes. Anne Bilson of the *Sunday Times* commented after *Benny & Joon* that he "might have been the next Tom Cruise except that his career choices are *so wilfully* noncommercial" (quoted in Goodall 1999, 138; emphasis added). "Tom Cruise," in this sense, is a theory of acting, and Johnny Depp has failed to turn himself into precisely that.

He is, perhaps, to the degree that cinematic acting is both musical and a performance, the Franz Liszt of his age. Just as Wilson claims about Liszt that he

may or may not have launched the powerful fixations on performers imbedded in our own cultural biases about professional music, but he certainly did his part to assist: to Liszt is attributed the remark, "Le concert, c'est moi!"—"*I* am the concert!" . . . He realized that the concert stage was ripe for conversion into a platform for the display of human prowess, and correctly guessed that people would come to concerts to see such a display as eagerly as Romans flocking to the Coliseum. (1998, 214)

one may claim about Depp that he realized the screen was ripe for a similar conversion. If, for Wilson, Liszt "threw his hat—and the career of the musician along with it—into the Darwinian universe" (214), it may be true that Depp has thrown his hat, and the career of the actor, into a universe more rife with social than with natural forces of selection, into a classed and racialized universe. If it is going too far to suggest that the "Johnny Depp film" can be isolated as a genre in itself, and that in each film of this genre Depp *is* the central force and attraction; still, as I have tried to suggest again and again in this book, in each "Johnny Depp film" there are moments in which he gives what can only be called a virtuoso performance, thereby transforming the relationship between actors and audiences, and in so doing transforming the definition of acting skill (to paraphrase what Wilson says of Liszt [215]). Indeed, Depp is a striking example of an actor whose selection of roles, whose infusion into the roles he plays, whose depth of commitment to his performance, whose subtlety of expression, whose range of athleticism and grace, whose physical plasticity and immense vocal range, contribute in sum to a performance style that is at once surprising, brilliant, unparalleled, unrepeated, and unrepeatable. "Performers now had to be capable of virtuosic performance because that was what audiences demanded," Wilson writes of Liszt (215), but the same can be said of Depp as a model for the new screen actor of the twenty-first century.

Depp is notably not garrulous or precise in his discussion of his performances. He tends to be anecdotal, elusive, suggestive, mysterious, or vague; leaving the impression that his acting is largely intuitive and that he would find any coherent theoretical formulation that attempted to make sense of what he does rather pointless. Discussing his transvestitism in *Ed Wood,* for example, he notes that he thought he was "the ugliest woman I had ever seen" and yet, at the same time, "I've got some nice slips and hosiery and garters, a couple of nice brassieres, and I love Angora sweaters. Oh man, they're unbelievable" (quoted in Goodall 1999, 177). This is very suggestive of the kind of transformation in sensibility and awareness that must have been effected by, and through, him; yet it doesn't offer the kinds of explicit and erudite grounds for rationalizing performance that theorists demand. Nevertheless the performance is striking and it is there. I might suggest the *thereness* is explicitly a central feature of an attractive image, that in being captivated by such a form we are made profoundly conscious of the space inhabited by the performer/ image as object of our vision and ourselves as viewing subjects being bipolar, being a field for an exacting and painful force that keeps us withdrawn *here* from the image that excites us and that is always *there*. In this sense, attractive performance taunts and simultaneously inflames the viewer, and confronts the scholar who would cling to theory with a serious challenge: as much as performance is deeply meaningful it is also coherent. One experiences the meaning with a sense of taste; but one experiences the coherence with pleasure and hunger. If critics think of "Depp films" as kitschy, this may be only because they have lacked a coherent theory from which to view them as high art. Or because their commitment to criticism has shriveled their pleasure and stripped their hunger.

In the end, we must take a different kind of approach to serve our subject, one that does not precisely encircle or encapsulate him, that does not define, that does not rationalize or predict. If the piety of narrative is theoretical formulation or decoding, the piety of attraction is description. And, indeed, while writing about cinema has become progressively denser and more self-reflexive, more prolix in its intimation of fractures and fragmentations of meaning and response; at the same time it has found itself tongue-tied in describing what it sees. Between the work of screenwriters, who compose the film, and critics who decompose it, there is little text that attempts to write the filmic experience *per se*. And, to be sure, the idea of "writing the filmic experience *per se*" is itself taken in the critical perspective as a useless venture.

This does not mean to suggest that Johnny Depp cannot be theorized, or that his performances are beneath or beyond theory. One theoretical avenue is laid in Guy Debord's *Cinema of Spectacle,* where the alluring is entirely devoured and digested according to a post-Foucauldian schema that incorporates not only the viewer and the object viewed but the entire social system of appropriation and containment through the gaze. I do not mean to suggest that theoretical formulation is pointless, or even that it does not have the power to assist us in our appreciation of what is onscreen. But I do mean to say that in the field of contemporary cinema, the screen performances of Johnny Depp seem to constitute a particularly enigmatic, challenging, and alluring point of focus, one that recalls the sensibilities and powers of the pre-theoretical. More than he is an obstruction to theory, then, Depp is an invitation to reexperience what it is that makes theory possible and desirable.

If we accept this invitation, we find ourselves as richly surrounded by provocation, intimation, and delight as in listening to the complete piano sonatas of Beethoven, watching the films of Jean Vigo or Preston Sturges, reading the fiction of Borges. But with Johnny Depp, the safely containing broader structure of narrative form entirely melts away when he comes onscreen. One has to remind oneself, indeed, of what is "going on." He is at once a bizarre insect (the grasshopper Leonardo DiCaprio is beheading in *What's Eating Gilbert Grape*), a flower, a dancer in motion, a tree, a surface, a song. However, given that his image onscreen is mass-produced, commercialized, and heavily mediated, it does appear inconceivable that so simple and pure a fascination could remain attached to it. Depp will surely enter a forward category soon enough, and his history will then be recorded, his image understood, his fascination laid bare for all to see and master. For now, the theoretically minded scholar can look down on these images as pure *kitsch*.

And the Johnny Depp that starts here keeps changing.

THE IMAGE VIEWS HIMSELF DISAPPEAR

L ike much of the rest of Western mainstream culture, the *New York Times,* once an admittedly too-cloistered sanctuary of informed opinion and haughty, self-congratulatory insider knowledge, has thrown itself brazenly at the feet of Hollywood— this, to a degree so flattering and self-deprecating, if also smarmily chic, that it now, apparently once *every* autumn, publishes an "annual movie issue" of its Sunday magazine. "Where id was, there shall ego be," Freud wrote. Here one might well say, "Where high culture's exclusivity was, there shall pop culture's shameless marketing be." On page 96 of the issue for November 9, 2003, for example, we learn that the British actor Paul Bettany, married to Jennifer Connelly and also 6 feet 3 inches tall, and soon to appear in *Dogville, Master and Commander,* and *Wimbledon,* is wearing a custom-made (scarlet) Ozwald Boateng suit valued at $1,590.

But on page 55, drawing to an end her profile of Tim Burton (in celebration of the then-forthcoming *Big Fish*), Lynn Hirschberg, "a kind of emissary to the entertainment world," after noting that for *Batman Returns* Burton used 70 "pretty insane" live penguins whose stage had to be kept cold enough to give many crew members the flu, that in his private studio he has a framed Hiroshi Sugimoto photograph of "an old movie theater on Catalina Island," that at one point his mother had "a gift store devoted to cats," and that the standard early critical approach to him was that he had "a brilliant eye and no ear" for a story, suddenly, and without either romance or preparation, without context or comment, brings up the topic of Burton's "next movie," a remake of *Willy Wonka & the Chocolate Factory.*

Burton had been negotiating since at least August 2003 to get Depp to play the title role in that film. Landing deftly on the actor's fascination for the Oompa Loompas, a tribe of mantra-chanting chocolate-covered dwarfs who slave in the factory for the benevolent capitalist Wonka—"What is Tim going to do with the Oompa

Loompas?" asked Johnny Depp (Hirschberg 2003, 55)—Josh Grossberg hinted August 20 on E! Online that it would "soon be Oompa Loompa time for Johnny Depp. . . . Burton and Warners sweetened on Depp following the blockbuster success of *Pirates of the Caribbean.* . . . Depp also has bona fides as a candy lover" (Grossberg 2003).

But after introducing *Willy Wonka* to her readers, those avid sycophants of the "Oscar-scheming, novel-adapting, release-date-juggling, upper-mid-brow-seducing, period-recreating, art-budget-breaking, grown-up-pleasure-making prestige film season" (to whom the magazine coyly but self-knowingly addresses itself), Hirschberg cannot resist quoting Johnny saying something else, something entirely more profound. "If the movie happens, with Tim directing me," says he, "well, maybe I should bow out gracefully after that. I doubt it will get any better" (55).

"I doubt it will get any better." Whatever are we to make of this? What are we to make, indeed, given the fact that other deals have been struck and acted upon: he will vocalize, in Tim Burton and Mike Johnson's *The Corpse Bride* (based on a Russian folktale) a man who inadvertently marries a corpse, and then, according to FilmStew.com of July 3, 2004, "return to the Walt Disney Co. where he will shoot back-to-back sequels to *Pirates of the Caribbean.* Meanwhile, *Ils se marièrent et eurent beaucoup d'enfants* is in post-production from Yvan Attal, as is Benicio Del Toro's *The Rum Diary* (from a Hunter S. Thompson novel), in which he will be joined by Del Toro, Nick Nolte, and Josh Hartnett. In production are Laurence Dunmore's *The Libertine* (where, if *www.iol.co.za* for March 30, 2004, can be believed, he will be accompanied by three hundred naked extras), *Charlie and the Chocolate Factory,* and Julian Schnabel's *The Diving Bell and the Butterfly,* about a forty-three-year-old Parisian magazine editor paralyzed in all but his left eye. In the face of all this, what can "I doubt if it will get any better" now be taken to mean? Yet it can hardly mean nothing.

Perhaps what Depp's readers in the *Times* could infer is that he was sold on *Chocolate Factory* and that they could look eagerly toward it in the very near future. That Depp has an immense respect for Burton, a fact unsurprising to anyone who has read his considerable interview comments on how the two guzzled black coffee and stared at one another on first meeting and on how Burton used his drawings to seduce Johnny with the idea of becoming Edward Scissorhands. That the experience of working with Burton is not only unsurpassable, but in fact good, very good, as good as it gets and is likely to get for him or, presumably, any other actor lucky enough to be alive and working while Burton is alive and working.

I hear something else, however. I hear that Johnny has had a new thought, something cool and gray, even eerie, and certainly a thought the media have never credited him with thinking before. Since the Johnny I am writing about is a creature of the media and a denizen of the screen—even the apparently enthused and spontaneous, one could say "authentic," Johnny who analyzes Chaplin's technique for Richard Schickel—and nothing if not a success, I claim it as a thought that has been waiting over his horizon, something so out of his reach no germ of it has infected a moment of his conscious experience. But now, suddenly, in the face of Willy Wonka of all things, he is wondering what might happen if he "should bow out gracefully." No matter the reason and no matter the moment, a thought has entertained his considerations, a new thought, a bold thought. Gracefully bow out.

Depp is now, and has always been, a person of flesh and blood with a civil life and a claim to privacy, a person most people do not know and have no likelihood of meeting, as is everyone else. That person may always have dreamed of the possibility of not acting, of sitting back and doing something else with his life, but he is not the figure I am referring to here. It is the Depp who speaks to me—who can be quoted in the *New York Times,* the Depp who will be seen onscreen in *Charlie and the Chocolate Factory,* or *The Diving Bell and the Butterfly,* the Depp who recounts fables about working with Tim Burton, about his relationship with Tim Burton, about the magnitude of the pleasure he derives from his association with Tim Burton, the Depp of print and sound bite, the image of Depp lounging grizzled at the Chateau Marmont in an expensive suit with his legs spread and a glass of Merlot—it is *our* Johnny Depp who is now, as the script has it, thinking of disappearing. The image of Depp, in fact, has had a vision of his own disappearance: dis-appearance here working as centrally, engagingly, rapturously for his own (very two-dimensional) imagination as his (two-dimensional) appearance works for ours.

I think this quotation, this moment in the *Times Magazine,* this reconsideration of his own presence, is important for a number of reasons, but principally two:

First, an image has mortality. We all know that the humans behind an image are mortal: that Vincent Price, after making *Edward*

Scissorhands as Edward's "father," passed away, that Ted Demme, who made *Blow,* is now dead, that Troy Donahue and Robert Mitchum, who worked on *Cry-Baby!* and *Dead Man,* respectively, are in their graves, that Brando is gone. But here, the image itself appears to see itself in time, to imagine a future, to imagine evanescing. Because, once again, the Johnny behind the Johnny onscreen is still a surface, a construct; yet that surface has a vision of its own future.

I am startled again and again, as I think of films I have seen in my life, to note various actors who seemed central to my consciousness while I was watching them and long afterward, certainly my consciousness as a moviegoer, and who suddenly were not there anymore to see in the sweet darkened vaulted rooms where the great images floated on the screen. Replaced by other actors, they would be imperceptible and intangible in their disappearance, until, many years later, I would suddenly start out of a daydream to recollect that I had not seen them for years! Thus it is that when images disappeared, they merely ceased to provide appearance, as though drawn off the stage of the field of my sight by unseen directorial hands. Where is Thomas Gomez? Where Katy Jurado? Where Barbara Stanwyck? Where Michael Pate? Wendy Hiller? Rex Harrison? Cornel Wilde? When did Charles Gray die, and how was that possible, so profoundly did he shine. One can look all this information up, of course, but I don't mean, "When in the calendar history that dates forward and backward from my own birth did an actor cease to live?" I mean, "When, in the image history that is the chain of cinematic moments I have seen and been touched by did an image shed its last life?" To see again old films made by actors who are not acting anymore is to see reflections, after all, not directness. Yet, too, these images are immortal, as long as celluloid is immortal, although it is also true that in generation after generation viewers bring new knowledge of the world, new expectations, to the images they confront and therefore see them differently. Suddenly the images of one's childhood seem to cease to be, and then the commodifying media step in and frame obituaries, documentary testimonials, festivals of films. But all my life I have experienced the death of images, and always it has been a blunt, chilling, echoing—and thus disturbing—fact of existence in an image-filled world. To open a book and see, suddenly, a photograph of Jeff Chandler; to know with a start that one possesses an image trace, because one can recognize that face, yet also that for years one has not called upon that trace, that it has been, as it were, buried or hidden; to realize, upon looking, that fifty years have passed; to know that the world I see before me is not filled with the face of Jeff Chandler the way it is filled with the face of Johnny Depp, that Ida Lupino's face is gone, Sterling Holloway, Olan Soule, Gloria Grahame—everlasting, all of them, yet at the same time gone—is to wonder where all those old images go when they leave the screen. To remember all the people one has met can be a challenge. But to remember all the images one has seen may not seem as difficult as it is until one is suddenly confronted with a face from a world long gone.

Now, however, an image can speak and give an interview about the eventuality of its own demise. (The marketing and publicity of stardom has become more self-reflexive.) And if the image can have mortality, perhaps it can also have—already does have—life.

Secondly, it is apparently the case that an image can in fact *imagine*. Publicity material now informs us not only where to find Johnny's face but what the mind behind that face is thinking about the past and future of that face. For the Johnny Depp who speaks out in the pages of the *New York Times* is an image, not a person, and now this image is turning his mind not to statements of fact (however constructed or repeatable)—where he grew up, what he thought of working on "21 Jump Street" or acting with Marlon Brando, why he smokes—but to the consideration of hypothetical possibilities. *Maybe I should bow out gracefully after.* The mind of the image is engaging the subjunctive, that state of trembling. Now, given that the man behind the image is unknown, the image itself, "the famous and quotable Johnny Depp," becomes even rounder and more intensive for us, possessed of a chilling premonition or anticipation of its own future. It seems, too—so matter-of-fact is its utterance—completely assured and in control of what is to come, able to decide eventuality and enact its own development and termination at will. The past and future of an image are harder and more distinct, more geometric, than the past and future of a person. When an actor dies, a person dies; but an image is not an actor, it is a picture of an actor. Once that picture gains a voice (thanks to the subjugations and blandishments of the press and media) and begins to speak its experience, we can be entranced not only by the look of images (the sexuality, the link to commodity culture) but by the history and philosophy that images articulate.

Before the age of "self-revelation" symbolized by Depp, actors speculated about their futures *privately,* to their families and agents, to their personal friends, just in the way that other people did. Now even images—that is, socially organized publicly accessible phantasms—can speculate, can see the future, can have will. Imagine that the girl in the pink dress, swinging through the glen of Arcady in the famous canvas by Fragonard, spoke to a gathering crowd of her "eyeball contact" with the painter, her soulful affinity shared with him; or that Emil Jannings was established by the press as a man with opinions of himself playing the role of doorman in *The Last Laugh* (1924). To say that what the "Depp" behind *Depp* is configured to be doing and thinking—this public mirroring—is, in essence, postmodernism itself is to escape into the deceptive simplicity of labeling. The experience of knowing him knowing "himself" is considerably more moving, and more troubling than that label implies; and now we are opened to the thought that he thinks of an end to that object of his own thinking. He has become a philosopher.

Celebrities, of course, may wither but it is difficult for them to bow out, gracefully or otherwise, and after *Pirates* Johnny is nothing if not a celebrity. Well-known now for his being well known (as Daniel Boorstin labeled the star), perhaps even more, by most people, than for his talents in performance, he has become an outsider of sorts even in the Hollywood system:

> For the industry, the star's economic value transcends the nature of their work and thus their wages far outstrip those earned by generally unionized film workers. The celebrity's independent connection to the audience permits the configuration of a separate system of value for his or her contribution to any film. This connection to the audience is on an affective or emotional level that defies clear-cut quantification of its economic import. (Marshall 1997, 83).

Is the "independent connection to the audience" an interminable one, especially if he chooses to terminate it? The issue, I think, is not whether Johnny persists in his career but how we can come to acknowledge, on our "affective or emotional level" if not also in our philosophical approach, that the thought of bowing out has crossed his mind. Crossed, that is, the "mind" of the being who is animating "Johnny Depp" for us so diligently.

Finally, it is shocking to think that the talent, bizarre and inexplicable as it is, that embodied the many characters I have written about in this book (and the many others I have omitted) might choose to discontinue making interesting characters for us to screen, that he might become, for instance, little more than a quite literal product of consumption, the template from which plastic surgeons model their craft. That "he smolders" appeals to *People* magazine (May 10, 2004) principally, it would seem, because his heat might generate inspiration for reshapings and "makeovers," those contemporary apocalyptic gestures: "'His cheek structure really stands out,' says Dr. Rod Rohrich, president of the American Plastic Surgeons and professor of plastic surgery at University of Texas Southwestern Medical Center. 'They're high, angular and very well defined, which is a bit unique, especially in a male'" (94). Certainly, Johnny will already not have been a shooting star like River Phoenix or the incomparable James Dean, but it may strangely also occur that he does not permit his career as a performer to mature in front of our eyes. He may never become what John Wayne became, or Mitchum, or Cary Grant, or Ralph Richardson, who if he stormed into civilization with his weapons brandished against the sky in William Cameron Menzies's *Things to Come* (1934) lived to slide down a staircase upon a silver platter in his dotage, in Hugh Hudson's *Greystoke* (1984). *Maybe I should bow out gracefully.*

Then we would have a few dozen glittering and very different performances in the youth and young adulthood of a mystery. He would be replaced and, by some, be forgotten, so that finally, and blissfully, he could walk at least some of the streets of Paris without being accosted by interviewers and paparazzi. His films would come to symbolize an era, as do those of Errol Flynn and Bette Davis. People would look back and say, "Ah, the early twenty-first century!" And the mouth behind Johnny Depp's mouth, that organ the interviewers love, would be, at least most of the time for most of us, silent. Who would take a moment to think, in such an eventuality, without posters and articles and photographs and celebrity sightings, that once behind all these shifting fabulous images there had been, no less attractive, the image of their engenderer? Who would recall the Johnny we now daily come to hope we are getting to know, the "inner Johnny" we try to reach, the Johnny interviewers dangle in front of us (because they dangle him in front of themselves, a cat's toy)? The images, after all, spreading everywhere, are linked to what we take to be an intentionality. Where will our escapade and game of trying to grasp Johnny go, when the countless pictures with which we must work are all that we have left?

Depp himself, meanwhile, whoever that gentleman was by then, would be off with a book and a glass of wine, or else a fishing rod and a portable radio, or else a puppy and a child, yet something none of us were prepared to understand, while what remained of him in cinema was replayed in festivals, taught in universities, aired on television late at night. A little startled, we could look back to see that the actor who had been the medium of all this, now become wholly imperceivable, was and ever would be a phantom.

WORKS CITED AND CONSULTED

Aaron, Stephen. 1986. *Stage Fright: Its Role in Acting.* Chicago: University of Chicago Press.

Barthes, Roland. 1981. *Camera Lucida: Reflections on Photography.* New York: Hill and Wang.

Baudelaire, Charles. 1983–85. "Le Peintre de la vie moderne." 1863; reprinted in *Oeuvres completes.* Paris: Gallimard.

Benjamin, Walter. 1986. *Reflections: Essays, Aphorisms, Autobiographical Writings.* Trans. Edmund Jephcott. New York: Schocken.

——. 1997. *Charles Baudelaire: A Lyric Poet in the Era of High Capitalism.* Trans. Harry Zohn. London: Verso.

Berman, Marshall. 1988. *All That Is Solid Melts into Air: The Experience of Modernity.* Harmondsworth, Middlesex: Penguin.

Bilger, Burkhard. 2002. "Waiting for Ghosts." *New Yorker* (December 23 and 30), 86–100.

Blackwelder, Rob. 1999. "Deppth Perception." SPLICEDwire interview of November 12, 1999. Available at .

Blake, William. 1969. *Complete Writings.* Ed. Geoffrey Keynes. 1802; reprint, London: Oxford University Press, 816–819.

Bordwell, David. 2002. "Intensified Continuity: Visual Style in Contemporary American Film." *Film Quarterly* 55: 3 (Spring), 16–28.

Bordwell, David, Janet Staiger, and Kristin Thompson. 1985. *The Classical Hollywood Cinema: Film Style and Mode of Production to 1960.* New York: Columbia University Press.

"Bravo! Profile of Johnny Depp." Directed by Michael Byrne. Broadcast June 22, 2003.

Brottman, Mikita. 1999. "Donnie Brasco." In *Johnny Depp: Movie Top Ten,* ed. Jack Hunter, 107–117. London: Creation Books International.

Burke, Kenneth. 1965. *Permanence and Change.* Indianapolis: Bobbs-Merrill.

Caron, Isabelle. 2003. "Johnny Depp: The Former Hell-Raiser Reveals How He's Found Happiness in His Role as a Doting Husband and Father." *Hello!* 775 (July 29), 86–89.

Carr, Steven Alan. 2001. *Hollywood and Anti-Semitism: A Cultural History Up to World War II.* New York: Cambridge University Press.

Cawelti, John G. 1974. "Savagery, Civilization and the Western Hero." In *Focus on the Western,* ed. Jack Nachbar, 57–63. Englewood Cliffs, N.J.: Prentice-Hall.

Chapman, Joan M., and Brian Chapman. 1957. *The Life and Times of Baron Haussmann.* London: Weidenfeld and Nicolson.

Clair, René. 1951. *Réflexion faite: Notes pour servir a l'histoire de l'art cinématographique de 1920 à 1950.* Paris: Gallimard.

Clark, Danae. 1995. *Negotiating Hollywood: The Cultural Politics of Actors' Labor.* Minneapolis: University of Minnesota Press.

Clark, Jason. 1999. "Johnny Depp in 'Edward Scissorhands.'" *Matinee Magazine* (October 18). Available at www.matineemag.com/jump.cgi?ID=95.

Cohan, Steven. 1997. *Masked Men: Masculinity and the Movies in the Fifties.* Bloomington: Indiana University Press.

Compton, Nick. 2001. "The Cat in the Hat." *Details* 20: 1 (October), 146–150.

Cooper, Henry S. F., Jr. 1973. *13: The Flight That Failed.* New York: Dial Press.

Courant, Curt. 2002. "Chef opérateur dans l'âge d'or du cinema." *Positif* 499 (September), 58–60.

Davis, Ronald L. 1993. *The Glamour Factory: Inside Hollywood's Big Studio System.* Dallas: Southern Methodist University Press.

DeAngelis, Michael. 2001. "Gender and Other Transcendences: William Blake as Johnny Depp." In *Ladies and Gentlemen, Boys and Girls: Gender in Film at the End of the Twentieth Century,* ed. Murray Pomerance, 283–299. Albany: State University of New York Press.

De Beauvoir, Simone. 1989. *The Second Sex.* Trans. H. M. Parshley. New York: Vintage Books.

De Cordova, Richard. 2001. *Picture Personalities: The Emergence of the Star System in America.* Urbana: University of Illinois Press.

Demme, Ted, and Johnny Depp. 2001. *Blow by Blow.* N.p.: Vision On.

Denby, David. 2003a. "Mild in the Streets." *New Yorker* (July 7), 84–85.

——. 2003b. "High Seas." *New Yorker* (July 28), 94–95.

Depp, Johnny. 1995. "Foreword." In *Burton on Burton,* ed. Mark Salisbury, ix–xii. Rev. ed. London: Faber and Faber.

——. 1999. "The Night I Met Allen Ginsberg." *Rolling Stone* 816–817 (July 8–22), 69–70.

De Vries, Hilary. 1993. "The Normalization of Johnny Depp." Available at http://ww.johnnydeppfan.com/latimes93.htm.

Diamond, Jamie. 1993. "Johnny Depp." Available at http://www.johnnydeppfan.com/cosmo.htm.

Dixon, Wheeler Winston. 1995. *It Looks at You: The Returned Gaze of Cinema.* Albany: State University of New York Press.

Doane, Mary Ann. 2002. *The Emergence of Cinematic Time: Modernity, Contingency, the Archive.* Cambridge: Harvard University Press.

Dunaway, Faye, with Betsy Sharkey. 1995. *Looking for Gatsby: My Life.* New York: Simon and Schuster.

Dyer, Richard. 1999. *Stars.* London: BFI.

——. 1997. *White.* New York: Routledge.

"Eavesdropping . . . Overheard in Hollywood." 2003. *Star* (August 19), 37.

Ebert, Roger. 1999. Review of *Sleepy Hollow. Chicago Sun-Times,* November 19. Available at www.suntimes.com/edbert/ebert_reviews/1999/11/111902.html.

——. 2000. Review of *The Ninth Gate. Chicago Sun-Times,* March 10. Available at www.suntimes.com/ebert/ebert_reviews/2000/03/031003.html.

——. 2001. Review of *Blow. Chicago Sun-Times,* April 6. Available at www.suntimes.com/ebert/ebert_reviews/2001/04/040601.html.

Fiedler, Leslie A. 1969. *The Return of the Vanishing American.* New York: Stein and Day.

——. 1978. *Freaks: Myths and Images of the Secret Self.* New York: Simon and Schuster.

Fischer, Craig. 2002. "Flaming Creature: Jerry Lewis and Screen Performance in *Hollywood or Bust.*" In *Enfant Terrible! Jerry Lewis in American Film,* ed. Murray Pomerance, 75–89. New York: New York University Press.

Foster, Gwendolyn Audrey. 2002. *Performing Whiteness: Postmodern Re/constructions in the Cinema.* Albany: State University of New York Press.

———. 2003. "Monstrosity and the Bad-White Body Film." In *BAD: Infamy, Darkness, Evil, and Slime on Screen,* ed. Murray Pomerance, 39–53. Albany: State University of New York Press.

Foucault, Michel. 1984. "What Is an Author?" In *The Foucault Reader,* ed. Paul Rabinow, 101–120. New York: Pantheon.

Freud, Sigmund. 1919. "The Uncanny." In *Collected Papers,* vol. 4, 368–407. Trans. Joan Riviere. London: Hogarth Press and the Institute of Psycho-Analysis.

Freydkin, Donna. 1999. "Burton and Depp: Wide Awake in 'Sleepy Hollow." Available at www.cnn.com/SHOWBIZ/Movies/9911/16/sleepy.hollow.

Giantis, Kat. 2004. "Depp's New Fan Base." From the "MSN Entertainment Guide to the 2004 Academy Awards." Available at http://entertainment.msn.com/netcal/?netcal=821.

Gibson, Walker. 1950. "Authors, Speakers, Readers, and Mock Readers." *College English* 11, 265–269.

Gifford, Sanford. 2004. "Freud at the Movies, 1907–1925: From the Piazza Colonna and Hammerstein's Roofgarden to *The Secrets of a Soul.*" In *The Celluloid Couch: Psychoanalysis and Psychotherapy in the Movies,* ed. Jerrold R. Brandell, 147–167. Albany: State University of New York Press.

Goffman, Erving. 1971. *Relations in Public.* New York: Harper and Row.

———. 1974. *Frame Analysis: An Essay on the Organization of Experience.* Cambridge: Harvard University Press.

Goodall, Nigel. 1999. *Johnny Depp: The Biography.* London: Blake.

Goodman, Paul. 1972. *Speaking and Language: Defense of Poetry.* New York: Random House.

Grady, Pam. n.d. "Johnny Handsome: From *Jump Street* to *Sleepy Hollow,* Johnny Depp Has Proven He's More Than a Pretty Face." Available at www.reel.com/reel.asp?node=features/interviews/depp.

Granger, Susan. 2002. "10 Stars Confess Their Bad Habits." *Famous* 3: 10 (October), 46.

Grant, Barry Keith. 2003. *Stagecoach.* New York: Cambridge University Press.

Grassin, Sophie. 2003. "Pirate Attitude." *Première* 318 (August), 51–57.

Grossberg, Josh. 2003. "Depp's Golden 'Wonka' Ticket?" Available at www.eonline.com/news/items/0,1,12351,00.html.

Gunning, Tom. 1994. *D. W. Griffith and the Origins of American Narrative Film.* Urbana: University of Illinois Press.

———. 1995. "Tracing the Individual Body: Photography, Detectives, and Early Cinema." In *Cinema and the Invention of Modern Life,* ed. Leo Charney and Vanessa R. Schwartz, 15–45. Berkeley: University of California Press.

———. 2000. *The Films of Fritz Lang: Allegories of Vision and Modernity.* London: BFI.

———. 2001. "New Thresholds of Vision: Instantaneous Photography and the Early Cinema of Lumière." In *Impossible Presence: Surface and Screen in the Photogenic Era,* ed. Terry Smith, 71–99. Chicago: University of Chicago Press.

———. 2004. "Flickers: On Cinema's Power for Evil." In *BAD: Infamy, Darkness, Evil, and Slime on Screen,* ed. Murray Pomerance, 21–37. Albany: State University of New York Press.

Halberstam, David. 1993. *The Fifties.* New York: Fawcett.

Haralovich, Mary Beth. 1999. "Selling *Mildred Pierce:* A Case Study." In *Boom and Bust: American Cinema in the 1940s,* ed. Thomas Schatz, 196–202. Berkeley: University of California Press.

Heard, Christopher. 2001. *Depp.* Toronto: ECW.

Heath, Chris. 1993. "Portrait of the oddest as a young man." *Details* (May). Available at www.johnnydeppfan.com/interviews/details.htm.

Hirschberg, Lynn. 2003. "Drawn to Narrative." *New York Times Magazine* (November 9), 50–55.

Holmes, Oliver Wendell. 1892. *The Works of Oliver Wendell Holmes,* vol. 2. Standard Library Edition. Boston and New York: Houghton Mifflin.

Horton, Andrew. 2002. "Dreaming of Jerry Lewis's Arizona Dream." In *Enfant Terrible! Jerry Lewis in American Film,* ed. Murray Pomerance, 43–57. New York: New York University Press.

Hunter, Jack, ed. 1999. *Johnny Depp: Movie Top Ten.* London: Creation Books International.

Jay, Martin. 1994. *Downcast Eyes: The Denigration of Vision in Twentieth-Century French Thought.* Berkeley: University of California Press.

"Johnny Depp Trashes America: Good Riddance!" 2002. *National Enquirer* (April 13).

Jousse, Thierry. 2002. "Icônes en tout genre." *Cahiers du cinéma* 566 (March), 8–9.

Kaplan, Abraham. 1961. *The New World of Philosophy.* New York: Vintage.

Kaylin, Lucy. 2003. "Johnny in Paradise." *Gentleman's Quarterly* (August), 92–97+.

Kerouac, Jack. 1991. *On the Road.* 1957; reprint, New York: Penguin.

King, Barry. 1986. "Stardom as an Occupation." In *The Hollywood Film Industry,* ed. Paul Kerr, 154–184. London: Routledge and Kegan Paul.

Kracauer, Siegfried. 1960. *Theory of Film: The Redemption of Physical Reality.* Princeton: Princeton University Press.

Leigh, Danny. 2001. "Johnny Be Good." *Guardian.* Available at http://film.guardian.co.uk/Print/0,3858,4191,780,00.html.

Lerner, Max. 1957. *America as a Civilization.* New York: Simon and Schuster.

Lifton, Robert Jay. 1969. *Boundaries.* Toronto: CBC.

Marshall, P. David. 1997. *Celebrity and Power: Fame in Contemporary Culture.* Minneapolis: University of Minnesota Press.

McCloskey, Robert. 1976. *Homer Price.* 1943; reprint, New York: Puffin.

Metz, Christian. 1974. *Film Language: A Semiotics of the Cinema.* New York: Oxford University Press.

Mills, C. Wright. 1951. *White Collar: The American Middle Classes.* New York: Oxford University Press.

Mitchell, Elvis. 2000. "'The Ninth Gate: Off to Hell in a Handbasket, Trusty Book in Hand." *New York Times* (March 10). Available at www.nytimes.com/library/film/031000gate-film-review.html.

"Most Wanted." 2004. *People* 61: 18 (May 10), 94.

Naremore, James. 1988. *Acting in the Cinema.* Bloomington: Indiana University Press.

Nashawaty, Chris. 2003. "Johnny Depp Has Twelve Tattoos." *Entertainment Weekly* 729 (September 19), 28–34.

Needleman, Deborah. 2001. "Mellow Drama." *House & Garden* 170: 11 (November), 140–147.

Offman, Craig. 1999. "Johnny Depp Battles Editor over Comma." (July 22). Available at www.cnn.com/books/news/9907/22/salon.depp.

Okwu, Michael. 2000. "Johnny Depp: Living Unconventionally Is *Magnifique*." "Showbiz Today," CNN, broadcast December 12, 2000. Available at www.cnn.com/2000/SHOWBIZ/Movies/12/12/chocolat.

Ortega y Gasset, José. 1968. *The Dehumanization of Art and Other Essays on Art, Culture, and Literature.* Princeton: Princeton University Press.

Overpeck, Deron. 2002. "From Hell." *Film Quarterly* 55: 4 (Summer), 41–45.

Poe, Edgar Allan. 1998. "The Man of the Crowd." In *Selected Tales,* ed. David Van Leer, 84–91. London: Oxford University Press.

Pomerance, Murray. 2002. "'Don't understand, my own darling': The Girl Grows Up in *Shadow of a Doubt.*" In *Sugar, Spice, and Everything Nice: Cinemas of Girlhood,* ed. Frances Gateward and Murray Pomerance, 52–67. Detroit: Wayne State University Press.

Rebello, Steven. 1990. "Johnny Handsome." *Movieline* (May).

Rice, Shelley. 1997. *Parisian Views.* Cambridge: MIT Press.

Richardson, John H. 2004. "The Unprocessed Johnny Depp." *Esquire* 141: 5 (May), 95–99.

Robb, Brian J. 1996. *Johnny Depp: A Modern Rebel.* London: Plexus.

Rosenbaum, Jonathan, ed. 1992. *This Is Orson Welles: Orson Welles and Peter Bogdanovich.* New York: HarperCollins.

Rosenblum, Robert. 1985. *Ingres.* New York: Harry N. Abrams.

Russell, Lisa. 2003. "The Sexiest Man Alive." *People* (December 8), 72–78.

Saada, Nicolas. 1996. "Entretien avec Jim Jarmusch." *Cahiers du cinéma* 498 (January), 25–31.

Sacks, Oliver. 1985. *The Man Who Mistook His Wife for a Hat.* London: Duckworth.

Sagan, Carl. 1994. *Pale Blue Dot: A Vision of the Human Future in Space.* New York: Random House.

Said, Edward W. 1979. *Orientalism.* New York: Vintage Books.

Sartre, Jean-Paul. 1956. "The Meaning of 'To Make' and 'To Have': Possession." In *The Self: Explorations in Personal Growth,* ed. Clark E. Moustakas, 140–146. New York: Harper and Row.

——. 1964. *La Nausée* [Nausea]. Trans. Lloyd Alexander, with an introduction by Hayden Carruth. Norfolk, Conn.: New Directions.

Schatz, Thomas. 1999. *Boom and Bust: American Cinema in the 1940s.* Berkeley: University of California Press.

Schickel, Richard. 1997. "Depp Charge." *Time* 149: 9 (March 3). Available at www.time.com/time/magazine/1997/dom/970303/depp_charge.html.

Schivelbusch, Wolfgang. 1986. *The Railway Journey: The Industrialization of Time and Space in the Nineteenth Century.* Berkeley: University of California Press.

——. 1993. *Tastes of Paradise: A Social History of Spices, Stimulants, and Intoxicants.* New York: Vintage.

——. 1995. *Disenchanted Night: The Industrialization of Light in the Nineteenth Century*. Berkeley: University of California Press.

Schneller, Johanna. 2004. "Depp Rules as the Actor Who Can Do No Wrong." *The Globe and Mail* (March 26), R1–R2.

Sebeok, Thomas A., and Jean Umiker-Sebeok. 1983. "'You Know My Method': A Juxtaposition of Charles S. Peirce and Sherlock Holmes." In *The Sign of the Three: Dupin, Holmes, Peirce,* ed. Umberto Eco and Thomas A. Sebeok, 11–54. Bloomington: Indiana University Press.

Sella, Marshall. "The Kid Stays in the Pictures: How Leonardo DiCaprio Finally Learned to Play the Hollywood Game." *New York Times Magazine* (November 24, 2002), 61–65+.

Simon, John. 2003. Personal conversation (November 22).

Sobchack, Vivian. 1991. "Postmodern Modes of Ethnicity." In *Unspeakable Images: Ethnicity and the American Cinema,* ed. Lester D. Friedman, 329–352. Champaign: University of Illinois Press.

Sontag, Susan. 1966. *Against Interpretation and Other Essays.* New York: Delta.

——. 2003. *Regarding the Pain of Others.* New York: Farrar, Straus and Giroux.

Sterritt, David. 1999. "Arts and Leisure Feature on *The Source.*" *New York Times* (August 29), sec. 2, p. 9.

Sterritt, David, and Mikita Brottman. 2004. "*Lost in La Mancha:* The Making, Unmaking, and Remaking of Terry Gilliam." In *Terry Gilliam Interviews,* ed. David Sterritt and Lucille Rhodes, 208–219. Jackson: University Press of Mississippi.

Tauber, Michelle, Ruth Andrew Ellenson, Michael Fleeman, Amy Gurvitz, and Marisa Laudadio. 2004. "A New Kind of Cool." *People* 61: 11 (March 22), 85–87.

Thompson, Hunter S. 1998. *Fear and Loathing in Las Vegas: A Savage Journey to the Heart of the American Dream.* 1971; reprint, New York: Vintage.

Toumarkine, Doris. 2001. Review of *Blow. Film Journal International* (n.d.). Available at www.filmjournal.com.

Truffaut, François. 1978. *The Films of My Life.* Trans. Leonard Mayhew. New York: Simon and Schuster.

——. 1985. *Hitchcock.* Trans. Helen Scott. New York: Simon and Schuster /Touchstone.

Tuan, Yi-Fu. 1997. *Space and Place: The Perspective of Experience.* Minneapolis: University of Minnesota Press.

Tyrangiel, Josh 2004. "Doing It Depp's Way." *Time* 163: 11 (March 15), 76–78.

Veblen, Thorstein. 1908. *The Theory of the Leisure Class: An Economic Study of Institutions.* New York: Macmillan.

Vertrees, Alan David. 1997. *Selznick's Vision: "Gone With the Wind" and Hollywood Filmmaking.* Austin: University of Texas Press.

Vidich, Arthur J., and Joseph Bensman. 1960. *Small Town in Mass Society: Class, Power, and Religion in a Rural Community.* Garden City, N.Y.: Doubleday Anchor.

Vidler, Anthony. 2001. "Warped Space: Architectural Anxiety in Digital Culture." In *Impossible Presence: Surface and Screen in the Photogenic Era,* ed. Terry Smith, 285–303. Chicago: University of Chicago Press.

Vonnegut, Kurt, Jr. 1971. *The Sirens of Titan.* New York: Dell.

Weinraub, Bernard. 2004. "Playboy Interview: Johnny Depp." *Playboy* 51: 5 (May), 59–65+.

Wilson, Frank R. 1998. *The Hand.* New York: Pantheon.

Worth, Sol, and John Adair. 1972. *Through Navajo Eyes: An Exploration of Film Communication and Anthropology.* Bloomington: Indiana University Press.

Zehme, Bill. 1991. "Sweet Sensation." *Rolling Stone* 595 (January 10), 30–35, 75.

Filmography

A Nightmare on Elm Street
1984
New Line Cinema
Eastmancolor (Technicolor), 91 min.

DIRECTOR: Wes Craven; WRITTEN BY: Wes Craven; EXECUTIVE PRODUCERS: Stanley Dudelson, Joseph Wolf; ASSOCIATE PRODUCER: John Burrows; MUSIC: Charles Bernstein and Steve Karshner, Martin Kent, Michael Schurig (song "Nightmare"); CINEMATOGRAPHY: Jacques Haitkin; EDITORS: Rick Shaine, Pat McMahon; PRODUCTION DESIGN: Gregg Fonseca; SET DECORATION: Anne Huntley; CASTING: Annette Benson; COSTUME DESIGN: Dana Lyman; MAKEUP DEPARTMENT: RaMona Fleetwood, Kathy Logan, David Miller, Mark Wilson, Louis Lazzara

CAST: John Saxon (Lieutenant Donald Thompson), Ronee Blakley (Margaret "Marge" Thompson), Heather Langenkamp (Nancy Thompson), Amanda Wyss (Christina "Tina" Grey), Jsu Garcia (Rod Lane [as Nick Corri]), Johnny Depp (Glen Lantz), Charles Fleischer (Dr. King), Joseph Whipp (Sergeant Parker), Robert Englund (Fred "Freddy" Krueger), Lin Shaye (Teacher), Mimi Craven (Nurse [as Mimi Meyer-Craven]), Jack Shea (Minister), Ed Call (Mr. Lantz), Sandy Lipton (Mrs. Lantz), David Andrews (Foreman), Jeffrey Levine (Coroner), Donna Woodrum (Tina's Mom)

Private Resort
1985
TriStar Pictures
Metrocolor, 82 min.

DIRECTOR: George Bowers; WRITTEN BY: Gordon Mitchell, Ken Segall, Alan Wenkus; PRODUCERS: R. Ben Efraim, Don Enright; CINEMATOGRAPHY: Adam Greenberg; EDITOR: Samuel D. Pollard; CASTING: Elisabeth Leustig; PRODUCTION DESIGN: Michael Corenblith; SET DECORATION: Gayle Simon; COSTUME DESIGN: Jill M. Ohanneson; MAKEUP: Donna Felix, Deborah Figuly, Peter Tothpal

CAST: Rob Morrow (Ben), Johnny Depp (Jack), Emily Longstreth (Patti), Karyn O'Bryan (Dana), Hector Elizondo (The Maestro), Dody Goodman (Mrs. Rawlings), Tony Azito (Reeves), Hilary Shapiro (Shirley), Leslie Easterbrook (Bobbie Sue), Michael Bowen (Scott), Lisa London (Alice), Andrew Clay (Curt), Ron House (The Barber), Greg Wynne (Mike), Nora Gaye (Kelly), Susan Mechsner (Aerobics Instructor), Matthew Levine (Georgie), Lucy Lee Flippin (Wanda), Phyllis Franklin (Dog Lady), Jonathan Prince (Fred), Jeremy Lawrence (Phillip)

Platoon
1986
Hemdale Film Corporation, Cinema 86
Color, 120 min.

DIRECTOR: Oliver Stone; WRITTEN BY: Oliver Stone; PRODUCERS: John Daly, Derek Gibson, A. Kitman Ho, Arnold Kopelson; MUSIC: Georges Delerue with additional music by Samuel Barber, Stephen Foster, and Otis Redding; CINEMATOGRAPHY: Robert Richardson; EDITOR: Claire Simpson; CASTING: Pat Golden, Warren McLean, Bob Morones; PRODUCTION DESIGN: Bruno Rubeo; ART DIRECTION: Rodell Cruz, Doris Sherman Williams; MAKEUP: Cecille Baun, Derek Howard, Gordon J. Smith, Gionilda Stolee

CAST: Tom Berenger (Staff Sgt. Bob Barnes), Willem Dafoe (Sgt. Elias Grodin), Charlie Sheen (Pvt. Chris Taylor), Forest Whitaker (Big Harold), Francesco Quinn (Rhah), John C. McGinley (Sgt. Red. O'Neill), Richard Edson (Sal), Kevin Dillon (Bunny), Reggie Johnson (Junior), Keith David (King), Johnny Depp (Lerner), David Neidorf (Tex), Mark Moses (Lt. Wolfe), Chris Pedersen (Crawford), Tony Todd (Sgt. Warren), Corkey Ford (Manny), Ivan Kane (Tony), Paul Sanchez (Doc), J. Adam Glover (Sanderson), Bob Orwig (Pvt. Gardner), Kevin Eshelman (Morehouse), James Terry McIlvain (Ace), Dale Dye (Capt. Harris), Peter Hicks (Parker), Basile Achara (Flash), Steve Barredo (Fu Sheng), Chris Castillejo (Rodriguez), Andrew B. Clark (Tubbs), Oliver Stone (Alpha Company Major in bunker)

Cry-Baby
1990
Imagine Entertainment, Universal Pictures
Color (DeLuxe), 85 min.

DIRECTOR: John Waters; WRITTEN BY: John Waters; PRODUCERS: Jim Abrahams, Brian Grazer, Pat Moran, Rachel Talalay; MUSIC: Patrick Williams and Doc Pomus (song "King Cry Baby"); CINEMATOGRAPHY: David Insley; EDITOR: Janice Hampton; CASTING: Paula Herold, Greg Mason, Pat Moran; PRODUCTION DESIGN: Vincent Peranio; ART DIRECTION: Dolores Deluxe; SET DECORATION: Virginia Nichols, Chester Overlock III; COSTUME DESIGN: Van Smith; MAKEUP: Betty Beebe, Nancy Broadfoot, Denise Cellucci, Christine Mason, Van Smith

CAST: Johnny Depp (Wade "Cry-Baby" Walker), Amy Locane (Allison Vernon Williams), Susan Tyrrell (Ramona Rickettes), Polly Bergen (Mrs. Vernon Williams, Allison's Grandmother), Iggy Pop (Uncle Belvedere Rickettes), Ricki Lake (Pepper Walker), Traci Lords (Wanda Woodward), Kim McGuire (Hatchet-Face, aka Mona Malrovawski), Darren E. Burrows (Milton Hackett), Stephen Mailer (Baldwin, Allison's Boyfriend), Kim Webb (Lenora), Alan J. Wendl (Toe-Joe Jackson), Troy Donahue (Hatchet's Father), Mink Stole (Hatchet's Mother), Joe Dallesandro (Milton's Father), Joey Heatherton (Milton's Mother), David Nelson (Wanda's Father), Patty Hearst (Wanda's Mother), Willem Dafoe (Hateful Guard at Maryland Training School for Boys), Jonathan Benya (Snare-Drum), Jessica Raskin (Susie-Q), Robert Tyree (Dupree), Angie Levroney (Dupree's Girlfriend)

Edward Scissorhands
1990
20th Century Fox
Color (DeLuxe), 105 min.

DIRECTOR: Tim Burton; WRITTEN BY: Tim Burton, Caroline Thompson; PRODUCERS: Tim Burton, Denise Di Novi, Richard Hashimoto, Caroline Thompson; MUSIC: Danny Elfman; CINEMATOGRAPHY: Stefan Czapsky; EDITOR: Colleen Halsey, Richard Halsey; CASTING: Victoria Thomas; PRODUCTION DESIGN: Bo Welch; ART DIRECTION: Tom Duffield; SET DECORATION: Cheryl Carasik; COSTUME DESIGN: Colleen Atwood; MAKEUP: Irene Aparicio, Fern Buchner, Bridget Cook, Selena Miller, Matthew W. Mungle, Ve Neill, Rick Provenzano, Kim Santantonio, Susan Schuler-Page, Werner Sherer, Liz Spang, Rick Stratton, Yolanda Toussieng, Mary Ann Valdes, Lynda Kyle Walker, Brad Wilder, Stan Winston

CAST: Johnny Depp (Edward Scissorhands), Winona Ryder (Kim Boggs), Dianne Wiest (Peg Boggs), Anthony Michael Hall (Jim), Kathy Baker (Joyce Monroe), Robert Oliveri (Kevin Boggs), Conchata Ferrell (Helen), Caroline Aaron (Marge), Dick Anthony Williams (Officer Allen), O-Lan Jones (Esmeralda), Vincent Price (The Inventor), Alan Arkin (Bill Boggs), Susan J. Blommaert (Tinka), Linda Perri (Cissy), John Davidson (Talk Show Host), Biff Yeager (George Monroe), Marti Greenberg (Suzanne), Bryan Larkin (Max), John McMahon (Denny, Van Owner), Victoria Price (TV Newswoman), Stuart Lancaster (Retired Man), Gina Gallagher (Granddaughter), Aaron Lustig (Psychologist), Peter Palmer (Editor)

Freddy's Dead: The Final Nightmare
1991
New Line Cinema
Color (DeLuxe), 96 min.

DIRECTOR: Rachel Talalay; WRITTEN BY: Wes Craven, Rachel Talalay, Michael De Luca; PRODUCERS: Michael De Luca, Michael N. Knue, Robert Shaye, Aron Warner; MUSIC: Brian May; CINEMATOGRAPHY: Declan Quinn; EDITOR: Janice Hampton; CASTING: Janet Hirshenson, Jane Jenkins, Roger Mussenden; PRODUCTION DESIGN: C. J. Strawn; ART DIRECTION: James R. Barrows

CAST: Robert Englund (Freddy Krueger), Lisa Zane (Dr. Maggie Burroughs), Shon Greenblatt (John Doe), Lezlie Deane (Tracy), Ricky Dean Logan (Carlos), Breckin Meyer (Spencer), Yaphet Kotto (Doc), Roseanne (Childless Woman), Tom Arnold

(Childless Man), Elinor Donahue (Orphanage Woman), Johnny Depp (Teen on TV, as Oprah Noodlemantra), Cassandra Rachel Frel (Little Maggie), David Dunard (Kelly), Marilyn Rockafellow (Maggie's Mother), Virginia Peters (Woman in Plane), Stella Hall (Stewardess), Angelina Estrada (Carlos's Mother), Peter Spellos (Tracy's Father), Tobe Sexton (Teen Freddy), Alice Cooper (Freddy's Father)

Arizona Dream (also known as *The Arrowtooth Waltz*)
1993
Constellation, Hachette Première, Le Studio Canal+, Union Générale
Cinématographique (UGC)
Color, 142 min.

DIRECTOR: Emir Kusturiça; WRITTEN BY: David Atkins, Emir Kusturiça; PRO-
DUCERS: Richard Brick, Paul R. Gurian, Yves Marmion, Claudie Ossard; MUSIC:
Goran Bregovic; CINEMATOGRAPHY: Vilko Filac; EDITOR: Andrija Zafranovic; CAST-
ING: Pennie DuPont; PRODUCTION DESIGN: Miljen Kreka Kljakovic; ART DIRECTION:
Jan Pascale; SET DECORATION: Jan Pascale; COSTUME DESIGN: Jill M. Ohanneson;
MAKEUP: Karoly Balazs, Deborah Ann Piper, Patty York

CAST: Johnny Depp (Axel Blackmar), Jerry Lewis (Leo Sweetie), Faye Dunaway
(Elaine Stalker), Lili Taylor (Grace Stalker), Vincent Gallo (Paul Leger), Paulina
Porizkova (Millie), Michael J. Pollard (Paul), Candyce Mason (Blanche), Alexia
Rane (Angie), Polly Noonan (Betty), Ann Schulman (Carla), Patricia O'Grady
(MC/Announcer), James R. Wilson (Lawyer), Eric Polczwartek (Man with Door),
Kim Keo (Mechanical Doll), James P. Marshall (Boatman), Vincent Tocktuo (Es-
kimo Man), Jackson Douglas (The Priest), Tricia Leigh Fisher (Lindy), Michael S.
John (The Doctor), Sal Jenco (Man at the phone), Emir Kusturiça (Man in the bar)

Benny & Joon
1993
Metro-Goldwyn-Mayer, Roth-Arnold Productions
Color (Eastmancolor), 98 min.

DIRECTOR: Jeremiah Chechik; WRITTEN BY: Barry Berman, Leslie McNeil; PRODUC-
ERS: Susan Arnold, Bill Badalato, Lesley McNeil, Donna Roth; MUSIC: Rachel Port-
man, Charlie Reid, Craig Reid; CINEMATOGRAPHY: John Schwartzman; EDITOR:
Carol Littleton; CASTING: Risa Bramon Garcia, Heidi Levitt; PRODUCTION DESIGN:
Neil Spisak; ART DIRECTION: Pat Tagliaferro; SET DECORATION: Barbara Munch;
COSTUME DESIGN: Aggie Guerard Rodgers; MAKEUP: Frida Aradóttir, Cindy J.
Williams, Patty York

CAST: Johnny Depp (Sam, Mike's Cousin), Mary Stuart Masterson (Juniper "Joon"
Pearl), Aidan Quinn (Benny Pearl), Julianne Moore (Ruthie), Oliver Platt (Eric),
C.C.H. Pounder (Dr. Garvey), Dan Hedaya (Thomas), Joe Grifasi (Mike, Card

Player), William H. Macy (Randy Burch), Liane Alexandra Curtis (Claudia), Eileen Ryan (Mrs. Smail), Amy Alizabeth Sanford (Young Joon), Brian Keevy (Young Benny)

What's Eating Gilbert Grape
1993
J&M Entertainment, Paramount Pictures
Color (DeLuxe), 118 min.

DIRECTOR: Lasse Hallström; WRITTEN BY: Peter Hedges (novel and screenplay); PRO-DUCERS: Alan C. Blomquist, Lasse Hallström, David Matalon, Bertil Ohlsson, Meir Teper; MUSIC: Björn Isfält, Alan Parker, Joseph S. DeBeasi; CINEMATOGRAPHY: Sven Nykvist; EDITOR: Andrew Mondshein; CASTING: Gail Levin; PRODUCTION DESIGN: Bernt Capra; ART DIRECTION: John Myhre; SET DECORATION: Gretchen Rau; COS-TUME DESIGN: Reneé Ehrlich Kalfus; MAKEUP: Toni G, Rodd Matsui, Deborah Ann Piper, Cindy Williams, Patty York

CAST: Johnny Depp (Gilbert Grape), Leonardo DiCaprio (Arnie Grape), Juliette Lewis (Becky), Mary Steenburgen (Betty Carver), Darlene Cates (Bonnie Grape), Laura Harrington (Amy Grape), Mary Kate Schellhardt (Ellen Grape), Kevin Tighe (Ken Carver), John C. Reilly (Tucker Van Dyke), Crispin Glover (Bobby McBurney), Penelope Branning (Becky's Grandma), Tim Green (Mr. Lamson), Susan Loughran (Mrs. Lamson)

Ed Wood
1994
Touchstone Pictures
Black and white, 127 min.

DIRECTOR: Tim Burton; WRITTEN BY: Scott Alexander, Larry Karaszewski, from *Nightmare of Ecstasy* by Rudolph Grey; PRODUCERS: Tim Burton, Denise Di Novi, Michael Flynn, Michael Lehmann; MUSIC: Ray Evans and Jay Livingston (song "Que Sera, Sera"), Howard Shore; CINEMATOGRAPHY: Stefan Czapsky; EDITOR: Chris Lebenzon; CASTING: Victoria Thomas; PRODUCTION DESIGN: Tom Duffield; ART DIRECTION: Okowita; SET DECORATION: Cricket Rowland; COSTUME DESIGN: Colleen Atwood; MAKEUP: Carrie Angland, Rick Baker, Bridget Cook, Jim Leonard, Lucia Mace, Jim McLoughlin, Ve Neill, Matt Rose, Yolanda Toussieng

CAST: Johnny Depp (Edward D. Wood, Jr.), Martin Landau (Bela Lugosi), Sarah Jessica Parker (Dolores Fuller), Patricia Arquette (Kathy O'Hara), Jeffrey Jones (Criswell), G. D. Spradlin (Reverend Lemon), Vincent D'Onofrio (Orson Welles), Bill Murray (John "Bunny" Breckinridge), Mike Starr (Georgie Weiss), Max Casella (Paul Marco), Brent Hinkley (Conrad Brooks), Lisa Marie (Vampira), George "The Animal" Steele (Tor Johnson), Juliet Landau (Loretta King), Clive

Rosengren (Ed Reynolds), Norman Alden (Cameraman Bill), Leonard Termo (Makeup Man Harry), Ned Bellamy (Dr. Tom Mason), Danny Dayton (Soundman), John Ross (Camera Assistant), Bill Cusack (Tony McCoy)

Don Juan DeMarco
1995
American Zoetrope, New Line Cinema, Outlaw Productions
Color (Eastmancolor), 97 min.

DIRECTOR: Jeremy Leven; WRITTEN BY: Lord Byron (character of Don Juan), Jeremy Leven; PRODUCERS: Francis Ford Coppola, Michael De Luca, Fred Fuchs, Robert Newmyer, Patrick Palmer, Brian Reilly, Jeffery Silver, Ruth Vitale; MUSIC: Bryan Adams (song "Have You Ever Really Loved a Woman?"), Michael Kamen, Robert John Lange; CINEMATOGRAPHY: Ralf D. Bode; EDITOR: Tony Gibbs; CASTING: Lynn Kressel; PRODUCTION DESIGN: Sharon Seymour; ART DIRECTION: Jeff Knipp; SET DECORATION: Maggie Martin; COSTUME DESIGN: Kirsten Everberg; MAKEUP: Ron Berkeley, Lucia Mace

CAST: Marlon Brando (Dr. Jack Mickler), Johnny Depp (Don Juan), Faye Dunaway (Marilyn Mickler), Géraldine Pailhas (Donna Ana), Bob Dishy (Dr. Paul Showalter), Rachel Ticotin (Dona Inez), Talisa Soto (Dona Julia), Marita Geraghty (Woman in Restaurant), Richard C. Sarafian (Detective Sy Tobias), Tresa Hughes (Grandmother DeMarco), Stephen Singer (Dr. Bill Dunsmore), Franc Luz (Don Antonio), Carmen Argenziano (Don Alfonzo), Jo Champa (Sultana Gulbeyaz), Esther Scott (Nurse Alvira), Nada Despotovich (Nurse Gloria), Gilbert Lewis (Judge Ryland), "Tiny" Lister, Jr. (Rocco Compton)

Dead Man
1995
12 Gauge Productions, JVC Entertainment, Miramax Films, Newmarket Capital Group LLC, Pandora Filmproduktion GmbH (Denmark),
Black and white, 121 min.

DIRECTOR: Jim Jarmusch; WRITTEN BY: Jim Jarmusch; PRODUCERS: Karen Koch, Demetra J. MacBride; MUSIC: Neil Young; CINEMATOGRAPHY: Robby Müller; EDITOR: Jay Rabinowitz; CASTING: Ellen Lewis, Laura Rosenthal; PRODUCTION DESIGN: Robert Ziembicki; ART DIRECTION: Ted Berner; SET DECORATION: Dayna Lee; COSTUME DESIGN: Marit Allen; MAKEUP: Clare Corsick, Scott W. Farley, Tom Irvin, Todd Kleitsch, Neal Martz, Patty York

CAST: Johnny Depp (William "Bill" Blake), Gary Farmer (Nobody), Lance Henriksen (Cole Wilson), Michael Wincott (Conway Twill), Mili Avital (Thel Russell), Robert Mitchum (Dickinson), Iggy Pop (Salvatore "Sally" Jenko), Crispin Glover (Train fireman), Jimmy Ray Weeks (Marvin), Mark Bringleson (Lee), Gabriel

Byrne (Charles Ludlow "Charlie" Dickinson), John Hurt (John Scholfield), Alfred Molina (Trading Post missionary), Gibby Haynes (Man with gun in alley), George Duckworth (Man at end of street), Richard Boes (Man with wrench), John North (Mr. Olafsen), Peter Schrum (Drunk), Thomas Bettles (Young Nobody #1), Daniel Chas Stacy (Young Nobody #2), Billy Bob Thornton (Big George Drakoulious), Jared Harris (Benmont Tench), Steve Buscemi (Bartender), Mickey McGee (Bartender)

Nick of Time
1995
Paramount Pictures
Color (DeLuxe), 90 min.

DIRECTOR: John Badham; WRITTEN BY: Patrick Sheane Duncan; PRODUCERS: John Badham, D. J. Caruso, Cammie Crier; MUSIC: Arthur B. Rubinstein; CINE-MATOGRAPHY: Roy H. Wagner; EDITORS: Frank Morriss, Kevin Stitt; CASTING: Carol Lewis; PRODUCTION DESIGN: Philip Harrison; ART DIRECTION: Eric Orbom; SET DECORATION: Julia Badham; COSTUME DESIGN: Mary E. Vogt; MAKEUP: Janice Alexander, Hazel Catmull, Clare Corsick, John Elliott, Sheila Evers, Jim Scribner, Patty York, Dale Miller

CAST: Johnny Depp (Gene Watson), Courtney Chase (Lynn Watson), Charles S. Dutton (Huey), Christopher Walken (Mr. Smith), Roma Maffia (Ms. Jones), Marsha Mason (Gov. Eleanor Grant), Peter Strauss (Brendan Grant), Gloria Reuben (Krista Brooks), Bill Smitrovich (Officer Trust), G. D. Spradlin (Mystery Man), Yul Vazquez (Gustino, Guest Services), Edith Diaz (Irene, Domestic Maintenance)

Cannes Man
1996
Cult DVD, Rocket Pictures Home Video, Eclectic DVD Distribution
Color, 88 min.

DIRECTOR: Richard Martini; WRITTEN BY: Deric Haddad, Richard Martini, Irwin Rappaport, Susan Shapiro; PRODUCERS: Tom Coleman, Holly MacConkey, Johan Schotte, Jon Turtle; MUSIC: Richard Martini; CINEMATOGRAPHY: Denise Brassard, Dean Lent; EDITOR: Richard Currie; CASTING: Aaron Griffith; MAKEUP: Lori Matyska; SOUND: Jon Ailetcher, Ross Levy

CAST: Seymour Cassel (Sy Lerner), Francesco Quinn (Frank "Rhino" Rhino-slavsky), Rebecca Broussard (Rebecca Lerner), Johnny Depp (Himself), Treat Williams (Himself), Jim Jarmusch (Himself), Lara Flynn Boyle (Herself), James Brolin (Himself), Nino Cerruti (Himself), Jon Cryer (Himself), Ann Cusack (Kitty Monaco), Marc Duret (French Actor), Benicio Del Toro (Himself), Robert Evans (Producer), Dennis Hopper (Himself), Therese Kablan (Tawny), Lloyd

Kaufman (Troma Chief), Julian Lennon (Himself), John Malkovich (Himself), Chris Penn (Himself), May Hall Ross (Investor), Kevin Pollak (Himself), Jim Sheridan (Exasperated Director), Frank Whaley (Himself)

The Brave
1997
Acapella Pictures, Brave Pictures Inc., Majestic Film International,
Color, 123 min.

DIRECTOR: Johnny Depp; WRITTEN BY: D. P. Depp, Johnny Depp, Paul McCudden, from a novel by Gregory McDonald; PRODUCERS: Diane Batson-Smith, Charles Evans, Jr., Buck Holland, Carroll Kemp, Jeremy Thomas; MUSIC: Mark Governor, Iggy Pop, J. J. Holiday and Chuck E. Weiss (song "Devil with Blue Suede Shoes"); CINEMATOGRAPHY: Vilko Filac; EDITORS: Pasquale Buba, Hervé Schneid; CASTING: Louis DiGiaimo; PRODUCTION DESIGN: Miljen Kreka Kljakovic; ART DIRECTION: Branimir "Bane" Babic; COSTUME DESIGN: Lindy Hemming; MAKEUP: Judy Yonemoto

CAST: Johnny Depp (Raphael), Marlon Brando (McCarthy), Marshall Bell (Larry), Elpidia Carrillo (Rita), Frederic Forrest (Lou Sr.), Clarence Williams III (Father Stratton), Max Perlich (Lou Jr.), Luis Guzmán (Luis), Cody Lightning (Frankie), Nicole Mancera (Marta), Floyd "Red Crow" Westerman (Papa)

Donnie Brasco
1997
Tristar Pictures, Baltimore Pictures, Mandalay Entertainment, Mark Johnson
Productions
Color (Technicolor), 127 min.

DIRECTOR: Mike Newell; WRITTEN BY: Paul Attanasio, Joseph D. Pistone, Richard D. Woodley, based on Pistone's book *Donnie Brasco: My Undercover Life in the Mafia;* PRODUCERS: Louis DiGiaimo, Alan Greenspan, Mark Johnson, Barry Levinson, Patrick McCormick, Gail Mutrux; MUSIC: Patrick Doyle, Ray Evans and Jay Livingston (song "Silver Bells"); CINEMATOGRAPHY: Peter Sova; EDITOR: Jon Gregory; CASTING: Louis DiGiaimo, Brett Goldstein; PRODUCTION DESIGN: Donald Graham Burt; ART DIRECTION: Jefferson Sage; SET DECORATION: Leslie Pope; COSTUME DESIGN: Aude Bronson-Howard, David Robinson; MAKEUP: Margo Boccia, Milton Buras, Nathan Busch II, John Caglione, Jr., Jay Cannistraci, Sharon Kalb

CAST: Al Pacino (Benjamin "Lefty" Ruggerio), Johnny Depp (Joseph D. Pistone/ Donnie Brasco), Michael Madsen (Dominick "Sonny Black" Napolitano), Bruno Kirby (Nicky Santora), James Russo (Paulie), Anne Heche (Maggie Pistone), Zeljko Ivanek (Tim Curley), Gerry Becker (Dean Blandford), Robert Miano (Alphonse "Sonny Red" Indelicato), Brian Tarantina (Bruno "Whack Whack" Indelicato), Rocco Sisto (Richie Gazzo), Zach Grenier (Dr. Berger), Walt MacPherson (Sheriff), Ronnie Farer (Annette), Larry Romano (Tommy Ruggerio)

L.A. Without a Map
1998
Dan Films, Euro American Films S.A., Marianna Films
Color (Deluxe), 107 min.

DIRECTOR: Mika Kaurismäki; WRITTEN BY: Mika Kaurismäki, Richard Rayner; PRODUCERS: Pierre Assouline, Julie Baines, Sarah Daniel, Mika Kaurismäki, Brent Morris, Deepak Nayar; MUSIC: Sébastien Cortella; CINEMATOGRAPHY: Michel Amathieu; EDITOR: Ewa J. Lind; CASTING: Steve Brooksbank, Randi Hiller; PRODUCTION DESIGN: Caroline Hanania; SET DECORATION: Marcia Calosio, Eliza Solesbury; COSTUME DESIGN: Yasmine Abraham; MAKEUP: Raqueli Dahan, Nicholas Serino

CAST: Steve Huison (Billy), David Tennant (Richard), Margo Stanley (Mrs. Blenkinsop), Vinessa Shaw (Barbara), Saskia Reeves (Joy), Malcolm Tierney (Joy's Dad), Margi Clarke (Bradford Woman), Monte Hellman (Himself), Jean-Pierre Kalfon (Jean-Mimi), Julie Delpy (Julie), Kevin West (Spielberg Man), Lisa Edelstein (Sandra), Michael Campbell (Young Porter), Joe Dallesandro (Michael), Cameron Bancroft (Patterson), Matthew Faber (Joel), Brent Morris (Aviator Shades Cop), Mista Taboo (Rapper), Dijon Talton (Kid), Vincent Gallo (Moss), Joey Perillo (McCrea), Amanda Plummer (Red Pool Owner), Dominic Gould (Music Store Clerk 1), Andre Royo (Music Store Clerk 2), Johnny Depp (Himself), Anouk Aimée (Herself)

Fear and Loathing in Las Vegas
1998
Fear and Loathing LLC, Rhino Films, Shark Productions, Summit Entertainment, Universal Pictures
Color (Rankcolor), 118 min.

DIRECTOR: Terry Gilliam; WRITTEN BY: Terry Gilliam, Tony Grisoni, Tod Davies, Alex Cox, from the book by Hunter S. Thompson; PRODUCERS: Harold Bronson, Patrick Cassavetti, Richard Foos, John Jergens, Laila Nabulsi, Stephen Nemeth, Elliot Lewis Rosenblatt; MUSIC: Ray Cooper, Michael Kamen; CINEMATOGRAPHY: Nicola Pecorini; EDITOR: Lesley Walker; CASTING: Margery Simkin; PRODUCTION DESIGN: Alex McDowell; ART DIRECTION: Chris Gorak; SET DECORATION: Nancy Haigh; COSTUME DESIGN: Julie Weiss; MAKEUP: Robb Bottin, Bridget Cook, Bill Fletcher, Lynn Del Kail, Matthew Mungle, Cheryl Nick, Ellen Powell, Cindy Rose, Bob Scribner, Danny Valencia, Victoria Wood, Patty York, Mike Smithson

CAST: Johnny Depp (Raoul Duke), Benicio Del Toro (Dr. Gonzo), Tobey Maguire (Hitchhiker), Ellen Barkin (Waitress at North Star Café), Gary Busey (Highway Patrolman), Christina Ricci (Lucy), Mark Harmon (Magazine Reporter at Mint 400), Cameron Diaz (Blonde TV Reporter), Katherine Helmond (Desk Clerk at Mint Hotel), Michael Jeter (L. Ron Bumquist), Penn Jillette (Carnie Talker), Craig Bierko (Lacerda), Lyle Lovett (Road Person), Flea (Musician), Laraine Newman (Frog-Eyed Woman), Harry Dean Stanton (Judge), Hunter S. Thompson (Other Duke in Matrix Flashback)

The Source
1999
Beat Productions, Calliope Films, WNET Channel 13 New York
Black and white/Color, 89 min.

DIRECTOR: Chuck Workman; WRITTEN BY: Chuck Workman; PRODUCERS: Mark Apostolon, Glen Tedham, Chuck Workman, Hiro Yamagata; MUSIC: David Amram, Philip Glass; CINEMATOGRAPHY: Andrew Dintenfass, Tom Hurwitz, Don Lenzer, José Louis Mignone, Nancy Schreiber; EDITOR: Chuck Workman; PRODUCTION DESIGN: Marc Greville-Masson

CAST: Steve Allen, William F. Buckley, William S. Burroughs, Neal Cassady, Walter Cronkite, Richard J. Daley, Johnny Depp (Jack Kerouac), Bob Dylan, Lawrence Ferlinghetti, Allen Ginsberg, Brion Gysin, Dennis Hopper (William S. Burroughs), Lyndon Johnson, Jack Kerouac, Ken Kesey, Martin Luther King, Timothy Leary, Robert Motherwell, Peter Orlovsky, John Sampas, Ed Sanders, Gary Snyder, John Turturro (Allen Ginsberg)

The Ninth Gate
1999
Araba Films, Bac Films, Kino Vision, Le Studio Canal+, Live Entertainment, Origen Productions Cinematograficas S.A., Orly Films, R.P. Productions, TF1 Films Productions, Via Digital
Color, 133 min.

DIRECTOR: Roman Polanski; WRITTEN BY: John Brownjohn, Enrique Urbizu Roman Polanski, from *The Club Dumas* by Arturo Pérez-Reverte; PRODUCERS: Mark Allan, Antonio Cardenal, Michel Cheyko, Wolfgang Glattes, Adam Kempton, Iñaki Núñez, Roman Polanski, Alain Vannier, Suzanne Wiesenfeld; MUSIC: Wojciech Kilar; CINEMATOGRAPHY: Darius Khondji; EDITOR: Hervé de Luze; CASTING: Howard Feuer; PRODUCTION DESIGN: Dean Tavoularis; ART DIRECTION: Gérard Viard; SET DECORATION: Philippe Turlure; COSTUME DESIGN: Anthony Powell; MAKEUP: Jean-Pierre Berroyer, Michel Demonteix, Paul Le Marinel, Bettina Miquaix, Liliane Rametta, Jean-Luc Russier

CAST: Johnny Depp (Dean Corso), Frank Langella (Boris Balkan), Lena Olin (Liana Telfer), Emmanuelle Seigner (The Girl), Barbara Jefford (Baroness Kessler), Jack Taylor (Victor Fargas), José López Rodero (Pablo and Pedro / 1st and 2nd Workmen), Tony Amoni (Liana's Bodyguard), James Russo (Bernie), Willy Holt (Andrew Telfer), Allen Garfield (Witkin)

The Astronaut's Wife
1999
Mad Chance, New Line Cinema
Color (DeLuxe), 109 min.

DIRECTOR: Rand Ravich; WRITTEN BY: Rand Ravich; PRODUCERS: Jody Hedien, Mark Johnson, Donna Langley, Andrew Lazar, Diana Pokorny, Brian Witten; MUSIC: George S. Clinton; CINEMATOGRAPHY: Allen Daviau; EDITORS: Tim Alverson, Steve Mirkovich; CASTING: Debi Manwiller, Richard Pagano; PRODUCTION DESIGN: Jan Roelfs; ART DIRECTION: Sarah Knowles; SET DECORATION: Leslie A. Pope, COSTUME DESIGN: Isis Mussenden; MAKEUP: Deborah K. Larsen, Candy L. Walken

CAST: Johnny Depp (Commander Spencer Armacost), Charlize Theron (Jillian Armacost), Joe Morton (Sherman Reese), Clea DuVall (Nan), Donna Murphy (Natalie Streck), Nick Cassavetes (Capt. Alex Streck), Samantha Eggar (Dr. Patraba), Gary Grubbs (NASA Director), Blair Brown (Shelly McLaren), Tom Noonan (Jackson McLaren), Tom O'Brien (Allen Dodge), Lucy Lin (Shelly Carter), Michael Crider (Pat Elliott)

Sleepy Hollow
1999
American Zoetrope, Mandalay Pictures, Paramount Pictures
Color (Deluxe), 105 min.

DIRECTOR: Tim Burton; WRITTEN BY: Kevin Yagher, Andrew Kevin Walker, from "The Legend of Sleepy Hollow" by Washington Irving; PRODUCERS: Francis Ford Coppola, Celia Costas, Larry Franco, Mark Roybal, Scott Rudin, Adam Schroeder, Kevin Yagher, Andrew Kevin Walker; MUSIC: Danny Elfman; CINEMATOGRAPHY: Emmanuel Lubezki; EDITORS: Chris Lebenzon, Joel Negron; CASTING: Susie Figgis, Ilene Starger; PRODUCTION DESIGN: Rick Heinrichs; ART DIRECTION: Ken Court, John Dexter, Andrew Nicholson; SET DECORATION: Peter Young; COSTUME DESIGN: Colleen Atwood; MAKEUP: Colleen Callaghan, Tamsin Dorling, Paul Gooch, Don Kozma, Bernadette Mazur, Peter Owen, Sue Parkinson, Astrid Schikorra, Kirsty Stanway, Elizabeth Tagg, Leda Shawyer

CAST: Johnny Depp (Constable Ichabod Crane), Christina Ricci (Katrina Anne Van Tassel), Miranda Richardson (Lady Mary Van Tassel / The Western Woods Crone), Michael Gambon (Baltus Van Tassel), Casper Van Dien (Brom Van Brunt), Jeffrey Jones (Reverend Steenwyck), Christopher Lee (The Burgomeister), Richard Griffiths (Magistrate Samuel Philipse), Ian McDiarmid (Dr. Thomas Lancaster), Michael Gough (Notary James Hardenbrook), Marc Pickering (Young Masbath), Steve Waddington (Mr. Killian), Christopher Walken (The Hessian Horseman), Claire Skinner (Midwife Elizabeth "Beth" Killian), Alun Armstrong (High Constable), Mark Spalding (Jonathan Masbath), Jessica Oyelowo (Sarah, The Servant Girl), Tony Maudsley (Van Ripper)

The Man Who Cried
2000
Adventure Pictures, Le Studio Canal+, Working Title Films
Black and white, Color, 100 min.

DIRECTOR: Sally Potter; WRITTEN BY: Sally Potter; PRODUCERS: Simona Benzakein, Tim Bevan, Linda Bruce, Eric Fellner, Christopher Sheppard; MUSIC: Osvaldo Golijov; CINEMATOGRAPHY: Sacha Vierny; EDITOR: Hervé Schneid; CASTING: Mary Colquhoun, Irene Lamb; ART DIRECTION: Carlos Conti, Laurent Ott, Ben Scott; SET DECORATION: Maggie Gray, Philippe Turlure; COSTUME DESIGN: Lindy Hemming; MAKEUP: Jan Archibald, Anita Burger, Gérard Carrissimoux, Reynald Desbant, Beya Gasmi, Karina Gruais, Melissa Lackersteen, Chantal Leothier, Sylvie Lonchamp, Morag Ross, Loulia Sheppard, Elizabeth Tagg, Nathalie Tissier

CAST: Christina Ricci (Suzie), Cate Blanchett (Lola), John Turturro (Dante Dominio), Johnny Depp (Cesar), Harry Dean Stanton (Felix Pearlman), Oleg Yankovsky (Father)

Before Night Falls
2000
El Mar Pictures, Grandview Pictures
Color (Technicolor), 133 min.

DIRECTOR: Julian Schnabel; WRITTEN BY: Cunningham O'Keefe, Lázaro Gómez Carriles, Julian Schnabel, from a memoir by Reynaldo Arenas; PRODUCERS: Matthias Ehrenberg, Olatz Lopez Garmendia, Jon Kilik, Julian Schnabel; MUSIC: Laurie Anderson, Carter Burwell, Ennio Morricone (song "Surrounding the Casbah"), Lou Reed; CINEMATOGRAPHY: Xavier Pérez Grobet, Guillermo Rosas; EDITOR: Michael Berenbaum; PRODUCTION DESIGN: Salvador Parra; ART DIRECTION: Antonio Muño-Hierro; SET DECORATION: Laurie Friedman; COSTUME DESIGN: María Estela Fernández; MAKEUP: Virginia Campos, Manolo García, Judi Goodman, Ana Lozano, Kerrie R. Plant

CAST: Javier Bardem (Reynaldo Arenas), Olivier Martinez (Lázaro Gómez Carriles), Andrea Di Stefano (Pepe Malas), Johnny Depp (Bon Bon / Lieutenant Victor), Michael Wincott (Herberto Zorilla Ochoa), Olatz Lopez Garmendia (Reynaldo's Mother), Giovanni Florido (Young Reynaldo), Loló Navarro (Reynaldo's Grandmother), Sebastián Silva (Reynaldo's Father), Carmen Beato (Teacher)

Chocolat
2000
David Brown Productions, Fat Free Limited, Miramax Films
Color (Technicolor), 121 min.

DIRECTOR: Lasse Hallström; WRITTEN BY: Robert Nelson Jacobs, from a novel by Joanne Harris; PRODUCERS: Alan C. Blomquist, David Brown, Mark Cooper, Kit Golden, Leslie Holleran, Meryl Poster, Michelle Raimo, Bob Weinstein, Harvey Weinstein; MUSIC: Rachel Portman; CINEMATOGRAPHY: Roger Pratt; EDITOR: Andrew Mondshein; CASTING: Kerry Barden, Billy Hopkins, Amy MacLean, Suzanne Smith; PRODUCTION DESIGN: David Gropman; ART DIRECTION: Louise Marzaroli,

Lucy Richardson; SET DECORATION: Stephanie McMillan; COSTUME DESIGN: Renee Ehrlich Kalfus; MAKEUP: Helen Barrett, Chrissie Beveridge, Naomi Donne, Sallie Jaye, Ray Marston, Peter Owen, Toni Walker, Norma Webb, Lizzie Georgiou, Patty York

CAST: Juliette Binoche (Vianne), Alfred Molina (Comte de Reynaud), Carrie-Anne Moss (Caroline Clairmont), Aurelien Parent Koenig (Luc Clairmont), Antonio Gil-Martinez (Jean-Marc Drou), Hélène Cardona (Françoise "Fuffi" Drou), Harrison Pratt (Dedou Drou), Gaelan Connell (Didi Drou), Elisabeth Commelin (Yvette Marceau), Ron Cook (Alphonse Marceau), Guillaume Tardieu (Baptiste Marceau), Hugh O'Conor (Pere Henri), John Wood (Guillaume Blerot), Lena Olin (Josephine Muscat), Peter Stormare (Serge Muscat), Leslie Caron (Madame Audel), Victoire Thivisol (Anouk), Judi Dench (Armande Voizin), Michèle Gleizer (Madame Rivet), Dominique MacAvoy (Madame Pouget), Arnaud Adam (George Rocher), Christianne Gadd (Chitza), Johnny Depp (Roux), Marion Hauducoeur (Gati)

Blow
2001
Apostle Pictures, Avery Pix, New Line Cinema, Spanky Pictures
Color (DeLuxe), 124 min.

DIRECTOR: Ted Demme; WRITTEN BY: David McKenna, Nick Cassavetes, from a book by Bruce Porter; PRODUCERS: Michael De Luca, Ted Demme, Tracy Falco, Georgia Kacandes, Denis Leary, Jose Ludlow, Susan McNamara, Hillary Sherman, Joel Stillerman; MUSIC: Money Mark, Graeme Revell; CINEMATOGRAPHY: Ellen Kuras; EDITOR: Kevin Tent; CASTING: Avy Kaufman; PRODUCTION DESIGN: Michael Z. Hanan; ART DIRECTION: David Ensley, Bernardo Trujillo; SET DECORATION: Melo Hinojosa, Douglas A. Mowat; COSTUME DESIGN: Mark Bridges; MAKEUP: Sheryl Blum, Desne J. Holland, Whitney James, Jamie Kelman, Candace Neal, Ve Neill, Martin Samuel, Rita Troy, Karl Wesson, Kevin Yagher

CAST: Johnny Depp (George Jung), Penélope Cruz (Mirtha Jung), Franka Potente (Barbara Buckley), Rachel Griffiths (Ermine Jung), Paul Reubens (Derek Foreal), Jordi Mollà (Diego Delgado), Cliff Curtis (Pablo Escobar a k a El Magico), Miguel Sandoval (Augusto Oliveras), Ethan Suplee (Tuna), Ray Liotta (Fred Jung), Kevin Gage (Leon Minghella), Max Perlich (Kevin Dulli), Jesse James (Young George), Miguel Pérez (Alessandro), Dan Ferro (Cesar Toban), Tony Amendola (Sanchez), Bobcat Goldthwait (Mr. T), Michael Tucci (Dr. Bay), Monet Mazur (Maria), Lola Glaudini (Rada), Jennifer Gimenez (Inez), Emma Roberts (Young Kristina Jung), James King (Kristina Sunshine Jung)

From Hell
2001
20th Century Fox, Underworld Pictures
Color (DeLuxe), 122 min.

DIRECTORS: Albert Hughes, Allen Hughes; WRITTEN BY: Terry Hayes and Rafael Yglesias, from a graphic novel by Alan Moore and Eddie Campbell; PRODUCERS: Thomas M. Hammel, Jane Hamsher, Albert Hughes, Allen Hughes, Don Murphy, Amy Robinson; MUSIC: Trevor Jones; CINEMATOGRAPHY: Peter Deming; EDITORS: George Bowers, Dan Lebental; CASTING: Joyce Gallie, Sally Osoba; PRODUCTION DE-SIGN: Martin Childs; ART DIRECTION: Jindra Koci; SET DECORATION: Jill Quertier; COSTUME DESIGN: Kym Barrett

CAST: Johnny Depp (Inspector Fred Abberline), Heather Graham (Mary Kelly), Ian Holm (Sir William Gull), Robbie Coltrane (Sergeant Peter Godley), Ian Richardson (Sir Charles Warren), Jason Flemyng (Netley, The Coachman), Katrin Cartlidge (Dark Annie Chapman), Terence Harvey (Benjamin "Ben" Kidney), Susan Lynch (Liz Stride), Paul Rhys (Dr. Ferral), Lesley Sharp (Kate Eddowes), Estelle Skornik (Ada), Nicholas McGaughey (Officer Bolt), Annabelle Apsion (Polly), Joanna Page (Ann Crook), Mark Dexter (Albert Sickert/ Prince Edward Albert Victor), Danny Midwinter (Constable Withers), Samantha Spiro (Martha Tabram), David Schofield (McQueen), Byron Fear (Robert Best), Peter Eyre (Lord Hallsham), Cliff Parisi (Mac Bartender), Sophia Myles (Victoria Abberline), Ralph Ineson (Gordie), Liz Moscrop (Queen Victoria)

Lost in La Mancha
2002
Eastcroft Productions, Low Key Productions, Quixote Films Limited
Color, 93 min.

DIRECTORS: Keith Fulton, Louis Pepe; WRITTEN BY: Keith Fulton, Louis Pepe; PRODUCERS: Rosa Bosch, Andrew J. Curtis, Lucy Darwin; MUSIC: Miriam Cutler; CINEMATOGRAPHY: Louis Pepe; EDITOR: Jacob Bricca; PRODUCTION DESIGN: Benjamín Fernández; SOUND: Michael Kowalski

CAST: Jeff Bridges (Narrator), Bernard Bouix (Himself), Bernard Chaumeil (Himself), René Cleitman (Himself), Johnny Depp (Himself), José Luis Escolar (Himself), Benjamin Fernandez (Himself), Pierre Gamet (Himself), Terry Gilliam (Himself), Tony Grisoni (Himself), Vanessa Paradis (Herself), Phil Patterson (Himself), Nicola Pecorini (Herself), Gabriella Pescucci (Herself), Jean Rochefort (Himself)

Pirates of the Caribbean: Curse of the Black Pearl
2003
Jerry Bruckheimer Films, Walt Disney Pictures
Color, 143 min.

DIRECTOR: Gore Verbinski; WRITTEN BY: Ted Elliott, Terry Rossio, Stuart Beattie, Jay Wolpert; PRODUCERS: Jerry Bruckheimer, Paul Deason, Bruce Hendricks, Chad

Oman, Paul Sandston, Mike Stenson; MUSIC: Klaus Badelt, Ramin Djawadi, James Michael Dooley, Nick Glennie-Smith, Steve Jablonsky, James McKee Smith, Blake Neely, Mel Wesson, Geoff Zanelli, Hans Zimmer; CINEMATOGRAPHY: Dariusz Wolski; EDITORS: Stephen Rivkin, Arthur Schmidt, Craig Wood; CASTING: Jennifer Alessi, Ronna Kress; PRODUCTION DESIGN: Brian Morris; ART DIRECTION: Derek R. Hill, James E. Tocci, Donald B. Woodruff; SET DECORATION: Larry Dias; COSTUME DESIGN: Penny Rose; MAKEUP: Barney Burman, Greg Cannom, David DeLeon, Joel Harlow, Anne-Maree Hurley, Mary Kim, Sarah Love, Ve Neill, Douglas Noe, Martin Samuel, Maria Sandoval, Brian Sipe, Keith VanderLaan, and others

CAST: Johnny Depp (Jack Sparrow), Geoffrey Rush (Barbossa), Orlando Bloom (Will Turner), Keira Knightley (Elizabeth Swann), Jack Davenport (Norrington), Jonathan Pryce (Governor Weatherby Swann), Lee Arenberg (Pintel), Mackenzie Cook (Ragetti), Damian O'Hare (Lt. Gillette), Giles New (Murtogg), Angus Barnett (Mullroy), David Bailie (Cotton), Michael Berry, Jr. (Twigg), Isaac C. Singleton, Jr. (Bo'sun), Kevin R. McNally (Joshamee Gibbs), Treva Etienne (Koehler), Zoe Saldana (Anamaria), Guy Siner (Harbormaster), Ralph P. Martin (Mr. Brown), Paula J. Newman (Estrella), Paul Keith (Butler), Dylan Smith (Young Will), Lucinda Dryzek (Young Elizabeth)

Once Upon a Time in Mexico
2003
Columbia Picture Corporation, Dimension Films, Troublemaker Studios
Color, 101 min.

DIRECTOR: Robert Rodriguez; WRITTEN BY: Robert Rodriguez; PRODUCERS: Elizabeth Avellan, Carlos Gallardo, Sue Jett, Tony Mark, Robert Rodriguez, Luz María Rojas; MUSIC: Robert Rodriguez, Johnny Depp; CINEMATOGRAPHY: Robert Rodriguez; EDITOR: Robert Rodriguez; CASTING: Mary Vernieu; PRODUCTION DESIGN: Robert Rodriguez; ART DIRECTION: Melo Hinojosa, COSTUME DESIGN: Graciela Mazón; MAKEUP: Allan A. Apone, Troy Breeding, Jake Garber, Barry R. Koper, Robert Kurtzman, Sandra Miguell, Gregory Nicotero, Roxie Norman, Ermahn Ospina, Carmen de la Torre

CAST: Antonio Banderas (El Mariachi), Salma Hayek (Carolina), Johnny Depp (Sands), Mickey Rourke (Billy), Eva Mendes (Ajedrez), Danny Trejo (Cucuy), Enrique Iglesias (Lorenzo), Marco Leonardi (Fideo), Cheech Marin (Belini), Rubén Blades (Jorge FBI), Willem Dafoe (Barillo), Gerardo Vigil (Marquez), Pedro Armendáriz, Jr. (El Presidente), Julio Oscar Mechoso (Advisor), Tito Larriva (Cab Driver), Miguel Couturier (Dr. Guevera), José Luis Avendaño (Alvaro)

Secret Window
2004
Grand Slam Productions, Columbia Pictures, Pariah Entertainment Group
Color, 96 min.

DIRECTOR: David Koepp; WRITTEN BY: David Koepp, from a story by Stephen King; PRODUCERS: Gavin Polone, Ezra Swerdlow; MUSIC: Philip Glass; CINEMATOGRA-PHY: Fred Murphy; EDITOR: Jill Savitt; CASTING: Pat McCorkle, John Papsidera; PRODUCTION DESIGN: Howard Cummings; ART DIRECTION: Gilles Aird; SET DECORATION: Francine Danis; COSTUME DESIGN: Odette Gadoury; Lyse Pomerleau

CAST: Johnny Depp (Mort Rainey), John Turturro (John Shooter), Maria Bello (Amy Rainey), Timothy Hutton (Ted Milner), Charles S. Dutton (Ken Karsch), Len Cariou (Sheriff Dave Newsome), Gillian Ferrabee (Fran Evans), Richard Jutras (Motel Manager), Kyle Allatt (Busboy)

Finding Neverland
2004
Film Colony
Color, 108 min.

DIRECTOR: Marc Forster; WRITTEN BY: Allan Knee, David Magee; PRODUCERS: Tracey Becker, Nellie Bellflower, Gary Binkow, Michael Dreyer, Richard N. Gladstein, Neal Israel; MUSIC: Elton John, Jan A.P. Kaczmarek; CINEMATOGRAPHY: Roberto Schaefer; EDITOR: Matt Chesse; CASTING: Kate Dowd; PRODUCTION DESIGN: Gemma Jackson: ART DIRECTION: Peter Russell; SET DECORATION: Trisha Edwards: COSTUME DESIGN: Alexandra Byrne, Mary Kelly; MAKEUP: Christine Blundell, Denise Kum, Sian Richards, Nuria Mbomio

CAST: Johnny Depp (J. M. Barrie), Kate Winslet (Sylvia Llewelyn Davies), Julie Christie (Mrs. Du Maurier), Nick Roud (George Llewelyn Davies), Radha Mitchell (Mary Barrie), Joe Prospero (Jack Llewelyn Davies), Freddie Highmore (Peter Llewelyn Davies), Dustin Hoffman (Charles Frohman), Kate Maberly (Wendy Darling), Luke Spill (Michael Llewelyn Davies), Kelly Macdonald (Peter Pan), Tony Way (Set Mover), Murray McArthur (Stage Hand), Ian Hart (Sir Arthur Conan Doyle), Paul Whitehouse (Stage Manager), Matt Green (John Darling)

The Libertine
2004
Mr. Mudd Productions, Isle of Man Film Commission, First Choice Film 2004, Isle of Man Ltd.
Color, 130 min.

DIRECTOR: Laurence Dunmore; WRITTEN BY: Stephen Jeffreys; PRODUCERS: Chase Bailey, Steve Christian, Louise Goodsill, Lianne Halfon, Ralph Kamp, Colin Leventhal, John Malkovich, Marc Samuelson, Peter Samuelson, Russell Smith, Donald A. Starr, Daniel J.B. Taylor; MUSIC: Michael Nyman; CINEMATOGRAPHY: Alexander Melman; EDITOR: Jill Bilcock; CASTING: Lucy Bevan, Mary Selway; PRODUCTION DESIGN: Ben van Os; ART DIRECTION: Patrick Rolfe, Fleur Whitlock; ART DEPARTMENT: Graham Caulfield, Gareth Cousins, Mark Hedges, Lisa McDiarmid, Daryn McLaughlin, Stuart Read, Nigel Salter

CAST: Johnny Depp (John Wilmot, aka the Earl of Rochester), Rupert Friend (Billy Downs), Tom Hollander (George Etherege), Shane MacGowan (seventeenth-century bard), John Malkovich (King Charles II), Samantha Morton (Elizabeth Barry), Rosamund Pike (Elizabeth Malet), Johnny Vegas (Charles Sackville).

Ils se marièrent et eurent beaucoup d'enfants
2004 (currently in post-production)
Pathé Renn Productions, Hirsch, TF1 Films Productions
Color

DIRECTOR: Yvan Attal; WRITTEN BY: Yvan Attal; PRODUCERS: Claude Berri, Pierre Grunstein, Nathalie Rheims; MUSIC: Christian Chevalier, Brad Mehldau; CINE-MATOGRAPHY: Rémy Chevrin; EDITOR: Jennifer Augé; CASTING: Antoinette Boulat, Laurent Soulet; PRODUCTION DESIGN: Katia Wyszkop; SET DECORATION: Sandrine Mauvezin; COSTUME DESIGN: Jacqueline Bouchard; PRODUCTION MANAGEMENT: Aimeric Bonello, Nicole Firn, Jerome Pinot

CAST: Charlotte Gainsbourg (Gabrielle), Yvan Attal (Vincent), Alain Chabat (Georges), Emmanuelle Seigner (Nathalie), and with Anouk Aimée, Claude Berri, Jérôme Bertin, Alain Cohen, and Johnny Depp (garage customers)

The Rum Diary
2005 (currently in post-production)
FilmEngine
Color

DIRECTOR: Benicio Del Toro; WRITTEN BY: Michael Thomas, from a novel by Hunter S. Thompson; PRODUCERS: Johnny Depp, A. J. Dix, Robert Kravis, Nick Nolte, Anthony Rhulen, Greg Shapiro

CAST: Johnny Depp (Paul Kemp), Josh Hartnett (Addison Fritz Yeamon), Benicio Del Toro (Bob Sala), and Nick Nolte (Lotterman)

The Corpse Bride
2005 (currently in production)
Warner Bros., Tim Burton Animation Co., Will Vinton Studios
Color

DIRECTORS: Tim Burton, Mike Johnson; WRITTEN BY: Pamela Pettler, Caroline Thompson; PRODUCERS: Jeffrey Auerbach, Tim Burton; MUSIC: Danny Elfman; CINEMATOGRAPHY: Pete Kozachik; PRODUCTION DESIGN: Alex McDowell; ART DI-RECTION: Nelson Lowry; VISUAL EFFECTS: Chris Watts

CAST: Helena Bonham Carter (voice), Johnny Depp (voice), Richard E. Grant (voice), Christopher Lee (voice), Emily Watson (voice)

Charlie and the Chocolate Factory
2005 (currently in production)
Warner Bros., The Zanuck Company, Plan B Films, Plan B Productions Inc.,
Basic Entertainment, Maverick Entertainment Inc.
Color

DIRECTOR: Tim Burton; WRITTEN BY: John August, from the novel by Roald Dahl;
PRODUCERS: Liccy Dahl, Derek Frey, Brad Grey, Patrick McCormick, Michael
Siegel, Richard D. Zanuck; MUSIC BY: Danny Elfman; CINEMATOGRAPHY: Philippe
Rousselot; EDITOR: Chris Lebenzon; CASTING: Susie Figgis; PRODUCTION DESIGN:
Alex McDowell; ART DIRECTION: François Audouy, Andy Nicholson, Kevin Phipps;
SET DECORATION: Peter Young; COSTUME DESIGN: Gabriella Pescucci

CAST: Johnny Depp (Willy Wonka), Jordan Fry (Mike Teavee), Freddie Highmore
(Charlie Bucket), David Kelly (Grandpa Joe), Missi Pyle (Ms. Beauregarde), Anna-
sophia Robb (Violet Beauregarde), Philip Wiegratz (Augustus Gloop), Julia Winter
(Veruca Salt)

The Diving Bell and the Butterfly
2006 (currently in production)
The Kennedy/Marshall Company
Color

DIRECTOR: Julian Schnabel; WRITTEN BY: Ronald Harwood; PRODUCERS: Kathleen
Kennedy, Frank Marshall

CAST: Johnny Depp (Jean-Dominique Bauby)

Pirates of the Caribbean 2 (also known as *Pirates of the Caribbean 2:
Treasures of the Lost Abyss*)
2006 (currently in pre-production)
Walt Disney Pictures, Jerry Bruckheimer Films
Color

DIRECTOR: Gore Verbinski: WRITTEN BY: Ted Elliott, Terry Rossio; PRODUCED BY:
Jerry Bruckheimer

CAST ANNOUNCED: Johnny Depp (Captain Jack Sparrow), Orlando Bloom (Will
Turner)

CREDITS

Page 3: *Cry-Baby* (John Waters, Universal, 1990). Collection of Murray Pomerance.

Page 19: *Benny & Joon* (Jeremiah S. Chechik, MGM, 1993). Collection of Murray Pomerance.

Page 107: Depp (left) with Darlene Cates, *What's Eating Gilbert Grape?* (Lasse Hallström, Paramount, 1993). Collection of Murray Pomerance.

Page 121: Depp (right) with Leonardo DiCaprio, *What's Eating Gilbert Grape* (Lasse Hallström, Paramount, 1993). Collection of Murray Pomerance.

Page 135: Depp (right) with Charlize Theron, *The Astronaut's Wife* (Rand Ravich, New Line Cinema, 1999). Collection of Murray Pomerance.

Page 142: *Lost in La Mancha* (Keith Fulton and Louis Pepe, Eastcroft/Quixote, 2002). Frame enlargement.

Pages 154 and 161: *Fear and Loathing in Las Vegas* (Terry Gilliam, Universal, 1998). Collection of Murray Pomerance.

Page 166: Depp (right) with Géraldine Pailhas, *Don Juan DeMarco* (Jeremy Leven, Zoetrope/New Line Cinema, 1995). Collection of Murray Pomerance.

Page 177: *Donnie Brasco* (Mike Newell, Tristar, 1997). Collection of Murray Pomerance.

Page 188: *A Nightmare on Elm Street* (Wes Craven, New Line Cinema, 1984). PhotoFest New York.

Page 194: *Arizona Dream* (Emir Kusturiça, Hachette Première/Le Studio Canal +, 1993). PhotoFest New York.

Page 201: *Dead Man* (Jim Jarmusch, 12 Gauge/Miramax, 1995). PhotoFest New York.

Page 206: from left: *Edward Scissorhands* (Tim Burton, 20th Century Fox, 1990), PhotoFest New York; Depp (left) with Jordi Mollà, *Blow* (Ted Demme, New Line Cinema, 2001), Collection of Murray Pomerance; *The Source* (Chuck Workman, Beat/Calliope/WNET, 1999), Collection of Murray Pomerance; *Before Night Falls* (Julian Schnabel, El Mar/Grandview, 2000), Collection of Murray Pomerance.

Page 222: Depp (left) with Orlando Bloom, *Pirates of the Caribbean: Curse of the Black Pearl* (Gore Verbinski, Disney, 2003). Collection of Murray Pomerance.

Page 233: Depp (left) with Cody Lightning, *The Brave* (Johnny Depp, Acapella, 1997). PhotoFest New York.

Page 237: *Secret Window* (David Koepp, Columbia, 2004). PhotoFest New York.

Page 243: *Sleepy Hollow* (Tim Burton, Zoetrope/Paramount, 1999). Collection of Murray Pomerance.

Page 261: *Nick of Time* (John Badham, Paramount, 1995). Collection of Murray Pomerance.

INDEX

Page numbers in italics indicate illustrations.

ABOUT THE AUTHOR

Murray Pomerance is the author of *An Eye for Hitchcock* (Rutgers) and *Magia D'Amore* (Sun & Moon), and the editor or co-editor of numerous volumes, including *Where the Boys Are: Cinemas of Masculinity and Youth* (Wayne State), *BAD: Infamy, Darkness, Evil, and Slime on Screen* (SUNY), *Enfant Terrible! Jerry Lewis in American Film* (NYU), *Sugar, Spice, and Everything Nice: Cinemas of Girlhood* (Wayne State), and *Ladies and Gentlemen, Boys and Girls: Gender in Film at the End of the Twentieth Century* (SUNY). Forthcoming are *American Cinema of the 1950s: Themes and Variations, Cinema and Modernity, City That Never Sleeps,* and *A Family Affair,* all edited by him, and, edited with Ernest Mathijs, *From Hobbits to Hollywood: Essays on Peter Jackson's "Lord of the Rings."* He is editor of the "Horizons of Cinema" series at State University of New York Press, and, with Lester D. Friedman, co-editor of the "Screen Decades" series at Rutgers University Press. He chairs the Department of Sociology at Ryerson University.